W9-CCE-289

Pre-publication REVIEWS, COMMENTARIES, EVALUATIONS . . .

"This book is a treasure and a creative resource for every therapist working with children and adolescents. An outstanding cast of authors covers so much ground and provides so many invaluable resources and applications that the book is a must for all clinicians who work with children and adolescents, and for all trainers of family therapy."

Volker Thomas, PhD
Associate Professor and Director,
Marriage and Family Therapy Program,
Department of Child Development and Family Studies,
Purdue University

"I wish I had this book when I was in training to be a child and adolescent therapist. I would have used it every day because I cannot see how any professional working with youths could do without it. This is an indispensable 'must' resource that is chock-full of ideas, plans, and suggestions that will enlarge the therapeutic armamentarium of any student or professional working with this population. To say 'I recommend it' is an understatement. Get this book ASAP!"

Luciano L'Abate, PhD
Professor Emeritus of Psychology,
Georgia State University;
President, Workbooks for Better Living

The Therapist's Notebook for Children and Adolescents
Homework, Handouts, and Activities for Use in Psychotherapy

HAWORTH *Practical Practice in Mental Health*
Lorna L. Hecker, PhD
Senior Editor

The Therapist's Notebook for Children and Adolescents
Homework, Handouts, and Activities for Use in Psychotherapy

Catherine Ford Sori, PhD
Lorna L. Hecker, PhD
and Associates

The Haworth Clinical Practice Press
An Imprint of The Haworth Press, Inc.
New York • London • Oxford

Published by

The Haworth Clinical Practice Press, an imprint of The Haworth Press, Inc., 10 Alice Street, Binghamton, NY 13904-1580.

PUBLISHER'S NOTE
Client identities and circumstances have been changed to protect confidentiality.

Cover design by Jennifer M. Gaska.

Library of Congress Cataloging-in-Publication Data

The therapist's notebook for children and adolescents : homework, handouts, and activities for use in psychotherapy / Catherine Ford Sori, Lorna L. Hecker, editors.
    p. cm.
Includes bibliographical references and index.
   ISBN 0-7890-1096-8 (alk. paper)
   1. Child psychotherapy—Handbooks, manuals, etc. 2. Adolescent psychotherapy—Handbooks, manuals, etc. I. Ford Sori, Catherine. II. Hecker, Lorna L.
RJ504 .T475 2003
618.92'8914—dc21
                                             2002027285

To my children, who have filled my life with joy and purpose: Jessica and Heather, Jeremy and Joel, Paul, Ann, Al, Marlene, and Marisa, and to all their children. . . . And to Cameron and Alexis, who have allowed me to enter their world during our "Special Play Time."

To my first family: my father, Marvin Ford, who shared his love of storybooks and make-believe; Elnora Updegraff Ford, my mother, who filled our home and my heart with her songs; and to Albert Annesser and my late sister, Cynthia, who shared my childhood and with whom I sang, danced, and explored the world of make-believe play.

Above all, to my husband, John, a "nonanxious presence," who encouraged me to pursue this dream, and whose steadfast love, encouragement, and support have sustained me throughout this process. CS

To my children, Aaron and Noah Schlossberger, who light my path with energy, creativity, and pure "joie de vivre." LH

And . . . to all the children and families who have allowed us the privilege of knowing them, and who continue to teach us so much! CS & LH

CONTENTS

ABOUT THE EDITORS

Catherine Ford Sori, PhD, is University Professor in the Division of Psychology and Counseling at Governors State University in University Park, Illinois. Her special interests include children in family therapy, children and families facing illness and bereavement, and divorce and stepfamily issues. Dr. Sori received her doctorate in child development and family studies with a specialization in marriage and family therapy from Purdue University. She is a past Fellow in Family Systems and Health through the Chicago Center for Family Health and the University of Chicago. Dr. Sori was formerly Director of Children and Family Services at the Cancer Support Center in Homewood, Illinois, where she implemented a program and services for children, adolescents, and families coping with cancer and bereavement. She has provided training to school professionals on children and families with cancer as well as children and bereavement. Dr. Sori has done research in the area of training family therapists to work with children in family therapy and has authored articles on both children in family therapy and couples therapy.

Lorna L. Hecker, PhD, is Professor in the marriage and family therapy master's program and Director of the Marriage and Family Therapy Center at Purdue University Calumet in Hammond, Indiana. She is the founding editor of the *Journal of Clinical Activities, Assignments & Handouts in Psychotherapy Practice* (The Haworth Clinical Practice Press). She (with Sharon Deacon and Associates) is the author of *The Therapist's Notebook: Homework, Handouts, and Activities for Use in Psychotherapy Practice* (1998, Haworth). In addition, Dr. Hecker is the founding editor of the Haworth Practical Practice in Mental Health: Guidebooks for In-Patient, Out-Patient, and Independent Practice book program. A resident of Munster, Indiana, she maintains a private practice. Her interests include trauma recovery, ethics and professional issues in family therapy, and gender and multicultural issues in family therapy.

CONTRIBUTORS

Lisa Abrahamson, MS, is a family therapist and substance abuse counselor at the Mid-Eastern Council on Chemical Abuse (MECCA) in Iowa City, Iowa. She counsels individuals, couples, and families with substance abuse issues and cofacilitates a dual-diagnosis group.

C. Everett Bailey, PhD, received his doctoral degree in marriage and family therapy from Purdue University, West Lafayette, Indiana. He is the editor of the book *Children in Therapy: Using the Family As a Resource* (2000). Clinically, he specializes in working with children, adolescents, and their parents. He currently is the Marriage and Family Therapy Program interim director at North Dakota State University, Fargo.

Nancee Biank, MSW, LCSW, is the program director and director of Children and Family Services at Wellness House, Hinsdale, Illinois, a nonprofit organization that offers psychosocial support to cancer patients and their families. Nancee developed the groundbreaking Family Matters Program for children who have a parent with cancer. She was recently invited to present this model to an international audience at the Eighteenth Congress of Psycho-oncology in Normandy, France, and is currently working with Catherine Ford Sori on a book for professionals titled *Tell Them That We Know . . . Children's Responses to Illness and Loss.* Nancee is also in private practice and is cofounder of Partners in Transition in Hinsdale, Illinois. She trained at the Institute for Psychoanalysis, Child and Adolescent Therapy Program, University of Illinois, Jane Adams College of Social Work in Chicago, Illinois, and also with Judith Wallerstein. Nancee lives with her husband, Vincent, in Hinsdale and enjoys spending time with her two grown sons.

Anna L. Bower, RN, MS, licensed marriage and family therapist, completed her undergraduate degrees in nursing and psychology at Purdue University, West Lafayette, Indiana. She received a graduate degree in community mental health counseling at Purdue and completed an internship in individual, family, and group therapy at Wabash Valley Hospital, West Lafayette. She received a graduate degree in psychiatric nursing and administration from St. Xavier University, Chicago, Illinois, and completed her internship for the master's in business administration at the Joint Commission on Accreditation of Healthcare Organizations, Oakbrook Terrace, Illinois. Anna has been working in the health care field for the past twenty-five years. She has been employed by Southlake Center for Mental Health as a nurse-therapist and outpatient psychotherapist. She was director of adult psychiatry at St. Margaret Mercy Health Care for five years and also practiced outpatient therapy there. Until recently, she was the assistant director, clinical operations, of University of Illinois Medical Center at Chicago for the Internal Medicine Center. Anna has experience in health care consulting and advice to hospitals, clinics, and physician practice models. She currently practices individual, family, and group therapy with the O. C. Professional Properties group in Munster and Valparaiso, Indiana.

Anna is a clinical member of the American Association for Marriage and Family Therapists; a member of the American Red Cross National Disaster Relief Team in the area of Crisis Intervention; a member of the University of Illinois Advanced Practice Association for Nursing; a clinical practice specialist for the Department of Psychiatry, University of Illinois Medical Center at Chicago; and adjunct faculty for the University of Illinois College of Nursing, Chicago.

Tammy B. Bringaze, PhD, LPC, NCC, is currently serving as the interim director of University Counseling Services and adjunct professor at Truman State University, Kirksville, Missouri. In addition, she has researched and published in the areas of sexual identity development, career development, and diversity.

Maia C. Coleman, MS, received her master's degree in developmental psychology in 1996 from the University of Michigan, Ann Arbor. She is currently pursuing a PhD in clinical psychology at Howard University, Washington, DC. She is a recipient of the Fredrick Douglass Fellowship and was previously funded by the American Psychological Association Minority Fellowship Program and the Rachham Merit Fellowship at University of Michigan. Her research interests include the effects of cultural identity and self-expression on the development and diagnosis of psychopathology in African-American children and adolescents. She enjoys mentoring and working with adolescent girls. She also is a member of Balaphone Women's Ensemble, an African dance company, and spends much of her time outside of school rehearsing and performing, as well as traveling abroad.

Megan L. Dolbin, MS, is a doctoral student in marriage and family therapy at Purdue University, West Lafayette, Indiana. She completed a bachelor's degree in human development and family studies from the Pennsylvania State University and a master's degree in marriage and family therapy from Purdue University. Her clinical interests include gifted children and adolescents, abused children and adolescents, family therapy, and sex therapy. Her research interests include sexual satisfaction, sexual communication, and attachment in adult relationships.

Barry L. Duncan, PsyD, is currently an associate professor in the family therapy program in the School of Social and Systemic Studies, Nova-Southeastern University, Fort Lauderdale, Florida. His current teaching interests include brief applications of systems theory, practical applications of the empirical literature, integration of different systemic models, and common factors across treatments.

Dana Edwards, PhD, has experience as a high school teacher and elementary school counselor. Currently, she is an assistant professor in the Department of Psychological Services at Georgia State University in Atlanta, Georgia. She primarily teaches courses on socialization and personality development, group processes, and school counseling. She has given numerous presentations to teachers, parents, and students on the topics of parenting, home and school behavior management, social interest and encouragement, and conflict resolution strategies. She has also published journal articles on these topics.

Eliana Gil, PhD, has been working on the prevention and treatment of child abuse since 1973. She currently is director of the Abused Children's Treatment Services at Inova Kellar Center in Fairfax, Virginia. She also provides intensive training on play therapy with abused children, family play therapy, and sand therapy. Eliana is bilingual and bicultural and originally is from Guayaquil, Ecuador.

Liddy B. Hope, MS, has a master's degree in marriage and family therapy from Purdue University Calumet, Hammond, Indiana. She is currently pursuing her PhD in family social sciences at the University of Minnesota, Duluth.

Julie Johnson, MS, is a family therapist in Family Services of the Greater Elgin Area in Elgin, Illinois. Her primary clinical focus is high-risk children and adolescents.

Jeanne Thibo Karns, PhD, CCLS, is a coordinator of the Child Life Program and assistant professor of Child Development at the University of Akron, Ohio. Child life specialists work with hospitalized children and their families, helping them to cope with the psychosocial and emotional stresses of medical care. Her research interests include coping methods for pain, the role of humor as a coping skill, and stress reduction and relaxation techniques for children and parents. She is a member of the American Psychological Association, Child Life Council, Society for Research in Child Development, and the International Society for Infant Studies.

Diane E. Karther, EdD, is an assistant professor of early childhood education at Ashland University. Her background includes development of various family education programs for parents of newborns through preteens as well as teaching child development in departments of pediatrics, family and consumer sciences, and education. She has been a consultant to Head Start for five years. Her research interests include fathers' influences on children's literacy and schooling, home-school relationships, and multiracial early childhood environments. Other interests include the influence of brain development on early childhood professional practice and collaborations between teachers and health and human service providers.

Jody R. Kussin, PhD, is a clinical psychologist, educator, writer, and lecturer. She enthusiastically advocates helping parents enjoy their roles as parents. Jody is the director of children's services for Verdugo Mental Health, Glendale, California, a nonprofit private behavioral health care agency. She is also the clinic director of the Glen Roberts Child Study Center, a community mental health center located in Glendale, California, that serves low-income and ethnic minority children and their families. Jody also has an active consulting practice, working with public school districts, independent schools, preschools, and religious institutions throughout Southern California. She is a frequent speaker and educator at various parent organizations as well as for mental health professionals. Jody is married to research psychologist Steve Shoptaw. Together they raise three children, two dogs, and various vegetable and flower gardens.

Stephanie Malench, MSW, is a student at Saint Louis University in St. Louis, Missouri. She has just finished working at West Central Outreach in St. Louis with low-income, special needs children ages five to twelve years old.

Ann-Marie Martinez, PhD, is a clinical and research psychologist and acts as the coordinator of research and outcomes for Verdugo Mental Health Children's Services, Glendale, California. She conducts training and supervision, oversees all research and outcomes evaluations projects that take place at the center, and presents information at conferences throughout the country. Ann-Marie and her husband have one child . . . so far.

Lenore McWey, MS, received her master's degree from the University of North Florida, Jacksonville, and is pursuing her doctorate in marriage and family therapy at Florida State University, Tallahassee. Lenore's interests include play therapy with children in crisis and working with families whose children are in foster care. She has presented at state and national conferences of the Supervised Visitation Network regarding her work with children in foster care. Lenore is currently employed by Florida State University as a teaching assistant and is a therapist at the Center for Marriage and Family Therapy, associated with the university.

Katherine A. Milewski-Hertlein, BA, is a master's candidate in the Marriage and Family Therapy Program at Purdue University Calumet, Hammond, Indiana. Her previous work includes publications in *College Student Journal* and *American Journal of Family Therapy,* as well as several presentations at local and national conferences.

Nancy Nickell, MS, received her master's degree in marriage and family therapy from Purdue University Calumet. She has practiced at agencies in northwest Indiana and currently owns and operates her own retail business in Waterloo, Iowa, where she resides with her husband, Kent Nickell, MD.

David Paré, PhD, is a chartered psychologist and assistant of educational psychology at the University of Ottawa in Ontario, Canada. For the past ten years, David has been interested and involved in narrative and social constructionist theory and practice.

Elisabeth Reichert, PhD, LCSW, is an assistant professor in the School of Social Work at Southern Illinois University at Carbondale. She came to the United States on a Fulbright scholarship and is a graduate of the University of Tennessee, Knoxville. She was a clinical social worker in a sex abuse treatment program, where she worked with children and survivors of sexual abuse. She now teaches undergraduate and graduate classes in social work practice. She has published articles in the *Journal of the California Graduate School of Marital and Family Therapy, Reflections: Narratives of Professional Helping, Journal of Law and Social Work, Journal of Baccalaureate Social Work, Child and Adolescent Social Work, Migration Worker, Social Development,* and *International Social Work.*

Linda L. Richardson, BS, received her bachelor's degree from the University of South Dakota in May 1999, with majors in both psychology and alcohol and drug abuse studies. She is currently working on her master of arts degree in community agency counseling, also at the University of South Dakota, Vermillion. Linda is married and the mother of three daughters, and she works for the university's Student Support Services. Linda's professional interests are in the areas of chemical dependency, family therapy, math anxiety, and trauma survivors.

Mary Ann Majchrzak Rombach, PhD, recently completed her doctoral dissertation on the subject of narrative supervision. Her specialties include narrative therapy in clinical work and in training counselors. Mary Ann has published "Defiance on the Armchair" in the *Journal of Family Psychotherapy* (10[1], 1999), has submitted "Men's Peace Project" to the International Family Therapy Conference in Oslo, and is working on two articles: "An Invitation to Therapeutic Letter Writing," in press with the *Journal of Systemic Therapies,* and "the Visible Web," in progress.

Nikki Ruble, MS, received her master's degree in marriage and family therapy from the University of Kentucky, Lexington. She is currently completing her doctoral degree in marriage and family therapy at Florida State University, Tallahassee. She also is employed by the university as a teaching assistant for an undergraduate family relations class and a research assistant for a grant-funded research project. Nikki's clinical focus is on the inclusion of children and the use of play in family therapy. She has presented workshops on this topic at the annual meetings of the American Association of Marriage and Family Therapy, the National Council on Family Relations, and the Florida Association for Marriage and Family Therapy.

Lee Shilts, PhD, is currently the associate dean and an associate professor in the School of Social and Systemic Studies, Nova-Southeastern University, Fort Lauderdale, Florida. His current teaching interests include brief solution-focused theory and therapy, supervision and training in systemic therapies, and the use of letter writing in therapeutic settings.

Robert Sholtes, MD, is the director of behavioral sciences at MacNeal Hospital Family Practice Residency Program and the codirector of the Family Systems and Health Post-Doctoral Fellowship Program provided jointly with the Chicago Center for Family Health. He also is in private practice as a family therapist at the Glen Ellyn Family Center. He received his medical degree from Loma Linda University in California in 1981 and graduated from Duke University, Durham, North Carolina, Child Psychiatry Fellowship, in 1986. While an associate professor of neuropsychiatry at the University of South Carolina, Columbia, he directed the child and adolescent inpatient services and the family therapy training program until 1990. He also supervised the first in-home intervention team working with severely distressed children and families through the South Carolina continuum of care. For the past fourteen years, he has been a consultant to numerous community mental health facilities, providing services to marginalized children and their families.

Susan K. Sholtes, LSCW, is codirector of the Glen Ellyn Family Center and associate faculty member of the Chicago Center for Family Health. She is currently a supervisor for the Family, Systems and Health Fellowship Program, Chicago, Illinois. Her special interests include chronic medical illness and disabilities work with individuals, families, and groups. Her background includes work with children and adolescents in both outpatient and inpatient settings.

Susan received her clinical social work degree from the University of Chicago in 1980. She is a member of the American Family Therapists Association, the Collaborative Family Health Care Coalition, and the National Association of Social Workers. She is currently studying and teaching narrative therapy practices with the Evanston Family Therapy Center, Evanston, Illinois.

Hemla D. Singaravelu, PhD, LPC, NCC, is currently an assistant professor at St. Louis University, Missouri. She teaches several courses, including career development, culture and gender, and assessment methods, in the Department of Counseling and Family Therapy. Prior to her position as the coordinator of Career and Mentor Programs at Fitchburg State College, Massachusetts, she worked as a career counselor for several years at Southern Illinois University, Carbondale, while completing her doctoral program. Her research interests include issues in career development; culture/diversity; and the gay, lesbian, bisexual, and transgender community.

Dominicus W. So, PhD, is a native of Hong Kong and received his doctorate in clinical/community psychology in 1997 from the University of Maryland, College Park. He is an assistant professor of psychology at Howard University in Washington, DC. He trains clinical graduate students in child and adolescent psychopathology and treatment and teaches abnormal psychology with a writing emphasis. He conducts research in the areas of spirituality, hope, alternative treatments, spiritual strategies in psychotherapy for adolescents and adults, and the holistic teaching of psychology. He is an author of and contributor to writings on spirituality, family therapy, adolescent girls, and cross-cultural and minority mental health issues. He has been awarded the Fund for Academic Excellence and Faculty Research Support Grant. Outside of academic work, he enjoys art and spirituality. He actively participates in church, gospel singing, pottery, and clay sculpture.

Philippa S. Stuart, BS, obtained her bachelor's degree in psychology from Bennett College in Greensboro, North Carolina. She currently is a Doctor Scholars Fellow, pursuing a doctorate in clinical psychology at Howard University in Washington, DC. Her research interests include examining depression as a function of self-concept formation, self-esteem development, and the parent-child relationship in the African-American adolescent female population. Philippa has traveled to many parts of Australia and North and South America. She loves music, the visual arts, and both the written and spoken word. She dedicates her life and knowledge to the elevation and actualization of the human spirit, particularly for children and adolescents.

Risë VanFleet, PhD, RPT-S, is a licensed psychologist and registered play therapist-supervisor. She is founder and director of the Family Enhancement and Play Therapy Center in Boiling Springs, Pennsylvania. Risë is the author of numerous filial play therapy books and articles and is featured on three play therapy training videos. She is the past president and board chair of the Association for Play Therapy and serves on the editorial board of the *Journal of Play Therapy.* She has trained thousands of professionals in play, filial, and family therapies throughout the world.

James Patrick Ward, MS, is a doctoral student in marriage and family therapy at Purdue University, West Lafayette, Indiana. He received his master's degree in marriage and family therapy from Abilene Christian University. His previous work includes the Integrating Stress Management into Therapy Workshop. Patrick enjoys working with couples and adolescents and has a particular interest in resilience and strengths-based therapy.

Linda Wark, PhD, LMFT, is an associate professor and Chair, Department of Human Services, Indiana University-Purdue University Fort Wayne, Fort Wayne, Indiana. Her areas of clinical and research expertise include children in family therapy, qualitative research methods and analyses, and family therapy supervision and training.

Daniel J. Wiener, PhD, is the founder and director of the method Rehearsals for Growth and is a professor in the Department of Health and Human Services at Central Connecticut State University, New Britain.

Toni Schindler Zimmerman, PhD, is a director of the Marriage and Family Therapy Program and an associate professor in the Human Development and Family Studies Department at Colorado State University, Fort Collins, as well as a licensed marriage and family therapist. She has published in the areas of women's issues, gender equity, dual-income couples, small business, and family systems theory as it applies to work and nonclinical environments. Toni examines how the workplace and families can create greater equity and support the balance between family and work. She was recently the co-recipient of a $206,000 grant from the Alfred P. Sloan Foundation to study the qualities of the strategies used by successful dual-earner couples. She is the past chair of the Women's Programs and Studies Board at Colorado State University, and she was recently named editor of the *Journal of Feminist Family Therapy*. She and her husband Craig have two daughters, Misha and Sage. She enjoys rock climbing, hiking, biking, and otherwise playing with her family.

Foreword

My high school English teacher was aghast when I began submitting poetry in the style of e.e. cummings. I would not be discouraged, however, imagining that great prose was emerging from the very depths of my dramatic adolescent self! She grew more and more intolerant until finally she stated, "Don't fancy yourself a writer because you imitate someone's style. Before you can consider crafting language as cummings does, you must understand the basic rules of poetry composition and syntax. . . . He makes something very complicated look very simple because it's based in solid structure." The message was: Know the basics, understand the foundation, and only then can you structure flights of fancy. I soon discovered how complex and carefully designed the prose of e.e. cummings was! I was crushed and inspired.

I remembered this adolescent lesson while reading this book and the memory seemed coincidental at first. I later realized the connection: the authors present a solid foundation from which creativity soars. Anchored in theory, clinicians in this book explore and invent ways to enlist the cooperation of all family members while decreasing resistance. They make it look easy but it's actually complex and promising. This process of moving from the traditional and familiar to what is less known and structured is both risky and rewarding. This book has abundant exploration, fun, creative spirit, and innovation. It was truly a treat to find a potpourri of playful therapeutic approaches with families in one text.

More memories surfaced as I read this book: I remembered my training in family therapy and the field's consistent lack of interest in young children. Over and over I learned that most family therapists are comfortable with older children who are verbal and cooperative. Younger children were often asked to wait while family therapy occurred, or they were literally placed out of sight with crayons and paper or a few token toys for entertainment. I remember thinking how odd this exclusion ritual seemed to be, especially for therapists who designated themselves as *family* therapists. We've truly come a long way!

This book is gratifying on many levels. It not only brings forward possibilities for meaningful participation by young children but also celebrates the originality that emerges from anyone who can tap into his or her own artistry to promote therapeutic goals. When I do trainings on the topic of play therapy, I find a consistent initial response from students: they want to learn techniques, they want definitive recipes for implementing the techniques, and they want to develop their comfort level through repetitive use. This need for clear instructions and a desire to implement correctly can become rigid and confining. That is why the assignment in my family play therapy class is to design a new family play therapy technique. The students work in groups of five and they develop an idea with clearly stated goals, within a theoretical framework, including safeguards and a stated intent. The projects have been skillful and unique. Students learn to take their own interests, their own experiential data, and shape them until they are comfortable that the techniques have the potential to provide useful assessment data or promote common therapeutic goals. *The Therapist's Notebook for Children and Adolescents* will similarly encourage practitioners to use their skills in creative ways.

The techniques in this book are drawn from a variety of theoretical frameworks such as narrative, behavioral, Gestalt, art therapy, and bibliotherapy. Included are illustrations of the techniques as applied to issues such as divorce, learning problems, nightmares, trauma, bereavement, overt conflict, stepfamilies, parent-child difficulty, and many others. Play is used as the central conduit for change with children and adolescents in a way that is positively engaging and efficient in both eliciting and maintaining their participation.

Catherine Ford Sori and Lorna Hecker have done an excellent job coordinating a diverse group of talented mental health professionals who illustrate the possibilities of integrating play therapy into their clinical practice. So often clinicians hesitate to attempt or blend new approaches for fear of feeling less confident than they do with their more practiced methods of information gathering, therapeutic conversation, and family interventions. This book opens a wide window into the utilization of play to optimize clinical work with parents and their children.

When I first started using play with families I did it out of self-defense. I found myself working too hard to make sure the children were included. The problem? I was using a style that was not user-friendly to young children, whose primary mode of communication is not verbal! In essence, I conspired with parents to keep therapy at an intellectual level and in so doing did not create a bridge that children could cross. Once I did my first family play therapy technique (a family collage) I was hooked! Families responded with some hesitation at first, but that soon gave way to enthusiasm, fun, and relaxation. Even the most conservative and resistant families will feel disarmed if they're asked to be playful.

This book is a resource for all clinicians who need a little inspiration and guidance to spice up family work and make it more accessible to clients. Even those of us who are more adept in this modality have days when the creative juices do not flow, so it's good to know we can lean on others' creativity to enhance our clinical work.

Play therapy is by definition playful and fun, but it is also serious and purposeful. It may look simple to the untrained eye but it is often very intricate. It's important to know how play can be curative, educational, abreactive, and capable of assisting with expression of thoughts and feelings. It's critical to understand the depth of feeling it can awaken and the power it has to be emotionally moving. I recommend that clinicians always do the play techniques themselves before involving their clients. Also, they must be sure to secure their clinical work to a chosen theoretical model. In this manner, they can navigate unhindered and explore freely without wandering too far or losing their way.

Eliana Gil, PhD
Director, Abused Children's Treatment Services
Inova Kellar Center
Fairfax, Virginia

Preface

When treating children individually or in family therapy, therapists often grapple with trying to discover methods to tap into the small souls that we each used to be. Every psychotherapist is aware that small children often carry some large burdens. And if problems are not dealt with effectively in childhood, they often go on to impact negatively adult life. Therapists' input can be vital at this tender time in development. This book was written to provide therapists with field-tested methods to use when working with children and/or adolescents in family, individual, or group therapy.

For those who work primarily with children individually or in children's groups, this book offers some creative new ideas and is especially useful in understanding why, when, and how to include families in your child-focused work.

For family therapists, this volume will greatly expand your repertoire of creative ideas to engage and intervene with families and children of all ages. Although many presume that family therapists are adept at working with children, in actuality, a great number of therapists feel uncomfortable with children and inadequately prepared to work with both children and adults simultaneously. In fact, research has shown that almost half of family therapists exclude children from family sessions (Johnson, 1995; Johnson and Thomas, 1999; Korner and Brown, 1990). The decision to exclude children is often based on therapists' personal preferences, instead of the needs of the children or families. This is largely due to therapists' discomfort with children, and therapists' feeling their training was inadequate to prepare them to work with the youngest family members.

The idea for this book grew out of our love for children and an understanding that to reach children one must tap creativity. Yet therapy must also be theory guided and, most important, effective. We created this book so therapists who regularly work with children can share ideas that work, that tap into the minds of children both in terms of understanding and playfulness.

We also were aware that many therapists who are "in the trenches" working with children on a regular basis seldom get the chance to share what they do in therapy. This book offers this opportunity. The homework, handouts, and activities within have been field-tested by therapists who indeed have—driven by both theory *and* trial and error (or sometimes just a fluke)—found what works. We are delighted that so many therapists have shared their work with us.

Probably the most common criticism of this type of book is that it is a "cookbook" approach to therapy. Trainers complain that students delight in "cookbook interventions" so that they can intervene quickly when they don't know what to do with clients. We are opposed to this approach to therapy ourselves and believe that each therapist should be firmly guided by his or her own theory of therapy as well as the needs of clients. Interventions such as the ones in this book should be theory driven. We believe that therapists are adept at taking useful information and adapting it to fit their preferred theoretical approaches. Some of the chapters in this book will be very clearly rooted in theory; for example, several chapters are guided by narrative theory or behavioral theory. Others are adaptable to various theories. In short, we firmly believe that creativity should not be bound by theory but encouraged by it. We hope this book will encourage therapist creativity and allow therapists (and their small clients and families!) to enjoy therapy and grow and develop with fervor.

Finally, we have encountered many psychotherapists of all affiliations who believe they are not creative or playful. For those of you who refuse to give up this "dominant story," you may use the interventions as they are presented. For others, we expect this book to be a springboard from which additional homework, handouts, and activities will be launched. Creative ideas beget more creative ideas, and we expect therapists will use this book as a tool to enhance the artistry of their work.

Organization

The book is organized into eight sections, although the intervention areas often overlap. It is difficult to categorize homework, handouts, or activities that could easily be adapted for use with various types of problems. Section I has some very useful ideas about helping children understand their feelings. Section II utilizes various forms of play in therapy. Section III deals with specific childhood problems such as those related to school, sleeping, separation anxiety, and social skills. Next, Section IV covers difficult topics such as illness, trauma, and bereavement. In Section V, those "tough" adolescents are engaged in therapy in some very fun and unique ways. Specific approaches in dealing with children are described in Section VI. Finally, in Sections VII and VIII specific family issues and parent education are considered with the knowledge that children do not live in a vacuum, and that context (parents and family) is an integral component to successful treatment of children.

Audience

This book is useful to any clinician whose practice includes children and families. Those in private practice and/or with limited exposure to other therapists may welcome this book as a source for ideas and insight into other therapists' styles and work. Experienced clinicians looking for new ideas and trying to develop some of their own may consult this book for inspiration. New therapists and trainees may find this book helpful as they are developing their own ideas about how to intervene with clients. Textbooks often have few specific examples that students can easily implement as they learn to conduct therapy. Supervisors and trainers may use this book as a text for their practicum and skills classes.

Because the contributors of this book come from various regions, professional backgrounds, and theories, the activities, handouts, and homework assignments in this book can be useful to therapists in many child-related fields, with various degrees, specializing in different problems. Most of these resources are broad enough to be easily adapted to different styles of psychotherapy.

Engaging Children in Therapy

Although some therapists specialize in seeing individual children, others treat children within the context of the family. As stated earlier, even well-trained family therapists sometimes have a difficult time engaging children in therapy. Many of the founding fathers and mothers of family therapy, such as Ackerman, Minuchin, Whitaker, Satir, and Haley, however, actively engaged both children and adults in the therapy process. In fact, Ackerman (1970) stated, "Without engaging the children in a meaningful interchange across the generations, there can be no family therapy. And yet, in the daily practice of this form of treatment, difficulties in mobilizing the participation of children are a common experience" (p. 403).

This raises the question of just what does go on in family sessions when children *are* included. Cederborg (1997) observed family therapy sessions that included young children, ages four to seven, and found that even when physically present, children are neither active nor equal participants in sessions. In fact, children uttered only 3.5 percent of all words spoken in the therapy sessions in this study! Cederborg concluded that children are not granted "full membership status" in family therapy and have been denigrated to the status of nonpersons, since they are "not talked to but rather talked about" (p. 37). Therapists in this study included children, but did not engage them as active participants, stating they were uncertain of children's role in family therapy.

How, then, do children feel about coming to family therapy? Stith and colleagues (1996) interviewed sixteen children between the ages of five and thirteen who had attended at least four family therapy sessions. They found that these children wanted to be involved in sessions, even when the problem was not directly related to them. They wanted to be not only physically present, and not left in the waiting room (which was both boring and sometimes worrisome), but also involved in the therapy process.

Research by Sori (2000) explored the views of experts in the field on training family therapists to work with children. A consensus of opinions was gathered among expert panelists, who emphasized the importance of including children and outlined specific skills necessary for therapists to work with children. Relational skills included how to join, build rapport, and engage both children and adults. Practical skills included how to talk to both children and adults, how to make the process of therapy meaningful to children and adults, and how to use creative ways to facilitate positive interactions among all family members. The importance of being able to engage both children and adults was emphasized by this diverse and renowned panel of experts' consensus that only one resource should be used to train family therapists in child-inclusive work: Chasin and White's (1989) "The Child in Family Therapy: Guidelines for Active Engagement Across the Age Span." This panel also agreed on the use of playful techniques that included speaking through puppets, storytelling, drawing, games, and nonverbal therapeutic art that can be discussed later among family members.

This book is an attempt to draw upon the recommendations of the expert panelists in Sori's (2000) study, and to fill a gap in the field. It also provides some creative solutions to Ackerman's dilemma of how to mobilize children to actively participate in the process of therapy. First, however, clinicians must consider another finding in the Sori study: Panelists agreed that therapists must "touch inside themselves their playful, spontaneous, forgiving, trusting, and creative parts, . . . [t]each parents to reconnect with their playful parts, and coach parents in playful interactions with their children." This is a tall order, and one not easily taught!

Attitude About Play

To facilitate therapists being in touch with their "playful, spontaneous, forgiving, trusting, and creative parts," we suggest clinicians explore their own attitudes about play, playfulness, childhood, and children. Zilbach (1986) discussed how therapists' own childhood experiences influence their reactions to statements such as, "Go outside and play" and "Where did you play in your house?" Reactions to these and other statements may have underlying roots in childhood, which may make it difficult to engage playfully with children and families. Children are amazingly perceptive and will be quick to sense a therapist's discomfort. It also is vital that therapists model comfort and playfulness to parents.

To help facilitate therapist growth and self-awareness, we have included "Therapists' Attitudes About Play" following this preface. This is a brief self-of-the-therapist assessment tool developed to help clinicians begin to explore the roots of their own feelings and attitudes about play. Zilbach (1986) believes that once therapists become aware of their attitudes, they may want to rediscover how to play—and may even learn to enjoy it!

At the same time, however, we caution therapists not to become so focused on play or playfulness, or the ideas in this book, that they lose sight of therapeutic goals and the specific needs of the children and families. The chapters in this book are meant to spark therapeutic creativity, and to serve as a resource to be drawn upon *if and when* they fit the specific child and family needs, as well as the presenting problem. Pittman (1984) suggests therapists' techniques should arise spontaneously, from the specific therapeutic situation. Minuchin (personal communication, 2000) cautions that when techniques are too specific therapists can "get wedded to the technique instead of responding to the stimuli that the family and the children send." Instead, Minuchin suggests that therapists need, first, to be "so comfortable with interviewing families with children that then they can include some techniques without that wagging the dog." We encourage readers to allow the ideas in this book to "lead from behind," while always maintaining a focus on the process of the interactions and specific therapeutic goals.

We leave you with a final thought, from one of the greatest authors of children's stories, on how to recapture the creative essence, spontaneity, and magic of the make-believe world of childhood:

> When I was ten, I read fairy tales in secret and would have been ashamed if I had been found doing so. Now that I am fifty I read them openly. When I became a man I put away childish things, including the fear of childishness and the desire to be very grown up. (C. S. Lewis, 1982, p. 34)

Someone once said that we don't stop playing because we grow old. We grow old because we stop playing. So, if you've somehow lost your playfulness, Zilbach (1986) reminds us, "It is not difficult to play! Most children are wonderful teachers" (p. 22).

REFERENCES

Ackerman, N. (1970). Child participation in family therapy. *Family Process, 9,* 403-410.

Cederborg, A.D. (1997). Young children's participation in family therapy talk. *American Journal of Family Therapy, 15,* 18-38.

Chasin, R. and White, T.B. (1989). The child in family therapy: Guidelines for active engagement across the age span. In L. Combrinck-Graham (Ed.), *Children in family contexts: Perspectives on treatment* (pp. 5-25). New York: Guilford Publications.

Johnson, L.J. (1995). The inclusion of children in the process of family therapy. Unpublished dissertation, Purdue University, West Lafayette, Indiana.

Johnson, L. and Thomas, V. (1999). Influences on the inclusion of children in family therapy. *Journal of Marital and Family Therapy, 25*(1), 117-123.

Korner, S. and Brown, G. (1990). Exclusion of children from family psychotherapy: Family therapists' beliefs and practices. *Journal of Family Psychology, 3*(4), 420-430.

Lewis, C.S. (1982). On three ways of writing for children. In W. Hooper (Ed.), *On stories and other essays on literature* (pp. 3-7). New York: Harcourt Brace Jovanovich.

Pittman, F.S. (1984). Wet cocker spaniel therapy: An essay on technique in family therapy. *Family Process, 23,* 1-9.

Sori, C. (2000). Training family therapists to work with children in family therapy: A modified Delphi study. Unpublished doctoral dissertation, Purdue University, Lafayette, Indiana.

Stith, S.M., Rosen, K.H., McCollum, E.E., Coleman, J.U., and Herman, S.A. (1996). The voices of children: Preadolescent children's experiences in family therapy. *Journal of Marital and Family Therapy, 22*(1), 69-86.

Zilbach, J.J. (1986). *Young children in family therapy.* Northvale, NJ: Jason Aronson, Inc.

Therapist Attitudes About Play

Catherine Ford Sori

For therapists to work successfully with children, they must first be comfortable with the world of childhood. To facilitate this, it is important to assess one's own attitude about play and playfulness. The following questions can be used as a springboard to begin this exploration. Responses can be used to generate discussions in supervision, and reflected upon whenever a clinician experiences difficulties touching his or her own playfulness, spontaneity, or creativity in child-related therapy. Reflecting on one's own childhood, answer these questions:

1. Describe your family's attitude about play. What influenced this attitude?

2. Were there any restrictions on play in your family (e.g., location, amount of noise, messiness, etc.)?

3. What do the words "Go outside and play" mean to you?

4. Where did you play *most often?* Describe this place, and your feelings while playing there.

5. Where was your *favorite* place to play, and what did you do there?

6. Did you prefer solitary play or play with friends or siblings? Who was your favorite playmate? Why? What did you play?

7. What were your favorite play activities? Who engaged in these play activities with you?

8. What were your favorite games? Were these active games (e.g., tag, hide and seek, statues), interactive games (i.e., LIFE, Monopoly, checkers, card games), or solitary games? Who played these games with you?

9. Describe your favorite toy as a child (color, texture, size, shape, and smell). Why was this your favorite toy?

10. What was (were) your favorite book(s) as a young child? In middle childhood? Adolescence? Why?

11. Were you read to as a child? If so, by whom? What was this experience like?

12. Check and rank the following play activities in order of your preference as a child:

_____ Books	_____ Board game: _____
_____ Make-believe	_____ Card games: _____
_____ Riding bikes	_____ Puzzles
_____ Dollhouse	_____ Puppets
_____ Stuffed animals	_____ Dressup
_____ Blocks, Legos	_____ Dolls
_____ Drawing	_____ Guns (i.e., army)
_____ Play-Doh/clay	_____ Other: _____
_____ Plastic figures	_____ Other: _____

What are your reflections on these activities?

Was there a toy you always wanted as a child but never got?

13. Describe your favorite childhood pet. What did this pet mean to you?

14. What types of make-believe play did you engage in as a child? With whom? What were the themes? What role did you often play?

15. Did you have imaginary playmates? If so, what were their names?

16. Did you play with imaginary hero(es) (e.g., Superman, Indiana Jones, Han Solo)?

17. What were your parents' reactions to your play? Did your parents play with you? If so, what, and how often? Describe these experiences with each parent.

18. What types of fun or playful activities did your family enjoy? Describe.

19. Who most influenced your attitudes about play? How?

20. What memories or feelings were evoked as you completed this exercise? What did you learn from this experience? What can you tap into from your own childhood experiences to carry with you into your adult world as you work with children?

Source: Adapted and expanded from Zilbach, 1986.

Acknowledgments

We would like to acknowledge all of the wonderful help in the compilation of *The Therapist's Notebook for Children and Adolescents*. Without these many hands and minds on this project, it would not have come to fruition. We would first like to thank all of our gracious authors who contributed chapters and gave of their time, creativity, and clinical skills. In addition, we would like to thank the wonderful folks at The Haworth Press for their tenaciousness and skills in assembling this book. Also, we would like to thank helpers along the way, including Judy Bates, Christina Dust, Debi Mitchell, Meghan Ryan, Patricia Geiger, and Diane Strange-Hoogeveen. Thanks also to our families, especially Marvin Ford and John Sori, for their encouragement, and for proofreading and commenting on some chapters. In addition, special thanks to Nancee Biank for sharing her passion for helping children in pain and their families, and to C. Everett Bailey, for his efforts to advance the field in this area. Others who have greatly inspired us include Eliana Gil and Risë VanFleet, and those who have long championed the needs of children and families: Lee Combrinck-Graham, Carl Whitaker, and, above all, Salvador Minuchin, whose research on psychosomatic families ignited my (CS) passion to enter the field of family therapy. I (CS) would also like to acknowledge the many leading experts who were panelists in my research on training family therapists to work with children, along with those who supported this research at Purdue University: Douglas H. Sprenkle, Fred P. Piercy, Volker Thomas, and Laura Johnson. Finally, thanks to the support of friends who have sustained us by calling and insisting we take time to play—Kathleen Hazlett, Cathy Mize-Spalding, Judy Stiff, Nancy Nickell, and Anna Bower.

SECTION I:
DEALING WITH CHILDREN'S FEELINGS

Feeling Faces Prevent Scary Places

Nancee Biank
Catherine Ford Sori

Type of Contribution: Activity, Handout

Objective

This activity is designed to help children, ages five to twelve, understand that everyone experiences a variety of feelings, and that children can have more than one feeling simultaneously. Children are taught to identify and recognize a wide range of feelings that can then be normalized and validated by the therapist.

Rationale for Use

Children are often exposed to a myriad of circumstances over which they have little or no control. Divorce in the family, being in a new stepfamily, the serious illness of a family member, or the death of a parent are examples of difficult circumstances faced by many children and their families. During such challenging times, children, as well as their parents, experience a variety of feelings, which are normal and need to be validated. Many adults have used the analogy of a roller-coaster ride to describe how quickly their feelings can shoot up and down when they are going through an experience such as cancer or divorce. Children are often unwilling passengers on this ride that, at times, may feel out of control. Helping children to express the full range of their emotions and to understand that they can feel two feelings simultaneously helps them maintain their sense of self. Children also benefit from learning that their concerns are valid and normal.

Instructions

On a sheet of paper, draw several different "feeling faces," or make copies of our Focus on Feeling Faces handout. Make sure to include examples of feelings such as sad, happy, mad, jealous, worried, and afraid. When making this sheet leave a few circles blank and ask the children for examples of additional feelings that they have experienced to add to the sheet. Feeling charts or cards that offer a wide range of emotions can also be used. Go over each feeling state with the children, asking them to explain what is meant by "sad," "happy," or "worried." Generate a discussion about circumstances when people might have each of these feelings, encouraging children to share times when they experienced some of these emotions.

Next, begin a dialogue on how people can experience two feelings at the same time, or pretend to act one way while really feeling another way inside. In other words, we may have an inside feeling and an outside feeling. To help children understand this concept it is helpful to use the analogy of wearing a mask. When we put the mask on, people think we feel the way we look, but when we take the mask off, we may reveal a set of feelings altogether different from our actions.

In the second part of the activity children will construct masks to represent both their inside and outside feelings. Hemmings (1995) suggests having children make paper plate masks to represent a feeling and its opposite. In the Feeling Faces activity children are purposefully *not* instructed to identify an "opposite" feeling from the one shown on the outside. Instead the choices for inside feelings are left open-ended, so that children may choose from the wide range of emotions discussed in the first part of this activity.

The masks may be constructed in advance, or the children can make their own. Give each child six paper plates and three straws. Staple two plates front sides together, and staple the straw between the plates to serve as a handle, similar to a lollipop. Then ask the children to draw three feelings, one on each of the three paper plates, to represent feelings that they feel on the inside. For example, sad, mad, and worried are all inside feelings that the children might not share with anyone, but that they do experience. Then ask them to turn the plates over and draw three feelings on the opposite sides that represent the feelings they use to cover up their inside feelings, in other words, the ones they use as a mask. For example, if children feel sad on the inside they may act silly on the outside to distract from their sadness. When the project is complete, each child will have three masks, each of which shows an inside feeling on one side and a corresponding outside feeling on the other side.

Once the children have completed the plates, begin a discussion about the feelings that they hide and the feelings that they allow others to see. Ask the children how they know the difference, and why they choose to hide those specific feelings. Also ask them to explore what it might be like to express their hidden feelings, and to whom they might feel safe doing so. Include a discussion about times it is probably wiser to wear a mask. For example, if children have been teased about being different, it would be unsafe to share their inner sad feelings with the persons doing the teasing. Reinforce that the individual, group, or family therapeutic settings are places in which it is safe to share, because all feelings are acceptable.

Vignettes

Child of Divorce in Individual and Family Therapy

Often children experiencing divorce have a difficult time coping with changes. One of the most difficult is seeing the emotional transformations their parents are experiencing. A parent who may have previously been stable, rational, and supportive may now exhibit volatile emotions that can be quite frightening to a young child. During a difficult and uncertain time children may feel as if the very foundation of their family has been shaken and now rests on shifting sand. With encouragement these children may be able to talk about how they have two feelings at the same time. For example, children may act happy on the outside in front of Mom and Dad, hoping to prevent their parents from arguing or fighting. In reality, however, on the inside, the children are sad and want to cry because they recognize they will never have complete access to both parents again.

Eight-year-old Audrey's mother and father were always fighting and threatening to take the other parent to court, or to call the police for some minor infraction of the visitation order. As children often do, Audrey interpreted her parents' anger in terms of herself and believed that she was somehow to blame. Audrey always acted pleasant in front of her parents because she believed that showing any negative behavior or emotions would lead to her parents having another fight. In therapy Audrey began to work with the feeling faces and demonstrated a good understanding of a variety of emotions, and that people could often have two feelings simultaneously.

She also recognized that she was hiding some of her feelings, especially the angry ones, from both of her parents.

In making her masks and in the discussion that followed, the therapist was able to validate and normalize Audrey's inside feelings. In a joint family session that included Audrey and both parents, Audrey was encouraged to express herself and her feelings to both her mom and dad. Both her parents were surprised to learn that inside she often felt scared that they would fight and angry because she wanted their lives to be as they were before. Both had believed that she was doing fine because the masks she wore portrayed her as "happy" and "normal." The therapist also helped the family understand divorce through the eyes of a young child.

Child Bereavement in Children's Group

When a parent dies a child's world changes forever. The innocence and security that other parents and children take for granted vanish, and the effect on the child is profound and lifelong. At the same time, often no one can help the child understand the shock and overwhelming feelings he or she is experiencing, since often the remaining parent is too overwhelmed to support the child (Christ, 2000). This is, however, an opportunity for a young child to begin to understand the plethora of emotions he or she is experiencing, and to learn how to share them with the remaining parent, who is also grieving (Webb, 1993; Shapiro, 1994; Smith and Pennells, 1995). Open communication between the surviving parent and child facilitates healthy adjustment for the child (Raveis, Siegel, and Karus, 1999; Christ, 2000; Shapiro, 1994).

Research indicates that the period of anticipatory grief in the terminal stage of a parent's illness is often the most difficult for a child (Christ et al., 1993). Furthermore, research also shows that intervening prior to the death of a parent greatly improves postdeath adjustment for both the child and the surviving parent (Christ, 2000; see also Bourke, 1984). Still, many parents remain blind to the anticipatory grief their children are experiencing (Rosenheim and Reicher, 1986).

Andrew, who was an only child, was nine years old when his mother died. In the months leading up to her death Andrew's father buried himself in his work and avoided talking about his wife's terminal cancer. He did eventually heed the advice of relatives to take Andrew to a children's group that offered support to children who have a parent with cancer. There Andrew learned how people can experience two feelings at the same time.

About two months after the support group ended Andrew lost his mother to ovarian cancer. Andrew asked his father to call the group leader to tell her the sad news. The leader attended the service, and at the coffin Andrew pulled her quietly aside. There he initiated a discussion about the loss and the many different feelings he had. Spontaneously, Andrew took a tissue and tore it in half. He stated that half of him felt like this part of the tissue—flat and regular, knowing that Mom was finally out of pain, and no longer felt so terrible. He then quickly crumbled up the other portion of the tissue, squeezing it into a tight ball. Andrew then said that the other half of him felt like this crumpled part of the tissue—angry that his mother was no longer with him, and that she would never be able to be alive to be his mother again!

Somewhat amazed, the group leader listened as Andrew so beautifully articulated his feelings. With empathy and care she validated and normalized all his emotions. Because Andrew had come to understand feelings and their different levels of expression in the group, at this crucial time he was able to seek out a safe person with whom to talk, rather than repress his overwhelming sadness and anger. With a little time and support, Andrew's father became more available to listen, tolerate, and validate the range of Andrew's emotions. This support opened the door for father and son to share appropriately their grief and support with each other, and to mourn their loss together as they began restructuring their family.

Suggestions for Follow-Up

Once the children initially use the Feeling Faces activity it becomes a resource that can be referred to at any time. The handout or masks can be used to check in with the child by asking questions such as, "What are you feeling today?" or "What feeling did you have inside this week that you weren't able to share?"

This idea can also be continued in follow-up by giving children a sheet of paper with six or eight blank circles in two rows and asking them to draw inside feelings on the top row and "masked" feelings underneath (see Speltz and Biank, 2001). Children can also be reminded of this exercise when learning about conflict resolution or assertiveness training. Giving children a solid understanding of emotions and encouraging them to express themselves verbally or with pictures lessens children's need to inappropriately act out their feelings.

Contraindications for Use

Learning about "feeling faces" should begin soon after the therapist has established a safe and comfortable therapeutic relationship, and when the therapist determines the child is open to learning new experiences. This activity is not recommended when the child or family is experiencing a crisis.

Professional References

Biank, N. and Beck, P. (1997). Enhancing therapeutic intervention during divorce. *Journal of Analytic Social Work, 4*(3), 63-81.

Bourke, M. P. (1984). The continuum of pre- and post-bereavement grieving. *British Journal of Medical Psychology, 57*(2), 121-125.

Christ, G. H. (2000). *Healing children's grief: Surviving a parent's death from cancer.* New York: Oxford University Press.

Christ, G. H., Siegel, K., Freund, B. and Langosch, D. (1993). Impact of parental terminal cancer on latency-age children. *American Journal of Orthopsychiatry, 63*(3), 417-425.

Hemmings, P. (1995). Communicating with children through play. In S. Smith and Sr. M. Pennells (Eds.), *Interventions with bereaved children* (pp. 9-23). Bristol, PA: Jessica Kingsley Publishers.

Raevis, V., Siegel, K., and Karus, D. (1999). Children's psychological distress following the death of a parent. *Journal of Youth and Adolescence, 28*(2), 165-180.

Rosenheim, E. and Reicher, R. (1986). Children in anticipatory grief: The lonely predicament. *Journal of Clinical Child Psychology, 15*(2), 115-119.

Shapiro, E. R. (1994). *Grief as a family process: A developmental approach to clinical practice.* New York: Guilford Publications.

Smith, S. C. and Pennells, Sr. M. (1995). *Interventions with bereaved children.* Bristol, PA: Jessica Kingsley Publishers.

Speltz, A. and Biank, N. (2001). *Kid support: A procedures manual for conducting support groups with the children of cancer patients.*

Wallerstein, J. and Blakeslee, S. (1990). *Second chances: Men, women, and children a decade after divorce.* New York: Ticknow and Fields.

Webb, N. B. (1993). *Helping bereaved children: A handbook for practitioners.* New York: Guilford Publications.

Readings for Children and Parents

Brown, L. K. and Brown, M. (1988). *Dinosaurs divorce: A guide for changing families.* Boston: Little, Brown and Co.

Brown, L. K. and Brown, M. (1996). *When dinosaurs die: A guide to understanding death.* Boston: Little, Brown and Co.

Buscaglia, L. (1982). *The fall of Freddie the Leaf: A story of life for all ages.* New York: Henry Holt and Company.

Cain, B. S. (1990). *Double-dip feelings: Stories to help children understand emotions.* New York: Magination Press.

Girard, L. W. (1987). *At Daddy's on Saturdays.* Morton Grove, IL: Albert Whitman and Co.

Ives, S. B., Fasler, D., and Lash, M. (1994). *Divorce workbook: A guide for kids and families.* New York: Talman Co.

Mundy, M. (1998). *Sad isn't bad: A good-grief guidebook for kids dealing with loss.* St. Meinrad, IN: Abbey Press.

Vigna, J. (1991). *Saying goodbye to Daddy.* Morton Grove, IL: Albert Whitman and Co.

Focus on Feeling Faces

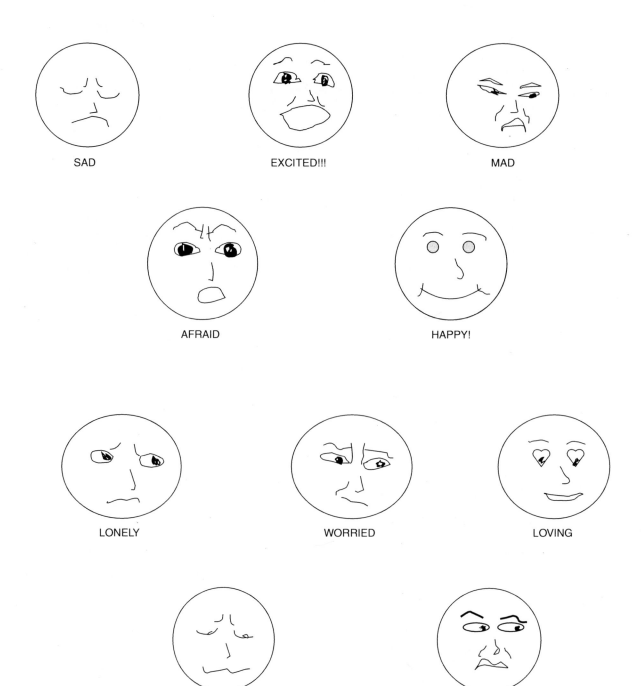

SAD

EXCITED!!!

MAD

AFRAID

HAPPY!

LONELY

WORRIED

LOVING

EMBARRASSED

JEALOUS

2

Deflating Fear

Catherine Ford Sori
Nancee Biank

Type of Contribution: Activity, Handouts

Objectives

The objective of this activity is to help children express their deepest fears, and to begin to find ways to manage fearful thoughts and feelings. This helps parents become more aware of the depth of the child's hidden worries and anxieties. This activity may offer the therapist leverage to involve parents in their child's therapy, and to increase parents' awareness of how unaddressed couple or family issues may be negatively impacting their child.

Deflating Fear also teaches children (and their parents) about the link between the mind, body, and emotions and helps them understand how negative thoughts can increase negative emotions, such as fear, guilt, or anger. Children learn to replace irrational beliefs with more rational thoughts, thus reducing fears and anxieties. They benefit further when their parents respond appropriately, and when parents begin to address the family dynamics that often underlie children's anxieties.

Rationale

When children experience traumatic events, such as divorce or the death of a parent or sibling, they often develop distorted beliefs that result from magical thinking. These children are more at risk for becoming symptomatic and developing serious problems. Unaddressed fears may lead to somatic symptoms, sleep disturbances, excessive worrying, depression, regressive behaviors, or other acting-out problems. Over time unaddressed magical thoughts can impede the children's development, resulting in more serious pathologies (Fogarty, 2000). Helping children to talk about their fears is the crucial first step in treating anxious, fearful children. However, young children may lack the language skills to express verbally their feelings (Gondor, 1957; Ariel, Carel, and Tyano, 1985; Sori, 1998, 2000). In addition, many symptomatic children, especially internalizing children who are anxious or depressed, keep their fears well hidden. This can lead to emotional isolation for these children, who have no one to counter their fears, address their thoughts, and help them learn to cope and soothe themselves.

Deflating Fear helps children first to identify and express their fears and then to understand how unchecked fears or worries can snowball into excessive worry. Children begin to understand that not talking about stressful feelings doesn't really work because the fear will show up in bodily symptoms. Some authors have used a body map to help children identify a variety of feelings (Gregory, 1990; Speltz and Biank, 2001). Here the My Body . . . My Feelings of Stress handout is used primarily to locate where in the child's body stressful feelings such as fear or worry are expressed. This activity provides children with a safe way to share their innermost stressful feelings with the very people who are best equipped to help them: their parents.

This activity is best suited for use when the therapist already has a trusting relationship with the child. Deflating Fear is designed first to be used with the child, with the goal of empowering the child to overcome fears, and then to increase parents' awareness of the child's unexpressed fears. This activity can provide leverage for motivating parents to work on their own individual or couple issues, once they realize how problems at home are affecting their child.

Originally the fear handout was used in a group format, and was part of a comprehensive program designed by Nancee Biank for children who have a close family member with cancer. Here it is described as part of an intervention to address children's fears in a family context.

Instructions

Step One: Identifying the Fears

The children should be comfortable with doing art or written work before beginning this activity. Begin this activity by engaging children in a discussion about feelings, telling them clearly that it is okay to have both good and bad feelings. Feelings charts or cards can be used to help children identify and understand many different feelings, and to introduce the idea that people can have two feelings at the same time (e.g., love someone and also be angry with that person).

The My Body . . . My Feelings of Stress handout shows an illustration of a human body, and asks children to choose a color to represent fear, and to color the places on the body where they physically experience stress or fear. They are also asked to rate how much fear, worry, or stress they feel in each body part they marked, using a scale of one to ten, with ten being the most negative emotion. Ask questions about how each of these (and possibly other) emotions is experienced. For example:

- How does stress make your head feel?
- What does that fear feel like in your heart?
- When it's at its worst, how bad does that worry make your heart hurt on a scale from one to ten?
- What is happening when you notice that feeling in your body?

The second handout, Everyone Has Fears, has three open-ended statements. First, the children are asked to complete the sentence that begins "There are times that I feel frightened when . . ." by either writing or drawing about those examples of when they felt afraid. Some children may first write about a more general fear before admitting to fears related to a family situation. Children who are strongly defensive probably will not initially bring up a family problem but are more likely to write about more universal fears, such as fear of monsters, the dark, or scary movies. This allows for a safe introduction to the topic of fears, and the children may need to test the waters before sharing deeper fears.

Next ask the children to complete the statement "When I feel frightened I . . . " Here children are asked to write or draw a picture of what happens when they feel frightened. For example, what do they say or do when they are afraid, who knows, and how do they respond? This gives the therapist valuable information about whom the child feels safe confiding in, and how the child's fears are addressed. It also offers insight into the child's coping skills and ability to self-soothe. The therapist can also trace the sequence of fearful thoughts or events to their conclusion by asking a series of questions about what happens next.

Finally, the child's fears are generalized by answering the third statement, "Everyone feels frightened when . . ." Here it is useful to ask for specific examples of things that frighten people. This may be when the child first names the family problem—but as it relates to "everyone." This bypasses children's natural defenses, offering them a safer way to disclose fears, while not directly "owning" their personal fears. At the same time, fears are normalized. The therapist may ask what they think some people might do when they feel frightened by that event. The children's readiness to discuss the impact of the problem on them directly may be tested by asking how frightened they feel about that issue, and what they do when frightened.

Step Two: Assessing and Expanding Coping Skills

Beginning with more general fears, talk with the children about times that they overcame a fear. Solution-focused questions that explore what they did and what they told themselves helps children begin to realize that they already have some experience defeating fear. For example, children may say they were afraid to go into the basement alone, but they put the light on, took their dog, told themselves nobody was down there, and went. Spend some time discussing each step in the process of overcoming this fear, congratulating the children on having such great fear-busting skills.

Next, focus on their self-talk. Ask children to think about the kinds of thoughts they had when they first felt afraid. The children may wish to write down such thoughts as, "I thought I heard a noise down there" or "I thought Freddie was in the basement." Next, explore what they were saying to themselves when they overcame the fear, such as "I told myself the noise was just the furnace" or "Freddie is just a movie character."

The metaphor of a balloon is useful for children to understand visually how fears can be inflated, by thinking bad thoughts, or deflated, by thinking good thoughts. Young children may not understand what an "irrational" or "negative" thought is, but they will understand "bad" thoughts and "good" thoughts. Explain that "bad" thoughts are ones that make you more afraid, and "good" thoughts are ones that help you feel less afraid.

Step Three: Deflating Fear

Once the children have identified specific "bad" and "good" thoughts, explain that fear is like a balloon. It rests on their chest but can get very big and heavy. Explain that bad thoughts fill the balloon up, as with heavy air that presses on their chest (or other body part where they experience fear). Explain that good thoughts are ways to deflate the balloon and empty out all the air compressing their chest, leaving just a deflated balloon! Ask the children to close their eyes and picture themselves during their last fearful event. Then suggest that they imagine a deflated balloon resting on their chest. For example, a child might picture himself or herself lying in bed at night, worrying about a piano recital. The bad thoughts that begin to inflate the heavy balloon might include statements such as, "I just know I am going to be nervous, I'll probably make a mistake, and I might even completely forget my piece!" Ask if the child can imagine how these bad thoughts would quickly fill that balloon.

Next ask the child to take a deep breath and imagine the balloon beginning to deflate as he or she begins to think good thoughts. Ask the child to exhale through the mouth as the therapist says aloud the good thoughts the child has identified. Good thoughts might be, "I have done my practicing and I know this music, Miss Walker said I play well and she thinks I will do fine, and Mom said it doesn't have to be perfect!"

Discuss how the children felt when the balloon was inflated. Ask questions such as these:

- How big was the balloon, and how heavy did it feel?
- How did they start to deflate the balloon?
- How did it feel when they started thinking the good thoughts?
- How quickly did the balloon deflate? How did that feel?
- How much did it weigh before? How much does it weigh now?
- Do they feel less afraid now than when the balloon was big?

The therapist should take a one-down position, emphasizing how the children already knew the "secret" good thoughts to overcome fear.

The next important step transfers this success to more serious fears. For example, therapists may ask, "What are some bad thoughts about divorce, illness, death, etc., that might inflate the fear balloon? How can they begin to deflate the balloon?" (Note: If a child is reluctant or unable, sometimes the therapist can help the child get started. For example, share that other kids have described thinking that they might not get to see their dad after the divorce inflates their fear balloon, but thinking "Dad promised I would visit every other weekend and holidays" deflates the balloon.)

This activity accomplishes several purposes. First, the child is playfully engaged using imagination, visualization, and positive self-talk to cope actively with fear. The child is helped to identify both bad and good thoughts, to realize the effects of each, and to picture what happens when he or she chooses to think both ways. The child is empowered to be in control of both inflating and deflating the balloon. Finally, the "as if," playlike quality of this activity changes the context of the problem. The problem can no longer occur in the same emotional context, since the child has role-played a more positive outcome. Ariel, Carel, and Tyano (1985) point out that the problem becomes "alien" and disowned by the child "because, by the definition of make-believe play, it is not true of him in the here and now" (p. 53).

Step Four: Involving Parents

While the previous activities are cathartic and help children to internalize new coping skills, this intervention is incomplete without this crucial last twofold step. First, parents who may have been unwilling or unable to realize the effects of the problem on their child are able to see and hear it for themselves in the child's fear handouts and balloon story. The child is less hesitant to share fears because it is in a nonblaming, playful context, and often because the child also trusts the therapist to be there to support the parents. As the child shares both fears and new coping skills, often the parents' eyes are opened to their child's pain. The child may be the motivation for parents to work harder at reducing marital conflict and/or improving family relationships.

Second, parents who may have been peripheral may be engaged in their child's therapy. Instead of the therapist having responsibility for positive change, that responsibility is now coshared with parents (Bailey and Sori, 2000). Just helping the child to share secret fears changes the family's communication rules. Parents can be coached to address directly the child's fears, suggest more good thoughts and coping skills, and practice soothing the child.

This activity can be expanded to help parents begin to address their own hidden fears and improve their coping skills. The balloon metaphor is excellent for adults to check their own self-talk. Parents can be encouraged to "check in" each night with their child, to see how big the fear balloon is, and if the child needs any help "blowing the air out."

Vignette

Paul, age ten, who was first seen with his mother, Pauline, had been referred by his pediatrician. Paul, an only child, had developed severe asthma over the past year, during the time that his parents had decided to divorce. The divorce had become increasingly bitter, and the couple's fights had become both more intense and more frequent. Paul's symptoms had worsened in direct proportion to his parents' conflicts. He had been hospitalized twice, and the doctor was concerned about the heavy doses of steroids currently being administered to prevent further crises.

Although the therapist requested that everyone attend sessions, since that was the best and fastest way to help Paul, Pauline insisted that wouldn't work. Her husband wouldn't come, even if she wanted him to—which she didn't! She knew all the fighting wasn't good for Paul, but she wasn't convinced it was linked to Paul's asthmatic condition. She hoped that some individual therapy sessions would help him be less anxious. Pauline also wanted some individual time to talk about her stress over the bitter battles.

For the first few sessions the therapist met first with the mother and son briefly and then with each alone. Paul was reluctant to talk directly about his feelings but drew pictures of his family before the divorce, as well as how they currently were. He also enjoyed the *Dinosaurs Divorce* book and the *Divorce Workbook*. Often first the therapist would read sections to Paul, and then Paul would read them to his mother. Sessions with Mom assessed her safety, identified her role in the fight sequences, and helped her explore ways to control her own emotions.

By the fourth session the therapist felt well joined with Paul and wanted to help him begin to express the fears that might be contributing to his medical condition. Paul had started a notebook to collect his artwork, and the therapist told him she had a new sheet to color. She offered him the My Body . . . My Feelings of Stress handout and asked him to color where in his body he felt fear, and to rate how severe the pain was in each body part. Paul colored his entire chest black, which was the color of his fear, and he rated this fear a ten when it was the worst.

Next the therapist gave him the Everyone Has Fears handout, and Paul identified two times when he feels frightened. The first was when he sees scary movies, such as *I Know What You Did Last Summer*. Paul wrote that he gets afraid that the scary guy in the costume is hiding under his bed at night. He's afraid to get out of bed to run to Mom because his leg will get chopped off! Then the killer will go after Mom and chop her head off!

He then wrote, "When I feel frightened I put the lamp on and say, 'It's not real, it's just a movie. There's nobody under my bed.'" Then he also wrote, "When Mom starts yelling at Dad I feel tight in my chest, and I can't breathe and start to cry. Then Mom comes and says it's okay. But sometimes I still have to go to the hospital."

For the third statement Paul wrote, "Everyone feels frightened sometimes when they can't breathe, and when their parents divorce."

The therapist validated all of Paul's feelings and remarked that fear is sometimes like a balloon that rests on our chest. When we aren't afraid, the balloon is empty. But when we get afraid, that balloon fills up with those fear thoughts, getting heavier and heavier, until we can hardly breathe! Then the therapist remarked how great it was that Paul already had found the "secret" to deflating a fear balloon and getting it off his chest. A discussion followed in which the therapist explained how the balloon fills from bad thoughts (e.g., "There's a scary guy under my bed") and deflates with good thoughts (e.g., "It's not real, it's just a movie").

In a previous session Paul and his mother had been introduced to relaxation training (see Chapter 4). He enjoyed this experience, and easily closed his eyes when the therapist asked him to imagine the deflated balloon on his chest. They went through the imagery of inflating and deflating the balloon, using Paul's own bad and good thoughts, and then discussed how he felt throughout this exercise. Paul was again complimented on being able to use this "secret" to deflate that fear balloon.

Paul was then asked what bad and good thoughts he had about his parents divorcing. His bad thoughts included, "I'll have to move away from my friends and change schools, and my parents are always going to fight. And Mom will always be mad if I want to see Dad." These thoughts were discussed and written on the back of his fear sheet.

Paul had more difficulty coming up with some good thoughts and agreed to ask for Mom's help. Mom was invited in and shown Paul's handouts. In explaining the body sheet, the therapist pointed out how thick and black fear was over the chest. She then asked Paul if he'd like to read his fear sheet. As he read, Pauline's expression softened, and she said she had no idea how many fears he had, especially about the divorce. The therapist coached Pauline to address each fear, especially his fear that his parents would always fight. Pauline also relieved Paul of his role as "referee," vigilantly standing guard to make sure Mom was okay. She promised him that she would do everything she could to stop the fighting, and that she believed Dad would help too.

Pauline now recognized how their fights were affecting Paul and was determined to do whatever it took to help her son. She made a commitment to talk to her husband and urge him to come to therapy to find better ways to resolve their conflicts. She also admitted that she often provoked her husband and wanted to work at controlling her own temper. The therapist used this opening to emphasize the importance of starting right away to develop a healthy postdivorce parenting relationship. Pauline was now motivated and aware of her crucial role in helping her son.

Paul was asked how high his fear scale was at the end of the session. It had gone from a ten, all the way down to a five! When asked what would help it go down further, Paul said, "Not fighting. And not worrying that someone will get hurt." Nothing further needed to be said.

Follow-up: This was a major turning point in family therapy. True to her word, Mom learned better ways to deal with her anger. Dad attended some sessions, in which Paul proudly showed Dad his work and read his fear handout to him. Both parents quickly learned to take time-outs when discussions began to escalate. As arguments decreased, so did Paul's asthmatic symptoms. Within three months the divorce was final, Dad had moved into an apartment, and the dosage of Paul's medicine had been reduced. Paul reported his fear was down to a two or three, and he enjoyed his time with both parents.

Suggestions for Follow-Up

The therapist can continue to explore the mind-body link, and the balloon metaphor may be expanded to include other situations or emotions. For example, a depressed child may identify where sadness is experienced in the body and what bad thoughts fill the sadness balloon. One very depressed and obese nine-year-old girl had sad thoughts about the mean things that her friends said whenever she got mad and complained about something. This made her stomach ache. These pains were relieved by food—particularly huge bags of cookies she carried in her knapsack. This was an opportunity to explore other ways to cope and soothe herself, as well as how to develop better nutritional and social skills.

Contraindications

This intervention is excellent for middle childhood to preadolescence. However, very young children often cannot trace their thoughts back to their origins, following Piaget's concept of irreversibility. This makes it difficult to undo magical thinking that is entrenched in the minds of young children. Therefore, very young children would not be able to verbalize the thoughts that preceded the emotions. However, they could benefit from the metaphor and visualization. The therapist and parents could address their fears directly and suggest good thoughts to deflate the fear balloon. Parents should be encouraged to practice this as an exercise with their child at home.

Finally, part of the purpose of this intervention is to help parents take responsibility for addressing family problems that are harming their child. If a child reveals abuse or neglect, extra care must be taken to ensure the child's safety. Often much work must be done to assess the availability of the nonabusive parent to support the child.

Professional Readings

Ariel, S., Carel, C., and Tyano, S. (1985). Uses of children's make-believe play in family therapy: Theory and clinical examples. *Journal of Marital and Family Therapy, 11*(1), 47-60.

Bailey, C. E. and Sori, C. E. F. (2000). Involving parents in children's therapy. In C. E. Bailey (Ed.), *Children in therapy: Using the family as a resource* (pp. 475-501). New York: W. W. Norton and Company.

Biank, N. and Beck, P. (1997). Broadening the scope of divorce mediation to meet the needs of children. *Mediation Quarterly, 14*(3), 179-199.

Fogarty, J. A. (2000). *The magical thoughts of grieving children: Treating children with complicated mourning and advice for parents.* Amityville, NY: Baywood Publishing Company, Inc.

Gil, E. (1994). *Play in family therapy.* New York: Guilford Publications.

Gondor, L. H. (1957). Use of fantasy communications in child psychotherapy. *American Journal of Psychotherapy, 5*, 323-335.

Gregory, P. (1990). *Body map of feelings.* Lethbridge, Alberta, Canada: Family and Community Development Program.

Sori, C. E. F. (1998). Involving children in family therapy: Making family movies. In L. Hecker and S. Deacon, (Eds.), *The therapist's notebook: Homework, handouts, and activities for use in psychotherapy.* Binghamton, NY: The Haworth Press, Inc.

Sori, C. E. F. (2000). Training family therapists to work with children in family therapy: A modified Delphi study. Unpublished dissertation, Purdue University, West Lafayette, Indiana.

Speltz, A. and Biank, N. (2001). *Kid support: A procedure manual for conducting support groups with the children of cancer patients.* Evanston, IL: Self-published.

Bibliography for Clients

Brown, L. K. and Brown, M. (1988). *Dinosaurs divorce: A guide for changing families.* Boston: Little, Brown and Co.

Cain, B. S. (1990). *Double-dip feelings: Stories to help children understand emotions.* New York: Magination Press.

Girard, L. W. (1987). *At Daddy's on Saturdays.* Morton Grove, IL: Albert Whitman and Co.

Ives, S. B., Fasler, D., and Lash, M. (1994). *Divorce workbook: A guide for kids and families.* New York: Talman Co.

Rofes, E. (1982). *The kids' book of divorce: By, for, and about kids.* New York: Lewis Publishing Company.

My Body . . . My Feelings of Stress

Everyone has stressful feelings, such as fear or worry. Pick a color to represent stress. Color the places in your body where you feel afraid, worried, or stressed. Then write each body part on a line and rate how much stress you feel in each place in your body.

STRESS SCALE

1 2 3 4 5 6 7 8 9 10

Place in Body . . . Amount of Stress

_____   _____
_____   _____
_____   _____
_____   _____
_____   _____

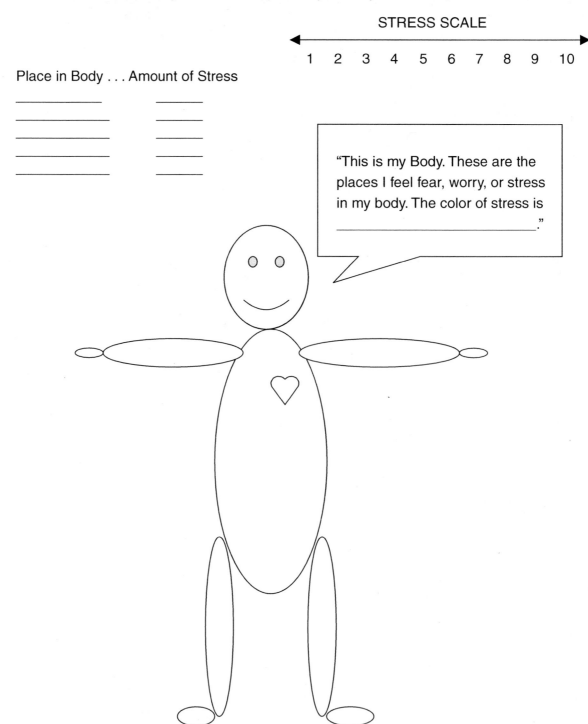

"This is my Body. These are the places I feel fear, worry, or stress in my body. The color of stress is _____."

Everyone Has Fears

"There are times that I feel frightened when . . ."

"When I feel frightened I . . ."

"Everyone feels frightened when . . ."

3

A Child's Impossible and Scariest Tasks

Nancee Biank
Catherine Ford Sori

Type of Contribution: Activity, Handout

Objectives

Children who find it difficult to talk directly about painful or difficult events in their lives can learn to express themselves safely by using playful methods, such as puppets and drawings. The purpose of My Impossible and Scariest Tasks activity and handout is to help children begin to articulate some of the difficult feelings they are experiencing. This activity may be used in children's groups as well as individual or family therapy. When done with other children (e.g., with siblings or in a group), a child has the additional benefit of hearing others share similar feelings. This information can be used to facilitate discussions among children, as well as to open communication among family members. Often this activity opens parents' eyes so they can see and begin to understand the depth of their children's hidden feelings and concerns.

Rationale

Children often struggle to make sense of events that occur as a result of serious problems in the family. In times of crisis, such as a serious illness, a divorce, or the death of a family member, parents often become so preoccupied with trying to cope themselves that they are not aware of how their children are affected. When parents are not available to explain things and answer questions, children may struggle to figure out what these events mean in terms of their own lives. Children often fear that their parents will become overwhelmed and will not be available to take care of them. Not only do these children feel emotionally isolated from their parents, but they also often feel different from their peers. With no one to help them sort out these perplexing emotions, they often struggle to cope. Unaddressed fears coupled with misinterpretations of events can interfere with children's normal development. This intervention serves to normalize and validate children's experiences and help them verbalize specific instances that cause them duress. It also identifies what is still good in their lives and punctuates children's strengths and positive ways of coping.

Children who are struggling to make sense of a family crisis often believe certain myths. Children sometimes believe that they did something bad and are therefore responsible for causing a problem in their family. An example of this type of egocentric thinking occurred in a family with two young boys, the younger of whom had recently been diagnosed with cancer. His older brother, who was eight, felt terribly guilty for months because he felt responsible for causing his brother's tumor. About two weeks before the diagnosis he had accidentally struck his brother in the leg with a ball when they were playing softball. This blow was not serious but left a slight bruise, and he was convinced that it was his fault that cancer was later discovered in his brother's leg. If these types of beliefs (or myths) are not addressed they often remain with the child for life, resulting in free-floating anxiety, depression, guilt, or even thought disorders.

An example of the long-term consequences of unchecked egocentric thinking occurred in a fifty-year-old woman who sought treatment for chronic pain and depression. Marge had experienced debilitating pain most of her life and could only hobble around on crutches, unable to function normally. Over the years she had seen hundreds of specialists from around the country and had endured hundreds of thousands of dollars worth of tests, yet no physician could find any physical explanation for her disabling pain. However, when discussing her family the therapist learned that Marge had experienced a very traumatic event in her childhood. When she was eight years old she was sent outside to pull her little brother up and down the sidewalk in a wagon. Without warning, a speeding car jumped the curb and struck both of the children. They were rushed to the hospital, and Marge recalled lying on a table, assuring the doctors and nurses that she was okay, and begging them to take care of her brother, who was lying asleep on a nearby table. She was reassured that her brother was fine. Both of Marge's legs were broken, and she was hospitalized for over a week. Her father picked her up from the hospital, but instead of taking her home, he took her to a cemetery to "see something." There he showed Marge her little brother's fresh grave, covered with wilting flowers. Her father said that her mother was sick with grief, and he forbid Marge to cry or ever talk about the accident or her brother. When she got home all of her brother's things were gone, and she stayed alone in her room for days, trying to understand what had happened. Marge had lost her only sibling and felt horribly responsible, yet no one comforted her. She was never allowed to express her grief or the tremendous sense of self-blame and guilt she felt for her brother's death. She suffered in isolation, and her emotional pain and disenfranchised grief were translated into a more acceptable physical pain. Her body spoke what her voice was not allowed to express (see Griffith and Griffith, 1994).

This activity provides an opportunity for therapists to address myths that children may develop when families experience situations such as illness, death, or divorce. As the children begin to talk, therapists can gain a truer understanding of what their beliefs are. As children hear others express similar thoughts they realize that other children also face difficult circumstances and have found ways to cope.

When a family experiences an emotional crisis parents often respond by creating an enormous denial system, insisting that everything is okay (as is often seen in substance-abusing families). While this false belief may help the parents feel better, it creates more anxiety in children. They see or hear things they can't make sense of, and they don't know how or if it is safe to talk about them. They may be frightened and confused, not knowing how to respond. Often children don't feel secure because they feel a sense of loss or emotional abandonment of their parents. Their sense of reality becomes distorted. My Impossible and Scariest Tasks helps children clarify and validate what is real in their world.

An additional benefit is the impact this activity often has on parents. When parents see the handout and hear their children discuss their own struggles, the family denial system is challenged, and they begin to recognize their children's hidden distress. Parents can then be supported to address their own emotional issues, while being encouraged to make adaptations that will accommodate the revealed needs of their children.

A final benefit is that the therapist can empower children by reinforcing and helping them expand coping mechanisms they are already using well. For example, Mary shared that when she was missing her mother it helped her to look at her picture and talk to someone about happy memories of Mom. The therapist congratulated Mary on having already discovered such good ways to Come Out of [Her] Shell. She encouraged Mary (and others) to draw pictures of several happy memories with Mom, and to make a list of everyone she could call to share these memories with when she felt like going into her shell. All the children brought pictures of their deceased parents the following week, drew a happy memory picture, and shared stories with one another.

Instructions

Two Hand Puppets: Bumblebee and small turtle (that can be pulled into its shell)

First introduce the children to the bumblebee puppet, saying you'd like them to meet Biggee Bee. Ask what they know about bumblebees. Tell them there is something they might not know—that bees perform an Impossible Task. Ask if they know what the Impossible Task might be. Then explain that, aerodynamically, bees can't fly! Their wings are too thin (you can almost see right through them), and their bodies are too big and round and heavy. But somehow they *do* fly—they do something impossible!

You can use the following dialogue to talk to the children:

> Lots of times children whose parents are divorcing [or whose parent is sick or who has lost a parent or sibling] are like Biggee Bee—they have impossible things they have to perform. Children are supposed to grow up with two parents. But when there's a divorce [death/unavailable parent], you may have to do some impossible things. [Give an example, such as serious illness: One parent is too sick to do everything he or she used to do, while the other parent is busy doing the work of two parents, and sometimes kids feel left out.] And so kids have to do some impossible things. What are some Impossible Tasks you've had to do?

Next introduce the children to the second puppet:

> This is Tuttle Turtle: What are some things that turtles do? Turtles hide. There are times when all of us want to hide. Who in this room has ever felt like hiding like Tuttle Turtle? Where's your favorite hiding spot? [Therapists might share their own to facilitate discussion.] What are things that make you feel like a turtle and want to hide?

Impossible and Scariest Task Handout

Give children the option of either drawing or writing this part of the activity. Use either a large sheet of paper or the handout, which is divided into four columns with four categories: Impossible Task, Still Possible Task, Hide Like a Turtle, and Come Out of Your Shell. The directions are as follows:

1. Impossible Task: Draw a picture or write a couple sentences about what has really been impossible for you during this whole experience.
2. Still Possible: Write or draw what is still possible. What things are still good or are okay?
3. Hide Like a Turtle: Draw or write about what has made you want to hide like a turtle.
4. Come Out of Your Shell: Draw or write about what has helped you to come out of your shell.

Have the children share their completed handouts if they are comfortable. It is important to make connections between similar experiences or emotions among children or family members. *Punctuate children's strengths and good coping skills.* Then say, "Sometimes when something bad happens in our family it makes us stronger." *Encourage children to think of positive things that have resulted, such as being more independent or caring.* This last step is crucial since children may have revealed some deeply painful material, and you want them to leave the session feeling stronger and more hopeful. For example, one bereaved eight-year-old boy drew a picture in his last column of Superman wearing his cape. But instead of the standard "S," his Superman had the word "Courage" on his cape because the boy's courage had helped him come out of his shell. The atmosphere of the room lightened as several boys realized that they too had a "secret courage cape" of which they previously were unaware.

Vignette

In children's bereavement groups Still Possibles always involve a part of their lives that has remained constant, such as school or sports. The Impossible Task always describes an aspect of having to go on without that person. Common examples are "going to bed at night without Mom to tuck me in," or "getting up in the morning knowing Dad's not there." Hide Like a Turtle responses often include watching Mom or Dad die, and having to say goodbye to a parent for the last time. Responses that help children Come Out of [Their] Shell often involve friends, other supportive family members, and knowing that the parent who died loved them and will always be in their heart.

Sarah was in a bereavement group for children who had lost a parent to cancer. She was nine years old, and her mother had died within three weeks of being diagnosed with lung cancer. Sarah, who had been very close to her mother, was the only girl in the family and had a younger brother. On the handout for her Impossible Task Sarah drew a picture of her in bed with her mom, who was singing her favorite bedtime lullaby, "Hush Little Baby." Below the picture Sarah wrote, "What is impossible is going to bed without my mommy." When sharing this, Sarah closed her eyes and spontaneously lifted her lyrical voice to share this most precious memory with the facilitators and group members.

What was Still Possible for Sarah was that she was able to do her homework (although sometimes it was hard to concentrate). In her Hide Like a Turtle column Sarah wrote, "Knowing I will never ever see my mommy again makes me want to hide." But what helped her to Come Out of [Her] Shell was remembering all the fun she had with Mom, such as going to the zoo a few weeks before her mother got really sick.

The therapist validated Sarah when she openly shared her My Impossible and Scariest Tasks handout. Other children resonated with Sarah's feelings, some saying they too really missed their mothers at bedtime. This led to a group discussion about what it was like to watch a parent die. Common feelings the children expressed were disbelief that it was really going to happen, numbness, fear that the other parent would also die and no one would be there to take care of them, and anger at the parent for getting sick and leaving them. Most children experienced tremendous anticipatory grief and felt helpless and out of control. And some felt responsible for the death (for further reading of children's responses see Christ, 2000).

Children's responses to the handout have a dual purpose. First, the material can be used to facilitate open discussions and to link common experiences among children. Second, this type of heartfelt sharing encourages children to ask questions about situations that may have arisen in their own family, but that they might not have raised if they were not in a safe place where feelings are normalized and validated. Once difficult questions are aired they can be answered honestly and age appropriately, and any underlying myths can be refuted.

In this case, during the discussion Sarah softly admitted that she believed it was her fault that her mother died. When questioned, Sarah revealed that she blamed herself for not making Mom stop smoking. She had learned in school about smoking and lung cancer, but she hadn't been able to make Mom stop, and smoking had killed her mother. This was the first time Sarah had ever told anyone of her belief, and the therapist spent some time easing her guilt by explaining why it wasn't Sarah's fault her mother died.

We often invite parents to do this exercise to determine where they are in their own grief process, and how they are coping. (Note: Parents should initially not share their own handout information with their children.) At the end of the children's bereavement group sessions the parents come in to see their children's work. Sarah's dad was amazed at the depth of his child's thoughts, and he was made more aware of how much of a loss this was for her. Dad also never knew Sarah's myth: that she felt to blame for Mom's death. He was able to elaborate further on the truth introduced by the therapist: that Mom couldn't stop smoking because substances in cigarettes cause people to become addicted, and that it's very difficult to conquer a smoking addiction.

Suggestions for Follow-Up

If possible, try to provide each child with bumblebee and turtle puppets to use in follow-up sessions. Children can talk through the puppets as they become more comfortable sharing additional impossible and scariest tasks, as well as sharing how they did the impossible and were able to come out of hiding. The puppets can even be used to enact a scenario. In family sessions each family member can take turns with the puppets, sharing their impossible and scariest tasks, and what helps them come out of their shells. Children can learn from their parents, just as parents begin to see ways they might further help and support their children.

Contraindications

It is important to offer children the choice of writing or drawing the handout. One way of responding could be contraindicated, for example, if a child's motor skills aren't good enough to do drawings. An important caution is that parents will see the real experiences of their children and might feel they have failed the children or have not been good parents. Take the time to talk through the children's responses, being sure to normalize these experiences. On the positive side, this type of reaction may be used as leverage to help the parents grieve their own losses so they can be more available for their children.

Professional Resources

Biank, N. and Beck, P. (1997). Enhancing therapeutic intervention during divorce. *Journal of Analytic Social Work, 4*(3), 63-81.

Christ, J. (2000). *Healing children's grief: Surviving a parent's death from cancer.* New York: Oxford University Press.

Fry, V. L. (1995). *Part of me died too: Stories of creative survival among bereaved children and teenagers.* New York: Dutton Children's Books.

Furman, E. (1974). *A child's parent dies: Studies in childhood bereavement.* New Haven, CT: Yale University Press.

Griffith, L. G. and Griffith, M. E. (1994). *The body speaks: Therapeutic dialogues for mind-body problems.* New York: Basic Books.

Visher, E. B. and Visher, J. S. (1988). *Old loyalties, new ties: Therapeutic strategies with stepfamilies.* New York: Brunner-Mazel Publishers.

Wallerstein, J. and Blakeslee, S. (1990). *Second chances: Men, women, and children a decade after divorce.* New York: Ticknor and Fields.

Recommended Client Resources

Brown, L. K. and Brown, M. (1988). *Dinosaurs divorce: A guide for changing families*. Boston: Little, Brown and Co.

Evans, M. S. (1986). *This is me and my two families: An awareness scrapbook/journal for children living in stepfamilies*. New York: Magination Press.

Girard, L. W. (1987). *At Daddy's on Saturdays*. Morton Grove, IL: Albert Whitman and Co.

Ives, S. B., Fasler, D., and Lash, M. (1994). *Divorce workbook: A guide for kids and families*. New York: Talman Co.

McCue, K. (1996). *How to help children through a parent's serious illness*. New York: St. Martin's Press.

Mundy, M. and Alley, R. W. (1998). *Sad isn't bad: A good-grief guidebook for kids dealing with loss*. St. Meinrad, IN: Abbey Press.

Visher, E. B. and Visher, J. S. (1982). *How to win as a stepfamily*. New York: Brunner-Mazel Publishers.

My Impossible and Scariest Tasks

IMPOSSIBLE TASK	STILL POSSIBLE	HIDE LIKE A TURTLE	COME OUT OF YOUR SHELL
Draw a picture or write a couple of sentences about what has been the hardest thing or the most impossible for you.	Write or draw what is still possible. What things are still good, or are still okay?	Draw or write about what has made you want to hide like a turtle.	Draw or write about what has helped you to come out of your shell.

– 4 –

Soaring Above Stress:
Using Relaxation and Visualization
with Anxious Children

Catherine Ford Sori
Nancee Biank

Type of Contribution: Activity, Handouts

Objective

The purpose of this activity is to teach children a method to reduce their fears and anxieties. By learning techniques to relax their bodies children can better cope with tension and stress either prior to, during, or after an anxiety-provoking event. This empowering activity may be used with individual children, with children and families, or in a group format.

Rationale

Anxiety problems are the most common psychological problems found in children (Kashani et al., 1989). Most children experience fears and anxieties throughout childhood. Common childhood fears include fear of the dark, test taking, monsters, scary movies, and bullies at school. However, when a child becomes so anxious or fearful that his or her well-being is affected the problem needs to be addressed, since severe anxiety can negatively impact a child's development (Wells and Vitulano, 1984). Anxiety does not always disappear as the child grows, and unaddressed childhood anxiety often leads to adult anxiety.

Although childhood anxiety is not well researched (Estrada and Pinsof, 1995), reports indicate that between 10 and 20 percent of school-age children develop internalizing disorders such as anxiety, depression, or hypersensitivity (Johnson, 1979; Orvaschel and Weissman, 1986; Werry, 1986). Anxious children are often seen in therapy for a variety of presenting problems, such as school phobia, separation anxiety, adjustment disorders, child or family illness, bereavement, post-traumatic stress disorder (PTSD), marital conflict, divorce, or stepfamily adjustment.

With increasing frequency, relaxation training is being incorporated into overall treatment plans for a variety of childhood anxiety problems. Relaxation training is a term that incorporates one or several techniques, such as breathing exercises, deep muscle relaxation, and visual imagery. Several authors have reported using relaxation techniques to treat anxious children with a variety of presenting problems. For example, Goodman (1991) includes relaxation in treating childhood cancer. Bevin (1991) describes her work with a child with PTSD: "Every therapy session started with a period of relaxation, one of the most important skills that survivors must learn to counteract the everyday stressors that create a domino-effect reaction relating back to the

25

original trauma" (p. 108). In this case, Bevin taught the child to tense and relax different muscle groups and helped him experience how different it feels when muscles are contracted as opposed to when they are relaxed.

Several researchers have found positive results in reducing childhood anxiety using relaxation training as part of an overall treatment design. Most of these studies use some type of cognitive or cognitive-behavioral interventions in addition to relaxation techniques. Components of relaxation have been used to treat impulsive, depressed, and fearful children (Deutschle, Tosi, and Wise, 1987; Kendall, 1993). Others have found it effective to involve parents in coaching their children to use imagery and relaxation prior to surgery or during hospital procedures (Peterson and Shigetomi, 1981). Even young children (ages four to five years) have experienced relief from fearful symptoms and sleep disturbances when they were taught relaxation training and imagery along with coping skills (McManamy and Katz, 1989). Taken together, these studies provide evidence that the different components of relaxation training can be useful as part of the overall treatment of anxious or fearful children.

In addition, Joyner (1991) points out that relaxation exercises empower children as they learn to control their physiological responses, even though they may not be able to control the precipitating event. Children learn not only an effective and lifelong skill but also how to manage their own emotional states (Wachtel, 1994). For children whose lives are impaired by anxiety symptoms, learning skills to self-soothe is a huge step toward developing a sense of mastery and self-efficacy. In addition, parents who are involved in this training also feel a sense of empowerment in being able to help reduce their child's level of distress.

Anxious children often have an anxious parent. Anxiety disorders are a common complaint among adults, and many report that their anxiety began in childhood (Rapee and Barlow, 1992). Systems theory teaches that parents and children have a reciprocal influence on each other. Thus, a child might become anxious in response to parental stress or anxiety, and an already-stressed parent becomes more distressed because he or she is concerned about the child's anxiety. Happily, the reverse is also true, as the child and parent each begin to relax. Parents' stress decreases as they see their child learning to relax, and the child who is aware that the parents are less stressed experiences an even greater ability to relax and let go of worries. Thus the positive effects are also mutually reinforcing. Breathing and relaxation programs are one of the mainstays of adult treatment of anxiety disorders, often used in combination with self-talk and other cognitive-behavioral approaches, as well as medication (Campbell, 2001). Relaxation skills have been shown to be an effective component of adult support groups for cancer patients. Studies show adult cancer patients experience reduced stress, increased coping ability, better response to treatment, and even increased life span (Spiegel et al., 1989; Fawzy et al., 1993; Shrock, Palmer, and Taylor, 1999).

We routinely incorporate relaxation training in our group work with children and parents, with adult cancer patients, as well as in family sessions. In family therapy, teaching relaxation skills often indirectly benefits the parents, as well as the children. Parents are encouraged to practice the exercises with their children, helping themselves learn to relax in the process of helping their children. In our experience children often love to have this special quiet time at home with parents.

When used in groups, children may have a bit harder time relaxing initially, since they may be self-conscious of other kids watching them. It helps to ignore any giggles, to space children far enough apart so their bodies don't touch, and to dim the lights to encourage children to focus. Relaxation tapes also help to soothe and set the stage to begin these exercises. We have found that children are proud to have learned a new skill that their parents don't know. After they have had a session or two to practice this skill, their parents are invited to participate. Children enjoy explaining this activity to their parents, and demonstrating how it works. They often insist their parents practice with them between group sessions. Both parents and children report that these techniques are especially helpful when the children are anxious at bedtime and have trouble falling asleep, and for sleep disturbances such as sleepwalking, nightmares, and night terrors. The children overwhelmingly rate relaxation training as one of the most helpful and/or the best part of their entire group experience.

Each of the three main types of relaxation training will be introduced here, and each may be used as a separate activity or in combination with other techniques. (We most often use the breathing and visualization exercises with children.) Handouts with suggestions on how to introduce each topic are included. We prefer to use the term "stress" rather than "anxiety" when working with children. It is less pejorative and normalizes rather than pathologizes their emotions. After all, everyone experiences stress!

Instructions

Introduction

It is wise not to introduce these exercises until the child seems fairly comfortable with the therapist. Wachtel (1994) warns that some children have a difficult time relaxing because they don't like feeling the loss of control when asked to lie down, relax, and take deep breaths. She suggests giving these children a soft, floppy stuffed animal to hold and asking them to try to relax their bodies as much as the animal's body is relaxed. We allow each child to select a Beanie Baby to hold at the beginning of each group or family session.

The topic of stress and relaxation and visualization can be introduced in a playful way by using a children's story, such as "Sammy the Seagull Soars Above Stress" (Biank and Sori, submitted). It is useful to preface this activity with a discussion about fears and stress, and how we physiologically respond to anxiety-provoking situations. In introducing the topic of stress, explain stress as a response we feel in our bodies when we tighten our muscles (see Handout 1: Introducing Stress).

Stress can then be normalized, as the therapist discusses how everyone experiences stress at different times in their lives. The children (and/or family) are encouraged to think of things that people find stressful, and to use the My Stress Handout (Handout 2) to record their ideas. Children may list taking tests or speaking in front of a class as general examples, and discussions can be guided to deeper fears (e.g., parents divorcing). Next each child is asked to describe where in his or her body that anxious, fearful, or stressful feeling is usually experienced. Children may say, "My heart was pounding" or "My stomach was in a knot." They are encouraged to check off those body parts on the My Stress Handout where this anxiety was experienced, and to use the scale to rate how stressed they feel. Next the therapist may explore both good and bad behavior adults and kids employ to feel less stressed. Bad ways to cope might include throwing a tantrum, hitting someone, or using alcohol or drugs. While outside the scope of this chapter, good ideas to reduce stress include exercise, finding someone to talk to, journaling, using positive self-talk, distracting oneself with an activity, playing music, and, of course breathing, relaxation, and visualization. These are listed on the handout, with room for children to generate more coping strategies. When working with families, parents should be encouraged to share their stress-reducing strategies with children.

Children are encouraged to practice the exercises at home between sessions. They may use the My Soaring Above Stress record (Handout 3) to record their between-session exercises, and parents are encouraged to participate and to coach their children. It is helpful to provide children with a tape of the therapist's voice to facilitate at-home practice.

Breathing

The first step to help anxious children (or adults) relax is often to teach them to pay attention to their breathing. Children should be in a relaxed position, either seated in a chair with their feet on the floor or lying on a comfortable cushion (Cautela and Groden, 1978). To help children focus, the room should not be too bright or have too many distractions. Soft music or relaxation tapes of soothing sounds are useful to set the mood and help induce a relaxed state. Therapists should also be aware of their vocal quality and try to use a soft, gentle, soothing voice that is somewhat monotonic. Handout 4 provides suggestions to teach children breathing exercises.

Progressive Muscle Relaxation

After children have relaxed by attending to their breathing, they are ready to learn to progressively tighten, hold, and finally relax different muscle groups. Encourage the child to continue to focus on breathing while he or she progressively tightens and relaxes the various muscle groups in the body (see Handout 5: Progressive Muscle Relaxation Instructions).

Visual Imagery

Along with Pennells and Smith (1995), we have found visual imagery to be an excellent way to close group sessions, especially when discussions have included difficult subjects, such as death or other losses. This activity may be prefaced by reading a poem, such as "Magic Carpet Ride" by Shel Silverstein, and then encouraging children to discuss and draw a picture of their favorite special place. This place may be real or imagined, but it is somewhere very special to them, someplace where they feel relaxed and happy (see Speltz and Biank, 2001).

First, have the children relax by focusing on their breathing, as described previously. Encourage them to close their eyes and use their imagination to "see" the story, such as the one described in Handout 6. Using music and a slow, soothing voice, the therapist begins to paint a visual image by taking the children (or family) through an imaginary sequence of events. Handout 6 offers one of our favorite examples of a visual imagery exercise.

Helping children to focus on their senses—the sights, sounds, smells, touches, and even tastes, brings this exercise to life. Just as it is important to set the stage by helping children relax by focusing on their breathing and closing their eyes, it is equally important to bring participants gradually back to the present (Pennells and Smith, 1995).

Vignette

Eight-year-old Jason Clarke was referred for family therapy because he had become anxious to the point that he was afraid to be separated from his mother, Dorothy, and did not want to go to school. Jason's father, Bill, had leukemia that was in remission. Jason had an older sister, Susan, age ten. The Clarkes reported that Susan was "doing fine," but Jason's symptoms had recently worsened. He often went to the nurse's office complaining of vague stomach pains, asking the nurse to phone his mother at work. Jason also had several panic attacks at home after school. Nearly hysterical, he would page his mother, terrified she had died in a car accident. Jason also had difficulty sleeping and had frequent nightmares. The family came to the first session in crisis, after Jason had been utterly distraught for two days while his mother was away on a business trip. He was convinced she was going to die in a plane crash.

In family sessions the therapist explored how each family member had coped with Bill's cancer. Special attention was paid to changes that occurred for each of them. Bill talked about how hard it had been to be off work for nine months, and even though he had now returned and was feeling pretty good, he still tired easily and needed a lot of rest. Dorothy had a more difficult time talking about how stressful the past year had been. She had been Bill's primary caregiver throughout, taking him to treatments, nursing him through the terrible side effects of chemotherapy, and still maintaining her full-time job as a surgical nurse. Although she had some limited outside help from family and friends with the children, she had shouldered most of the parenting and household responsibilities. The therapist also spent time explaining to the parents how children may be negatively affected when a family member has a serious illness.

With the children, the therapist spent some time using drawing, puppets, and writing to explore their fears and worries. Most children feel abandoned by both parents when one has cancer, since so much of the family's time and resources must necessarily be focused on the patient. With some encouragement, Jason was able to express his fears—which included the fear that *both* his parents would die (his dad of cancer, his mom and sister in a car or plane accident), and that he would be an orphan, with no one to love or care for him. Susan also had fears, but they had been well hidden by this straight-A student. She too was afraid "everyone would die," including herself, but she was even more afraid to share her fears with her parents. Susan explained that they were already too stressed, worried about Dad, and now they were also concerned about her brother! She couldn't bear to add to their worries, but she secretly cried herself to sleep many nights and had terrible nightmares of a huge monster sucking her down into a black, bottomless hole.

When the children were first introduced to relaxation training, they simply loved it. They were excited to share their new skills with their parents, whom they believed would also benefit from learning to relax more. First, however, the children shared their My Stress Handouts with their parents, who were surprised the children experienced so much stress, especially in their heads and stomachs. They also shared examples of what they experienced as stressful. For example, Jason wrote, "I get stressed when I think everyone will die." One of Susan's comments was, "I feel stressed because I worry that they haven't told us everything." The parents were very moved by the children's open comments. The family had a good discussion about helpful ways to reduce stress. Dad shared that going to the putting green helped him relax, while Mom said talking to her best friend always helped her feel better. The parents encouraged their children to talk to them when they were stressed and assured Susan that they would not hold back information about Dad's health. They encouraged her to share her worries and assured her they were *more* stressed if she didn't talk!

The children then excitedly explained the relaxation exercises to their parents. They read "Magic Carpet Ride" to Mom and Dad and shared pictures of their own special places. During the exercise the children lay on cushions, while their parents sat in chairs close by. At the end of the exercise everyone reported on where they had "been" and what they had "seen" during the visualization. Jason had been in Disney World, while Susan was in the woods where the family had gone camping the previous summer. The children enjoyed hearing that Mom had "visited" the ocean and brought back a seashell, while Dad had gone to the top of a mountain, where he felt "on top of the world." Everyone talked about how they had been able to relax and to picture the scenes described. The children were clearly delighted that their parents participated in this activity with them.

Relaxation became a regular part of family sessions and fostered a much more intimate, open atmosphere. The children loved hearing about the "special places" their parents visited, and what objects they brought back. Jason was soon insisting that they all do this in Mom and Dad's bed—every night!

Susan and Jason had been able to use the My Stress Handout to express their worries and were encouraged to continue to share their feelings with Bill and Dorothy. Once everyone's stress was out in the open and acknowledged, the family could work together to reduce its effects. The parents discussed asking for occasional outside support and considered joining a cancer support group. They also explored ways to "put cancer in its place" by restoring more pockets of normalcy in their marital and family lives.

The parents took turns practicing relaxation with the children before bed each night, using a tape provided by the therapist. As the parents felt less stressed they were better able to address the children's fears. They were coached to answer their children's questions about cancer and Dad's remission. They even suggested the children attend a doctor's appointment so they might ask the doctor about anything they didn't understand. The parents promised they would keep the children up to date on Dad's medical condition. This greatly reduced the children's fear that something terrible was being hidden from them. The children were also assured that in the unlikely event that something happened to both of them, arrangements had been made for a favorite aunt and uncle to care for them.

Within two months Jason's symptoms were remarkably reduced. There were no more panicked pages to Mom, and trips to the nurse's office at school were rare. The nightmares had all but disappeared, and he was sleeping well. Susan rarely cried anymore, and when she did she now turned to Mom for support. She was visibly more relaxed, having lost the tense, fearful look she'd had initially. She was no longer having nightmares and had started spending more time with friends. Both parents were relieved and happy that their children were less anxious, and that they too were handling the stress in their lives much better.

At termination the children were asked what they thought had been the most helpful part of therapy. Without hesitation, both happily replied, "The relaxation!" And they pointed out it hadn't just helped them, it had helped their parents too.

Guess how they wanted to end the final session?

Contraindications

Caution should be exercised in doing visual imagery with a child who may be dissociative. Also, hyperactive children often have a more difficult time relaxing, especially in a group situation. These children, as well as the developmentally delayed, should first be taught preliminary focus skills one-on-one, using the suggestions in Cautela and Groden (1978). Rewards, such as treats or holding a special toy, are also good ways to motivate impulsive children.

Initially some adults may not want to participate in relaxation training. While not everyone is able to benefit from relaxation exercises, we have found that reluctant parents can often be persuaded to give it a try when they understand how their participation may help their child. And once they are engaged, they often learn to enjoy the benefits for themselves.

References for Professionals

Bevin, T. (1991). Multiple traumas of refugees—Near drowning and witnessing of maternal rape. In N. B. Webb (Ed.), *Play therapy with children in crisis* (pp. 92-110). New York: Guilford Publications.

Biank, N. and Sori, C. F. (submitted). "Sammy the Seagull Soars Above Stress."

Campbell, G. (2001). The anxious client reconsidered. *Psychotherapy Networker, 25*(3), 40-45.

Cautela, J. R. and Groden, J. (1978). *Relaxation: A comprehensive manual for adults, children, and children with special needs.* Champaign, IL: Research Press.

Deutschle, J. Jr., Tosi, D., and Wise, P. (1987). *The use of hypnosis and metaphor within a cognitive experiential framework: Theory, research, and case applications with impulse control disorders.* Paper presented at a meeting of the American Society for Clinical Hypnosis, Las Vegas, NV.

Estrada, A. U. and Pinsof, W. (1995). The effectiveness of family therapies for selected behavioral disorders of childhood. *Journal of Marital and Family Therapy, 21*(4), 403-440.

Fawzy, F. I., Fawzy, N. W., Hyun, C. S., and Elashoff, R. (1993). Effects of an early structured psychiatric intervention, coping, and affective state on recurrence and survival 6 years later. *Archives of General Psychiatry, 50,* 681-689.

Goodman, R. F. (1991). Diagnosis of childhood cancer. In N. B. Webb, (Ed.), *Play therapy with children in crisis* (pp. 310-332). New York: Guilford Publications.

Graziano, A. M., and Mooney, K. C. (1982). Behavioral treatment of children's "nightfears": Maintenance of improvement at 2- to 3-year follow-up. *Journal of Consulting and Clinical Psychology, 50,* 598-599.

Johnson, S. B. (1979). Children's fears in the classroom setting. *School Psychology Digest, 8*(4), 382-396.

Joyner, C. D. (1991). Individual, group, and family crisis counseling following a hurricane. In N. B. Webb, (Ed.), *Play therapy with children in crisis* (pp. 396-415). New York: Guilford Publications.

Kashani, J. H., Orvaschel, H., Rosenbert, T. K., and Reid, J. C. (1989). Psychopathology in a community sample of children and adolescents. *Journal of the American Academy of Child and Adolescent Psychiatry, 28,* 701-706.

Kendall, P. (1993). Cognitive-behavior therapies with youth: Guiding theory, current status, and emerging developments. *Journal of Consulting and Clinical Psychology, 61,* 235-247.

Lohaus, A. and Klein-Hebling, J. (2000). Coping in childhood: A comparative evaluation of different relaxation techniques. *Anxiety, Stress, and Coping, 13,* 187-211.

McManamy, C. and Katz, R. C. (1989). Brief parent-assisted treatment for children's nighttime fears. *Journal of Development and Behavior Pediatrics, 10,* 145-148.

Orvaschel, H. and Weissman, M. (1986). Epidemiology of anxiety in children. In R. Gittleman (Ed.), *Anxiety disorders of childhood* (pp. 58-72). New York: Guilford Publications.

Pennells, Sr. M. and Smith, S. C. (1995). Creative groupwork methods with bereaved children. In S. Smith and Sr. M. Pennells (Eds.), *Interventions with bereaved children* (pp. 141-159). Bristol, PA: Jessica Kingsley.

Peterson, L. and Shigetomi, C. (1981). The use of coping techniques in minimizing anxiety in hospitalized children. *Behavior Therapy, 12,* 1-14.

Rapee, R. M., and Barlow, D. H. (1992). Generalized anxiety disorder, panic disorder, and the phobias. In P. B. Suther and H. E. Adams (Eds.), *Comprehensive handbook of psychopathology* (Second edition, pp. 109-127). New York: Plenum.

Shrock, D., Palmer, R. F., and Taylor, B. (1999). Effects of a psychosocial intervention on survival among patients with stage I breast and prostate cancer: A matched case-control study. *Alternative Therapies, 5*(3), 49-55.

Speltz, A. and Biank, N. (2001). *Kid support: A procedures manual for conducting support groups with the children of cancer patients.* Evanston, IL: Self-published.

Spiegel, D., Bloom, J., Kraemer, H. C., Gottheil, E. (1989). Effect of psychosocial treatment on survival of patients with metastatic breast cancer. *Lancet, 2,* 888-891.

Taffel, R. (2001). The wall of silence. *Psychotherapy Networker, 25*(3), 52-64.

Thompson, C. L. and Rudolph, L. B. (1996). *Counseling children* (Fourth edition). Pacific Grove, CA: Brooks/Cole Publishing Company.

Wachtel, E. F. (1994). *Treating troubled children and their families.* New York: Guilford Publications.

Wells, K. C. and Vitulano, L. A. (1984). Anxiety disorders in childhood. In S. Turner (Ed.), *Behavioral theories and treatment of anxiety* (pp. 413-433). New York: Plenum.
Werry, J. S. (1986). Diagnosis and assessment. In R. Gittleman (Ed.), *Anxiety disorders of childhood* (pp. 73-98). New York: Guilford Publications.

Suggested Readings for Clients

Naparstek, B. (1995). *Staying well with guided imagery*. New York: Warner Books.
Silverstein, S. (1974). *Where the sidewalk ends*. New York: HarperCollins Publishers.
Silverstein, S. (1981). *A light in the attic*. New York: HarperCollins Publishers.

Handout 1: Introducing Stress

Therapists may paraphrase the following to introduce the topic of how stress may be experienced as bodily tension, and how this new skill can be used, before, during, or after a stressful event:

Whenever we become afraid, nervous, or upset, the muscles of our body tighten up, and this is why we feel tense or stressed. But we can learn how to identify and relax those tense muscles, which will help us feel less stressed. The skills we are going to learn can help us relax at different times: *After* we've been in a situation that has upset us, *before* an event that we know will make us anxious, and even *while* we are in a stressful situation. We can use this anytime! Relaxation is a skill that we can practice and learn, just like other skills you may have learned (such as bouncing a ball, pounding clay or a pillow, or playing a video game). And the more we practice, the better we get!

Handout 2: My Stress Handout

What things make you feel stressed?	Stress is often felt in your body:
(Draw or write)	Check How Much Stress (0 = None; 1 = Some; 2 = Much) ___ Head ___ Neck ___ Shoulders ___ Arms ___ Hands ___ Chest ___ Stomach ___ Hips ___ Legs ___ Feet

Check ways that help you feel less stressed:

___ Talking positively to myself. What do you say that is helpful?

_____

_____

___ Exercise (for example, riding bikes, playing basketball, rollerblading, punching bag). List your favorite activities:

_____

_____

___ Talking to someone. List whom: _____

_____

___ Doing something to take my mind off the stress. List things you do: _____

_____

___ Writing in a journal

___ Playing music

___ Drawing

___ Breathing, relaxation, and visualization

___ Playing with a friend. Name friends: _____

_____

___ Others: _____

_____

Handout 3: My Soaring Above Stress Record

NAME: _____

DATE	ACTIVITY*	ALONE or WITH WHOM	COMMENTS	STRESS LEVEL**	
				BEFORE	AFTER

* List the letters for the type of activities you did (for example, B and V = breathing and visualizing):
   B = Breathing exercise
   R = Relaxing muscles
   V = Visualizing exercise
** = Stress Level (place the numbers on the chart that fit your stress level *before* and *after* exercise):

     Less Stress   **More Stress**

     1   2   3   4   5   6   7   8   9   10

Handout 4: Deep Breathing Instructions

To introduce children to deep breathing, therapists may paraphrase the following instructions, speaking slowly and softly:

Notice what it feels like to sit or lie there . . . the sensation of where your feet are resting . . . your legs . . . hips . . . backs . . . arms . . . and heads. [Pause] Now take a deep breath, hold it for a few seconds, and let the air out slowly, through your mouth. . . . Put one of your hands lightly on top of your tummy, and feel your tummy slowly go up . . . and down . . . as you breathe in and out. . . . Let your tummy guide your breathing, which should be slow . . . silent . . . and regular. Now use your imagination to picture a balloon that is resting on your tummy . . . notice what color your balloon is . . . and imagine that the balloon begins to fill up with air as you breathe out, or exhale . . . and notice how big the balloon gets. Now picture the balloon emptying of air or deflating as you breath in, or inhale, and notice how small and limp it looks when all the air is out. Can you blow out twice as much air as you breathed in? . . . Now imagine your whole body relaxing as you breathe out, until you are as limp as that deflated balloon . . . and as you sink deeper and deeper onto the cushion. Can you imagine stardust being sprinkled over your heads . . . and drifting down to your feet, helping you feel quieter and more relaxed? Each new breath brings in air that travels throughout your body . . . and that air is searching for any stress or worry . . . and that breath takes those stressful feelings and carries them away as you exhale. With each breath your body feels more and more relaxed. . . .

Handout 5: Progressive Muscle Relaxation Instructions

After children (and parents) have been able to relax their bodies by focusing on their breathing, introduce progressive muscle relaxation. Encourage the children to continue to focus on their breathing, and use the following guide to introduce progressive muscle relaxation:

Now you are ready to learn to tighten, hold, and finally relax all the different muscle groups in your body. As you continue to breathe, and keeping your eyes closed, notice the feeling in your relaxed feet and ankles. Now flex or tighten your ankles and toes, and become aware of how it feels when those muscles are tensed. After holding for a few seconds, slowly relax your ankles and toes, noticing how different the muscles feel when relaxed. Now, once again, tighten your ankles and toes . . . hold . . . and relax. Continue to breathe, and now move up to notice the feeling in your relaxed calf muscles. . . . Now tighten or flex your calves . . . and hold for a few seconds, noticing how it feels in your calves when the muscles are tightened . . . and now relax . . . and be aware of how different it feels in your calves when the muscles are not tensed. . . . Now repeat, tensing your calves . . . holding . . . being aware of that sensation . . . and now relaxing.

This process of tensing, holding, and releasing muscle groups is continued, moving upward to include the thighs, hips, stomach, chest, arms, shoulders, neck, head (top and temples), and face (forehead, eyes, cheeks, mouth, and jaws).

At the end, an additional breath is used to scan the body from head to toe, searching for any places where stress has hidden. These areas are given an additional flex-hold-and-release.

At the end encourage the child and parent to just lie there for a moment, enjoying this restful, peaceful, relaxed state.

Encourage children and parents to practice this exercise at home together, between sessions.

Handout 6: Visual Imagery Example

Children often enjoy lying down on a soft cushion and closing their eyes for this activity, which may be done with individual children, in groups, and/or in family sessions. Therapists may read or paraphrase the following example of a visual imagery exercise:

Imagine you are very relaxed and lying on a giant, fluffy white feather pillow. It is so soft and comfortable, and you can feel the softness gently caressing you. Using your imagination, you can allow the pillow to turn into a cloud that slowly begins to lift off the ground and rise up into the air. Feeling very safe on the cloud you peer over the side and notice that you are floating above a beautiful garden. You are aware of the warmth of the sun and the gentle whisper of the breeze on your skin as you continue to look down at the garden . . . and you notice many beautiful flowers there, in all your favorite colors . . . blues, yellows, pinks . . . and you love their wonderful smell. Perhaps you also see a birdbath with two blue jays splashing and singing . . . and you notice a bunny hiding beneath a rosebush, twitching his nose at you. You are aware of your cloud moving now, over grass . . . and ahead you might see a forest with tall pine trees . . . and you notice the smell of pine cones . . . and ahead you might see a majestic mountain, and you can choose to float right up to and over the mountain, noticing the colors, the trees and grass, and the animals . . . deer, raccoons . . . and you can see snow on top of the mountain, and the air that brushes your cheeks feels fresh and cool.

Maybe you can also see the sea ahead and are floating on your cloud toward a beach. And you notice the color of the sand . . . and the blueness of the water . . . and the gentle rhythm of the waves . . . the salty smell of the sea. . . . Perhaps as you look down you can see seashells, or brightly colored fish darting about near the surface of the water.

Now you just lie back . . . looking up at the blue sky, aware of the birds singing and flying about, of the white clouds slowly drifting by, of the warmth and brightness of the sun, and of the gentle touch of the ocean breeze. . . . And you are very contented . . . and relaxed.

And now you are approaching your own special place . . . real or imagined, this is a place where you feel happy and stress free. . . . You gently lower your cloud and look around, and it feels so good to be here. . . . As you climb off your cloud you feel light and carefree, and you slowly turn from side to side . . . noticing all the sights . . . the colors . . . textures . . . the sounds. . . . Perhaps you are in someone's kitchen and can smell something special baking . . . or you might be sitting by a roaring fire. . . . Or maybe your special place is a park or a garden . . . there might be animals . . . or people that you know and care about. You just take time to enjoy being there. [Pause]

Now you look around for something to take back with you . . . something perhaps that can fit in your pocket, to remind you of this place, your own special place, to help you remember that you can return anytime.

And you feel wonderful as you climb back onto your cloud, which slowly begins to lift . . . and move up . . . and back over the water. And again you can hear the soothing sounds of the waves, smell the salty sea air . . . as your cloud carries you back over the sandy beach . . . over the green forest

. . . and over the majestic mountain. . . . And you take in all the colors and sights and sounds . . . and then ahead you see your garden and all the colorful flowers . . . and you can smell the sweet fragrance of flowers . . . and hear the birds singing, calling out to you, and splashing in the birdbath, and the rabbit hiding in the garden . . . and you feel the breeze and the warmth of the sun. And as your wonderful cloud gently comes to rest it is transformed back into the huge, soft feather pillow.

But you just enjoy lying there feeling relaxed . . . peaceful . . . feeling refreshed . . . and knowing you are free to take this special journey again . . . whenever you wish. . . .

[Using a more animated tone of voice] Now you take a deep, energizing breath, stretch your arms up in the air, and you are aware of the sounds of this room . . . of others here who want to share with you . . . and you open your eyes and sit up.

Throughout this exercise, encourage children to focus on their senses—the sights, sounds, smells, touches, and even tastes of this "journey," all of which bring this exercise to life. At the end it is important to orient the children to the present, by gradually bringing them back to reality and becoming aware of their surroundings, and by inviting them to share their experiences with other children or family members.

5

Getting to Know the Characters Inside Me: Children Coping with Thoughts and Feelings

Megan L. Dolbin

Type of Contribution: Activity

Objectives

The purpose of this activity is to provide a concrete and visual way for children to understand how different, and sometimes conflicting, thoughts and/or feelings can exist at the same time. As the child becomes more aware of the existence of his or her many thoughts and feelings about a given problem, the therapist can then help the child learn to cope with any thoughts and/or feelings that are conflicting or problematic.

Rationale for Use

When exploring a presenting problem, therapists commonly hear clients talk about different parts of themselves. Clients will often say that, in relation to a given problem, part of them feels one way while another part of them feels the total opposite. For therapists, the fact that clients have ambivalent or conflicting thoughts and feelings about a presenting problem is certainly nothing new or surprising. Unfortunately, the process of negotiating these conflicting feelings and thoughts is often very confusing and challenging for clients as well as therapists. Internal family systems therapy, a model of therapy developed by Richard Schwartz (1995), directly deals with this issue by focusing on helping clients become aware of and develop new relationships between the parts (i.e., thoughts and feelings) of themselves. By accessing and empowering the self, which is an active leader and the seat of consciousness, clients can resume leadership of their parts (Schwartz, 1995). To take a very simplistic view, internal family systems therapy posits that when clients become self-led they are most able to resolve their conflicting thoughts and feelings (i.e., parts), and, in turn, their presenting problems.

Just as adults often have conflicting feelings and thoughts within the context of a given presenting problem, children are also likely to struggle with ambivalent feelings, thoughts, and behaviors. However, it is often extremely difficult for children to acknowledge and understand the complexity of their thoughts and feelings. Moreover, talking directly about their thoughts and feelings in relation to a problem is often difficult for children. Therefore, through the use of play techniques and imagination, it is often much easier for children to express themselves openly and honestly. This activity combines the use of play techniques with the basic principles of internal family systems therapy as a means for helping children explore and cope with their many, and sometimes conflicting, thoughts and feelings about a given problem.

Instructions

This activity is designed for use during individual work with the child and is likely to take several therapy sessions. It is critical that the therapist move at a slow pace so that the child does not become overwhelmed or confused. Before beginning this activity, be sure to have a substantial understanding of the child's presenting problem. That is, it is important to understand what is bothering the child and how the presenting problem is impacting the child's emotional and social lives.

1. Have the child stand against a large piece of paper that is taped to the wall. Trace an outline of the child's body. Once the outline is finished, remove the drawing from the wall.
2. Ask the child to think of his or her favorite movie or cartoon. Then, ask the child to describe the different characters in that movie or cartoon. Discuss how there are many different types of characters in the movie or cartoon—good characters, bad characters, funny characters, scared characters, sad characters, wise characters, and so on.
3. Explain to the child that everyone has their own set of characters inside of him or her. Stress that, as with his or her favorite movie or cartoon, everyone has good characters, bad characters, happy characters, scared characters, sad characters, and angry characters.
4. Ask the child to think about all of the different types of characters that he or she might have inside of him or her. As the child describes the characters, ask the child to draw a picture of each character inside the outline of the child's body. Depending on the child's age and cognitive ability, it is also possible to have the child draw the character into the body part where the child most often notices or feels the character. For example, if the child describes an anxious character, he or she might be asked how that character makes its presence known. If the child says that he or she gets stomachaches when the anxious character is around, the child might be encouraged to draw the anxious character on the stomach area of the drawing.

Note: Although it is possible to ask the child to focus on the presenting problem before he or she lists all of his or her characters, this activity is based on the assumption that through the language of play and imagination, the child will make the appropriate linkages between his or her characters and thoughts and feelings about the presenting problem without direct instruction. Therefore, therapists should not be overly concerned if the child does not appear to be making direct links between the characters and the presenting problem. In all likelihood, the child is making those linkages—even if he or she is not consciously aware of them.

5. Once the child has drawn all of the characters, the next step of the activity is to ask the child questions about each character. The purpose of these questions is to help the therapist and the child to get to know all of the characters and how they relate to the child's current difficulties. Depending on the child's level of creativity and interest, there are two approaches for getting to know the characters. Because the second approach allows children to distance themselves from their thoughts and feelings, it may be safer, more engaging, and may generate more information.

Approach #1: To introduce this portion of the activity to the child, it may be helpful to ask the child to pretend to be a newspaper reporter who has interviewed all of the different characters. Explain to the child that you want to find out what the child learned about the characters. Proceed by asking the child questions *about* each of the characters. Some example questions include these: What is the character's name? What is it like? What does it like? Dislike? Are their certain times when the character likes to remind the child that it is around? How does it let the child know? Why does it act like that? How does the character feel about the child's problem? What does the character do to make the problem better? Worse? What does the character want to have happen in relation to the child's problem? How would the character like things to be different?

Approach #2: Ask the child to pretend to be the characters. Explain that, similar to someone on the news, each character will be interviewed by a news reporter (therapist). With each character, conduct an interview. Some example questions include these: What is your name? What are you like? What do you like? Dislike? Are there certain times when you like to remind [child's name] that you are around? What do you say or do to [child's name] in relation to [presenting problem]? What do you make [child's name] think, do, or feel in relation to [presenting problem]? How do you feel about [child's name]? How do you think [child's name] feels about you? What do you think about [child's name]'s problem? How do you help make the problem better? How do you help make the problem worse? What do you want to have happen in relation to [presenting issue]? How would you like things to be different? What changes would you make?

6. Once all of the characters have been interviewed, ask the child to talk about how his or her characters get along with one another. It may be helpful to precede this exploration with a discussion about how the child gets along with other people in his or her life. Some example questions that can be used when asking the child about the relationships between the characters include these: Are there certain characters who always get along? Are there certain characters who always fight? How do specific characters feel about one another? Which character is most often in charge? When is this character in charge? How can the child tell? Which character is never in charge? Which character is the loudest? The quietist? Which character feels the happiest? The saddest? The most scared? The angriest?

Note: During the discussion of the relationships between the characters, the therapist must be very careful not to imply that any of the characters are "bad." Similarly, the therapist should avoid stating or implying that the child should get rid of "bad" characters. Rather, the therapist should stress that every character has an important role in the child's life. Therefore, the child should be encouraged to find a way to make friends and work with the "bad" characters.

7. Next, explain to the child that, as in the movies, a director is always in charge of making sure that all of the characters get along and do what they are supposed to do. Ask the child if she or he is interested in being the director of her/his different characters.
8. Assuming that the child agrees to become the director of the characters, the purpose of this portion of the activity is to help the child develop specific plans for making sure that the characters get along with one another and that they do not get the child (as the director) into trouble. Although there is no particular form that the plans should take, it is critical that the child has a role in creating the plans and believes that they will work. For example, one child had time-outs for a character who was angry and volatile. With a character who was scared, another child devised a plan in which he gave that character a hug. For characters who do not get along, the child can hold a trial with the child as the judge.

Helpful Hint #1: Because the child may have many characters, it is important to determine which characters are causing the most trouble. Since these characters are likely to be resistant to making change, it is recommended that the therapist focus first on characters who are not causing as much trouble.

Helpful Hint #2: While making plans, the therapist must be very careful not to overload the child. Overloading the child with too many plans reduces the probability of success. Therefore, each week, the therapist should focus on only one or two specific plans. As the child proceeds in therapy, other plans can be added.

9. To make the plans "official," have the child (or, if necessary, the therapist) write the plans in a notebook or on a piece of paper. Have the child take the notebook or paper home and put it in a place where he or she can refer to it on a daily basis.
10. Ask the child to follow the plans until the next therapy session.

Vignette

Jenny, age nine, entered therapy because of behavior problems at school and at home. At school, she had been avoiding social activities and often cried during class. At home, Jenny was very withdrawn and abusive toward the family dog. In terms of family factors, the therapist learned that Jenny's mother had recently suffered a miscarriage. Jenny's parents were still coping with the grief of the miscarriage and Jenny's mother had become severely depressed. Until the time of the miscarriage, Jenny had no major behavioral problems.

In therapy, Jenny exhibited several notable behaviors. As the family discussed its reactions to the miscarriage, the therapist noted that Jenny became aggressive with the toys in the therapy room. Guessing that Jenny was struggling with her feelings about the miscarriage, the therapist proposed that they try an activity where Jenny would learn more about herself and her thoughts and feelings. Jenny agreed. When asked to talk about her favorite movie or cartoon, Jenny immediately began talking about *The Little Mermaid*. She talked about how the sea-witch Ursula was scary and mean. She also talked about the brave and good prince, who saved Ariel (the mermaid) from Ursula. The therapist asked Jenny about the characters of Sebastian the crab and Flounder the fish. Jenny grinned and said that they made the movie funny.

The therapist then traced an outline of Jenny and asked her to think about whether she had characters inside of her who were similar to the characters in *The Little Mermaid*. Jenny was having trouble coming up with some characters, so the therapist asked her to think of characters who might be around when she thinks about the baby who died or about how her mother spends a lot of time in bed. With this guidance, Jenny said that there was a baby bunny character. As she drew the bunny, the therapist asked Jenny to pretend to be the baby bunny. When the therapist interviewed the baby bunny, it said that it was sad because the mother bunny went away and would never come back. The baby bunny also said that when she got scared and sad, she made Jenny cry and made her not want to play with her friends or go to school. According to the baby bunny, things would be better if the mother bunny would come back and take care of her.

After exploring a variety of other characters, the therapist and Jenny determined that the baby bunny was involved with a portion of Jenny's trouble at school and at home. The therapist asked Jenny if she would be willing to be a big sister to the baby bunny. Being a big sister to the baby bunny meant that Jenny would have to take care of her and help her to stop getting Jenny into trouble. Jenny enthusiastically agreed to help the baby bunny. To help Jenny have a sense of ownership and control over her situation, the therapist asked Jenny if she had any ideas that she could use to help the baby bunny. Jenny suggested that the baby bunny would not cry as much if she knew that the mother bunny was going to come back. When asked how the baby bunny would know that the mother bunny was coming back, Jenny said the baby bunny would know if she received a letter from the mother bunny. At this point, the therapist consulted with the parents to see if Jenny's mother would be willing to write a letter from the perspective of the mother bunny. Jenny's mother agreed. In the planning phase of the activity, it was decided that Jenny's mother would give the letter to Jenny. Then, Jenny would take the letter to school and, whenever the baby bunny started to get sad or worried, she would pull out the letter and remind the baby bunny that the mother bunny was coming back.

During the next therapy session, Jenny reported that the baby bunny liked the letter. Jenny's parents reported that, although she was still withdrawn at home, her behavior at school had improved. The therapist congratulated Jenny for being a good big sister and reminded her to keep working on it. After celebrating the week's success, the therapist asked Jenny if another character wanted to be interviewed. Jenny said his name was Brutus, he was very mean and scared her and the baby bunny. Brutus's interview and plan became the focus of that therapy session.

Suggestions for Follow-Up

1. At the beginning of each session, assess how the child did with his or her plan for the character(s). If the plan was successful, consider having a small celebration or ritual. If the plan was not successful, explore what went wrong and if some of the other characters might have messed up the plan. In addition to using this information to develop a new set of plans, this information can also help the therapist and the child identify other characters who might need attention and work.
2. Each time the child comes for therapy, ask if the characters were able to get along between sessions. If the characters were able to get along, ask how the child managed to do such an excellent job as director. If the characters were unable to get along, ask if any of those characters has anything important to say. From there, it is possible to begin devising plans for any problematic and conflicting characters.
3. Have the child introduce his or her characters to the rest of the family. In addition, have the child share the plans for directing the characters with family members. The family can be recruited to help the child act as the director and implement these plans.
4. Have the child keep a notebook about all the characters and the plans that were developed in therapy.
5. Over time, new characters (representing new thoughts and feelings) can be added to or old ones removed from the drawing.
6. Throughout therapy, the child can be encouraged to tell stories about or draw pictures illustrating the experiences of the characters.
7. As a culmination of the therapy process, the child can create his or her own movie about the characters and their adventures. The child can perform the movie for friends, family, and others who are important to the child.

Contraindications for Use

This activity is most useful for children who have reached a stage of cognitive development where they can pretend to be others and imagine the perspectives of others. Therefore, this activity would be contraindicated for use with very young children or children with severe cognitive impairment.

Professional Readings and Resources

Brooks, R. (1993). Creative characters. In C. E. Schaefer and D. M. Cangelosi (Eds.), *Play therapy techniques* (pp. 199-210). New York: Jason Aronson.

Gil, E. (1994). *Play in family therapy.* New York: Guilford Publications.

Schwartz, R. C. (1995). *Internal family systems therapy.* New York: Guilford Publications.

SECTION II:
THE USE OF PLAY IN THERAPY

6

Play Genograms

Eliana Gil

Type of Contribution: Activity, Handout

Materials: Large paper, miniatures (or an alternative)

Objectives

The Play Genogram expands the already well-established assessment tool developed by McGoldrick, Gerson, and Shellenberger (1999). The genogram enables clinicians to construct a graphic representation of family history, patterns, and significant events. In addition, clinicians unfamiliar with a case can look at genograms and gather vast information about family members and their relationships to one another. A variety of symbols (such as boxes for males, circles for females, and straight and broken lines for types of relationships) are used to illustrate information about family composition and membership, closeness or estrangement, substance abuse, violence, mental illness, and death. McGoldrick, Gerson, and Shellenberger (1999) state that the standardized genogram provides "a quick gestalt of complex family patterns; as such as they are a rich source of hypotheses about how a clinical problem may be connected to the evolution of both the problem and the family's context over time" (p. 1).

The goal of the Play Genogram is to give clients an opportunity to expand the data provided on a genogram through a clinical interview that elicits information from a client's conscious level (i.e., information that is acknowledged or understood). The Play Genogram invites individuals to choose from a collection of miniatures those which best show their thoughts and feelings about everyone in their family, including themselves, and later challenges them to choose symbols to represent the nature of their relationships with others. Thus a resistant adolescent who claims that she and her mom get along "fine," and everything at home is "okay," is able to construct a jack-in-the-box out of clay to describe her mother as "all wound up and you never know when she'll flip her lid."

Rationale for Use

When using the genogram as an assessment tool the clinician must rely on information that clients are willing or able to provide, particularly in early sessions when trust is still forming. At times, individuals are reluctant to offer information for a variety of reasons, including feelings of family loyalty, privacy, or fear that family members may appear in an unfavorable light or less than "normal." In addition, sometimes individuals are resistant to the therapeutic process and may find that withholding information gives them a greater sense of control. Moreover, some individuals are not necessarily comfortable with verbal communication and may feel constricted when asked to offer verbal descriptions of family members or feelings about their intimate relationships.

Play therapy makes fewer demands for verbal communication and instead incorporates symbolic and metaphoric language. Play therapists believe that play has many curative qualities, not the least of which is providing a vehicle for expanded communication (Schaefer, 1993). Play has often been thought to allow individuals to externalize their internal world by depicting it through symbolic language, story, miniature scenarios, or metaphor language. Innumerable resources in the play therapy literature promote the theory and application of play therapy (see, for example, Landreth, 1982; O'Connor, 1991; O'Connor and Braverman, 1997). In addition, over the past decade, more and more attention has been given to integrating play therapy techniques for use with families (Gil, 1994; Schaefer and Carey, 1994). The Play Genogram was a natural outgrowth of my familiarity with both sand therapy and family genograms (Gil and Sobol, 2000).

Instructions

There are two distinct uses of Play Genograms. The first is the individual Play Genogram, in which a single child or adult is asked to create a genogram of his or her family on easel-size paper. The clinician assists young children to provide information about their biological, foster, or adoptive family. Many of my child clients have lived in a variety of home situations and need to make a number of genograms on the large easel paper. I have experimented with helping the child make genograms on different pieces of easel paper or trying to fit everyone on one page. Putting many genograms on the page may actually give the child a sense of continuity and history, particularly in cases of multiple placements that leave children feeling confused or fragmented about their own history. Putting all important caretakers and family relations on one page creates a sense of order and containment, which may be therapeutic for the child.

The instruction is simple:

> I'd like you each to choose a miniature that best shows your thoughts and feelings about everyone in the family, including yourself. Place the miniature on the circle or square that represents the person for whom you chose the miniature.

I purposely use this phrase so that it is broad, yet structured enough so that younger or older individuals understand the directives. I avoid asking clients to choose "one" miniature because I find that people have difficulty limiting their choice to one miniature, preferring to use two or more. Some clients ask permission to use more than one miniature, others simply do what they wish, while yet others comply with what they perceive to be a rigid demand. The quantity of miniatures chosen therefore becomes diagnostic.

Once the first task of choosing miniatures to represent thoughts and feelings about each person is complete (this may take a full session), the person is given this additional instruction:

> Now choose a miniature that best shows your thoughts and feelings about the relationship you have with every person in your family, and place that miniature somewhere between you and the other person on the genogram.

Younger children may have a more difficult time with this task because they are being asked to move from a concrete to an abstract task. Children over the age of seven are usually more responsive to this directive, but I never underestimate younger children's ability to make brilliant representations of perceived relationships with family members. One six-year-old child placed a brick wall between herself and her father. "You're always far from me," she said to him when he asked about the wall.

The second type of Play Genogram is the family Play Genogram, in which all family members are asked to choose miniatures and place them on the genogram drawing. The instructions are exactly the same:

> I'd like you each to choose a miniature that best shows your thoughts and feelings about everyone in the family, including yourself. Place the miniature on the circle or square that represents the person for whom you chose the miniature.

A couple of issues can surface with family Play Genograms that don't typically arise when working with individuals. First, family members usually want to know if they should all work at the same time or if one family member should go first. My experience with this is that if one family member works alone, he or she is more likely to feel self-conscious about choices and adjust them based on the reactions or directives of family members. When family members work together, there appears to be greater fluidity and less opportunity for censorship.

The next issue is the potential for family conflict when and if individuals choose miniatures that may be perceived as negative, insulting, or critical. The clinician observes the process among family members during this task, noting communication patterns, types of interactions, alliances and collusions, triangulations, and other systemic information.

Once all family members have made their choices, clinicians can express therapeutic curiosity and engage in a therapeutic dialogue congruent with their theoretical approach. Clinicians are advised to use open-ended versus closed questions, refrain from making interpretations and giving explanations, and take every opportunity to help expand the metaphors that are chosen, rather than moving away from metaphors too quickly. The true advantage of Play Genograms is that they provide an opportunity for deeper understanding of each individual's perception of self and others, which allows family members to see one another in a new light. Individual choices must be honored and protected. I have often told families that this activity allows them to communicate with one another in different ways, and that everything which comes forward can be used toward some positive goal.

The metaphors that evolve during Play Genograms can inform the treatment process and can become an integral part of promoting treatment goals and moving the therapy in a positive direction. The clinical vignettes that follow will illustrate the value of using Play Genograms.

Note: Over time I have found it to be important to record information that is presented as soon as the session is complete. At times I videotape family sessions and review the tapes to make sure that family interactions are observed and understood.

Case Vignette: Individual Play Genogram

Nine-year-old Oscar was referred for treatment after his thirteen-year-old brother Ignacio sexually abused and beat him. Oscar was born in the United States, but his Central American parents had left three other children back in their mother country when they traveled to the United States. Ignacio had been raised by his maternal grandparents and was brought to this country when he was twelve. Needless to say, he was not happy about being dislocated from the only family he had known. He felt quite angry that he did not speak the language, could not succeed in school, and often had to rely on a younger brother whom he hardly knew to translate even the most basic information.

Ignacio was a troubled child, resentful, and in a great deal of pain over the loss of everyone important to him. Motivated by aggression, he assaulted his brother Oscar. Ignacio was placed in a juvenile facility and referred to sex offender treatment. Both his parents were shocked and distressed about not only what Oscar had done to his brother but that he was in danger of being placed outside their home.

Oscar was very tight-lipped about what had happened to him, not unlike most sexually abused boys, who present in treatment with a combination of shame and guilt. Sexually abused boys often feel as if they should have protected themselves, and being unable to stop the abuse suggests something about their vulnerability that may be less tolerated by boys. In addition, Oscar was quite intent on minimizing his abuse and often shrugged his shoulders, stating "It was no big deal" when he spoke about what Ignacio had done to him.

Through a nondirective play therapy approach early in treatment, Oscar was allowed to explore the play therapy office and choose what he wanted to work with. His preferred activity was doing sand worlds and then telling elaborate stories about the wars he set up in the sand. For a child who offered monosyllabic responses to most personal questions, it was amazing to watch Oscar weave wonderful and imaginative stories that then became an entry point for understanding his internal world.

Since he used miniatures so well, I asked him to do an individual Play Genogram, and what he offered was quite informative. He chose a very large Godzilla creature for himself, literally towering over other miniatures on the genogram. He chose a cobra for his brother Ignacio and, to my surprise, a smaller snake for his mother. Initially he did not choose a miniature for his father but later added a very small ant to represent him.

When he finished I said, "Tell me about your family," and in typical conservative language he said, "This is me. I'm a very large dinosaur and nothing can hurt me. This is my brother, 'cause he can be mean sometimes, this is my mom, and this is my dad." I said, "Tell me about the ant. What's it like to be an ant when you live with two snakes and a big dinosaur?" "I don't know." I then stated, "I wonder what makes this snake get mean sometimes?" "I don't know," Oscar repeated. I stopped asking questions at this point, although it's important to note that when people place their miniatures on the easel paper they have already spoken volumes; therefore, questions may be perceived as redundant. At the same time, it is important to facilitate an exploration of the metaphor, which sometimes provides very critical information. In this example, other exploratory questions might have been these:

- What's it like to be a dinosaur that never gets hurt?
- Has the dinosaur ever been hurt before?
- What happens when the snake wants to be mean to the dinosaur?
- I notice that there are two snakes, in other words, two creatures from the same species. What do they have in common and how are they different?
- What do the snake and the ant do when the big snake gets mean?
- What do you think makes the snake get mean?
- What's it like to be an ant in this family of larger animals?

In time Oscar answered several of these questions and he carried the metaphor into other play activities, allowing me to truly understand family dynamics and construct some interventions accordingly. My favorite technique with Oscar was "wondering out loud." I would make simple statements such as, "I wonder how those two snakes get along" or "I wonder what those two snakes have in common." Eventually, Oscar began to offer curt responses that allowed me to proceed with reflective listening as well as additional exploratory comments. His expressive communication skills never became expansive, but he did develop a level of comfort with me that allowed him to tell me some of what he felt, and he even began to use his sense of humor to communicate underlying emotions.

Case Vignette: Family Play Genogram

Janina is a ten-year-old girl who was sexually molested by her father, Bill, with whom she had enjoyed a close and supportive relationship prior to the abuse. When her acute discomfort with her father's new behavior precipitated her disclosure, her mother's reaction was appropriate: Mary made a child abuse report and emphasized her alliance with Janina. As time passed, however, Mary was more and more interested in reunification after Bill completed his prison sentence. Although she believed and supported Janina, she also made herself emotionally available to her incarcerated husband.

Janina had a series of problems associated with the abuse, including an acute sense of betrayal and subsequent anger toward her father. She also developed oppositional behavior with her mother, who felt tremendous stress about her situation and her daughter's difficult behaviors. When I asked Janina and Mary to create a family Play Genogram, Mary placed a pixie fairy for Janina, and Janina placed a teenager on the phone for her mother and one for her father. This was a not too veiled attempt at criticizing her mother's phone relationship with her father, which was against court order. Mary placed a farmer leaning on a rake for her husband; this farmer looked like he was resting or pensive. Janina's and Mary's symbols for their relationship with each other provided us with ample opportunity to explore important issues: Mary chose a mirror, which she placed between herself and her daughter; Janina chose a man digging. Mary said, "When I look at Janina I see myself," and Janina said, "My relationship with Mom is such hard work." Both metaphors were brought into verbal therapy, with Mary's discussion of enmeshed feelings toward her daughter and Janina's acknowledgment that she spent too much time worrying and feeling stress about her mother. At one point Janina said, "I just want her to be okay." Mary likewise began to realize that Janina experienced her mother's worry as intrusive or distrustful. The family Play Genogram provided robust metaphors for further exploration, and these metaphors served as code language for discussing difficult issues. Mary, for example, would often say, "Oops, I'm looking at the wrong mirror again," while Janina would make the motion of digging with her arms whenever she felt that conflicts were emerging with her mother.

Sometimes individuals who observe their symbol choices have remarkable insight after reflecting on the obvious and less obvious meanings implied by their symbols. Other times, individuals need directives that lead them toward less obvious meanings or stimulate their curiosity. It's always best when clients arrive at their own interpretations about symbols selected by themselves or others. Other times, clinicians need to nudge clients by articulating questions or broad observations to ignite conscious awareness.

The family Play Genogram is easy to do and adds a valuable level of information to that provided by constructing a genogram in the traditional way. There are many places to buy inexpensive miniatures, such as bakeries (miniatures used for decorating foods) and dollar stores, but clinicians who find buying and displaying miniatures expensive or cumbersome may want to experiment with other types of Play Genograms. For example, I have experimented with three useful alternatives: collage, button, and crystal Play Genograms. In the first, you simply cut out pictures from magazines (or make magazines available to clients for them to select and cut) and give the same instructions, replacing the word "picture" for "miniature." In the second, you provide a large array of buttons (different colors, shapes, and sizes) and ask clients to choose the buttons that best show their thoughts and feelings about self and others. I've also purchased multicolored crystals, rocks, and metals and made them available to clients for use in completing the Play Genogram, by choosing from the multicolored crystals of different shapes, smooth and hard rocks, and different types of metals. Although these are more abstract concepts, they yield interesting results as well.

Family and play therapists will find Play Genograms powerful and fascinating. In addition, this concept lends itself to expansion through clinical creativity. In the earliest stages, there is little rigidity and constriction about its use, so possibilities abound.

References

Gil, E. (1994). *Play in family therapy*. New York: Guilford Publications.

Gil, E. and Sobol, B. (2000). Engaging families in therapeutic play. In C. E. Bailey (Ed.), *Children in therapy: Using the family as a resource* (pp. 341–382). New York: W. W. Norton.

Landreth, G. L. (Ed.) (1982). *Play therapy: Dynamics of the process of counseling with children*. Springfield, IL: Charles C Thomas.

McGoldrick, M., Gerson, R., and Shellenberger, S. (1999). *Genograms: Assessment and intervention*, Second edition. New York: W. W. Norton.

O'Connor, K. J. (1991). *The play therapy primer: An integration of theories and techniques*. New York: John Wiley and Sons.

O'Connor, K. J. and Braverman, L. M. (Ed.) (1997). *Play therapy theory and practice: A comparative presentation*. New York: John Wiley and Sons.

Schaefer, C. E. (Ed.) (1993). *The therapeutic powers of play*. Northvale, NJ: Jason Aronson.

Schaefer, C. E. and Carey, L. J. (Eds.) (1994). *Family play therapy*. Northvale, NJ: Jason Aronson.

Play Genogram Tips

Because this is a technique that can be used with individuals or with families of varying sizes, it becomes important to have a way of documenting choices made by each family member. The following Recording Form is an attempt to facilitate this documentation, although I suggest that readers make necessary improvements as they use this form. The Recording Form allows clinicians to record each person's choice for other family members. Thus, mother/stepmother chooses a miniature for herself, her spouse or partner, and the child(ren). You may need to add additional columns if you are seeing extended family members of families with large numbers of children. Photo 6.1 is an example of a Play Genogram.

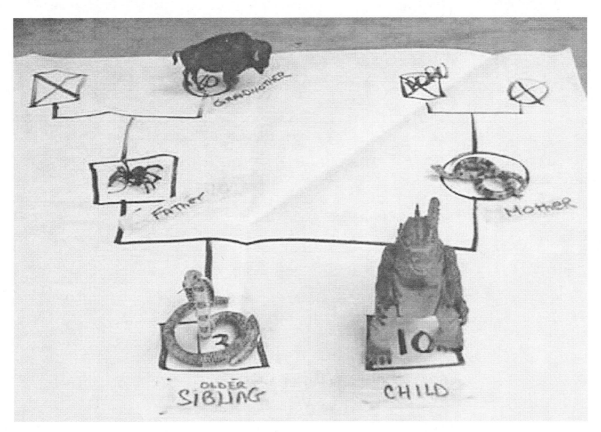

PHOTO 6.1. A family Play Genogram that uses miniatures.

Family Play Genograms Data Recording Form

MOTHER/STEPM	Self	Spouse	Child 1	Child 2	Child 3
FATHER/STEPF	Self	Spouse	Child 1	Chlid 2	Child 3
CHILD 1	Self	Mother/Stepm	Father/Stepf	Child 2	Child 3
CHILD 2	Self	Mother/Stepm	Father/Stepf	Child 1	Child 3
CHILD 3	Self	Mother/Stepm	Father/Stepf	Child 1	Child 2
PATERNAL GM	Mother/Stepm	Father/Stepf	Child 1	Child 2	Child 3
PATERNAL GF	Mother/Stepm	Father/Stepf	Child 1	Child 2	Child 3
MATERNAL GM	Mother/Stepm	Father/Stepf	Child 1	Child 2	Child 3
MATERNAL GF	Mother/Stepm	Father/Stepf	Child 1	Child 2	Child 3

7

Strengthening Parent-Child Attachment with Play: Filial Play Therapy

Risë VanFleet

Type of Contribution: Activity (overview of comprehensive treatment approach)

Objective

Filial play therapy, conceived and developed by Doctors Bernard and Louise Guerney, is designed to accomplish three primary goals: (1) improve child psychosocial adjustment on many levels, (2) improve parenting practices and confidence, and (3) strengthen the parent-child relationship.

Rationale for Use

Filial play therapy is a psychoeducational therapeutic approach that can be used for prevention and intervention with a wide range of psychosocial difficulties. Positive attachment between parent and child promotes mental health and provides a buffer for life stresses. Because filial therapy facilitates the continuing development of healthy parent-child attachment, it is applicable to many types of child/family problems, including anxiety, depression, oppositional behavior problems, attachment/adoption/foster care issues, attention deficits, divorce/single parenting, trauma, abuse, blended families, family illness, and so on.

In filial play therapy, the therapist engages parents as therapeutic partners, assisting them as they serve as the primary change agents for their own children. In essence, the filial play therapist trains the parents to hold special, one-on-one, child-centered play sessions with each of their children; supervises them as they conduct the play sessions; and eventually helps them transfer the play sessions to the home setting, in which they can generalize what they've learned.

Instructions

Following a thorough assessment, after which filial play therapy is recommended, the therapist works closely with parents through the following phases of therapy.

Play Session Demonstration

The therapist first demonstrates brief child-centered play sessions with at least one (and preferably all) of the family's children while the parents observe. This typically takes a single one-hour session. After holding the demonstration play session(s), the therapist discusses it thoroughly with the parents alone. The therapist encourages parents' reactions and questions and points out various aspects of the session that might relate to the family's goals. The therapist then reconfirms the family's interest in continuing.

Training Phase

In this phase, the therapist meets with the parents alone and trains them in the four basic child-centered play session skills: (1) structuring, (2) empathic listening, (3) child-centered imaginary play, and (4) limit-setting. The training typically consists of three one-hour sessions. In the first training session, the therapist discusses each of the skills in detail, providing examples. This is followed by practice of the empathic listening skill. The therapist uses toys and encourages the parents to say aloud what is happening and how the therapist seems to be feeling. For example, the therapist piles the blocks into a tall column, encouraging the parents to say things such as, "You're building it even taller. You're having fun piling on the blocks." The therapist exaggerates the expression of feelings to ensure that parents succeed. If the parents are quiet, the therapist prompts them by saying, "Just describe out loud what I'm doing. Look at my face [showing an exaggerated expression]—how do you think I'm feeling?" If the parents have difficulty with this, the therapist actually models a statement for them, "Try this: You're worried the blocks are going to tip over." The therapist maintains a lighthearted atmosphere and ensures that parents are successful.

The next two training sessions involve "mock play sessions." In these, the therapist role-plays a child and helps the parents practice all four skills. Parents take turns practicing while the other parent observes. The therapist breaks out of the child role periodically to coach the parents as they learn the skills. At the end of the fifteen-minute mock play session, the therapist discusses the parents' reactions to it and gives more detailed feedback. The therapist provides primarily positive feedback and gives the parent only one or two suggestions for improvement. The first mock session is kept relatively easy, while the second is made more challenging, using the basic behavioral principle of shaping. Although three sessions is the average length of the training phase, sometimes additional sessions are needed to help the parents learn the skills.

The training phase of filial play therapy is actually quite complex, requiring advanced clinical and educational/training skills. It should be attempted only by therapists who have had prior training in the approach.

Supervised Parent-Child (Filial) Play Sessions

When parents have demonstrated a basic understanding of the four play session skills, they hold one-on-one play sessions with their own children while the therapist observes. When two parents are involved, they observe each other's play sessions as well. The therapist refrains from intervening in the actual play session but meets with the parents afterward to discuss it. Parents are encouraged to share their reactions—good and bad—at the start of the discussion. The therapist then provides more detailed skill feedback, once again focusing on the positive and providing one or two suggestions for improvement. After the skill feedback, the therapist discusses possible meanings of the child's play with the parents. In-depth psychological interpretations are not needed, but the therapist helps the parents understand their children better by understanding their play. For example, the therapist helps parents recognize and understand play themes of control, power, affective expression, loss, winning and losing, rescue, and so on. Often this part of the discussion can begin by asking the parents, "What did you notice about the way your child was playing? What feelings did he or she seem to be expressing?"

The therapist directly supervises approximately five or six filial play sessions. Supervision continues until the parents seem to be competent in the use of all four skills and have a basic ability to recognize play themes when they occur. When these criteria are met, the parents begin to hold unsupervised play sessions at home.

Home Play Sessions

One session is usually spent planning the transition to the unsupervised home play sessions. The parents plan where and when to hold the sessions, and the therapist ensures that they have collected a (mostly) separate set of toys for use in the filial play sessions. Separate toys are used to help maintain the "special" flavor of the play sessions. The therapist and parents jointly plan how they will handle interruptions and other common problems that arise with the home sessions.

Early in filial therapy, the therapist provides parents with a list of toys they need to obtain for their home filial play sessions (VanFleet, 2000). Inexpensive toy substitutes are discussed, and filial therapists often provide "loaner" toy kits for families who cannot afford to provide their own. The list of toys is basically the same as the toys used in nondirective play therapy, with a number of items from each of the following categories: family-related and nurturance toys, aggression-related toys, expressive and construction toys, emergency and rescue items, and other multiuse toys. There are three main considerations for including toys in the filial play kits. First, the toys must be *safe* for the children's developmental levels. Second, there needs to be a *variety* of toys that encourage the expression of a wide range of childhood feelings and concerns. Third, the majority of play items must have the potential to be used readily in *imaginative* ways.

The parents then hold one half hour play session (still on a one-on-one basis) with each child each week. The therapist asks them to record some basic observations after each play session: what went well, what didn't, a self-critique of their play session skills, and the basic play themes noted during the session. The parents then meet with the therapist following the first home play sessions for a full discussion of them. If all has gone well, the home play sessions continue. Ideally, the therapist meets with the parents each week following their home sessions, but it's possible to stretch this out if costs or "approved number of sessions" is an issue. In this case, the parents hold two play sessions with each of their children over a two-week period and then meet with the therapist to discuss them.

By this time, parents are usually noticing significant positive changes in their children and in themselves. Sometimes the therapist must help parents understand and work through their own reactions to the play sessions. The filial play sessions commonly trigger important psychosocial issues of the parents, and the therapist uses a variety of therapeutic skills to help them express their concerns and solve problems. In this way, filial play therapy helps produce significant positive changes in the parents as well. For example, a somewhat distant father became extremely bored and "irritated" after his six-year-old daughter played "tea party" for the full thirty minutes of one of their play sessions. After sensitive guided questioning by the therapist, the father said that he preferred more active pastimes and that was why he wished they had had a son. The therapist eventually was able to help him realize he could engage in more action-oriented activities with his daughters. His disappointment about not having a son, triggered by a boring play session, helped him reach a more involved and rewarding relationship with his girls.

During the home play session phase, the therapist also helps the parents generalize the four play session skills to everyday life. Additional parenting skills are also taught. Because the parents have already seen how well the skills work, they usually are motivated by this time to use them outside the play sessions as well. Although there is wide variation, the home play session phase typically lasts for six to twelve home play sessions per child (three to six therapy sessions with the parents if the biweekly approach is used).

Ending Phase

When the home play sessions are going well, the child's presenting problems are showing resolution, the parents are able to generalize use of the skills, and the parents report satisfaction with the way things are going, it's time to phase out the therapy. The therapist explains that the parents can continue the play sessions at home and also suggests ways to broaden the play sessions to "family fun nights" and other playful family activities. The importance of some one-on-one time with each child is still stressed, however. Sometimes therapists ask the family to have play sessions for a longer period of time, perhaps a month, before returning for a final session. Many families continue to hold their filial play sessions long after formal therapy has ended.

Vignette

Danny was a four-year-old child whose father had been killed in an industrial accident. He had been very attached to his father, although he had also been quite close with his mother, Betsy. Since the accident, Danny had become increasingly dependent upon Betsy. He expressed anxiety that she would "go away and not come back." He engaged in tantrum behaviors whenever she left for work or other engagements. Betsy had begun limiting her time away from him, including reducing her work hours, but realized this was not necessarily the most healthy route. Danny had also been more aggressive since his father's death and had been scratched by the family cat after pulling its tail. His mother realized his reactions were probably related to the loss of his father, but she was uncertain how to help him.

After a thorough assessment and some other educational interventions, such as children's books about death issues, the therapist suggested filial play therapy to Betsy. The goals were to strengthen the mother-son attachment in a way that would help them work through their grief and face the future together.

Betsy learned the four play session skills readily. The therapist additionally prepared her for the possibility that Danny might play out accident and death themes. They practiced this in the second mock play session until Betsy felt comfortable with it.

During their first filial play session, Danny played quite aggressively. He broke several limits during the session, but Betsy handled this well. During the post-play session discussion with the therapist, Betsy expressed concern about his aggressive play and guilt about having to set limits. The therapist helped her realize that although some aggressive play was acceptable, when he became destructive her limits had been appropriate. When Betsy began to understand that her firm and consistent limit setting could actually help Danny feel more secure, she felt less guilty about it.

In subsequent sessions, Danny's play remained aggressive but became more focused. He reenacted a variety of industrial accidents in which heavy equipment tipped over on the figures, people fell, were squished, and so on. He also buried some of the figures in the sand in a manner reminiscent of funerals. His mother readily recognized these themes as being related to his father's death and burial. The therapist gave Betsy ample opportunity to express her own feelings of sadness following the play sessions. Although Danny's play saddened her, she also became fascinated with his ability to re-create the various scenes and his clear enjoyment in doing so.

After three sessions of injury, death, and burial play, Danny shifted his interest to the ambulance and hospital figures. His play reflected more rescue themes. The therapist helped Betsy realize this was probably Danny's way of gaining mastery over the death of his father. As she understood more of his play, Betsy became more able to be accepting of it. She reported shortly after the rescue play began that she and Danny had begun making a "Remember Daddy" scrapbook at home. She also reported that his inappropriate aggressive play and tantrums had lessened considerably. She had returned to working a full schedule, and Danny was more easily re-assured that she would indeed return home after work.

Themes of rescue and "daddy play" continued when Betsy and Danny began their home play sessions. Eventually Danny's play became more focused on present-time issues such as pre-school, friends, favorite TV shows, and sports. At the time of discharge after seventeen sessions, Danny's presenting problems had been resolved and Betsy reported that she believed their relationship was closer than ever before.

Suggestions for Follow-Up

Follow-up in filial play therapy usually involves spreading the parent meetings (following several home play sessions) over progressively longer periods of time. If gains are maintained, then discharge takes place. It is best if filial play therapists follow up with phone calls three and six months after therapy has ended.

One of the beneficial features of filial play therapy is that the therapist teaches the parents how to be the primary change agent for their own child(ren). As such, they are better prepared to handle new situations as they arise. Filial play therapy is an empowerment approach that increases the capability and confidence of parents.

Thirty-five years of research on filial play therapy (e.g., Bratton and Landreth, 1995; Chau and Landreth, 1997; Costas and Landreth, 1999; Ginsberg, 1976; Glover, 1996; B. G. Guerney, 1964; B. G. Guerney and Stover, 1971; L. F. Guerney, 1976, 1983, 2000; Jang, 2000; Landreth and Lobaugh, 1998; Oxman, 1971; Reif and Stollak, 1972; Rennie and Landreth, 2000; Sensue, 1981; Stover and B. G. Guerney, 1967; Stover, B. G. Guerney, and O'Connell, 1971; Sywulak, 1978; VanFleet, 1992; VanFleet and L. Guerney, 2002) have consistently shown it to be effective in (1) reducing child presenting problems, (2) improving parents' skill knowledge and use, (3) increasing parents' acceptance of their children, (4) reducing parents' stress, and (5) reducing utilization of mental health services. Long-term studies have shown these gains are frequently maintained over several years.

Contraindications for Use

Filial play therapy has wide applicability. It would not be the initial treatment, however, for children who are not yet engaging in imaginary or symbolic play. Children who are unable to tolerate the stimulation of the child-centered playroom might need more directive play therapy or a modified version of filial play therapy in which the number of toys is limited. Filial play therapy would also be contraindicated for parents who are *totally* emotionally unavailable to their children. If they cannot focus on their child for at least fifteen minutes, perhaps they could benefit from individual therapy themselves. Finally, filial play therapy would not be the initial treatment used for families in which the parents are the perpetrators of abuse. In most of these cases the child and parents would benefit from their own separate therapies at first. Filial play therapy would be ideal, however, as a later intervention. It can be a wonderful tool for family reunification and healing.

Professional Readings and Resources

Bratton, S. C. and Landreth, G. L. (1995). Filial therapy with single parents: Effects on parental acceptance, empathy, and stress. *International Journal of Play Therapy, 4*(1), 61-80.

Chau, I. and Landreth, G. (1997). Filial play therapy with Chinese parents. *International Journal of Play Therapy, 6*(2), 75-92.

Costas, M. and Landreth, G. (1999). Filial therapy with nonoffending parents of children who have been sexually abused. *International Journal of Play Therapy, 8*(1), 43-66.

Ginsberg, B. G. (1976). Parents as therapeutic agents: The usefulness of filial therapy in a community psychiatric clinic. *American Journal of Community Psychology, 4*(1), 47-54.

Ginsberg, B. G. (1997). *Relationship enhancement family therapy.* New York: John Wiley.

Glover, G. J. (1996). "Filial therapy with Native Americans on the Flathead Reservation." Unpublished doctoral dissertation, University of North Texas, Denton.

Guerney, B. G. Jr. (1964). Filial therapy: Description and rationale. *Journal of Consulting Psychology, 28,* 303-310.

Guerney, B. and Guerney, L. (1989). Child relationship enhancement: Family therapy and parent education. *Person-Centered Review, 4,* 344-357.

Guerney, B.G. Jr. and Stover, L. (1971). "Filial therapy: Final report on NIMH grant 1826401." Unpublished manuscript, The Pennsylvania State University, University Park, PA.

Guerney, L. F. (1976). Filial therapy program. In D. Olson (Ed.), *Treating relationships* (pp. 67-91). Lake Mills, IA: Graphic Publishing Co., Inc.

Guerney, L. F. (1983). Introduction to filial therapy: Training parents as therapists. In P. A. Keller and L. G. Ritt (Eds.), *Innovations in clinical practice: A source book,* Volume 2 (pp. 26-39). Sarasota, FL: Professional Resource Exchange.

Guerney, L. (2000). Filial therapy into the 21st century. *International Journal of Play Therapy, 9*(2), 1-17.

James, B. (1994). *Handbook for treatment of attachment-trauma problems in children.* New York: The Free Press.

Jang, M. (2000). Effectiveness of filial therapy for Korean parents. *International Journal of Play Therapy, 9*(2), 39-56.

Landreth, G. L. (1991). *Play therapy: The art of the relationship.* Muncie, IN: Accelerated Development Inc.

Landreth, G. and Lobaugh, A. (1998). Filial therapy with incarcerated fathers. *Journal of Counseling and Development, 76*(2), 157-165.

Oxman, L. (1972). "The effectiveness of filial therapy: A controlled study." Doctoral dissertation, Rutgers University, New Brunswick, NJ, 1971. *Dissertation Abstracts International, 32,* 6656.

Reif, T. F. and Stollak, G. E. (1972). *Sensitivity to young children: Training and its effects.* East Lansing, MI: Michigan State University Press.

Rennie, R. and Landreth, G. L. (2000). Effects of filial therapy on parent and child behaviors. *International Journal of Play Therapy, 9*(2), 19-37.

Sensue, M. (1981). "Filial therapy follow-up study: Effects of parental acceptance and child adjustment." Doctoral dissertation, The Pennsylvania State University, University Park, PA. *Dissertation Abstracts International, 42,* 148.

Stinnett, N. and DeFrain, J. (1985). *Secrets of strong families.* New York: Berkley Books.

Stover, L. and Guerney, B. G. Jr. (1967). The efficacy of training procedures for mothers in filial therapy. *Psychotherapy, 4,* 110-115.

Stover, L., Guerney, B., and O'Connell, M. (1971). Measurements of acceptance, allowing self-direction, involvement, and empathy in adult-child interaction. *Journal of Psychology, 77,* 261-269.

Sywulak, A. E. (1978). "The effect of filial therapy on parental acceptance and child adjustment." Doctoral dissertation, The Pennsylvania State University, University Park, PA. *Dissertation Abstracts International, 38,* 6180-6181.

VanFleet, R. (1992). Using filial therapy to strengthen families with chronically ill children. In L. VandeCreek, S. Knapp, and T. L. Jackson (Eds.), *Innovations in clinical practice: A source book,* Volume 11 (pp. 87-97). Sarasota, FL: Professional Resource Press.

VanFleet, R. (1994). Filial therapy for adoptive children and parents. In K. J. O'Connor and C. E. Schaefer (Eds.), *Handbook of play therapy,* Volume 2. *Advances and innovations* (pp. 371-385). New York: John Wiley and Sons.

VanFleet, R. (1994). *Filial therapy: Strengthening parent-child relationships through play.* Sarasota, FL: Professional Resource Press.

VanFleet, R. (1997). Play and perfectionism: Putting fun back into families. In H. G. Kaduson, D. Cangelosi, and C. Schaefer (Eds.), *The playing cure* (pp. 61-82). Northvale, NJ: Jason Aronson.

VanFleet, R. (1998). *Introduction to filial play therapy: A video workshop.* Boiling Springs, PA: Play Therapy Press.

VanFleet, R. (2000). Short-term play therapy for families with chronic illness. In H. G. Kaduson and C. Schaefer (Eds.), *Short-term play therapy interventions with children* (pp. 175-193). New York: Guilford Publications.

VanFleet, R., and Guerney, L. (Eds.) (2001). *Casebook of filial therapy.* Boiling Springs, PA: Play Therapy Press.

Bibliotherapy Sources for the Client

VanFleet, R. (2000). *A parent's handbook of filial play therapy.* Boiling Springs, PA: Play Therapy Press.

VanFleet, R. (2001). Parents' page. Web site: <http://www.play-therapy.com/parents.htm>.

VanFleet, R. (in production). *An overview of filial play therapy: A video for parents.* Boiling Springs, PA: Play Therapy Press.

8

Using Play to Help Parents Share Difficult Information with Young Children

Catherine Ford Sori
Nancy Nickell

Type of Contribution: Activity

Objectives

1. To help parents break difficult news to their young children
2. To help children understand and express their reactions to the news and address any magical thinking that could interfere with normal development
3. To facilitate parents' appropriate responses to children's questions and concerns, thus strengthening the parent-child bond and promoting healthy attachment

This may also be used as a live supervision training activity.

Rationale for Use

Often parents have difficult news that they need to share with their young children regarding issues such as decisions to divorce, changes of custody, adoption, the relocation of one parent, or other major changes in the family. Many parents struggle with whether to share this news, when to share it, and how to best break the news to their children. Some reasons parents have difficulty sharing such news with children include the following:

- A fear of hurting the children
- Not knowing how much information is appropriate to share or what is the best way to tell young children
- Fearing the children's emotional or behavioral reactions
- Being uncertain of how to respond appropriately to their children
- Feeling too overwhelmed themselves to have the resources to cope with children's reactions
- Not understanding children's need to know what's happening in the family

Children can sense tensions in the family and often overhear bits of information that they may misinterpret. They will often distort reality and imagine things are much worse than they actually are.

Therapists may first address these issues with parents using traditional "talk therapy" to help them decide what, when, and how to share difficult information, and they may even use role-play to help parents feel more comfortable. However, direct "talk" methods may not be the most appropriate modality to share sensitive information with young children for several reasons:

- Children may not have reached the stage of cognitive development where they are able to comprehend what the news means, and they may lack the language and verbal skills to ask questions and to express their emotional reactions (Piaget, 1975; Fogarty, 2000).
- Egocentrism and magical thinking may not be adequately uncovered and addressed. For example, children may believe that they caused their parents' divorce because of something they did.
- Young children lack adult coping skills and can't turn to peers as adults can.
- Children often sense how upset their parents are and are reluctant to add to their parents' burden. They often want to protect their parents or may fear that their parents may become too overwhelmed to take care of them.
- Children's magical thinking may lead them to believe that saying something out loud will make it happen. For example, a young child may believe that expressing the fear that "Daddy is divorcing me too, and he's going away and I'll never see him again" may make that exact event come true.

This intervention is best for children age eight or nine and younger. The goals are to

- offer the therapist and parents the opportunity to address magical thinking that, if left unaddressed, could develop into serious pathology (Fogarty, 2000);
- increase parents' awareness of their children's needs, and sensitize parents to respond in age-appropriate ways;
- empower the parents, who function as cotherapists, to soothe and reassure their children;
- increase parental self-esteem at a time when they may feel overwhelmed, powerless, or ineffectual in helping their children; and
- improve communication and strengthen the parent-child bond, which increases the likelihood that parents will be able to address future concerns that may arise with their children.

This intervention offers a way to involve parents in their children's therapy (Bailey and Sori, 2000) by employing a modality that offers a common ground by using children's language: play. It enables parents to access their children's understanding of events and emotions in a safe, nonthreatening way that sidesteps children's natural defenses. Play is how young children learn to understand their world, how they work through problems, and how they best communicate. When serious issues are addressed in a playful way, the "as if" quality sidesteps children's natural defenses and prevents them from becoming overwhelmed. Unspoken thoughts and feelings can be safely expressed through play in both individual and family sessions using various modalities, such as puppets (Irwin and Malloy, 1975; Gil, 1994; Oaklander, 1988) and stories (Gardner, 1971; Gil, 1994; Oaklander, 1988).

Instructions

The Setup

First, the therapist should work with the parents to clarify the information they want to convey to the children. Careful attention should be given to providing honest and accurate information that is age appropriate, but that does not overwhelm the children. It is important to ensure that the parents are able to share the news without decompensating, which might lead to the children trying to take care of the parents' emotional needs. Parents can be encouraged to share their own emotions honestly but calmly, and in a manner that reassures the child with the message that they will be okay, and that they are strong enough to take care of the children.

Next, parents should be given some brief, general information about children's cognitive abilities, such as the fact that children who think concretely have a difficult time comprehending more abstract concepts such as divorce, custody, or death (Piaget, 1975; Fogarty, 2000). Parents should then be given the rationale and an explanation of the intervention, and why it is a less threatening way to share difficult information with young children. It may then be helpful to role-play with the parents how the information can be shared through play. Parents should be encouraged to ask questions, and therapists should address any concerns to ensure that parents feel they are part of a "team" effort to help their children.

Materials

Materials for this intervention can be puppets, stuffed animals, or dolls, and they should be assembled prior to the family session. Care should be taken to ensure that there are enough toys to represent each family member. If dolls are used they should represent, if possible, the genders of the parents and the children.

The Intervention

Step one. Invite the family to sit on the floor in a circle, with the parents sitting by the therapist. Using one of the toys, the therapist may engage the children by introducing them to the toy, which could represent a child. For example, the therapist may say, "This is Benny Bear [or Betty Bear]. He helps kids talk about things that are hard to talk about." (*Note:* Do not use actual names of family members, as this may be threatening to the child. Remember that this is play and should *initially* retain the "as if" quality, as discussed earlier.)

Talking through the bears, spend a few minutes letting the bears get to know the children, asking what their favorite snacks are (bears love honey!), their favorite TV shows (*Winnie the Pooh*?), and who their friends are. Then introduce another bear, which represents a parent.

Next, use the toys to create a parallel story to what the family is currently experiencing. At this point, the information the parents and therapist have prepared to share is enacted by the therapist through the puppets, retaining the "as if" play quality. For example, the mommy and daddy bears may gather their "children" and share the news that they are getting a divorce. Mommy Bear might say, "Daddy Bear and I have decided that we should not live together anymore because we are so unhappy. . . ." The therapist then engages the children to imagine how the Bear children react to this news.

The therapist might encourage the children to hold and talk through the puppets by saying, "Susie, would you like to hold Betty Bear? What questions do you think she wants to ask Mommy Bear?" In this manner issues can be explored and concerns addressed. The therapist models appropriate responses to concerns and feelings expressed by the children through the parent bears.

Cognitive distortions resulting from magical thinking and egocentrism in young children can be addressed using this play modality. For instance, the toy representing a parent should tell children that they didn't cause the problem (e.g., a divorce). Children need to be given explicit permission to express a wide range of feelings, and strong emotional reactions should be normalized. Mommy or Daddy Bear can also reassure the children that they will always be cared for and loved. And they can begin to be prepared for how the changes will affect their lives (e.g.,

"Daddy won't live at our house, but he will have his own apartment. You will get to stay with him on weekends, and you can call him whenever you want.")

Step two. After using the toys to model a discussion about the implications of the news, the therapist offers the parent-toys to the parents and asks them to share with the puppet children (being held by the children) the information about what's happening *in their own family.* The parents begin by engaging the puppet children in a dialogue about their situation. The therapist may help the children respond through the puppets, or they may directly address their parents. The therapist's role is also to help by prompting the parents to respond appropriately, first to the puppets, and then directly to their children. Parents are coached to explain how the changes will affect the family and the individual children's lives, to balance reality with reassurance and hopefulness that, although these changes may be difficult, the family will get through them, and there will be joy and happiness in the future. The therapist also offers emotional support to all the family members by affirming their strengths and encouraging ongoing parent-child dialogues.

This activity empowers parents to meet their children's emotional and cognitive needs, thus strengthening the parent-child bond.

Vignette

Pauline was a single, African-American mother of two young girls, Toni and Tanya, ages six and eight. Toni had been diagnosed with attention deficit hyperactivity disorder (ADHD), and Tanya was a "slow learner" with several learning disabilities. The family lived with Pauline's mother in an inner-city neighborhood. The girls' father, who had been physically abusive to the mother, was serving time in prison for armed robbery. Pauline initiated individual therapy for herself to talk through her decision to leave the girls with her mother and move in with her boyfriend, who lived about a half hour from the girls.

The therapist (NN) thoroughly explored this issue with Pauline. They discussed the potential impact this decision might have on her and her children, who had already suffered the loss of their father and had other difficulties. Pauline, however, believed this was her "second chance for a happy life," and that the girls would be better off living with her mother. She and her mother often had conflicts over disciplining the girls, and she frequently gave up and gave in to her mother's criticism of her parenting efforts. Although the therapist had strong reservations about the advisability of her plan, Pauline had made up her mind and it was Pauline's decision. Pauline also resisted all efforts to involve her mother in the therapy until after her move. The immediate goal of therapy then shifted to how to share the news of her impending move to lessen the negative effects on the children.

The therapist had already seen the girls in an earlier family session, in which the children spent most of the session talking with Pauline while exploring the playroom. They were loud and disruptive and made talk therapy difficult. One interesting incident occurred during that session, which demonstrated the children's egocentrism and magical thinking. The supervisor, who was observing behind a one-way mirror, noticed Tanya touch the white board with a permanent marker and quickly telephoned in to alert the therapist. The buzz of the phone startled Tanya, who jumped back from the board. The therapist exchanged the permanent marker with the appropriate marker. Tanya, however, moved on to another activity. Later in the session Toni approached the white board and picked up the marker. Tanya quickly rushed over to her sister, saying, "Watch out! Touching that board makes the telephone ring!"

The therapist and supervisor agreed that play would be the most appropriate modality to engage these children and decided on this intervention to empower Pauline to tell her children, and to help her appropriately handle their reactions. The therapist helped Pauline clarify what information she needed to tell the girls and explained that "talking through" the toys would help the children be able to listen better without feeling as threatened as if they were told directly.

At the beginning of the family session the therapist greeted Pauline and the girls and attempted to ask them questions about what had happened since she'd last seen them. However, they were quickly out of their seats, and it was difficult to focus their attention long enough to engage them in a conversation. The therapist, wisely, had not used the playroom, so there would be fewer objects to distract the children. She pulled out one big brown bear and two smaller bears, which immediately got their attention. The family was invited to sit on the floor in a circle, and the therapist introduced the children to the Bear family, mentioning that Mom already knew the bears.

The children quickly quieted down as the therapist began to interact with the children through Momma Bear, asking them general questions about their likes and dislikes. She introduced the other kid bears and, at their squeals of delight, allowed each of them to hold a bear. Continuing to talk through Momma Bear, the therapist told the children that she had some news to tell the Bear children. She said that sometimes momma bears can't live in the same house with their kid bears, and that they have to move to a different house. Momma Bear then explained that the child bears will live with their Grandma Bear during the week, so they can go to school. However, they will visit with Momma Bear on weekends and holidays, and during the summer. Momma Bear also said that she would always be their momma, and that they could call her on the phone whenever they wanted.

The therapist handed Momma Bear to Pauline and then asked the children what their bears were thinking. Tanya responded rather tentatively that she was sad that Momma Bear was moving away. Toni's bear quickly agreed and said that she was worried they might not see Momma Bear again. The therapist coached Pauline in how to respond, for example, saying, "Momma Bear, it sounds like your children are sad and worried. How can you reassure them . . .?" The therapist interjected comments to help label the children's feelings, to normalize their reactions, and to encourage Pauline to address their fears. For example, at one point the therapist said, "Sounds like you bears are still worried about not seeing Momma Bear enough. Lots of bears would feel that way. Momma Bear, what can you say to help these little bears not be so worried?" These discussions continued, with Momma Bear assuring the children that they had done nothing wrong to cause this to happen. The children became increasingly freer in asking questions and expressing how the Bear children felt about the move.

Interestingly, Pauline spontaneously shifted at an appropriate moment from the role of Momma Bear to herself, with no prompting from the therapist. At a moment when the children seemed to have no further comments, Pauline took the lead, telling her children that she too, just like Momma Bear, would be moving a short distance away. The therapist encouraged Pauline to gather the children closer to her, and to ask the children how they felt. She told the children, "Sometimes it's hard to talk, but maybe your bear can help you talk about how you feel." The children, using the bears at first, began asking questions about when Pauline was moving, where she was moving to, and when they would see her. Pauline assured the children that they had not done anything bad that caused her to move, but that she was moving to live with Dan, and to be closer to work. Gradually the children dropped the puppets and talked directly to their mother. The therapist asked questions at the end of the session to ensure that the children understood the reality of the move, and that they had done nothing to cause this to happen. She ended on a positive note that the Bears, as well as Pauline and her children, would always be a family who loved one another and would have happy times together.

Another therapist took the children briefly to the playroom while the therapist spent a few minutes debriefing Pauline. When asked for her reactions to the session Pauline beamed. She stated that she was amazed at how attentive the children had been, how actively they had participated, and how they made the shift from the bear story to their own situation so naturally. She admitted she had been nervous at first but was overjoyed that it had gone so well, and she felt good about her part in helping her children. The therapist complimented Pauline on her active role, her sensitivity in responding to her children, and her good parenting skills. She encouraged the children to express their feelings, she addressed their concerns, and she answered all their questions. The therapist encouraged Pauline to continue these conversations on an ongoing basis, since the change would still be difficult for them.

Suggestions for Follow-Up

In future sessions the therapist can continue to use the toys to assess and address children's adjustment to changes in the family. Children often enjoy the toys and will usually look forward to using them to express their thoughts. This strengthens their ability to cope and provides them with a sense of security. At the same time, the therapist can provide ongoing support and guidance in helping parents respond to their children's needs. Parents' self-esteem increases as they are able to take emotional care of their children during a difficult time, and as they effectively manage difficult circumstances in their children's lives.

This activity also helps to reinforce an appropriate parent-child hierarchy, by continuing to put the parents in charge of the play dialogue with their children. It also is easy to transfer this modality to other issues, such as how the children are functioning at school, how they are sleeping, and their peer relationships.

It should be noted that this intervention could be used as a training activity. For example, the therapist in this case used a "bug-in-the-ear," through which the supervisor coached her regarding how to use the bears with the family.

Contraindications

Care must be taken not to use this intervention before the parents are ready and all their concerns have been addressed. Parents who are too overwhelmed themselves may need individual support to address their emotional issues before they will be emotionally available for their children. Often it is helpful to balance the parents' individual needs with individual child and family sessions throughout the course of therapy.

Parents who are low functioning and incapable of or not motivated to help their children may just want to turn this responsibility over to the therapist. However, therapists should not assume this responsibility without first trying to help the parents to feel better and to see the benefit of their involvement (see Bailey and Sori, 2000, for a discussion on involving reluctant parents).

Some parents continue to resist this activity because they are uncomfortable using play materials. Therapists should discuss these attitudes with parents, being careful not to judge them. For example, when the supervisor explored this with one mother she disclosed that the day after her own mother's death (she was seven), her father handed her a box and told her she had to give all her toys to charity—her childhood was over. Sometimes the therapist can model how to use play materials with the children, and the parents gradually are won over when they see how much their children enjoy this modality.

Finally, some young children, such as gifted and talented children, may prefer a talk modality. However, we have yet to see a young child who does not respond well to play materials, even if they are used as a temporary bridge to talk therapy.

When a therapist enters the world of "make-believe," few children—or parents—can resist following!

Professional Readings

Ariel, S., Carel, C., and Tyano, S. (1985). Uses of children's make-believe play in family therapy: Theory and clinical examples. *Journal of Marital and Family Therapy, 11*(1), 47-60.

Bailey, C. E. and Sori, C. E. F. (2000). Involving parents in children's therapy. In C. E. Bailey (Ed.), *Children in therapy: Using the family as a resource* (pp. 475-501). New York: W. W. Norton and Company.

Chasin, R. and White, T. B. (1989). The child in family therapy: Guidelines for active engagement across the age span. In L. Combrinck-Graham (Ed.), *Children in family contexts: Perspectives on treatment* (pp. 5-25). New York: Guilford Publications.

Fogarty, J. A. (2000). *The magical thoughts of grieving children: Treating children with complicated mourning and advice for parents.* Amityville, NY: Baywood Publishing Company, Inc.

Gardner, R. A. (1971). *Therapeutic communication with children: The mutual storytelling technique.* New York: Science House.

Gil, E. (1994). *Play in family therapy.* New York: Guilford Publications.

Irwin, E. C. and Malloy, E. S. (1975). Family puppet interview. *Family Process, 14,* 170-191.

Oaklander, V. (1988). *Windows to our children.* New York: The Gestalt Journal Press.

Piaget, J. (1975). *The origins of intellect: Piaget's theory* (Second edition). San Francisco: W. H. Freeman and Company.

Resources for Clients

Cain, B. S. (1990). *Double-dip feelings: Stories to help children understand emotions.* New York: Magination Press.

9

Explaining to Parents the Use of Play
in Family Therapy

Linda Wark

Type of Contribution: Activity

Objective

This chapter provides information that therapists can use to provide a rationale to parents for the use of play in therapy. It discusses the nature and multiple benefits of play and presents ideas for helping adults respond to a play orientation in therapy. With this information, clinicians should also be able to answer basic questions that parents might have regarding play and therapeutically oriented play. The information presented here primarily has children between the ages of four and eleven in mind.

Rationale

Play is a feature that unites many child therapies. Four strains of therapy employ play (Wark, 1999). Play therapy may be the most well known. It is primarily focused on children, traditionally to the exclusion of adult family members. Children take the lead in playing as they wish, while the therapist sets limits on destructive behavior and makes interpretations regarding pretend play and the children's own lives (Brody, 1996). All play therapy shares a common goal: the reestablishment of the child's ability to engage in play behavior (O'Connor, 1991). Some play therapists consider the family context by having parents join in the play while the child leads (Wachtel, 1994). This joining in is a major characteristic of filial therapy, known for its involvement of parents in the process of therapeutic pretend play. One of the goals of filial therapy (Guerney, 1964; VanFleet, 1994) is to make the parents cotherapists by honing the same skills that the therapist uses. Theraplay (Jernberg and Booth, 1999) uses play rooted in attachment-based behaviors to create new relationship experiences for parents and children. Adults take the lead in Theraplay. Pretend play is not used in Theraplay because the play behaviors, based on those common in healthy parent-infant relationships, are intended to foster secure attachment, parent to child and child to parent. Finally, playful family therapy (Wark, 1998) is a play-integrated family therapy that combines mainstream family therapy models with playful interpretations of well-known family therapy interventions and session activities. The therapist structures the therapy with pretend play to better include children, using developmentally appropriate techniques. Playful family therapy is the context for this chapter. However, the adult's comfort with play is important to many orientations, and the information presented here has potential use for other therapies that employ play.

Although many elements are necessary for effective therapy with children and their families, play has the potential to integrate both children and adults in the same therapy sessions. Since reputable evidence suggests that play between parents and children is a universal experience (Singer and Singer, 1990), the information on play presented here holds general relevance for a multiethnic and multiracial population (Gibbs and Huang, 1998). Clinicians, however, should become familiar with culture-specific interpretations of play when implementing play in therapy (Van Hoorn, 1987; Martinez and Valdez, 1992; Nguyen, 1992) and view any therapeutic play within all of its contexts (Sutton-Smith, 1986).

Occasionally, parents are uncertain about the relevance and efficacy of play in therapy sessions, believing that children play merely for entertainment. One challenge for therapists who use play in therapy can be to convince parents that play can help achieve resolution of serious concerns. Some parents who are frustrated with their children are reluctant to give credibility to play, hoping that therapy will cause their children to sit quietly and respond promptly to all questions from adults. Still other parents are uncomfortable with the idea of play for themselves in therapy. These parents fear that they will be asked to do something that is embarrassing to them and may envision play in therapy as purposeless, silly behavior. Erroneous beliefs regarding the use of play in therapy can be challenged with information. Information will also start therapy off on the right track for parents who are simply unfamiliar with the implementation of play in therapy. It is often useful to offer this information to parents prior to the first session because play in therapy may be unexpected and, thus, uncomfortable for parents. Preparation of clients prior to the first therapy session can help prevent dropouts (Schwartzbaum, 1999).

Parents should understand that play is often incorporated into therapy that includes children because children know how to play better than they know how to do almost anything else. Play in therapy is helpful to the therapeutic process because play is how children feel the most expressive, the most competent, and the most childlike. Thus, therapists who use a playful style in therapy communicate to children that therapy belongs to them and that they are worth spending time with (James, 1989). Play also increases the participation of children in the activities of therapy sessions. During therapy sessions, children's behavior that is annoying to adults (e.g., not answering questions when asked) or play that seems designed to disrupt (e.g., throwing wads of paper) are often children's attempts to create an environment in which they can participate (Montalvo and Haley, 1973). Thus, play provides children with an opportunity to control themselves (Fein, 1981). Further, play in therapy is useful for both children and adults. Play has neurophysiological effects on children and adults, and emotions are released safely in play (Fein, 1981). Children and adults feel less intimidated by novel experiences when they are playing. In addition, play increases the flexibility that family members have in solving problems (Sutton-Smith, 1982). Children benefit emotionally from their parents' interest and involvement in their play activities. In addition, parents stimulate a huge potential for cognitive and emotional growth by modeling and encouraging play (Armstrong, 1991). Finally, play can be carried over to daily life (Amster, 1943), and the therapeutic uses of play eventually assume a natural place in family interactions.

Although play is more than an idle or pleasure-evoking activity, some parents are unaware of the benefits of play and are more accepting of the idea of play in therapy when they are provided with an intellectual explanation. Thus, therapists can inform them that play has developmental benefits for children, providing a necessary component in cognitive, affective, and sensorimotor development (Singer, 1996). Some desirable correlates of pretend play for younger children include general positive emotionality, enhanced language skill, persistence in completing tasks, distinguishing reality from fantasy, strengthened empathy, cooperative relationships, leadership skills, impulse control, willingness to take turns, trying out different roles, ordering and sequencing skills, and anticipating consequences (Singer, 1996). Even Albert Einstein addressed the cognitive contributions of play, saying that "play is an essential feature of productive thought" (cited in Pearce, 1992, p. 72).

Children engage in several types of play (Bergen, 1988). *Sensorimotor play* is the domain of infants who explore their environment by visual observation, handling objects, and physical movement. *Practice play* contributes to the acquisition of physical and mental skills through playful repetition of various behaviors. For preschoolers practice play is a process, whereas elementary school children use practice play to achieve certain competencies. Thus, preschoolers hop on one foot for the sake of hopping, while school-age children might hop to play the game of hopscotch. Sensorimotor play on its own is confined to infancy (Santrock, 2002). However, it is later combined with practice play and pretend play to form *constructive play.* Constructive play can be found in both the preschool and school years. For example, a group of school-age children might implement their imagination, repetitive/practice skills, and physical abilities to create a neighborhood circus and charge admission to their parents. *Social play* begins in the preschool years, and remnants of it continue into adulthood. This play focuses primarily on the engagement of another person in a play activity. Finally, *pretend play,* dependent on the cognitive ability of children to use symbolism, begins during late infancy and the toddler stages. Elements of pretend play can be observed throughout the life span. Pretend play is the reason that cigar bands can become engagement rings and that Tom Cruise plays the air guitar in *Risky Business.*

Pretend play is characterized by metaphor and creativity, and it can figure prominently in therapy for both children and adults (Madanes, 1981; Mills and Crowley, 1986). Interchangeable terms for pretend play are pretense play, symbolic play, imaginative play, make-believe play, and fantasy play (Fein, 1981). Pretend play offers the opportunity for children and adults to act "as if" and suspend behaviors and perspectives long enough to gain new experiences (Ariel, Carel, and Tyano, 1985). The play of preschoolers is what most people think of when they think of pretend play. However, when children make the transition to grade school pretend play does not disappear; it just takes on a different quality. The symbolic representation that was cast on objects by the preschooler is now more internalized because children can now be cognitively aware of their thinking. Thus, fantasy is not observable as often (Singer and Singer, 1990). During the grade school years, play is consciously experimental and many possibilities are explored in play contexts (Pearce, 1992). Children over the age of eleven can be thought of as foregoing the play of their childhood for reality-based activities that are expected by society. Even though numerous skills and abilities in adolescence began as play activities in childhood, dominating tasks in adolescence are to construct bodies of knowledge and to develop abstract thinking. Although adolescents can be quite creative in work, social, or school activities, most of them are too close to this developmental shift to feel comfortable engaging in early imaginative play behavior unless it is constructed around activities such as role-playing, board games, and playing "for the sake of" younger siblings. Adults are highly capable of recapturing play in their behavior, but socialization often inhibits them.

Some adults adapt quite easily to a playful venue in therapy and others do not. Some therapies for children and their families require the participation of adults in play (Griff, 1983; Safer, 1965; Wark, 1999), but parents may feel uncomfortable playing because they believe that they lack specific skills to play. These parents can be guided to observe their children, let them lead, and then join in on their children's terms. Entry into children's ongoing play includes asking children questions about their ground rules for play ("What does the monster do when she needs to eat?" "What is the baby duck supposed to do now?") and not deviating sharply from these parameters (Armstrong, 1991). Other parents are uncomfortable playing because they think that play is just for children. However, most adults engage in play in some way but do not recognize their activities as play. Therapists can assist parents to identify the ways that they play through the recognition of their activities. Examples of adult play are creative writing; daydreaming; painting; reading metaphorical stories, such as the *Chronicles of Narnia* (Lewis, 1950) or the recent *Harry Potter and the Sorcerer's Stone* (Rowling, 1997); watching films, such as *The Wizard of Oz, Star Wars, E.T.,* or *Mulan;* scavenger hunts; running model trains; dressing up for costume parties; backyard sports; reading mystery books; party games; singing in the shower; acting in community theater; social clubs (which may have symbolic rituals such as secret handshakes); and dancing. Even visualization exercises to reduce stress and board games such as Monopoly have pretend elements (Singer and Singer, 1990). These adult play activities could not have occurred without the developmental link to childhood play. Parents who engage in these types of activities can compare them with their children's play to see the commonalities. These parents have a difficult time denying that play is already a part of their behavior.

Instructions

The following are instructions on how to approach parents to introduce the concept of play in therapy. They are presented as somewhat sequential, but therapists can arrange them to fit their own clinical situations.

1. Call prior to the first session. Set up an initial appointment or a phone call to inform parents that the therapy sessions will include playful activities to help their children feel included. Give examples of how play is incorporated into your therapy style.
2. Try to get a feel for how accepting the parents are of a playful therapy style. Ask for their reaction if it is not volunteered. If parents seem doubtful of the usefulness of play, go to step three.
3. Acknowledge to the parent(s) that what you have said may be a challenge to the image they have of therapy. Ask them to describe their images of therapy with such questions as "What are your ideas of what therapy should be like for families? What do you think would help your child feel comfortable in therapy? Do you think your child will sit still in a chair while we talk? What would help him or her participate?"
4. Explain to parents that play in therapy is structured around activities that have therapeutic importance. The structure will provide opportunities for their children to participate more fully. Play will ultimately be the glue that helps children stick with the important concerns that the family must confront.
5. Ask parents if you can share some time-honored child developmental knowledge related to play. Explain the connections between play and their children's development.
6. If your therapy includes parents in play, and the parents balk at the idea, stress that no one has to do anything playful that is uncomfortable for him or her. Explore how parents already play with their children at home. Provide ideas on how adults can join in children's play. Use their ideas to demonstrate that they will have a natural ability to participate in play during therapy.
7. Follow the phone call or initial appointment with a letter summarizing what you discussed.

Vignette

Aaron and Phoebe called to begin therapy because their two children, Rachael, age eight, and Alan, age ten, fought constantly. The therapist agreed to see all of the family for most of the therapy sessions. She asked if she could provide an explanation of how she conducted therapy before they arrived, either by phone or during a first session. They consented but said that it would be easier to talk with her by phone. The therapist asked if they had an extension phone so that they could both hear her at the same time.

The therapist explained that she would be using a number of playful activities in the therapy sessions that children typically like so the children would feel included and comfortable. For example, she might use board games, activities involving physical movement, and art supplies, all of which would help the children participate more fully in the therapy. She would include all family members in these activities, and she suggested that the family members wear comfortable clothing.

At the end of the explanation, Aaron said that it was just fine for the therapist to do whatever she could to help his children stop fighting, and if therapy with play was the answer that was okay with him. He said that it didn't seem that her therapy was really *his* style, but he agreed to attend the sessions. Phoebe said that she didn't think that she would know how to play, but she was very comfortable with her children playing while she and her husband watched. The therapist was disappointed that the parents wanted to be observers of their children in play, but she expected that exposure to play in therapy would change their minds.

After the phone call, the therapist mailed printed information to the parents summarizing what she had presented by phone. Her cover letter asked them to call if something did not make sense. Phoebe and Aaron did not call and arrived with their children for the first therapy session. The therapist had arranged the room so that a large tentlike structure was in one corner, a sleeping bag was opened and spread out on the floor, and a few chairs of different sizes were lining the wall on one side of the room. The therapist asked if everyone could sit on the sleeping bag. Rachael and Alan looked pleased at the invitation and sat on it immediately. The parents pulled up chairs next to the sleeping bag. Then, Phoebe moved from her chair to the sleeping bag. The therapist sat on the sleeping bag with the children. Before the therapist could begin the session, Rachael said, "Daddy, you're supposed to sit on the sleeping bag!" Aaron looked surprised and joined everyone else on the floor. Two other times at play junctures in the therapy session, Rachael said, "Everybody has to do this!" and her parents adopted her behavior. Alan cheered his father on several times when his father followed the playful style of the session activities. After the session, the therapist briefly addressed the parents privately. She asked them if they thought that their children wanted them to engage in playful activities in therapy. The parents said that it was their perception that the children seemed very pleased when they joined in the playful activities. They were also surprised how calm and happy the children were in therapy. Phoebe noted after the first therapy session that she thought a special kind of play was used in therapy. After the session, she realized that all of the play was familiar and comfortable to her. Alan still appeared reserved regarding play but expressed that he was impressed with how his children behaved in the therapy session. He also did not realize how much his children enjoyed having him play with them.

Suggestions for Follow-Up

A letter or second phone call can be used to facilitate parents' acceptance of play before meeting with the family the first time. Some therapists prefer to meet with adults alone at the beginning of therapy before including the children (Wachtel, 1994). The parents' comfort with play should be assessed both prior to the first session and after the first therapy session that includes play. Adults who still balk at play for themselves should be treated with patience and given time. Children will tolerate their parents' observing their play without actively participating with them, but if parents outwardly denigrate play, the children's play can be inhibited due to lack of support.

Contraindications for Use

Even after explanations regarding play and its benefits are given, some parents display reluctance to participate in therapy using a playful venue, and they should not be forced or coaxed to participate. Almost all parents are at least willing to attend therapy sessions where their children can behave playfully, even when they are uncomfortable engaging in play themselves. Often, when parents experience the play in therapy described by the therapist, those who previously declined will join in fully, or at least to some extent.

In therapy, when asking adults to engage in playful activities with their children, therapists should note whether adults or children have any physical concerns that may prevent certain types of involvement. For example, if Phoebe or Aaron suffered from chronic back pain, their ability to sit on the floor would be prohibited.

Finally, if the child clients do not play at home, this may be reason to conduct therapy sessions solely centered on play itself before proceeding with play-integrated family therapy. Children who do not play may have inhibited their normal play activity in response to family problems (Stern, 2002), or play has been stifled due to abuse (Mann and McDermott, 1983). Winnicott (1971) noted the connection between play and healthy relationships. If children have not been able to play to work through difficulties and cope with challenges, then the play behavior must first be established. Children can be trained to play, and readers are referred to other sources (O'Connor, 1991).

Professional Readings and Resources

Fein, G.G. (1981). Pretend play in childhood: An integrative review. *Child Development, 52,* 1095-1118.
Montagu, A. (1983). *Growing young.* New York: McGraw-Hill.
Singer, D.G. and Singer, J.L. (1990). *The house of make-believe: Children's play and the developing imagination.* Cambridge, MA: Harvard University Press.

Bibliotherapy Sources for Clients

Armstrong, T. (1991). *Awakening your child's natural genius.* New York: Putnam Publishing.
Nelson, E.L. (1975). *Movement games for children of all ages.* London: Oak Tree Press Co., Ltd.
Pearce, J.C. (1980). *Magical child.* New York: Bantam.
Silberg, J. (1993). *Games to play with toddlers.* Beltsville, MD: Gryphon House.

References

Amster, D. (1943). Differential uses of play in treatment of young children. *American Journal of Orthopsychiatry, 13,* 62-68.
Ariel, S., Carel, C., and Tyano, S. (1985). Uses of children's make-believe in family therapy: Theory and clinical examples. *Journal of Marital and Family Therapy, 11,* 47-60.
Armstrong, T. (1991). *Awakening your child's natural genius.* New York: Putnam Publishing.
Bergen, D. (1988). *Play as a medium for learning and development.* Portsmouth, NH: Heinemann.
Brody, V. (1996). Play therapy as an intervention for acting out children. In G.L. Landreth, L.E. Homeyer, G.G. Glover, and D.S. Sweeney (Eds.), *Play therapy interventions with children's problems.* New York: Jason Aronson.

Fein, G.G. (1981). Pretend play in childhood: An integrative review. *Child Development, 52,* 1095-1118.

Gibbs, J.T. and Huang, L.N. (1998). *Children of color: Psychological interventions with culturally diverse youth.* San Francisco: Jossey-Bass.

Griff, M.D. (1983). Family play therapy. In C.E. Schaefer and K.J. O'Connor (Eds.), *Handbook of play therapy* (pp. 153-168). New York: John Wiley and Sons.

Guerney, B. (1964). Filial therapy: Description and rationale. *Journal of Consulting Psychology, 28,* 304-310.

James, B. (1989). *Treating traumatized children.* New York: Free Press.

Jernberg, A. and Booth, P. (1999). *Theraplay: Helping parents and children build better relationships through attachment-based play.* San Francisco: Jossey-Bass.

Lewis, C.S. (1950). *The chronicles of Narnia.* New York: HarperCollins.

Madanes, C. (1981). *Strategic family therapy.* San Francisco: Jossey-Bass.

Mann, E. and McDermott, J.F. (1983). Play therapy for victims of child abuse and neglect. In C.E. Schaefer and K.J. O'Connor (Eds.), *Handbook of play therapy* (pp. 174-181). New York: John Wiley and Sons.

Martinez, K.J. and Valdez, D.M. (1992). Cultural considerations in play therapy with Hispanic children. In L.A. Vargas and J.D. Koss-Chioino (Eds.), *Working with culture: Psychotherapeutic interventions with ethnic minority children and adolescents* (pp. 102-119). San Francisco: Jossey-Bass.

Mills, J.C. and Crowley, R.J. (1986). *Therapeutic metaphors for children and the child within.* New York: Brunner/Mazel.

Montalvo, B. and Haley, J. (1973). In defense of child therapy. *Family Process, 12,* 227-244.

Nguyen, N.A. (1992). *Living between two cultures: Treating first-generation Asian Americans.* San Francisco: Jossey-Bass.

O'Connor, K.J. (1991). *Play therapy primer: An integration of theories and techniques.* New York: John Wiley and Sons.

Pearce, J.C. (1992). *Evolution's end: Claiming the potential of our intelligence.* New York: HarperCollins Publishers.

Rowling, J.K. (1997). *Harry Potter and the sorcerer's stone.* New York: Scholastic Press.

Safer, D. (1965). Conjoint play therapy for the young child and his parent. *Archives of General Psychiatry, 13,* 320-326.

Santrock, J.W. (2002). *Children.* New York: McGraw-Hill.

Schwartzbaum, S. (1999). "The pre-therapy orientation model for low income and minority clients." Presentation at the American Association for Marriage and Family Therapy. Chicago, Illinois. October 8.

Singer, D.G. and Singer, J.L. (1990). *The house of make-believe: Children's play and the developing imagination.* Cambridge, MA: Harvard University Press.

Singer, J.L. (1996). Cognitive and affective implications of imaginative play in childhood. In M. Lewis (Ed.), *Child and adolescent psychiatry: a comprehensive textbook* (pp. 196-199). Baltimore, MD: Williams and Wilkins.

Stern, M. (2002). *Child-friendly therapy: Biopsychosocial innovations for children and families.* New York: W.W. Norton and Company.

Sutton-Smith, B. (1982). The epistemology of the play theorist. *Behavioral Brain Science, 5,* 170.

Sutton-Smith, B. (1986). *Toys as culture.* New York: Gardner Press.

Van Hoorn, J. (1987). Games that babies and mothers play. In P. Monighan-Novrot, B. Scales, and J. Van Hoorn (Eds.), *Looking at children's play* (pp. 117-127). New York: Teachers College Press.

VanFleet, R. (1994). *Filial therapy: Strengthening parent-child relationships through play.* Sarasota, FL: Professional Resource Press.

Wachtel, E. (1994). *Treating troubled children and their families.* New York: Guilford Publications.

Wark, L. (1998). "Developmentally appropriate interventions with children and their families." Presentation at the American Association for Marriage and Family Therapy, Dallas, Texas. October 17.

Wark, L. (1999). "Child-inclusive family therapy: Three approaches for helping children in family therapy." (Manuscript under review)

Winnicott, D.W. (1971). *Play and reality.* London: Tavistock.

10

Family Sandplay: Strengthening the Parent-Child Bond

Lenore McWey
Nikki Ruble

Type of Contribution: Activity

Objective

The main objective of this activity is to strengthen the parent-child bond through a structured sandplay activity. Family play activities allow for an environment in which parents, children, and families may connect and/or enhance their relationship through the use of play, a language that both adults and children can understand. During a family sandplay activity, therapists can use symbolic figures and sandplay creations to discuss family topics, process their meanings, and initiate family change. The use of symbolic sandplay figures as the characters in these discussions allows for a safe and creative environment to discuss and process a variety of family issues. Sandplay may be used with family members of varying ages and development, from toddlers to adults.

Rationale for Use

In 1981, David Keith and Carl Whitaker co-authored an article that introduces play therapy as a paradigm to work with whole families together in session. Keith and Whitaker refer to play as the "as if" clause that can make dangerous emotions playful and allow for a more free-flowing release of emotional affect within the family. In a similar fashion, Gil (1994), in her book *Play in Family Therapy,* describes "play" as the essential component for actively involving young children in the family therapy process. Children use play to communicate with the world around them and to express thoughts, emotions, and feelings. Play allows children (and adults) the opportunity to solve problems, release tension, discover alternative behaviors, and heal emotional injuries. More simply, play grants children and adults permission to experience pleasure, joy, laughter, and fantasy. When children and play are included in family sessions, it often lowers defenses and unlocks deeper levels of interaction in which metaphors and symbolism can surface.

Carey (1991) lists at least four possible benefits for utilizing family sandplay activities in therapy: (1) the dimensions and the structure of the sand tray itself can provide a containment to discuss issues of boundaries in the family; (2) family dynamics may be observed more quickly during the play process; (3) unconscious material may surface quickly, allowing the therapist and the family to recognize and discuss the material; and (4) sandplay appeals to both the children and the inner child of adults in the family system.

In addition, Botkin and Ruble (1998) discuss a number of therapeutic values present in family sandplay activities: (1) the sand itself can provide a healing and soothing medium for the family; (2) the family can use the miniatures to project feelings, thoughts, and emotions; (3) the sand tray allows for the symbolic communication among family members; (4) family play activities foster cohesion and teamwork; and (5) family sandplay provides an opportunity for family solutions to be processed "in the sand."

Instructions

Materials for Sandplay

The therapists should obtain a sand tray with the dimensions 19 ½ by 20 ½ by 3 inches deep, with blue bottom and sides to represent water and sky. Plastic Rubbermaid boxes can be found at a number of stores and seem to work well as sand trays. The sand tray should be filled about three-fourths of the way with sand. The therapist may provide the family with a variety of miniatures to use in the sandplay. Miniatures might include people, cars, boats, animals (aggressive and tame, domesticated and wild), trees, fences, bridges, fantasy figures, police and fire workers, ambulances, fire trucks, weapons, and houses.

Implementation

The therapist should explain briefly the sand tray and the use of the figures, setting as few limits as possible. For example, with children, the therapist may state that "the sand must stay in the sand tray" and "the participants must be gentle with the figures." In a nondirective manner, ask the family or individual to create a world in the sand tray using the figures. Other ideas may include (1) create something happy, sad, safe; (2) create someone else's world (Mom's, Dad's); (3) create your family's world; and (4) create the perfect world. Nurture their experience by sitting back and observing. Create a very safe and accepting environment. For example, if asked what a figure is, the therapist could reply "anything that you want it to be." Or if asked, "What should I make?" one response could be, "It is your world . . . create anything that you want to create." Allow the family to work on the sand tray until they suggest that they have completed the activity.

Processing the Sand Tray

The family process that can be observed during a family sand tray activity is an excellent assessment tool. Pay attention to who leads, who participates, the figures used, who works together, or who disengages. When the family indicates that they have finished the sand tray, begin processing the sand tray by asking an open-ended question, such as, "Tell me about what you have created" or "Tell me about the world you have created." Ask nondirective questions and remember to stay in the realm of the family's fantasy. For example, the therapist may want to say, "Tell me about the lion, the snake, or the horse in your world." If a family member gives a figure a name, stay in that person's symbolic world by referring to that figure with the name chosen. Be careful not to place your own interpretations on the sand tray creation. The therapist may then use the symbolic figures to discuss topics that might be going on in the family. Allow the figures to save, comfort, or confront other figures. Using the symbolic figures to process family issues allows the family to have a parallel process occur within their own family reality.

Vignette

A very unique and determined family afforded us the opportunity to work with them. The therapy sessions involved a father and his three children. The oldest child was an eight-year-old female, her brother was five, and the youngest sister was four. The family had undergone a series of life changes, and the children's relationships with their father seemed in be in a state of flux. In recognizing the opportunity of this position of fluidity, the therapists encouraged specific activities to strengthen the bonds among family members.

The father and son's relationship for several weeks had seemed particularly strained. Thus, during one session a sand tray activity was devised to encourage the father and son's collaboration. The father and son were invited to create a sand tray depicting the son's long-term illness, a seemingly difficult subject for the family to address. The father and son gathered around the sand tray and began to interact. In the sand tray, the father and the son chose to situate a whale and a fish in the center and to create an ocean landscape by sculpting the sand as waves using their hands. They also added trees to depict "algae," sticks as "fishing poles," boats, a turtle, and other aquatic creatures that they discovered in the box of sand tray toys.

The whale and fish swam around other figures and objects arranged in the sand tray and then reconvened in the middle. There in the center, the whale and the fish enacted a scene where the fish, voiced through the son, told the whale how he felt "littler" than the other fish in the ocean. He "couldn't swim as fast" because of his illness, and he felt "sad." The whale, narrated by the father, told the fish how proud he was of the fish for being "smart, fun, and loving." The fish moved closer to the whale and the dialogue continued. The whale told the fish that he hadn't been aware of the fish's feelings, and the fish told the whale that he loved having a "big friend." Through this chosen medium, the selected characters enacted a discussion about this sensitive topic. In the process of the activity, the whale and fish were able to discover the other's perspective. At the end of the session, the father and son transcended the metaphor in the sand tray and gave each other a hug.

Suggestions for Follow-Up

Using the sand tray to depict real-life situations allows clients to discuss real-life situations in a safe, nonthreatening atmosphere. Other play therapy modalities may be used to reinforce the progress made through the use of the sand tray. These activities may include art activities, puppet play, games, or a variety of other interventions. Other sand tray activities may also be integrated into therapy. The sand tray may be further used to strengthen sibling bonds, address family triangles, process family scapegoating, and illuminate family patterns and trends. Any relevant theme can be addressed through the use of the sand tray, and the nature of the activity may provide a safe opportunity for challenges to be faced and family bonds to be strengthened.

Contraindications

One challenge with the use of the sand tray may be a lack of participation from one or more of the family members. The therapist may invite the parents or children to participate in the activity; however, family members may choose not to. Thus, further effort by the therapist may be needed to encourage participation. The therapist may also model participation in the activity for the reluctant participant. Conversely, one or more persons may dominate the project and restrict the participation of other individuals. Noting who is involved in the project and to what extent each participates, however, provides insight as to how the family functions during other activities that require family participation.

Another potential difficulty is the conflict that may arise among family members as to what to place in the sand tray to represent objects in their lives. There may be disagreement if, for example, one person wants to use a toy tree to depict something while another wants to use a toy boat. Such an occurrence may be used as an opportunity to explore problem-solving strategies of the participants.

Another aspect to consider when utilizing the sand tray is the emotional state of the parents or guardians involved in the sessions. If the parents or guardians are overwhelmed with their own personal struggles, then introducing an activity that involves tending to the needs of their children may be difficult. Thus, inviting parents who are experiencing individual struggles to share in a play activity with their children may be counterproductive. In addition, if therapy involves an abusive situation in which the parent is the perpetrator and the child is the victim, therapeutic modalities other than play therapy may be recommended until healing has begun (Botkin and Ruble, 1998).

Professional Readings and Resources

Carey, L. (1991). Family sandplay therapy. *The Arts in Psychotherapy, 18,* 231-239.
Gil, E. (1994). *Play in family therapy.* New York: Guilford Publications.
Kalff, D. (1980). *Sandplay: A psychotherapeutic approach to the psyche.* Santa Monica: Sigo Press.
Mitchell, R. and Friedman, H. (1994). *Sandplay: Past, present, and future.* New York: Routledge.
Thompson, C. and Rudolph, L. (1996). *Counseling children* (Fourth edition). Pacific Grove, CA: Brooks Cole Publishing.

Resources for Materials

Playrooms, P.O. Box 2660, Petaluma, CA 94953
Sandplay Therapists of America, P.O. Box 4847, Walnut Creek, CA 94596
Sandplay Toys, 4320 Edgewood Ave., Oakland, CA 94602
World Toys and Miniatures, P.O. Box 20288, Oakland, CA 94620

References for Parents

Diamant, R. (1992). *Positioning for play: Home activities for parents of young children.* Therapy Skill Builder. San Antonio, TX.
Kraft, A. and Landreth, G. (1998). *Parents as therapeutic partners: Listening to your child's play.* Northvale, NJ: Jason Aronson.
Morin, V. and Sokoloff, D. (1999). *Fun to grow on: Engaging play activities for kids with teachers, parents, and grandparents.* Chicago: Magnolia Street Publishers.
Sawyer, J. and Rogers, C. (1988). *Helping young children develop through play: A practical guide for parents, caregivers, and teachers.* Washington, DC: National Association for Education.

References

Botkin, D. and Ruble, N. (1998). "Family play therapy." A workshop presented at the annual meeting of the American Association of Marriage and Family Therapy, Dallas, Texas.
Carey, L. (1991). Family sandplay therapy. *The Arts in Psychotherapy, 18,* 231-239.
Gil, E. (1994). *Play in family therapy.* New York: Guilford Publications.
Keith, D. and Whitaker, C. (1981). Play therapy: A paradigm for work with families. *Journal of Marital and Family Therapy, 7,* 243-254.

11

Spin Me a Yarn:
Breaking the Ice and Warming the Heart

Catherine Ford Sori
Nancee Biank

Type of Contribution: Activity

Materials: One ball of yarn

Objective

Spin Me a Yarn can be used in children's groups or in family sessions. This activity is a playful way for even very shy children in a new group to begin to connect with others and to talk about themselves. It is an excellent icebreaker, and a way to overcome children's fear and resistance to talk in a group. Children's self-esteem is also enhanced as they begin to talk about themselves and they receive validation from the therapist and group members. The therapist also has an opportunity to begin to normalize children's problems and concerns.

When used in family sessions this activity serves three main purposes. First, it "loosens up" the family by encouraging everyone to participate in a playful way that both children and adults can enjoy. Second, the therapist sees and hears firsthand how family members think and interact with one another. Finally, when used at the end of an intense session this activity helps shift the atmosphere to a more positive and hopeful note. Strengths are spread among the family members, taking some of the focus off of the identified patient, and implying that problems don't reside in just one individual.

The use of yarn as an icebreaker was introduced to the first author (C.S.) by Janice DaLucia-Waack, PhD, as a way for adult group members to learn one another's names and to share something about themselves. Others (Speltz and Biank, 2001; Brandes and Phillips, 1990; Pennells and Smith, 1995) suggest throwing a soft ball or cushion to group members to aid in learning members' names. Here we have adapted and expanded this simple activity for use in children's groups and in family sessions.

Rationale

Anyone who has attempted to start a children's group knows how wary most children are in a group of their peers, especially if they are strangers (Thompson and Rudolph, 1996). Children may be looking forward to drawing pictures, hearing stories, making crafts to take home, and (of course) having a treat, but introduce the idea that they are expected to share or discuss difficult or painful subjects, and often the room falls deadly silent. The skillful group leader must discover playful ways to establish trust and to create a safe context for children to begin sharing with one another. Introducing a game is an excellent method to liven up a subdued group and begin the therapeutic process (Pennells and Smith, 1995). (See Brandes and Phillips, 1990, for game ideas.)

Recent research reveals common factors across therapies that account for positive therapeutic outcome (Blow, 1999). Very high on the list are relational factors between the therapist and clients, such as warmth, positive regard, and empathy. In family therapy, "joining" (Minuchin, 1974) with each member of the family has long been seen as the foundation of any therapeutic work that is to follow. Although family therapists have emphasized the importance of connecting with and hearing from every family member, therapists often have the most difficult time engaging children (Chasin and White, 1989). They often struggle with how to talk to children and adults simultaneously in ways that are meaningful (Sori, 2000). When asked a direct question, many children respond with a shrug, an "I don't know," or at best perhaps a one-word answer. Yet engaging only the children in play during family sessions runs the risk of leaving adults out of the process. It is especially difficult very early in therapy to find meaningful ways to engage both parents and children. In addition, beyond joining, therapists must assess the family interactions among both adults and children.

Often, parents drag a reluctant child to therapy and then spend much of the session trying to convince the therapist of how hopeless the child's situation is (Bailey and Sori, 2000). This deficit focus may reflect the parents' feelings of hopelessness, since many have already "tried everything, and nothing works." Parents might also be implying that the problem can't possibly be *them*—it has to be this impossible child. The "expert" therapist who moves too quickly to succeed where parents have failed runs the risk of demoralizing the parents even further and/or having their work subtly sabotaged by parents who feel upstaged. Other times parents are too overwhelmed to see any strengths—in themselves or in their child. The problem may loom so large that it has blocked out the sun, and the family needs help in balancing their vision to include strengths as well as problems.

Sometimes sessions focus on important but emotionally laden topics, such as bereavement or the impending death of a family member. All family members, but especially children, need to grasp that there is hope—maybe not hope for a cure or for things to return to "normal," but hope that things eventually will get better. Children need to know that there will once again be joy in life. Without diminishing the seriousness of these difficult subjects, illness or death can be "put in its place" as the family makes room for "pockets of normalcy," or more happy family moments.

This activity is useful in any of these situations: to establish a safe and playful therapeutic atmosphere for children new to a group, to engage multiple generations of family members in a playful and meaningful activity, to allow the therapist to see how family members view themselves and respond to one another, and to shift the mood or focus of a session to a positive and hopeful note.

Instructions

Introducing the Activity for Groups

The therapist asks a group of children to sit in a circle on the floor so they may play a game. The children are told that when they are tossed the ball of yarn they are to answer the question, hold a strand of the yarn in one hand, and toss it at random to another group member, making sure everyone gets a turn. Although children are encouraged to participate, a child may choose not to answer a question. In that case he or she still holds onto the end of the yarn and tosses the ball to another group member. After each child has had a turn the ball is tossed back to the therapist. The group facilitator participates in the activity and begins by answering the first question, and then tossing the ball. It is often helpful to give the first toss to a more vocal child, to "get the ball rolling"!

Each time the yarn cycles back to the therapist, the content of the statements changes. Statements start with very general information, which most children contribute willingly. As the children become more comfortable with the game, the questions gradually elicit more therapeutic information.

The following are examples of statements for group members, ages six to twelve years:

- Tell us your name? How old are are? What grade and school are you in?
- Name your favorite color/TV show/game, etc.
- Name something that you like to do for fun.
- Name something that you are proud of.
- Name something that you don't like to do.
- Name your favorite/least favorite thing about school.
- Name everybody who lives at your house.
- Name one thing that's special about your family.
- [If an illness group] Name who in your family has cancer/multiple sclerosis (MS), etc.
- Tell what has been the biggest change in your family.
- Tell what has been the hardest for you since _____ [the divorce, illness, etc.].
- Name one thing you wish was different (in your life/at school/at home).
- Name one thing you hope to have happen in this group.

During the activity the therapist may point out certain similarities among group members. For example, "It's interesting that both Bill and Sue are on swim teams! That takes a lot of practice and hard work!" or "Tom, Pete, and Mary all have brothers with leukemia, while Sue's and Bill's moms both have breast cancer, and Freddie, Tyler, and Katie have dads with different cancers. And it sounds like several of you are hoping to learn more about cancer, and to get to know other kids whose families are going through similar things."

Introducing in Family Session As a Joining/Assessing Activity

Family members are asked to place their chairs in a circle. The therapist begins by explaining that this is a way to get to know the family members, and to hear some unique things about each one. The therapist first asks each family member to say something that he or she likes to do and begins by saying something he or she likes to do for fun, holding on to a strand of yarn and tossing the ball to a family member. It is often helpful to start with the most outgoing or playful family member. Each time the ball returns to the therapist, another statement is given.

During the activity the therapist can assess the family's playfulness or rigidity, their attitudes (e.g., Is one child criticized for how he or she plays, or told he or she is doing it wrong?), the roles the family assumes (e.g., Does someone attempt to take charge, take over, or refuse to play?), and the family relationships (What are the alliances? Coalitions? Is one family member always last? Is someone left out? Are his or her remarks invalidated? How does this family communicate?).

One round of questions focuses on individual family members:

- What is something special about you (an accomplishment, something you like about yourself)?
- What was the happiest day of your life?

- What was your favorite vacation and why?
- If you could do anything for your birthday, what would it be?
- Name someone outside your family whom you care about.
- What is one important thing you do to help in your family?

Other questions focus on individual and family strengths:

- What is one way your family has fun together?
- What is one special thing you like about your family?
- Name one special thing you like or love about each family member.
- Name one kind or loving thing each family member does.
- Name one kind or loving thing you do for someone in your family.
- If you could change one thing about your family, what would it be?
- Who do you talk to/play with most in your family?
- What is something special your family does on your favorite holiday?
- What is something fun your family has done in the past that you wish you could do again?

Other questions can be generated, based on the family or group situation. At the end of the questions, everyone should be holding several strands of yarn, and an intricate web of yarn should connect the group or family members.

Processing the Information

The therapist can ask the family or group to look at what they have made and discuss what the yarn resembles. Answers may vary, from a crisscross to a dream catcher to a spiderweb. The therapist might then say:

> This web shows how we are really connected to other people in our lives. We connect when we are in the same family, or are friends, or share about ourselves and others share with us. We became more connected as we shared more things about what is important to us.

Then the group or family as a whole is asked to move the yarn high up in the air and look at it from underneath. After discussing what the yarn looks like from that angle, they then move it back down. The therapist might comment:

> Notice how everyone worked very carefully together not to drop any of the connections as we moved the yarn up and down. It looked different when we looked from underneath, didn't it? Sometimes coming to group/family counseling is like that—we see things differently when we all work together. And sometimes life is like the web; it has its ups and downs, but there will always be others with us to help and care for us. And look how important each and every one of you was in holding your pieces of yarn. What would have happened if someone had dropped his or her yarn? The web would not be the same, would it? And that is how important each one of you is to the group/family. It wouldn't be the same if someone were missing, would it?

This playful analogy prepares children and family members to share, and to see how valuable each member's role is in working together to solve problems. It builds a sense of connection and cooperation and uses a language that children, as well as adults, can understand. It also introduces a sense of wonder and anticipation that things may not always be as they first appear.

Vignettes

Group Vignette

Spin Me a Yarn is a great icebreaker to start building connections in groups of children who have a parent or sibling with cancer. One group of six- to eleven-year-olds was particularly quiet during the first session. Although the facilitator had met with each child and family at least once for an intake session, none of the children previously knew one another, and several were quite shy and afraid to talk, especially about cancer. The therapist had even been warned that one girl, nine-year-old Julia, had been particularly reticent to attend the group. Her mother had finally persuaded her, but only after promising she just had to "try it once."

The first session began with the children quietly decorating their name tags, reluctant to even say their names out loud. After everyone was assembled the children were invited to sit on cushions in a circle on the floor.

The group facilitator explained that they were going to start with a game. She would call out a question and toss the ball of yarn to someone. That person could answer if he or she chose, keep hold of one strand of yarn in one hand, and toss the ball to someone else in the group. Children were told they didn't have to answer if they couldn't think of anything to say, but they could still play by holding the yarn and tossing the ball to another child. (Telling kids they don't have to talk works amazingly well. Since children are given permission not to participate, they don't have to "resist" by not talking! It also gives children a sense of control and power over their choice of when and how to participate. Lack of control over life is often an important theme for children experiencing serious family illness.) When everyone had one turn, the yarn was tossed back to the therapist, who asked the next question.

The first few questions invited the children to share their names, class, schools, favorite activities (e.g., sports, band), TV shows, and movies. Several kids said they collected Pokemon cards, played soccer or a musical instrument, or were on the swim team. Children were then asked to say something special about themselves, something of which they were proud. Julia quietly passed on this question. Some children shared they had won a race, gotten an A on a math test, or made a goal in soccer. The game continued in this manner until all the children, including Julia, seemed to be comfortable and enjoying the activity. Questions eventually led to who in their families had cancer, what type of cancer, and what treatment they were receiving. Although it was still a little difficult for some, the facilitator helped with the names of some of the cancers and treatments. There were looks of relief as children heard others give voice to what was so difficult for them to discuss. Finally they were asked what they hoped to get out of the group. This last question brought a surge of happy responses, as the children listed some of the anticipated activities (e.g., making dream catchers), getting to choose snacks, learning about cancer, and hearing the experiences of other kids and their families.

The facilitator then asked the children as a group to look down at what they had created together. With excitement one child said it looked like telephone wires, and another said like a giant spiderweb. An eight-year-old girl amended, "Yes! Like Charlotte's web!" The facilitator commented that it showed how connected they all were. Some had similar interests or hobbies, liked the same TV shows, or were in the same grade in school, and all had someone with cancer in their families.

The group was then invited to move the web high up into the air. Instinctively the children rose to their feet, laughing as they raised the web. When they were asked to notice how it looked different from underneath, one girl said that they looked connected to one another, but in a different way—like they were reaching to hold something up. Another child said it looked like they were under a canopy. The facilitator commented that, similar to this web of yarn, problems sometimes look entirely different when we see them in a new way. She asked the group then to lower the web, being careful not to drop any strands of yarn. When they were all seated, smiling expectantly, the facilitator complimented them on working so well together, and how careful they had been not to let go of their important strands of yarn.

The group was then asked to think about how different it would have been if some of them were missing or had dropped their yarn. The whole web would be different! She said, "That's how important each one of you is to this group. Each of you has an important role, and if one of you is missing, it affects everyone."

By the end of this activity the entire atmosphere of the room had changed, from quiet dread to playful anticipation. When asked what they thought of today, the responses were overwhelmingly positive. Hands shot up, asking what fun things were planned for the next group meeting. As the group was saying goodbye and getting up to leave, Julia, who had been the quietest and most hesitant, sidled over to sit very close to the facilitator. Leaning over she whispered, "At first I didn't want to come today. I was pretty scared. But now I'm so glad I came. I really liked it! Can we please come back tomorrow? I don't want to wait a whole week!"

Family Vignette

The following is an example of how this activity was used to end a difficult family session on a note of strength, hope, and loving connection. Teresa had just completed treatment for stage one breast cancer. Her husband, Roberto, initiated family therapy for the couple and their two children, Alicia (age eight) and Robertocito (age thirteen). The parents had difficulty discussing Teresa's illness and were worried about how all the changes in the last six months had affected the children.

The session began with the therapist exploring what changes had occurred for each family member. Teresa tearfully explained how much of the time she had been too sick really to "be there" for her children. Roberto had struggled to keep working, while needing to take time off to take Teresa for treatments. Meals, laundry, and household talks had become pretty haphazard since Teresa's mom had returned to her native country of Costa Rica. Clearly Teresa felt guilty for not being able to care for her family, while Roberto still felt overwhelmed with all his responsibilities.

Alicia, a beautiful and expressive child, was quick to reassure Mom that she loved just sitting by her, even when she was too sick to play or talk. And she didn't mind canned soup and peanut butter sandwiches for dinner! Robertocito didn't have much to say, shrugging and mumbling that it didn't seem to affect him much. Teresa then turned to the therapist, saying that this was exactly one of her worries—Robertocito "seems like he doesn't care, or just isn't affected!"

Other worries were explored. Alicia admitted she was worried about money, since she'd overheard some snatches of her parents' conversation. Teresa was worried about treatment ending, since she would no longer have the security of seeing her doctor weekly. Robertocito said he didn't really know if he had any worries, and Roberto said right now that he was just thankful that Teresa's cancer was gone.

The therapist asked Alicia what she thought her brother's biggest worry might be. Alicia finally voiced everyone's greatest fear—one they had been unable to express. She said, "I think Robertocito is really scared that Mom's cancer will come back." No one said anything. When the therapist wondered if Alicia and others might also share that fear, tears fell as Alicia nodded a silent yes. When asked what she thought they needed to reduce this fear, Alicia said that she and Robertocito needed to be able to ask questions and know that their parents were telling them what was really going on with Mom.

With support both Alicia and Robertocito were encouraged to ask questions of their parents about the cancer (e.g., What is breast cancer? How do you get it? Can I catch it? Do boys get breast cancer?), and how Mom will continue to monitor her health (e.g., How often will you see the doctor? What kinds of tests will you take? How will you know for sure that you don't have cancer again?). The parents were coached and supported to alleviate their children's worries by offering honest and age-appropriate answers. Most important, they assured both children that they would be kept up to date on Mom's medical condition. Robertocito even got up the courage to ask Dad to please get a checkup for his high blood pressure, and to quit smoking!

It had been a tearful and emotional session in which the family communication had opened enough to allow some tough emotional questions to surface and begin to be addressed. However, the therapist sensed that the parents might have felt they had "blown it" by not addressing these issues earlier, and allowing the children to worry alone and without much support.

The therapist chose this activity to shift the focus to the family's individual and collective strengths, and to further cement the new levels of intimacy that had been forged. She explained the yarn activity and began by asking each one to say something he or she liked to do for fun that they hadn't already talked about. From there each one said something special he or she was proud of, and something he or she was looking forward to in the next week.

When asked to share something positive about each family member, Alicia begged to go first. The therapist tossed her the ball of yarn, and she began. "Well, I love my daddy—can I sit by him for a minute? [moving over to his lap, she snuggled up close and continued]—because he makes me feel so safe, and he takes me to the park sometimes . . . and he reads stories to me." Dad's eyes filled with tears and he hugged her tightly for a long moment. Alicia handed him a strand of yarn and next moved over to wrap her arms around Mom. "And I love my mommy because she is so very brave and strong, and yet soft and gentle . . . and when she feels better she plays Barbie dolls with me, and we eat ice cream and watch cartoons, even when she's tired." Now both parents were crying and had moved together to hug Alicia. Smiling through her tears, Alicia gave Mom a piece of yarn and moved toward Robertocito, who looked wide-eyed and uncertain. "And my brother. I love him because he thinks he is big and tough, but I know how much he loves all of us, and he doesn't talk about it because he tries to be so strong for Mom and me, but I know he cries sometimes . . . and I love him because he looks out for me and helps take care of me, and gave me his favorite jersey, and sometimes he even lets me hug him!" With this she gave him a huge bear hug, which he returned, turning his face away as he struggled to blink back tears.

As the activity continued, everyone shared what they appreciated about one another, how everyone did important and loving things for one another, and how they had helped one another through the cancer experience. Emotional shifts occurred, especially for Robertocito, when Mom said how much she appreciated him fixing dinner some nights, and for offering to stay up when she was sick and Dad worked late, and for watching out for Alicia. Dad, following Alicia's lead, walked over to hug his son as he said how much he appreciated Robertocito keeping up with the yard work, and even helping with laundry. Robertocito looked embarrassed, yet hugely pleased. And he was also able to voice quietly his love and appreciation for his family.

The family had several good laughs, for example, about the time Robertocito tried to make lasagna and set off the smoke alarm, and when Alicia made Mom's instant coffee using three heaping teaspoons—which was just how Alicia liked her hot chocolate! The therapist commented that although she had known that this family had many strengths, she was amazed at how much love and support everyone showed one another.

When the ball of yarn ran out the family just sat for a moment, gazing with smiles and damp eyes at one another. When the therapist asked them to look at what they had made with the yarn, they commented with surprise on how many strong connections there were among all of them—

connections that were there all along, but which they had never seen that clearly before. When asked what this experience had been like, Mom said she now saw that focusing on cancer had left each of them feeling disconnected, and unable to see the strong connections that were there. They all agreed that although cancer is a terrible experience for a family, it gave them the opportunity to see strengths they never knew they had, and to appreciate one another in new ways.

As the session ended the family wanted to continue to learn how to talk to one another about cancer. Teresa and Roberto warmly thanked the therapist for helping everyone to talk, and most of all for helping them to see how, despite the trials of the past six months, they were still a strong and loving family. Teresa commented, "I came in here feeling so emotionally depleted and alone—at a time when I should be so happy the cancer's gone! Now I feel so happy to know how to help my kids, and I feel confident that we are strong enough to get through anything!"

Suggestions for Follow-Up

Group Sessions

This activity can be used again in the last group to cement what was learned and to help children say goodbye. For example, when tossing the yarn the children can say what they like best about the group, what was their favorite activity, what was the most important thing they learned, and so on. Children can also be encouraged to say something positive about each group member, perhaps to offer a special wish for each person, or to share what they will miss most about each member.

Family Sessions

The rich therapeutic information gleaned during this activity can provide much material to guide the process of therapy. Issues that arise, communication problems that become evident, or systemic information can be addressed in future sessions.

Spin Me a Yarn can also be used when a family is ready to terminate therapy. As the yarn is tossed family members are invited to say what is different, what they learned in therapy, and what they hope will continue to happen in their family. The family can then be asked to look at the web of yarn and reflect on what has changed and how it feels different now from when they first did this activity. Finally, as an active participant, the therapist has a chance to punctuate individual and family changes he or she has seen during the course of therapy, to clarify strengths, and to deepen the meaning of new ways of relating.

Contraindications

In Group Sessions

Children who are hyperactive may be overstimulated by tossing the ball of yarn. The therapist can help by sitting behind the child, helping to guide gentle tosses. If several children seem very wound up, prefacing Spin Me a Yarn with some breathing exercises to relax the children is helpful (see Chapter 4).

If a child just refuses to participate simply allow the child to watch the activity. Perhaps the child might be offered a more passive role, such as "turn keeper"—making sure every child gets a turn for each question. The child could be invited at the end to comment on what he or she saw happen during the game.

In Family Sessions

Some families may be so problem focused or rigid that they find it difficult to play or talk about positive strengths in the family. These parents may need extra time to feel they've been listened to and understood. Parents who don't want to participate because they believe it is the therapist's job to "fix" the child can sometimes be encouraged to take a more active role as they are educated about the therapeutic benefits of playfulness, and how vital their role is to facilitate change for their child (see Bailey and Sori, 2000, and Chapter 9).

Professional Readings

Bailey, C. E. and Sori, C. E. F. (2000). Involving parents in children's therapy. In C. E. Bailey (Ed.), *Children in therapy: Using the family as a resource* (pp. 475-501). New York: W.W. Norton and Company.

Blow, A. (1999). "Common factors across theories of marriage and family therapy: A modified Delphi study." Unpublished doctoral dissertation, Purdue University, West Lafayette, Indiana.

Brandes, D. and Phillips, H. (1990). *Gamesters' handbook.* Cheltenham, England: Stanley Thornes.

Chasin, R. and White, T. B. (1989). The child in family therapy: Guidelines for active engagement across the age span. In L. Combrinck-Graham (Ed.), *Children in family contexts: Perspectives on treatment* (pp. 5-25). New York: Guilford Publications.

Minuchin, S. (1974). *Families and family therapy.* Cambridge, MA: Harvard University Press.

Pennells, M. and Smith, S. C. (1995). Creative groupwork methods with bereaved children. In C. Smith and Sr. M. Pennells (Eds.), *Interventions with bereaved children* (pp. 141-159). Bristol, PA: Jessica Kingsley Publishers.

Sori, C. E. F. (2000). "Training family therapists to work with children in family therapy: A modified Delphi study." Unpublished doctoral dissertation, Purdue University, West Lafayette, Indiana.

Speltz, A. and Biank, N. (2001). *Kid support: A procedures manual for conducting support groups with the children of cancer patients.* Self-published.

Thompson, C. L. and Rudolph, L. B. (1996). Counseling Children (Fourth edition). Pacific Grove, CA: Brooks/Cole Publishing Company.

Resources for Families

The Ungame (1975). Anaheim, CA: Ungame Company.

12

Co-Art: A Joining Activity for Therapists and Younger Clients

Liddy B. Hope

Type of Contribution: Activity

Materials: Drawing paper and markers, pencils, or crayons

Objective

This activity helps bridge the age gap between the child client and adult therapist. In addition, the activity aids in joining and can help ease anxiety surrounding difficult issues and the therapeutic process in general.

Rationale for Use

Therapy can be an uncomfortable experience for clients of all ages, but for children, initially, it can be an especially difficult experience. Often, it was not the child's idea to come to therapy, yet once there the child is expected to discuss issues that may be difficult or uncomfortable for him or her to express. Finally, this is done in an unfamiliar context with a person who is much older than the child. All of these factors combined can make therapy an unpleasant and unproductive situation. This activity can alleviate discomfort while also aiding in the joining process and promoting an egalitarian client-therapist relationship.

The aim of this activity is for the child and therapist to draw a picture together, taking turns. Through this, the client and therapist can ask questions about the other's contribution, as well as practice taking turns. This aspect of the activity mimics the give-and-take of the therapy room, thus offering a nonthreatening way for children to adjust to the therapeutic environment. By first asking questions regarding the picture, rather than the presenting problem, the client is able to adjust and become comfortable with the process before potentially difficult issues are introduced. Also, the therapist is able to control the rate at which such issues are introduced to maintain the level of comfort and the process of assimilation.

The therapist may opt to draw something and then ask the client about it, thus introducing a new topic. Through this, a subject that may need to be discussed is gently introduced. Since children often express themselves through art, questions about their artistic creations may help the therapist gain insight. Finally, because this is a collaborative effort, the therapist can use his or her own drawing to steer the activity in a particular direction, if needed.

Because the end result is a cocreated product, equity in the relationship is established. The final picture is tangible proof that the client has as much control over the session as the therapist. Often children who are brought to therapy (even if it is willingly) are essentially forced into a situation and may feel powerless. Typically it is the decision of the adult, not the child, to attend therapy. Although children may not be cognitively aware of a need to maintain some control, it is an important part of the therapeutic process. This activity helps empower clients, despite their young age.

Finally, drawing pictures can get pretty silly, creating a fun way to join with children. Joining is a vital part of any therapy, but especially when the therapy involves children. Drawing a picture with the child will allow him or her to see the creative, artistic, and fun side of the therapist. In other words, this activity enables the therapist to show his or her human side. Allowing the child client to see this side can help establish the similarities between therapist and client, which in turn will aid in the joining process. Where adult clients and therapist may use "small talk" to establish common ground, therapists and children can use drawing.

Instructions

This activity can be used as part of a session or for the entire session. Typically the participants will include the therapist and the identified young client (between the ages of three and twelve). Other children and adult clients may also be included, as the therapist deems appropriate. Materials needed for this activity are drawing paper and markers, pencils, or crayons. The client and therapist can decide on the number of pictures to create. The therapist introduces the activity by asking the client if he or she would like to draw a picture together. The client and therapist then take turns adding to the picture until it is decided that the picture is complete.

Vignette

Sue brought her eight-year-old daughter, Brianna, to therapy following her divorce from Brianna's father. Originally, only Sue attended therapy, but within the first few sessions she recognized that her daughter might also benefit from therapy. Sue's main motivation in bringing Brianna to therapy was to provide her with a safe place to discuss her feelings about the divorce. She reported that Brianna was eager to begin therapy, once it had been suggested.

Although Brianna did appear motivated to attend, her apprehension was evident. In an attempt to ease her apprehension and aid in joining, several board games were played. Brianna seemed to enjoy the games but was also entirely distracted by them and unable to discuss much except the games. Although this was helping the joining process, little progress was being made toward the mother's goal of providing a safe place for Brianna to talk about her parents' divorce.

Attempts to put away the games and simply talk were even less productive. Although Brianna was willing to answer the therapist's questions, she did so with obvious discomfort. For example, when the therapist asked Brianna how she felt about moving to a new house, she quickly replied, "Kind of happy, kind of sad." The therapist continued by asking what part of moving made her sad, to which Brianna stated, "The moving part," but would not elaborate. This exchange was typical of the conversations held by therapist and client. Brianna appeared to be comfortable with the therapist, but not with the process of therapy. In an attempt to alleviate Brianna's discomfort, the therapist asked if she would like to draw a picture together.

Brianna was intrigued by the idea of creating a drawing together. She asked the therapist to draw the first part. The therapist chose to draw a picture of a house. While drawing the house, the therapist shared with Brianna that this was a picture of her old house. The following is a paraphrase of the dialogue between therapist and client while the therapist continued to draw.

BRIANNA: When did you live in that house?

THERAPIST: Until I was twelve. Then we moved to a different town.

BRIANNA: Do you miss your old house ever?

THERAPIST: Sometimes, but it was pretty neat to move to a new house, and get a new room. Do you think you will miss your old house, too?

BRIANNA: Maybe, but my new room has a really big closet—that will be fun.

At this point the therapist finished her house, and slid the paper to Brianna for her turn.

BRIANNA: I don't know what to draw.

THERAPIST: Draw whatever you like; it doesn't even have to make sense.

BRIANNA: I know. I'll draw a road from your old house to your new one.

THERAPIST: Good idea. Is your new house very far from your old one?

BRIANNA: Not really.

THERAPIST: Close enough to ride your bike or walk?

BRIANNA: No, but you could drive.

The drawing and conversation exchange continued for the rest of the session. The therapist added a car that could be driven to the new or old house; Brianna added a pool at the new house, and a dog at the old one. Therapist and client were both pleased with the final product, and through the creation of the picture the therapist was able to learn that Brianna would miss her dog, since he couldn't come to the new house (which was an additional loss). Her new house had a pool, however, which made her excited. It is clear then that the use of this activity enabled Brianna to disclose emotions more readily than through a "normal" conversation.

This activity was incorporated into future sessions, usually as a way to begin each session. The therapist used specific drawings as a way to introduce important topics. For example, when Brianna's mother began dating, the therapist drew a picture of two people having dinner and explained to Brianna that this was her idea of what a date looked like. She then asked Brianna to add anything that was missing. By using this picture as a way to introduce the idea of her mother dating, the therapist and client were able to explore the feelings of all the individuals in the picture. Through this Brianna was able to view some of her mother's feelings about dating, but, more important, Brianna was able to express her own feelings. Brianna drew herself outside the scene, indicating that her mother's dating made her feel left out. She was later able to use the picture as a way to convey these feelings to her mother.

In general, this activity provides a method to join during initial sessions or can be used as an entire family group activity. Finally, this activity is a useful tool of communication with clients who have difficulty verbalizing. What is uncomfortable to say is often easier for children to draw. Through this activity, the initial goal of providing a safe place for Brianna's feelings was achieved.

Suggestions for Follow-Up

Just as this activity can be used as a way to ease young clients into the therapy process, it can also be used as a way for young clients to open up emotionally with their parents or other family members. This can be achieved either through sharing an already created picture with the family or by cocreating a picture with the family. By using this activity in a therapeutic environment, children and parents may feel more comfortable broaching difficult subjects or emotions. As already shown, the activity is a nonthreatening form of expression, and the therapist may provide an additional layer of security for the family by leading the discussion.

Also, the pictures can be saved and used as a way to revisit topics when necessary. For example, the therapist could use the house drawing as a way to explore Brianna's feelings about her parents' divorce. Brianna might be asked where her father's house would be in the drawing, how it is to be at Dad's house, and what it's like to go back and forth between houses. Clients also can use old pictures as a way to introduce topics or express feelings. Brianna often used the first house picture as an example when trying to explain the feeling of being torn between happy and sad.

Finally, this activity may be used as a "reward" at the end of a session. If a client is reluctant to participate or discuss an issue, the therapist may use drawing as an incentive. This may be a particularly effective way to convince younger children to take part in family sessions.

Contraindications

Using this activity as a reward may reinforce the child's belief that therapy or expression of emotions is unpleasant. Therapists should be careful when setting up such an incentive program.

Because this activity can be a great deal of fun, it is important that the therapist ensure the maintenance of a therapeutic environment. If the activity is being used only as a way to fill the session, and no actual therapeutic progress is being made, clinicians may need to reevaluate their use of the activity.

References for Professionals

Gil, E. (1994). *Play in family therapy*. New York: Guilford Publications.
Oaklander, V. (1988). *Windows to our children*. Highland, NY: Gestalt Journal Press.

13

Using LIFE to Explore Children's Worlds

Stephanie Malench
Lorna L. Hecker

Type of Contribution: Activity

Objective

Board games are a favorite activity for young children everywhere. By observing a child playing a board game, the therapist can learn a number of things about the child that may not be learned during an interview, such as susceptibility to peer pressure, leadership skills, confidence, competitiveness, and so on. In addition, games offer an entertaining and nonthreatening way to talk to children about important topics that affect their lives now and in the future. Frey (1986) cites eleven potential functions of board games in therapy:

1. Rapport establishment
2. Diagnostic value
3. Ego enhancement
4. Catharsis
5. Sublimation
6. Reality testing
7. Insight
8. Progression in therapy
9. Fantasy
10. Group play
11. Efficient use of time

In this activity, Milton Bradley's board game LIFE is used as a springboard to therapeutically relevant topics. Although it is unlikely that any one game will stimulate all these functions, LIFE offers the opportunity to open discussions in relevant areas (e.g., life goals, finances, rules, and thoughts about one's future) that other board games may not. This intervention can be used in individual sessions, children's groups, or family therapy.

Rationale for Use

According to a study by the Carnegie Council on Adolescent Development (1992), successful students spend twenty to thirty-five hours a week in high-yield leisure activities, such as playing board games (Munger, 1998). High-yield leisure activities are "activities that provide youngsters practice in reading, writing, discussing, problem-solving, decision-making . . . such as talking with parents about political elections, or about why it is important to get a good education, or about ways of successfully handling a problematic job situation" (Munger, 1998, p. 113).

By facilitating a game of LIFE, the therapist creates a forum for children to learn and talk about important life events. Some of these events can include those which stimulate abstract thinking, such as whether to go to college or enter the workforce directly after high school, what marriage means, or thoughts about having children. Other topics that LIFE suggests are more practical in nature, such as understanding what a loan is, what interest is, why insurance is important, and why we save money. By playing LIFE and integrating therapeutic questions into the game-playing process, children are (1) allowed to discuss topics parents may avoid, in a neutral environment; (2) learn about skills; and (3) be allowed to express their understanding of various life events that may be impacting their own lives. In addition, playing LIFE has a diagnostic value throughout the therapeutic process. Skills that can be informally assessed during the game include fine motor skills, reading, counting, critical thinking, reasoning, coping strategies, and social skills.

In working with children in groups, the goal of this intervention is to build rapport, provide a pleasurable experience, relax defenses, and elicit creative energies (Reid, 1993). In addition, feelings can be elicited and elucidated, assessment of beliefs or patterns may occur, and children's strengths and hopes can be tapped. Social skills can be developed by teaching appropriate turn taking and proper game etiquette. LIFE can help children see how others (1) respond to the same situation (anger or pleasure at landing on the Get Married space), (2) rationalize making a particular decision (going to college or getting a job), and (3) feel about events such as marriage, having children, the importance of education, and responsibility. The therapist can also observe how the child interacts with his or her peers or siblings, and playing the game itself can foster social and relational skills. Playing LIFE with small groups of two to four children is a most effective use of therapy time. This activity can also be used in family sessions.

In using the game of LIFE during family therapy sessions, family structure can be assessed, family communication can be observed, and family rules may be observed or discussed. The therapist can facilitate the discussion of important family topics such as educational beliefs, financial dreams and realities, and family values.

Instructions

The game is used as a springboard for discussion, and typically the game is not played according to directions. The therapist may place the LIFE tiles, cards, insurance policies, bank loans, or money aside, but players should have the correct number and correct color pegs in their cars. The therapist can either be a player, banker, or facilitator. The therapist's main role is to ask the players what the different spaces on the board mean to them, and what the consequences could be if one of the "rules of life" is broken.

For children in a group setting, rules of the game should be established. The following questions can then be integrated into the game:

- Why is it important for each of us to wait for his or her turn? What happens in life if you don't? Does anyone have examples of times when they were able to wait patiently for their turn? Are there times when it is hard to wait your turn? Why?
- What are some rules you are required to follow at home? At school? Why do we have rules such as don't drink and drive?
- Why are good deeds important? What type of good deeds do you do at home or at school?
- Why are drugs bad for you? What do you think you should do if someone wants you to take drugs? Give me an example of what you might say.
- In this game, we try to dodge bad luck. What type of bad luck have you had in your life? What type of good luck have you had?

- In this game, we try to make money. What else do you think is important to get in life besides money?
- If you were to get a tattoo, what would you like it to be? Would your mother or father approve? Would your grandmother or grandfather approve? Why or why not?
- What would you do if you won the lottery? How do you think your friends would react if you won the lottery? How would you react if your friend won the lottery? Why?
- How do you think you will make money as an adult? Have any of you made money already? How? Do any of you have a piggy bank or other ways to save money? Why is it important to have money? How do you decide whether to save or spend your money? Why do we pay taxes? What do you think taxes should be used for?

Questions may be made simpler or more complex depending on the children's intellectual level. Children can be taught by the therapist that LIFE is like a game, that we don't know how it will turn out, but it is important that we have fun and feel good about ourselves as we play. The therapist may then give the children an assignment to do one thing during the coming week to feel good in their lives, such as deciding to do a good deed for someone else.

When using this game in family therapy, the following questions can be asked:

- Who has the easiest time in this family waiting for his or her turn? Who has the hardest?
- What are the rules in your family? What happens in this family when you break the rules?
- What do you (or your mom, dad, sister, brother, grandfather, and so on) think about making money? If your family won the lottery, what do you think you would spend the money on?
- If this family could go anywhere on vacation, where would you go?
- Who in this family wants to go to college? What does each person think about college?
- If your mother (brother, sister, father, aunt, and so on) were to get a tattoo, what do you think it would be? What would your reaction be?
- Who handles the money in this family? How do you decide what money goes where? Who is involved? How are children involved in learning about money?
- How does this family handle bad luck? What type of bad luck have you had? When bad luck happens, on whom do you rely? When bad things happen, what do people in your family do to feel better?
- What type of good luck have you had in this family? Who celebrates good luck the most in this family? How do you celebrate?

Family topics may be developed as the game continues. Parents should ultimately decide the rules of the game of LIFE, after soliciting children's input. They may change the rules of the game if needed. The therapist can stress the development of family rules and begin to integrate the need for rules and play in family life. Homework assignments may be developed from topics that arise during the play of the game.

Suggestions for Follow-Up

It is helpful to talk to children individually if something comes up during the game that the therapist would like to learn more about, such as being hit, threats, inappropriate comments about drugs or alcohol, and so on. Whenever the children are talking to one another about the future, it is important to take time to discuss whether their dreams represent good, positive decisions about life. Families can be encouraged to develop their own game of life, which means clarifying their rules, hopes, dreams, and celebrations. If money and space permit, obtain extra copies of the game for parents or children to "check out" to play at home.

Contraindications for Use

In a group setting, this game is not recommended for children who cannot read or are severely emotionally disturbed. In a family setting, a family needs to have a basic working structure and be able to set minimal rules and consequences to benefit from this type of activity.

Professional Readings and Resources

Frey, D.E. (1986). The talking, feeling, and doing game. In C.E. Schaefer and S.E. Reid (Eds.), *Game play: Therapeutic use of childhood games* (pp. 21-40). New York: John Wiley and Sons.

Glasberg, D.S., Maatita, F., Nangle, B., and Schauer, T. (1998). Games children play: An exercise illustrating agents of socialization. *Teaching Sociology, 26,* 130-139.

Johnson, M.L. (1998). Use of play group therapy in promoting social skills. *Issues in Mental Health, 9,* 105-112.

Knell, S.M. (1993). *Cognitive-behavioral play therapy.* London: Jason Aronson.

Schaefer, C.E. and Reid, S.E. (Eds.) (1986). *Game play: Therapeutic use of childhood games.* New York: John Wiley and Sons.

Singer, D.G. (1993). *Playing for their lives: Helping troubled children through play therapy.* New York: The Free Press.

Bibliotherapy Sources for Children

Fano, K. (1993). *Jenny the penny: A story to teach children about the value of money.* Boulder, CO: Horizon Publications.

Fassler, J. (1971). *The boy with a problem.* New York: Human Sciences.

Velder, M. and Cohen, E. (1973). *Open-ended stories.* Englewood Cliffs, NJ: Globe Book Co.

References

Carnegie Council on Adolescent Development (1992). A matter of time: Risk and opportunity in non-school hours (Report of the Task Force on Youth Development and Community Programs). New York: Carnegie Corporation of New York.

Frey, D.E. (1986). The talking, feeling, and doing game. In C.E. Schaefer and S.E. Reid (Eds.), *Game play: Therapeutic use of childhood games* (pp. 21-40). New York: John Wiley and Sons.

Munger, R.L. (1998). *The ecology of troubled children.* Cambridge, MA: Brookline Books.

Reid, S. (1993). Game play. In C. E. Schaefer (Ed.), *The therapeutic powers of play* (pp. 323-348). Northvale, NJ: Jason Aronson.

SECTION III:
SPECIFIC CHILDHOOD PROBLEMS

14

Learning and School-Related Problems in Childhood

Robert Sholtes

Type of Contribution: Intervention and Handouts for Clinicians

Objective

The objective of this chapter is to provide the mental health professional with information and tools from which they can assess and treat learning and school-related problems. The tools and information presented aid the professional in establishing a cooperative venture between the parents and the school system to help a child overcome learning and/or school problems.

Rationale for Use

Our children are now expected to excel and achieve more than ever. In our high-pressure culture, parents, teachers, and children become driven, feel inadequate, and fear the student may be left behind if he or she is not achieving at an accelerated pace. Our public schools are struggling with violence, drug abuse, childhood depression, federal regulations, and heightened expectations, while many communities decline to support increased funding for education. As mental health professionals encounter the elementary school-age child, the simple tools described in this chapter will help them identify effective approaches with families and teachers facing the many obstacles that resulted in the referral.

When children enter the school system, they present with widely varying skills, family experiences, support, and educational needs. They also enter the system eager to learn and socialize, far more accepting of differences, and less aware of developmental differences. As children mature both physically and emotionally, they become painfully more self-aware of learning and behavioral problems in comparison to their peers. There are marginalizing metamessages in our culture about mental health problems, underachieving either in school or in athletics, and appearing different. Since these messages begin to have greater influence from fourth grade onward, to provide effective services it is vital that children with learning problems be identified as early as possible. Unfortunately, schools and families may delay consultation, or mental health professionals may delay suggestions for intervention in the hope that the child may "mature out of" a problem noticed at an early age. Earlier interventions are more efficacious than waiting until the problem behaviors are more established as habits (Reynolds and Temple, 1998; Lerner, 1989; Lyin, 1996). The sooner a young child is thoroughly evaluated, the sooner appropriate interventions by the parents and the school result in substantial improvements.

Although early evaluation is imperative, therapists must also be sensitive to the stigmatizing influence of the evaluation process itself. As mental health professionals, we expound our expert knowledge, the "truth speaking" Michel Foucault described as dangerous (Rabinow, 1994). We must be mindful of the danger of limiting our clients' options as we approach questions about the diagnoses and treatment of grade school children, especially given the powerful societal discourses described earlier. The health care industry and our schools demand diagnostic labels for reimbursement of health care services and to qualify children for special services in the school. Although it may be necessary to provide the appropriate diagnostic label, the therapist must be on the lookout, with the child, school, and family, for unexpected outcomes consistent with more "thickly described" (Geertz, 1973; White, 1997) experiences. One approach to diagnostic considerations is to consider the criteria and terminology as tools of communication while being alert to the problems of constraining discourses (e.g., labeling the child). The reader is referred to the DSM-IV (American Psychiatric Association [APA], 1994) for details on each diagnostic category.

Instructions

A simplified but adequate approach for the uninitiated mental health professional is to consider the following principles in assessing a child for a learning disability ("disorder" according to DSM-IV [APA, 1994]):

1. *The school system is responsible for the testing.* Federal law requires each school district to provide a comprehensive psychoeducational test (see description following) for any child identified as experiencing learning problems. Since school authorities may resist testing first-graders, some persistence and coaching of the parents may be in order so that timely testing can be achieved.
2. *A learning disorder (LD) is simply defined as achievement (in reading, math, writing, coordination, or communication) below ability,* determined by standardized measures.
3. *Attention deficit hyperactivity disorder (ADHD) is associated with a learning disorder 30 percent of the time* (APA, 1994). Any child referred for an evaluation of ADHD should be screened for a learning disorder unless the child has no difficulty learning. Do not assume a problem with learning is part of ADHD.
4. *School-related behavioral problems beginning after third grade are less likely to be associated with ADHD and are more likely to be related to LD, social stress, and/or depression.*
5. *The local community is your best resource.* CHADD (Children and Adults with Attention-Deficit/Hyperactivity Disorder) chapters, learning centers, coaches, scout leaders, and churches provide additional support to the family and school.

It is essential that the family work closely with the school in the process of evaluating and planning services for children experiencing school-related problems. Parents are the best advocates for their children. Most of the time, parents and educators work together, developing individualized plans well suited to the child's educational needs, with little or no involvement from the therapist. This collaborative process is achieved only with the best efforts of all parties. Sometimes parents may benefit from coaching regarding what to expect from their child and from the school. Here are some basic considerations:

1. Educators have many parents demanding special consideration for their child, while their resources are increasingly limited. Parents may feel stonewalled as they seek help for their child. Explain to timid parents that courteous persistence works.
2. Educators respond to reminders of the federal mandates for evaluation and services clearly stated in the Individuals with Disabilities Education Act (IDEA). Sometimes a letter from the therapist (see Appendix B for sample letter) helps parents advocate for an evaluation.
3. Complete psychoeducational testing includes a full battery of tests (IQ, achievement, coordination, and speech tests). If a parent says, "My child was tested," ask for a copy of the report. Initially, children referred for testing may be "screened" or observed by an evalua-

tor for a brief time in class. This observation may be considered "testing," with a report generated describing no need for further action. In order to rule out a learning disorder, a full battery of tests will be needed.

4. Educators do not evaluate ADHD; rather, various medical and mental health professionals provide this service. Psychologists, pediatricians, family practice doctors, neurologists, and psychiatrists provide widely varying approaches to evaluating and treating ADHD.

5. Classroom observations may not be included in the report. Have the teacher(s) complete a behavioral rating scale (the Conner's [1973, 1989, 1994, 1998] Teacher Rating Scale, for example). Also review report cards from previous years. Report cards have information about academic achievement, classroom behavior, and homework completion. This information is important in distinguishing ADHD and LD (persistent from preschool) from depression or a reaction to stress (often acute, having a distinct onset).

6. There is no "test" for ADHD. Parents or health care providers may demand a test. Computerized tests of attention and reaction time are available, but these tests are unnecessary for the evaluation or treatment of ADHD. The tests may burden parents with additional expenses without benefit. ADHD is diagnosed from observation and behavioral description, not performance on a test (APA, 1994). If the child experiences significant problems with attention span, hyperactivity, and/or impulsivity with clear evidence of impaired functioning, medical treatment with stimulants may substantially improve the child's functioning.

Once a child is identified as having a learning problem, a variety of services are available in the school and in the community. There are key words used in discussions about educational planning, defined in Appendix A and italicized here. School services include various forms of *special education* or *accommodations*. A *psychoeducational evaluation* is required to qualify a child for special education. Based on the evaluation, an *Individualized Education Plan* (IEP) is formally discussed with the parents. Special educational services are available for *learning disabilities* and for *behavioral disorders* or *emotionally handicapped* children. Some children may qualify for services to address learning and behavioral problems. These may be provided separately or in *cross-categorical* services. Special education teachers may visit the *mainstream* class or have the child visit them for *resource* support. This approach is consistent with *inclusion* of the child in the *mainstream* rather than sending the child to a *self-contained* classroom. Self-contained classes may be designated for learning, behavioral, or cross-categorical services. Inclusion in the mainstream class is preferred; however, children with severe problems may not be manageable in the mainstream class.

Schools are required to make accommodations for children with handicaps, including ADHD. The laws governing accommodations under Section 504 (U.S. Department of Labor, 1973) and the IDEA (Office of Special Education and Rehabilitative Services, 2001) do not require psychoeducational testing or an IEP. Accommodations may be as simple as having the child sit in the front of the room or giving extra time for tests. Parents and teachers may develop behavioral programs with daily feedback to parents regarding classroom behavior and homework completion. If special educational services are not needed, parents, teachers, and students may prefer the flexibility of accommodations. See the sample letter in Appendix C.

Suggestions for Follow-Up

The Conner's (1989, 1994, 1998) Teacher Rating Scales have been standardized with scoring, however a more common sense approach is suggested. The scales are very useful in obtaining information from generally objective observers. Having this information is essential to diagnose ADHD (especially items numbered 1, 2, 3, 4, 7, 8, 9, 14, 15, 16, 17, 21, 22, and 28) and may also help identify mood problems (especially items numbered 3, 4, 5, 6, 10, 11, 12, 13, 17, 19, 23, 24, 25, 26, and 27). If there is only one teacher, ask for separate scales for morning and afternoon observations. Ordinarily, the responses from teachers are very positive, and there is little ambiguity about the "diagnosis" of ADHD. Once the underlying problems are more clearly identified, the therapist is better positioned to negotiate a treatment plan with the family.

Fortunately, the therapist is not alone; indeed "it takes a village" (Clinton, 1996) to raise a child. Therapists are part of this village, as are coaches, church leaders, music teachers, neighbors, and families in the community with similar challenges. Children experiencing school-related problems often also have problems within the community as well. Parents should be encouraged to make the most of community support. If the child is reluctant to socialize, encouraging structured social experiences such as sports, scouts, and church groups helps the child overcome the reluctance. Parents and therapists may be inclined to shelter the child from "experiences of failure" yet more children feel like a failure when they avoid social activity and often feel relief and pride after overcoming their reluctance. A "spoilsport" is more likely to become a good sport when guided by an understanding coach. Anxiously avoidant children experience relief after enjoying a social experience with other children guided by an encouraging, sensitive adult scout or church leader. Rambunctious or defiant children may enjoy themselves and learn about team effort, discipline, and self-control in sports or martial arts classes. Parents may find relief and discover resources from grassroots organizations such as the local CHADD chapter.

Contraindications

A small but significant number of families struggle with serious and often chronically challenging children with autistic disorder, Asperger's disorder, and other pervasive developmental disorders (Kephart, 1998). At times more than one school district will combine to form specialized schools with staff trained to work with these children and families. The quality of the programs may vary widely even within a region. Parents should be advised to consult with other parents in the area, as well as researching other sources of information.

Childhood onset bipolar disorder may resemble ADHD with prominent hyperactivity and impulsivity. The bipolar child is more aggressive, hypersexual, and may be well behaved for weeks or years in contrast with the ADHD child. This condition is reportedly more common and more severe than just ten years ago (Papolos and Papolos, 1999). In addition, anxiety disorders in childhood are often overlooked, since these children are usually well-behaved, diligent students. However, when a child refuses to go to school, parents are often asked to seek professional help for their child. It is not uncommon to discover a reciprocal process of the family blaming the school and the school blaming the family for exacerbating the child's phobia of attending school. After ruling out any well-founded fear of real danger in the school setting, plans to expedite the child's return to school are almost always the best approach. Narrative (Freeman, Epston, and Lobovits, 1997) or behavioral family therapy (Falloon, 1991) approaches are recommended for school refusal. If an adolescent presents with school refusal, the treatment process often is more complicated and prolonged. Older children may be struggling with LD, depression, and/or highly stressful family problems. A very brief day hospital treatment may be indicated if initial attempts to negotiate a speedy return to school last longer than a week. The therapist may be hesitant to suggest such a deadline, resulting in more absences from school and increased rather than decreased anxiety for the child. The child may also experience panic attacks or psychosomatic symptoms. A calm, deliberate approach, in collaboration with the child, parents, school nurse, and primary care physician, usually works. Sometimes teaching the child progressive relaxation or trying systematic desensitization (McEwan, 1998) helps calm the family and the child. Externalization of the anxiety builds agency, a wonderful antidote to the influence of anxiety (Freeman, Epston, and Lobovits, 1997).

Appendix A

accommodations: Supportive strategies modifying the educational experience negotiated between the school and student to address specific educational needs. For example, allowing tests to be taken in a private area, more time for tests, having the student sit in the front of the room, and so on. For a more complete list of accommodations, see <http://www.ldonline.org/index.html>, or, more specifically, <http://www.ldonline.org/ld_indepth/teaching_techniques/mod_checklists.html>.

behavioral disorder (BD): A specific designation by the school team, qualifying the child for special educational services to support behavioral development and control.

cross-categorical: Children who have more than one category of qualifying condition (for example, LD and BD) may be placed in a self-contained classroom designated as cross-categorical.

emotionally handicapped (EH): May be the same as BD in some school districts. Other districts will use this designation for children who may not be disruptive but are emotionally ill equipped to manage in mainstream classes. Children in this category (for example, the severely depressed or anxious) may be enrolled in therapeutic schools staffed with educational and mental health professionals working in coordination.

individualized educational plan (IEP): This is a multidisciplinary plan developed after the psychoeducational testing is completed. A team, usually including the school psychologist, teacher(s), educational specialists, and parents, meets to discuss the evaluation or progress in meeting previously planned goals. A plan is developed to meet the child's individual educational needs, including specific and measurable goals.

learning disability (LD): A specific designation by the school team qualifying the child for special educational services to support learning.

psychoeducational evaluation: To qualify for special educational services, children with learning problems are evaluated with a battery of tests, usually including a WISC-III (Wexler Intelligence Scale for Children) or IQ test, a WRAT (Wide Range Achievement Test), a VMI (Developmental Test of Visual-Motor Integration), and screening tools for emotional problems, and the child must be found to have a qualifying condition to merit special educational services.

resource: A term usually reserved for support services provided either directly in the mainstream classroom (for example, a specialist aid) or to children who are seen for brief periods outside the mainstream class. Most special educational services are provided as a resource support to the mainstream classroom.

self-contained: Children with more severe educational and/or behavioral needs may be removed from the mainstream setting. These classrooms may be primarily LD, BD, or cross-categorical. There are advantages (for example, having more intensive support) and disadvantages (for example, stigma and negative peer influences) to this approach.

special education: Educational services for children who qualify under Public Law 94-142. These services are provided under federal guidelines and require a written plan developed by an interdisciplinary team and approved by the parent(s) in the IEP meetings.

Appendix B: Sample Letter to Teachers or Other School Officials

Your Name
Address
Fax and Voice Phone #

Date: _____

_____

_____

_____

Regarding: _____

To Whom It May Concern:

I am working with Dr. [name of medical doctor you consult] to evaluate the student named above for potential medical treatment of behavior problems consistent with attention deficit hyperactivity disorder (ADHD). Our hope is to work with the student, the family, and the school to promote educational and emotional development. In order to complete the evaluation, we will need your help. Please complete the Conner's Teacher Rating Scale for the morning and afternoon hours of school on one day prior to any medication trial.

Additionally, copies of any psychoeducational evaluations completed are needed to help differentiate ADHD from learning disabilities. If psychoeducational testing has not been completed, please arrange to have a full battery of IQ and achievement tests completed as soon as possible. Approximately 30 percent of children with ADHD have an additional specific learning disability. Treating the ADHD with appropriate individualized educational support for commonly associated learning disabilities is the optimal collaborative approach. If there is no indication of a learning disability from the testing and learning problems persist even after treatment we may discuss possible accommodations.

If a medication trial is initiated, the teacher(s) will be asked to complete Conner's Teacher Rating Scales during the morning and afternoon for each dose of medication administered.

Please call or write if you have any questions.

Sincerely,

Appendix C: Sample Letter to School Officials

Your Name
Address
Fax and Voice Phone #

Date: _____

_____

_____

_____

To Whom It May Concern:

I am treating _____ for attention deficit hyperactivity disorder. Students with this disorder may not perform up to their ability on tests, assignments, or in distracting surroundings.

Please provide accommodations for this student during scan format tests, such as allowing handwritten answers to questions on the test paper, taking tests in a separate room free of distractions, and allowing extra time, if needed. This letter is intended to validate the diagnosis and to suggest accommodations, which may be individualized according to the experience of the student and the school.

Please call or write if further clarification is necessary.

Sincerely,

Professional Readings and Resources

Hallowell, E. and Ratey, J. (1995). *Driven to distraction: Recognizing and coping with attention deficit disorder from childhood through adulthood.* New York: Simon and Schuster.

Kelly, K. and Ramundo, P. (1993). *You mean I'm not lazy, stupid or crazy?* New York: Simon and Schuster.

McEwan, E. K. (1998). *When kids say no to school: Helping children at risk of failure, refusal, or dropping out.* Wheaton, IL: Harold Shaw Publisher.

White, M. (1997). *Narratives of therapists' lives.* Adelaide, South Australia: Dulwich Centre Publications.

Bibliotherapy Sources for the Client

Hallowell, E. and Ratey, J. (1995). *Driven to distraction: Recognizing and coping with attention deficit disorder from childhood through adulthood.* New York: Simon and Schuster.

Kelly, K. and Ramundo, P. (1993). *You mean I'm not lazy, stupid or crazy?* New York: Simon and Schuster.

McEwan, E. K. (1998). *When kids say no to school: Helping children at risk of failure, refusal, or dropping out.* Wheaton, IL: Harold Shaw Publisher.

References

American Psychiatric Association (1994). *Diagnostic and Statistical Manual of Mental Disorders* (Fourth edition). Washington, DC: Author.

Clinton, H. (1996). *It takes a village.* New York: Simon and Schuster.

Conners, C. K. (1973). Rating scales for use in drug studies with children. *Psychopharmacology Bulletin* [Special issue on children], 24-42.

Conners, C. K. (1989). *Manual for Conners' rating scales.* North Tonawanda, NY: Multi-Health Systems.

Conners, C. K. (1994). The Conners rating scales: Use in clinical assessment, treatment planning and research. In M. Maruish (Ed.), *Use of psychological testing for treatment planning and outcome assessment.* Hillsdale, NJ: L. Erlbaum.

Conners, C. K., Sitarenios, G., Parker, J. D. A., and Epstein, J. N. (1998). Revision and restandardization of the Conners Teacher Rating Scale: Factor structure, reliability, and criterion validity. *Journal of Abnormal Child Psychology, 26.*

Falloon, I. R. H. (1991). Behavioral family therapy. In A. S. Gurman and D. P. Kniskern (Eds.), *Handbook of family therapy* (Volume 2). New York: Brunner/Mazel.

Freeman, J., Epston, D., and Lobovits, D. (1997). *Playful approaches to serious problems: Narrative therapy with children and their families.* New York: W.W. Norton and Company.

Geertz, C. (1973). *The interpretation of cultures.* New York: Basic Books Classics.

Kephart, B. (1998). *A slant of sun: One child's courage.* New York: W.W. Norton Company.

Lerner, J. (1989). Educational interventions in learning disabilities. *Journal of the American Academy of Child and Adolescent Psychiatry, 28,* 326-331.

Lyin, G. R. (1996). Learning disabilities. *The Future of Children, 6,* 54-76.

McEwan, E. K. (1998). *When kids say no to school: helping children at risk of failure, refusal, or dropping out.* Wheaton, IL: Harold Shaw Publisher.

Office of Special Education and Rehabilitative Services (2001). Individuals with Disabilities Education Act. Access: <http://www.ed.gov/offices/OSERS/Policy/IDEA/the_law.html>.

Papolos, F. and Papolos, J. (1999). *The Bipolar child: The definitive and reassuring guide to childhood's most misunderstood disorder.* New York: Broadway Books.

Rabinow, P. (1994). *Cambridge companion to Foucault.* New York: Cambridge University Press.

Reynolds, A. J. and Temple, J. A. (1998). Extended early childhood intervention and school achievement: Age thirteen findings from the Chicago longitudinal study. *Child Development, 69,* 231-246.

U.S. Department of Labor (1973). Section 504, Rehabilitation Act of 1973. Access: <http://www.dol.gov/oasam/regs/statutes/sec504.htm>.

White, M. (1997). *Narratives of therapists' lives.* Adelaide, South Australia: Dulwich Centre Publications.

15

Superman versus the Monster:
Assisting a Young Child with Nightmares

Lorna L. Hecker

Type of Contribution: Activity/Intervention

Objective

The objective of this activity is to help a child deal with recurring nightmares of monsters or other evil villains. Many parents awakened by children suffering from nightmares feel ill equipped to handle the depth of the fear that can accompany a child's nightmare. This intervention provides parents with a conceptual tool for handling nightmares in a way that helps children settle back down into sleep.

Rationale for Use

Developmentally, it is normal for young children to encounter a nasty monster or evil villain. In addition, with children witnessing so much violence in our society, it is not unusual for some of the violence to recur at an unconscious level in a child's dreams. In the recesses of a child's mind may lurk a hideous monster, a villain, or an ogre. Nighttime can be a frightening time for children, and even after a child is asleep, these scared feelings may surface in the form of nightmares. This intervention is best taught to a parent who will be with the child when a nightmare occurs. It may also be used by the therapist to teach a coping mechanism directly to a child for recurring, frightening nightmares.

When the child awakens, the parent comforts the child, perhaps by holding, cuddling, or rocking, to give the message, "You're okay; it will be okay." "Daddy won't let anything hurt you" or "Mommy is here for you" are good responses in attempting to calm a child. Sometimes for children who have experienced a very unsettling nightmare, these attempts are just not enough, and the parent feels helpless in knowing how to calm the child so all can return to sleep. Indeed, children may need to be protected in a very specific way from the monster in the dream before they feel able to rest again. One advantage of this approach is that it empowers the child and teaches him or her to self-soothe in the future when scary events or feelings occur.

One way parents can accomplish targeting a specific villain is through metaphor. Young children love superheroes. In this intervention, the solution is for a superhero to come to the rescue; not just any superhero should be chosen, but one who can take care of the specific nightmare problem at hand.

Instructions

Parents are given the following instructions:

1. When the child wakes you up, have the child describe the nightmare. Ask the child specifically about the monster (or villain, ogre, and so on). Ask the child to describe the nightmare to you much as you would ask a friend to describe a car accident: Who was involved? What happened? Did anyone get hurt? Are you okay? How are you feeling now?

2. Find out what this monster looks like, and what it was doing in the dream. Discuss what special talents this villain has that may make it hard to overpower. Then find out what aspect of the dream is still scaring or threatening the child. For example, the parent may find out that the monster can slide under the door to get into the house, and no matter where the child goes to hide, the monster is still able to get in. It is very powerful and never goes away. So if a parent reassures the child that the doors are locked and no monsters can get in, the child knows that this is not true because this particular monster has special abilities that the parent just does not understand. It is imperative to empathize with the child's fears. The key to making this intervention work is being sure you understand the main fear of the child so that you can devise a way to alleviate that fear.

3. After you have learned the details sufficiently (enough to know the enemy, but not enough to further wake or frighten the child), devise a plan to eradicate this pesky monster. Your child may have a favorite superhero who could do the trick depending upon what his or her special talents are and what the weaknesses are of the monster at hand. Devise a plan for the superhero to get rid of the monster using his or her own special powers. For example, Spider-Man might spin a web around a monster, or Batman might tie it up with his special bat cable and tow the monster away in his Batmobile. Wonder-Woman might run steel bands around the monster. One superhero who usually comes through well is Superman. Children may see lapses in power in many superheroes, but with the exception of kryptonite, Superman is "invincible."

4. After having the child describe the dream, ask him or her which superhero would be able to handle the monster. Provide suggestions that fit the child's personality. Have the child describe the encounter of the monster with the superhero. Then ask if the superhero can handle this monster (if the child says no, find a stronger superhero, or give the superhero an extra-turbo treatment!). Have the superhero do battle with the monster, and then have the superhero remove the monster and take it to a far-away place (e.g., the moon, Pluto, a star, and so on). Then talk with the child about how tired the superhero must be after traveling all that way, using voice tone and breathing in a way that calms the child down for sleep. The parent can reassure the child that the superhero has taken care of that mean monster.

Example

PARENT: What is the scariest thing about the dream?

CHILD: The monster will come back to eat me!

PARENT: So you're afraid that he will come back and get in your bedroom and eat you?

CHILD: Yes.

PARENT: Wow, that does sound scary. Can you think of anything you could do with that monster so he doesn't come back? Can we tie him up?

CHILD: No, he'll eat through the ropes.

PARENT: Oh, that won't do. Can you think of anything else? How about we put him in jail?

CHILD: No, he'll get out, he's very strong.

PARENT: Oh, he must be strong to be able to get out of jail by himself. What do you think Superman would do to the monster?

CHILD: I don't know. He'd fight him.

PARENT: Oh, is that so. He'd fight the monster . . . How would he fight the monster? Could we have Superman fight the monster?

CHILD: No, he may fight the monster, but the monster will still come back.

PARENT: Wow, he's an ornery monster! That monster is quite a dickens, isn't he? Hey, how about we have Superman fly the monster to the moon?!!! Do you think that Superman could do that?

CHILD: Uh-huh!

PARENT: [Lying down with child] Well let's imagine that Superman gets a hold of this monster and takes the monster and begins flying.

CHILD: Yeah . . .

PARENT: And because we don't want that old monster here on Earth, we have him fly it to the moon. Do you think Superman is strong enough to do that?

CHILD: Superman is very strong, and he's faster than a speeding bullet, more powerful than a locomotive, and able to leap tall buildings in a single bound!

PARENT: Yes, he is. And he has a hold of this naughty mean monster, and he begins to fly the monster to the moon. Can you imagine that? Do you see Superman flying with the monster clenched in his arms?

CHILD: Yeah, he's flying fast!

PARENT: Yes he is. It's the monster that looks scared now, doesn't he? I bet he is afraid Superman may drop him. Do you think he is?

CHILD: Yeah. He's scared.

PARENT: But Superman has a good hold on him and they are almost to the moon, flying by lots and lots of stars. Do you see the stars?

CHILD: Yeah, I do.

PARENT: Let's imagine Superman gets to the moon, lands on the moon with the monster, and tells the monster off. What do you think Superman might say?

CHILD: "You will never come back to Earth, Monster. You are stuck on the moon forever!" That monster is getting what he deserves.

PARENT: That's exactly right. He was a mean monster and now he is punished and won't have any friends.

CHILD: Yeah . . .

PARENT: Can you imagine Superman flying back to Earth? His cape blowing behind him in the wind and his arms held straight out front while he flies?

CHILD: Hmmmmm.

PARENT: [Gently] Superman is back on Earth, safe and sound. That monster is all gone.

CHILD: Yeah . . .

PARENT: I'll bet Superman is really tired after flying to the moon. He's so tired, it was such a long trip. He can hardly move he is so tired. He's going to sleep. He needs his sleep to be strong. [Parent lowers voice.] He's going to sleep . . . he's so, so tired. Superman is tired and going to sleep . . .

CHILD: [Deeper breathing]

PARENT: . . . so, so tired, going to sleep. His head is on the pillow, he's going to sleep . . .

PARENT: [Yawning] . . . so tired . . . so tired . . .

The latter part of the intervention can be geared toward the child and his or her sleeping style as appropriate.

Suggestions for Follow-Up

If the parent is unable to come up with a superhero who can manage the adversary at hand, the therapist may need to help in understanding the villain's special powers. In this way, the therapist can guide the parent into finding just the right superhero, or even inventing one specifically for the villain at hand.

Note: If the child fails to awaken the parent but mentions the nightmare the next day, the parent can ask the child to draw or paint the bad dream. This makes it more concrete and less threatening, and helps the parent really "see" the dream (Gil, 1994; Oaklander, 1988). It also aids in discussing elements of the dream. The child may then be asked to draw the superhero defeating the monster, or the parents may encourage the child to "be" the superhero and "tell" or act out how the superhero defeats the monster (Oaklander, 1988). This helps the child "internalize" the superhero's special powers. As the superhero, the child could even destroy the monster picture, reducing the monster to shreds and destroying his monster power. Another, gentler approach is to help the child understand the monster and why the monster is so angry. The parent and child can befriend the monster, inviting the unruly character to "tea" or over for pizza to conquer it with kindness and void the need for the monster to be unkind.

Contraindications for Use

This intervention may not be appropriate or useful for children who are suffering from a specific trauma. The trauma itself will need to be addressed; otherwise the nightmares will likely recur. However, when traumas are adequately addressed, this type of intervention may be useful in dealing with recurring nightmares by helping the parent protect, nurture, and comfort the child in both real and imaginary ways.

Professional Readings and Resources

Weissbluth, M. (1999). *Healthy sleep habits, happy child.* New York: Fawcett Books.

Bibliotherapy Sources for the Client

Ferber, R. (2002). *Solve your child's sleep problems.* New York: Fireside.
Mindell, J. (1997). *Sleeping through the night: How infants, toddlers, and their parents can get a good night's sleep.* New York: HarperCollins.

References

Gil, E. (1994). *Play in family therapy.* New York: Guilford Publications.
Oaklander, V. (1988). *Windows to our children.* Highland, NY: Gestalt Journal.

16

"Mommy Is a Restless Sleeper"

Lorna L. Hecker

Type of Contribution: Activity/Intervention, Handouts

Objective

The objective of this activity is to help put parents back in charge of sleeping behaviors in the home. Parents, often with the best of intentions, allow young children to sleep in the parental bed. This can quickly become a habit, and it can be very difficult to get young children to sleep in their own beds once again. Sometimes, a child begins sleeping with a parent or parents when the child has a period of illness. The parent comforts the child, but then the child is often very reluctant to leave the comfort of the parental bed, and the parent, for a myriad of reasons, can have terrible difficulty getting the child to return to his or her own bed.

Children love the warmth and snuggly security of the parental bed, and parents indulge children in treating them to the parental bed for several reasons. One common reason is that the child, once sick, is well but refuses to sleep in his or her own bed. Another common pattern is for a single parent to allow a child into his or her bed. Although in two-parent homes this may be more readily discouraged for practical reasons (e.g., crowding or romance), in single-parent homes there is less of a barrier to this behavior. In addition, when parents are going through a separation or divorce, they are reluctant to push their child to separate, feeling that the child has already suffered the loss of the other parent. Likewise, for many parents, having a child in the bed can be very comforting to them. It is comforting for some to wake up and see that their child is okay, breathing, and happily in slumber when the rest of life can feel like constant turmoil.

Dysfunctional marital patterns can also play a role, such as when a child is triangled into marital strife and is led into the parental bed to provide a buffer against an alienated spouse. There are numerous reasons why children are allowed in the parental bed, and an equal number of reasons why it is difficult to get them out.

Rationale for Use

Children who are reluctant to sleep in their own beds at night have gained expertise in manipulation. Their expertise, combined with parental guilt, makes this problem a particularly difficult one to break. Indeed, parents may be hesitant to bring up the issue in therapy, as sharing a family bed is commonly unaccepted behavior in our culture. Although the concept of the family bed deserves debate, the premise of this chapter is that children need their own beds to rest peacefully, be taught independence, and establish an identity separate from parents. However, breaking a habit that is highly reinforcing to a child will not come without its price.

There are several ways to try to break the pattern of the family bed:

1. Parents can try *asking* the child. Many parents accept that the child will not like moving back to his or her own bed, and then don't discuss it with the child. Although some parents will find it preferable to tell a child to go to his or her own bed, a first try might be to simply ask a child to sleep in his or her own bed. The parent can cite advantages for the child: the child won't have to hear Daddy's snoring, it means the child is growing up and can sleep alone and is showing more independence, the child has a nice bed to sleep in with favorite cartoon character sheets, and so on. In addition, the parent can list the reasons why it is difficult for the parent if the child remains in the parental bed: the parent gets grouchy and is more prone to yelling or scolding, the parent can't do his or her job as well during the day, and so on. The parent can emphasize how he or she does not want to be grouchy but simply needs good sleep and cannot get it with the child in the bed. The parent can joke that a foot in one's face does not make for a good night's sleep. Children often like to do favors for parents. For this type of child, asking may be a good option. For others, telling the child to go to sleep in his or her bed is more hierarchically effective.
2. Incentives can also be attempted to lure the child into his or her own bed. Parents can make the child's bed and room very desirable. They can help the child pick out decorations for the room, choose a favorite comforter, and arrange stuffed animals and books around the bed, as the child likes. Nighttime rituals such as reading books with a parent propped in the child's bed can also be a nice transition to bedtime as well as making settling into bed a rewarding experience for a child.
3. Punishments can be put in place if the child does not stay in his or her bed. Favorite toys may be taken away if a night is spent in the parental bed (to be returned on nights when the child succeeds in sleeping alone), or a privilege may be taken away (to be returned upon success).
4. Another option is to attempt to have the child sleep in his or her own bed by successive approximation. For a child who is used to sleeping in the parent's bed, the parent might say, "You have been sleeping in Daddy's bed for some time now. You are a big boy, and I think we can get you ready to go to your big-boy room. When you are a big boy, you can sleep totally in your room by yourself, but until then, I want you to get in training for sleeping by yourself. From now on, you can't sleep in Daddy's bed, but you can bring your pillow and blanket and sleep on the floor next to Daddy's bed." The child is then allowed to sleep next to the parental bed, with praise or a reward given when he or she is able to stay on the floor next to the bed. Then the parent gradually starts to move the pillow and blanket further from the bed, toward the door, with continued praise and rewards given for successes in staying on the floor. (If the child complains of the hardness of the floor, the parent can remind the child he or she is "in training" for a soft bed. If the child "rebels" and insists on sleeping in his or her own bed as a result, so be it!) Eventually the pillow and blanket are moved into the child's room until, finally, "the big event" arrives. Praise and celebration should ensue when the child finally masters a night in his or her own bed.
5. For the more difficult child, a more difficult intervention may be in order. This is where "Mommy is a restless sleeper" comes in. At some point, the parent gets (literally) tired of fighting the child who constantly begs to be in the parental bed. The problem with curbing this behavior is that it generally occurs when parents are equally or more exhausted than the child! They may have tried sending the child to his or her own bed; they may have tried punishments, reinforcers, and anything else they can think of, to no avail. It is for these parents that "Mommy is a restless sleeper" can be of the most help. This intervention is

equally successful when "Daddy is the restless sleeper." The goal of this intervention is to make the parental bed so uncomfortable for the child that his or her own bed will be a welcome respite from the discomforts of the parental bed.

Instructions

First, the previous options to try to get the child to bed should be attempted. If those fail, parents are instructed to remind the child of the agreement that they had (e.g., child is to sleep on the floor, the child is to sleep in his or her room but can have the light on, or whatever the prior agreement was). However, after the child has made several attempts to join the parental bed, a weary parent will often give in. When this happens in reality, therapists are to suggest to parents that they *pretend* to "give in." That is, when the child appears at the side of the bed of the exasperated, sleeping parent, the parent is to say to the child, "OK, Angela, I guess it would be all right this once if you sleep with Mommy, as long as you don't wake me up. If you wake me up, you have to go back to your own bed. Remember how Mommy said she gets grouchy if she doesn't get her sleep? You can stay here as long as you don't wake me up. Deal?" The relieved child will soon crawl in and get comfortable. The parent is then instructed to go quickly to "sleep." The parent is to pretend that she has fallen asleep; she is to close her eyes, breathe deeply, and even snore a little. In the process, it is important not to let much time pass for the child to get comfortable and fall asleep. The second order of business is that the therapist should instruct the parent to become "a restless sleeper." The sleeping parent then carefully moves about the bed, with the express goal of making sleep near to impossible and the bed uncomfortable for the child. A limb may be placed over the child, gently pinning him or her. Suddenly, the parent rolls over and pushes the child toward the edge of the bed. The parent pushes until the child is nearly dangling off the bed. The parent will of course notice the child repositioning to get comfortable but is expressly aware the child is not to wake up the parent because he or she does not want to be instructed to return to his or her bed. Loud snoring may be another option. The goal of this intervention is to make the parental bed an uncomfortable place to spend the night. Parents know the limits of what they can do before they hurt a child, and this intervention allows for some physical manipulation of the child without any pain, but not without some discomfort. The parent must be reminded that this is all done "as they sleep." If the child tries to "wake" the parent, the child is to be reminded that he or she was told if the child woke the parent, he or she agreed to return to his or her own bed so the parent could get a good night's sleep. If the child does wake the parent, and the child states he or she is too scared to return to his or her bed, the parent may make an exception, stating again, "Well, OK, as long as this time you don't wake me." Then the whole "restless sleeping" procedure is repeated. The procedure is repeated until the child falls asleep, the parent falls asleep, and/or the child gets disgusted with the poor accommodations and returns to his or her room on his or her own volition (while the parent is slumbering). Although it would be ideal for the parent to stay awake and continue being restless, realistically that does not always happen. The next morning the parent may simply comment at the breakfast table about what a restless sleeper she's become and try again the next night. It should not take too many nights of a parent being a "restless sleeper" before the child's fears of sleeping alone should miraculously disappear. What also happens in this intervention is that even when parents cannot successfully complete the restless parent routine, they are so enabled with their newly found "restless power" that some of the previous methods can be employed with success.

In addition, charts for success when a child sleeps in his or her bed can be utilized to reinforce the changes made. A chart is provided as a handout at the end of this chapter. The child may put a checkmark for success or stickers may be adhered to the days of success (child stays in his or her bed), and a reward may be given per sticker or for a certain amount of stickers. Verbal praise should be the main reinforcer. Additional reinforcers can include stickers, money given for each sticker (e.g., twenty-five or fifty cents per success), small collectibles (e.g., baseball cards; Pokemon cards), TV privileges, dessert, and so on. Therapists can give the child certificates marking success, such as the one provided at the end of the chapter.

Vignette

Sherry was a single parent who had been divorced for two years. Her youngest child, four-year-old Joshua, had established a fairly good routine of sleeping in his own bed, with occasional trips to his mother's bedroom in the middle of the night because he was "scared of monsters." Sherry tried many things to calm the monsters, but Joshua increasingly became more "scared" and soon almost every night, shortly after bedtime, would appear at Sherry's bed requesting to sleep with her. For a while, Sherry accommodated Joshua but grew tired of being awakened by the kicks and other antics of an active sleeper. While in therapy for other divorce-related issues, Sherry brought up the stress of Joshua sleeping with her. She was exasperated and feeling as though she had tried everything to get Joshua to sleep in his bed. She felt guilty trying to get him back to his bed because he was extremely afraid of monsters. Sherry had tried various tactics to get Joshua to stay in his bed, and she and her therapist worked together on the steps of asking, reinforcing, punishing, and successive approximation to sleeping in his bed (such as those listed under "Rationale for Use"). When she asked her ex-husband if Joshua slept with him, she found out that Joshua almost always slept with his father when he stayed with him. This information made it even more frustrating for Sherry to try to break this habit, as it appeared her ex-husband was not very concerned about the sleeping arrangements. In addition, all attempts to calm Joshua about monsters met with no success, and Sherry was fairly sure he was using his "fear" to manipulate her into letting him into the bed.

She was getting so frustrated at not getting her rest that the therapist suggested that she "give in" but with a twist. She was instructed to give in the next time Joshua approached her about sleeping in her bed but to tell Joshua that there would be some *rules* about sleeping with her. This was to be done without expressing anger or disappointment, but in a matter-of-fact manner. First of all, Sherry was to tell Joshua that he could sleep with her, *provided* that he did not wake her. Sherry was to remind Joshua that indeed if he did wake her, she would likely be grouchy, and she really needed her rest. She was instructed to tell Joshua that she understood he was scared, and to assure him that he could sleep with her, but to warn him that "Mommy is a restless sleeper." The therapist then instructed Sherry that when Joshua did try to settle into her bed, she should welcome him, snuggle with him a bit, and then pretend to go to sleep. She was to breathe deeply, do whatever else she might normally do when sleeping, and begin to spread out in slumber. She was to make sleeping in her bed as uncomfortable as she could for Joshua by being "restless." This included throwing a leg over him, or having her arm thrown out over his head, or even snuggling up next to him to the point where she pushed him (safely) off the bed. When Joshua tried to reposition, she should reposition herself and get in his way. She should continue to snuggle him and push him toward the edge of the bed. If Joshua found an empty spot on the bed, she was to roll over and throw a limb into that spot. She was to snore loudly. If Joshua protested, she was told he was to be scolded for waking her up and reminded that he could sleep with her only if he didn't wake her. Even if either person fell asleep, this routine was to be continued for a week. The mother was cautioned to be careful to not physically hurt Joshua in the course of being restless, which of course she understood.

Sherry was also told that *if* Joshua did fall asleep, she was to carry him to his bed and compliment him for overpowering the monsters the previous night enough to sleep in his own bed (it is likely that a child will not remember *how* he or she got to bed, and there is no harm in letting the child think it was of his or her own volition).

Sherry listened intently and started smiling. She doubted it would make a difference, but she said she would try it.

In our next session, Sherry relayed the following story:

I really didn't think anything was going to work, and one night I was so tired, and Joshua came in when I wasn't quite asleep yet. I was already mad just because I was exhausted and thought that I was going to suffer through yet another night of interrupted sleep. But I pretended to be asleep. He stood beside my bed, just waiting. Finally I opened my eyes and chided him: "Joshua, you are supposed to be asleep in your bed!" Joshua replied, "But I am afraid of the monsters in my room." Rather than convincing him there were no monsters, which always proved fruitless in the past, and rather than yelling at him to get to his bed, which always ended up with him in tears and me giving in, I decided to try your suggestion.

So I said, "Joshua, you can get in *as long as* you don't wake up Mommy. And just so you know, Mommy is a restless sleeper. And you know how Mommy gets grouchy when she doesn't get enough sleep." Joshua agreed he would not wake me up and he crawled in and started to snuggle down. My exasperation now turned to amusement because I started to breathe deeply and even let out an occasional snore. I also started to encroach on Joshua's territory. I snuggled close to him but, in the process, pushed him to the edge of the bed. He finally had one leg hanging off and decided to get out and reposition himself somewhere else on the bed. As soon as he would get comfortable, I would roll over and let my thigh rest over his body, effectively (but gently) pinning him. I would hold the position for a while, and then I would move and snuggle close to him again, pushing him further toward the edge of the bed. These antics went on for some time. At one point I rolled over and had my arm over his face, and I could feel his little eyelashes blinking under my arm. Luckily he was too small to know that the vibrations of the bed were from me laughing silently to myself! At one point, he tried to "wake me up." I said loudly, "Joshua! I told you that you could sleep with me as long as you didn't wake me up!" Joshua replied in exasperation, "But your skin keeps touching my skin!" I reiterated, "Okay, you can sleep with me as long as you don't wake me up." Unfortunately, I fell asleep but woke up a couple of hours later. There lay Joshua, and I thought I had screwed up. But I did what you said, and I put him in his bed. In the morning, I couldn't believe it, but Joshua walked into my room and said, "Mommy, guess what! I was able to sleep in my room!" I said, "Wow, Joshua, I am so proud of you for not being afraid of the monsters!" Joshua replied, "I figured out what to do. What I did was throw a blanket over the monsters, and then I nailed the blanket to the floor." I continued to be impressed (after I realized he didn't really use any nails!) and fawned over his monster-trapping abilities. We had one more night of Joshua coming to my bed, but as soon as I became a restless sleeper, he retreated to his room. He has been sleeping in his bed ever since!

Suggestions for Follow-Up

The therapist can follow up by complimenting the child on his or her monster-slaying ability and may even want to generalize and find other ways that the child has been brave and overcome problem situations. A congratulatory certificate may also be of use. Finally, the focus could move from the child to the parent and how he or she is doing with his or her problem of "restless sleeping." The parent can reinforce in therapy that having the child sleep in his or her own bed has been a tremendous help with the "restless sleeping" problem, and he or she can discuss feeling more rested and what a help the child was in assisting him or her.

Contraindications for Use

The therapist needs to be sure that the child has not been traumatized by other factors that may be causing him or her not to want to sleep alone. Certainly the goal of this intervention is not to retraumatize a child by sending him or her away from the comfort of a parent. Typically, parents can recognize when the child is really fearful and when the child is being manipulative. If a child is really fearful, he or she will stay in the parental bed no matter how uncomfortable, and if that happens, it is diagnostic and other avenues of treatment should be explored, and the restless sleeping intervention should be aborted. Finally, this intervention should not be suggested for very overweight parents, or those who could not do this activity in a playful and non-punishing manner.

Professional Readings and Resources

Messer, D. (1993). The treatment of sleeping difficulties. In I. St. James-Roberts and G. Harris (Eds.), *Infant crying, feeding, and sleeping: Development, problems, and treatment.* Hertfordshire, England: Harvester Wheatsheaf.
Weissbluth, M. (1999). *Healthy sleep habits, happy child.* New York: Fawcett Books.

Bibliotherapy Sources for the Client

Cohen, G. (1999). *Guide to your child's sleep: Birth through adolescence.* New York: Random House.
Ferber, R. (2002). *Solve your child's sleep problems.* New York: Fireside.
Mindell, J. (1997). *Sleeping through the night: How infants, toddlers, and their parents can get a good night's sleep.* New York: HarperCollins.

Child's Chart for Sleeping

SUNDAY	MONDAY	TUESDAY	WEDNESDAY	THURSDAY	FRIDAY	SATURDAY
☐ Yeah, I slept in my bed! ☐ I'll try harder tonight!	☐ Yeah, I slept in my bed! ☐ I'll try harder tonight!	☐ Yeah, I slept in my bed! ☐ I'll try harder tonight!	☐ Yeah, I slept in my bed! ☐ I'll try harder tonight!	☐ Yeah, I slept in my bed! ☐ I'll try harder tonight!	☐ Yeah, I slept in my bed! ☐ I'll try harder tonight!	☐ Yeah, I slept in my bed! ☐ I'll try harder tonight!
☐ Yeah, I slept in my bed! ☐ I'll try harder tonight!	☐ Yeah, I slept in my bed! ☐ I'll try harder tonight!	☐ Yeah, I slept in my bed! ☐ I'll try harder tonight!	☐ Yeah, I slept in my bed! ☐ I'll try harder tonight!	☐ Yeah, I slept in my bed! ☐ I'll try harder tonight!	☐ Yeah, I slept in my bed! ☐ I'll try harder tonight!	☐ Yeah, I slept in my bed! ☐ I'll try harder tonight!
☐ Yeah, I slept in my bed! ☐ I'll try harder tonight!	☐ Yeah, I slept in my bed! ☐ I'll try harder tonight!	☐ Yeah, I slept in my bed! ☐ I'll try harder tonight!	☐ Yeah, I slept in my bed! ☐ I'll try harder tonight!	☐ Yeah, I slept in my bed! ☐ I'll try harder tonight!	☐ Yeah, I slept in my bed! ☐ I'll try harder tonight!	☐ Yeah, I slept in my bed! ☐ I'll try harder tonight!
☐ Yeah, I slept in my bed! ☐ I'll try harder tonight!	☐ Yeah, I slept in my bed! ☐ I'll try harder tonight!	☐ Yeah, I slept in my bed! ☐ I'll try harder tonight!	☐ Yeah, I slept in my bed! ☐ I'll try harder tonight!	☐ Yeah, I slept in my bed! ☐ I'll try harder tonight!	☐ Yeah, I slept in my bed! ☐ I'll try harder tonight!	☐ Yeah, I slept in my bed! ☐ I'll try harder tonight!

THIS CERTIFIES THAT

HAS SUCCESSFULLY SLAYED
NIGHTTIME MONSTERS!
WAY TO GO!!!

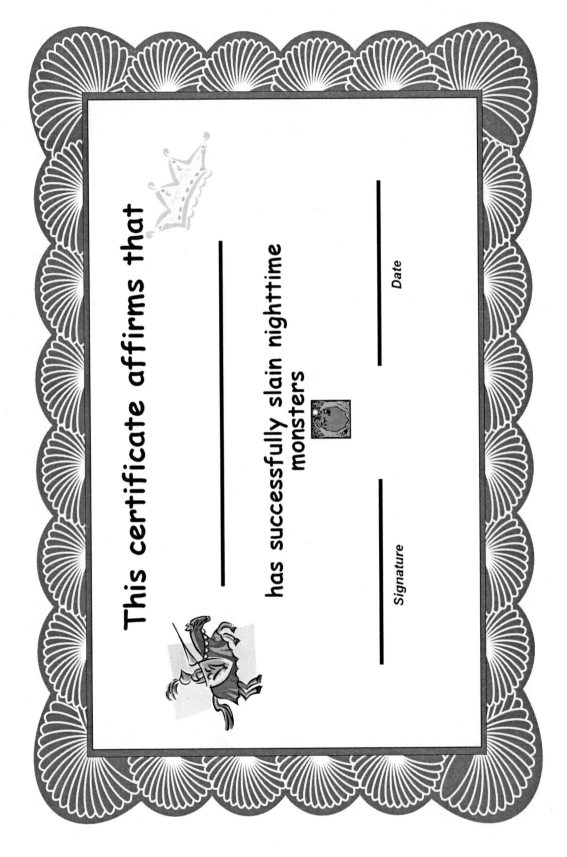

This certificate affirms that

_____

has successfully slain nighttime
monsters

_____
Date

_____
Signature

17

Secret Signals Soothe Separation Stress

Linda L. Richardson

Type of Contribution: Homework, Handout

Objective

Some children feel a great deal of stress when separated from their primary caregivers. Separations can be extremely hard on both the children and the caregivers. When children become distressed, all who are involved with them can feel at a loss for what to do. The objective of this homework assignment is to help ease the stress felt by children (and their caregivers) dealing with separation anxiety. The use of secret signals between a child and the primary caregiver may help the child feel privileged to information that most people do not have, thus making the child feel special. These secret signals represent the promise of the caregiver's return to the child. Because the signals are kept a secret between only the primary caregiver and the child, the child feels a special sense of camaraderie with the caregiver that no one else shares. This makes it more likely that the child will trust the promise being made by the primary caregiver—the promise that the caregiver will return to the child.

Rationale for Use

Children's stress at times of separation can be due to any number of events in their lives. These events could include (but are not limited to) a new or unfamiliar child care provider, a new day care location, or simply the children being inexperienced in staying with someone other than the primary providers. It is also common for separation anxiety to come about for no apparent reason at all. Children may have simply had a dream that has made them feel anxious about being away from their primary caregivers.

Separation anxiety can occur at most any time during childhood. An event such as moving to a new place, the loss of a family member or pet, or the birth of a sibling can trigger feelings of insecurity that may make it difficult for children to separate from their primary caregivers. This activity involves prescribing a ritual that may help instill security for children experiencing separation anxiety. According to Giblin (1995), rituals help to facilitate "developmental transitions, maintenance of stability and continuity, healing processes, and connectedness. . . . Healthy ritual life can also serve to buffer families from toxic effects of stress and pathology" (p. 37). This activity provides a stable signal for children in what may be an unstable transition. It can be used to give children a sense that things are only changing in some areas of their lives, but they do not change the bond between the primary caregivers and the children.

Children are often exposed to words or events that they do not fully understand and can easily feel excluded from many things because of this lack of understanding. Allowing children to have information that they *do* understand, and having the children realize that not everyone is privy to this information (thus, the secrecy of the signal) will give children a special feeling of inclusiveness that, in turn, builds trust. Papp (2000) believes that repeating daily rituals helps family members demonstrate who they are to one another in reliable ways. Daily rituals also help establish a boundary between the family and the outside world.

Instructions

Before giving this assignment, the counselor should be familiar with the structure of the child's family. The counselor should be aware of the dynamics in the family and determine whether the child would be better helped by working on other areas (e.g., the marital relationship). The counselor should keep in mind that this is an activity that will require cooperation from all parties involved.

Set up a secret signal, such as a hand signal or handshake, between the child and the primary caregiver, something that no one else knows. This signal stands for a promise of the caregiver's return to the child. This signal could be the "thumbs up" sign, a pinkie lock, the American Sign Language's symbol for "I love you" (the thumb, forefinger, and pinkie finger up with the two middle fingers down), bumping elbows three times, or any other signal that a child can perform. With older children who are dealing with separation anxiety, these signals could become quite elaborate, such as complex handshakes or a particular exchange of dialogue that is known to only the child and the primary caregiver (e.g., the words to a certain song, a scene from a favorite movie, or an inside joke). Have the child and parent practice using the secret signal.

Once a signal has been mutually established, the caregiver should inform the child of the meaning of the signal. This signal is a sign that when the child and the primary caregiver are separated there is always this promise of the caregiver's return. The signal should act as the reminder of that promise. The child should know that each time the signal is performed it means that he or she should remember the promise.

The child should also be informed that if he or she starts to worry about the return of the caregiver sometime during the caregiver's absence, then the child can remind himself or herself of the promise by using the secret signal.

The caregiver should keep in mind that if it becomes necessary for someone else to pick up the child, this other person might be informed of the secret signal so that the child is assured of reuniting with his or her primary caregiver soon. After this it may become necessary to change the signal so that it is once again a secret.

It is not the specific signal that is important here. What is important is the development of a ritualistic pattern. According to Imber-Black and Roberts (1988), rituals, in and of themselves, can be beneficial in that they reinforce specific components essential to family health: membership, belief expression, identity, healing, and celebration.

Vignette

Calvin, a four-year-old boy, had been in the care of his mother all of his life. His father had worked outside of the home and his mother had taken time off from her career to raise Calvin. Calvin's mother had recently decided to go back to work outside of the home. She found child care that she felt would be a good environment for Calvin and decided that it would be best to get Calvin used to the child care setting gradually, leaving him there for only a couple of hours while she was shopping and running errands. Each time she left, Calvin was frantic. He cried hard enough to take his breath away, clung to his mother, and pleaded for her to take him with her.

Two hours passed and Calvin's mother returned only to find her son exhausted from all the crying. His eyes were still red and swollen, he would not eat or drink anything, he did not play with any of the other children, and he had stayed near the window waiting for his mother's return the entire time. She was heartbroken.

After five weeks of similar scenarios at the child care facility and trying many things up to this point to help Calvin, the child care director referred them for family therapy. The therapist explained Secret Signals to his mother. With coaching, she told Calvin how special he was to her and shared a story about a time when she was little and she and her sister used a secret hand signal. She told Calvin that only very special people could know about the hand signal. She showed Calvin how to position his hand with hers to create the secret signal. Calvin was thrilled to know this secret with his mother. Then Calvin's mother explained to Calvin that "whenever we make this handshake, it means that we are very special to each other and that we will be together again soon." For practice, Calvin's mother did the handshake with Calvin and then left the room. After only a minute or so she returned to the room where Calvin was and held out her hand to make the signal again. Calvin smiled and then he did the same for his mother, leaving the room and then returning again to do the handshake. It was at this point that Calvin's mother explained to him that when she dropped him off at day care he was to remember, by way of the hand signal, that he is very special to her and that they would be together again soon. "This handshake is our secret promise," she told Calvin.

Calvin was still reluctant to go to day care, but when his mother reached out her hand and they did their secret handshake he smiled and quietly said to his mother, "See you later." When his mother returned later that day, Calvin ran to her smiling and held out his hand to do the handshake.

Suggestions for Follow-Up

It may take a few tries for this activity to begin to work. Children may need time to develop trust in the secret signal.

It may be helpful periodically to change the secret signal to keep the meaning fresh in the child's mind. The caregiver should remind the child of what is meant by the signal or ask the child to tell him or her.

When the caregiver returns, he or she should show the secret signal to the child again as a reminder of the kept promise. This will help to reinforce trust and will be especially useful during the initial stages of implementing this activity.

Should the adult forget to give the secret signal the child could become quite upset. The adult may need to go back to where the child is or make a special phone call to the child. The adult should use care to assure the child that if he or she forgets to give the signal that the promise is still there. Time needs to be spent assuring the child that forgetting to make the signal is a real possibility and that if this occurs it in no way means that the primary caregiver will not return. If one or the other of the parties forgets to give the signal, then the child needs to know that there will be a phone call, or that the primary caregiver will give the signal to the child twice upon return. The child should be informed that this is a lasting promise and is always there whether they do the signal or not. The child should be assured that the signal is just a *reminder* of the promise, not the promise itself.

It may be helpful for the signal to be something that is easily explained over the phone. If the child care provider contacts the parent because the child is upset, then the parent can send a *message* to the child through the child care provider. The child care provider can tell the child, "I don't know what this means but your mom [or other caregiver] said I should show you this and tell you it is from her." The child care provider can show the signal to the child and the child will know what it means and that it is from his or her primary caregiver (the child knows this because the signal is a secret that only his or her primary caregiver knows).

This activity can also be used to prevent separation anxiety. If the caregiver knows in advance of an upcoming event that will be a transition in the child's life, the primary caregiver can start using the signal with the child, thus preparing the child for a new event that will require adjustment. The primary caregiver can explain the promise to the child and allow time for the child to understand the signal (by practicing during different occasions) so that when the transition is actually taking place the child will already be aware of what the signal means and know that the primary caregiver will return.

Contraindications for Use

Children must be old enough to perform and understand the meaning of the signals (e.g., the sign language symbol for "I love you").

Another area of concern may be that older children (perhaps ten and older) may not place as much importance on a signal as do younger children. This activity may not be as helpful for older children and alternative actions may need to be taken.

Alternate Method

Some children may need something more tangible as a reminder of the promise of their primary caregiver's return. The secret signal could be replaced with a secret coin or charm for the child to see as a reminder. It should be something small that can be kept in a pocket such as a note, coin, charm, or a small picture, so that the child is free to do other activities without the reminder being a burden for the child to carry around. Small items are also advantageous because the child can participate in other activities without a constant reminder of the absent caregiver. This allows the child to make new associations that are not connected to the primary caregiver (e.g., new friends at day care).

Vignette

Debbie, age seven, had recently moved with her family to a new town. The first day in her new school was frightening for her. Debbie pleaded with her mother to stay at school with her, but her mother explained that was not possible. Although Debbie reluctantly trudged off to school, she felt sick to her stomach and could not concentrate on anything the teacher was saying. When recess came Debbie went out with the other children, but she stood by the building alone and crying. Debbie was afraid that, because they were in a new town, her mother would not be able to find her school again when it was time to pick her up. Debbie felt lost and did not know what to do. Then, Debbie remembered the playing card in her pocket. It was the ace of hearts. Her mother had given this card to her that morning to remind her of how much they love each other. Debbie looked at the card and began to feel somewhat better. Debbie thought, "Even if Mom can't find my school I know she will ask for help to find it because she loves me."

Professional Readings or Resources

American Psychiatric Association (1994). *Diagnostic and statistical manual of mental disorders* (Fourth edition). Washington, DC: Author.

Giblin, P. (1995). Identity, change, and family rituals. *The Family Journal, 3,* 37-41.

Imber-Black, E. and Roberts, J. (1988). *Rituals in families and family therapy.* New York: W. W. Norton and Company.

Papalia, D. and Olds, S. (1995). *Human development* (Sixth edition). New York: McGraw-Hill, Inc.

Papp, P. (2000). *Couples on the fault line: New directions for therapists.* New York: Guilford Publications.

Bibliotherapy Sources for the Client

ERIC = http://ericps.ed.uiuc.edu
Internet Mental Health = http://www.mentalhealth.com
Northern County Psychiatric Associates = http://www.ncpamd.com
Parenthood.com = http://www.parenthood.com

What Is Separation Anxiety?

Stress at times of separation can be due to any number of events in a child's life. These events could include (but are not limited to) a new or unfamiliar child care provider, a new day care location, or simply the child being inexperienced in staying with someone other than the primary care provider(s). It is also common for separation anxiety to come about for no apparent reason at all. The child may have simply had a dream that has made him or her feel anxious about being away from his or her primary caregiver(s).

Separation anxiety can occur at most any time during childhood. An event such as moving to a new place, the loss of a family member or pet, or the birth of a sibling can trigger feelings of insecurity that may make it difficult for the child to separate from his or her primary caregiver(s).

Children experiencing separation anxiety often feel distress about actual or impending separation from their home or their caregivers. Younger children may display a general sense of worry or fear. Older children often display fears of specific dangers. These children may worry about their parents becoming very ill or being in an accident, and concerns about death or dying are common.

It is not uncommon for children with separation anxiety to cry when separating from their parents, have a need to know where their parents are or be in continual contact with their parents, excessively cling to their parents, or have difficulties at bedtime (e.g., wanting to sleep with parents or siblings, having nightmares, not being able to fall asleep). These children may also display physical symptoms such as headaches, stomachaches, or feeling faint when experiencing anxiety about separation.

Parents who have children with separation anxiety generally experience a variety of feelings ranging anywhere from concern to frustration. They may witness times when it seems that their children may be overcoming their anxiety, and then see the anxiety heightened again without any clear explanation. However, parents can show consistency in their approach to handling their children's more anxious and less anxious times.

What Can Parents or Other Caregivers Do?

The Secret Signal

Set up a secret signal between yourself and your child—something that no one else knows about. This signal is a symbol that represents your promise to always return to your child when there is a need to spend time apart (e.g., school, work, etc.). But remember, it's a secret! Only your child is special enough for this information.

Suggestions for signals:

1. *Hand signals or handshakes*

    - "Thumbs up"
    - Bumping elbows three times
    - A pinkie lock
    - "High fives" that miss on purpose
    - The American Sign Language symbol for "I love you" (the thumb, forefinger, and pinkie finger up with the two middle fingers down)
    - Be creative!

2. *Tangible items (reminders)*

- A charm
- Ribbon
- Picture
- Favorite marble
- A small item that will fit nicely in a child's pocket

3. *Dialogue*

- An inside joke
- A promise
- A made-up word
- A question and answer
- A line from a song or movie
- Anything encouraging, funny, sincere, or even silly

This signal should be mutually established between yourself and your child, and your child should be made aware of the meaning of the signal. When you and your child separate there is always this promise of your return. Inform your child that each time this signal is performed he or she should remember the promise.

It may take a few tries for this activity to begin to work. Spend time practicing your new handshake or other signal, and have your child tell you what it represents. Make sure your child knows that this symbol is only a reminder of your promise to return, not the promise itself. Then, if there comes a time when you forget to perform the secret signal it will help your child to know that you did not forget your promise also—"The promise is always there. We only use the signal as a reminder."

When you do return to your child (or when your child returns to you) show the secret signal to your child again as a reminder of the promise you kept. This will help to reinforce trust and will be especially useful during the initial stages of implementing this activity.

18

A Brief Assessment of Social Competency Skills in Preschool and Early Elementary School Children

Diane E. Karther
Jeanne Thibo Karns

Type of Contribution: Observation Checklist

Objective

The ability to interact effectively with others is critical for life success. Social competency skills often are underdeveloped in young children. This checklist will assist in identifying specific knowledge and social skills that need to be strengthened. It can be used as a basis to plan intervention strategies to increase children's abilities to understand others and successfully engage in group activities. The Play Interaction Checklist is an assessment tool to identify discrete social interaction behavior problems in children between the ages of three and six years.

Rationale

Children learn through play. Informal, child-initiated, child-directed play offers opportunities for learning about emotions and social relationships as well as about the physical world. Through the give-and-take of social play, children learn to read the social cues of others, to try on emotions, and to discover ways to express their own needs. Children need to learn the cultural-specific methods of negotiation and compromise. Play enables children to learn the wide variety of social skills needed for friendship formation (Frost, Wortham, and Reifel, 2001; Katz and McClellan, 1997).

> Children's growing capacities for communicating, carrying on a discussion, negotiating, taking turns, cooperating, initiating interaction, articulating their preferences and the reasons behind their actions, accepting compromises, and empathizing with others are all based on types of understanding, all of which play a part in effective social interaction. (Katz and McClellan, 1997, p. 5)

As with physical skills, social skills do not develop evenly. Some children may be advanced in using language while immature in self-regulation or taking the perspective of others. Identifying specific delayed or missing social interaction skills may lead to more effective interventions than individual therapy or adult-led, broad-based social behavior therapy. By using the developmentally appropriate context of play for both the assessment and the intervention, the child's social skills are more easily recognized and enhanced. For example, children with poor or lagging social skills may benefit from children's group interventions or filial play therapy (see Chapter 7).

Instructions

The Play Interaction Checklist can be used to assess the play social skills of children between the ages of three and six years. The tool can be used by a therapist, teacher, or parent. The observer should be near the group to see and hear interactions but distant enough not to impede the ongoing play. When approached by children, the observer should reply but not encourage continued conversation. The observer should not interfere with the ongoing play, including conflicts and other expressions of emotion.

The observer should observe the child on two or more occasions to obtain an accurate sample of the child's social skills. If the observer is unfamiliar with the normal progression of the development of social skills in young children, other children of the same age should also be observed for comparison. The observer should keep in mind that play involves a variety of social skills, and at any given time a normally developing child may be slightly ahead of or lagging behind age-mates in the development of specific skills.

The child should be observed playing in his or her familiar play group. Children will display more developmentally mature play skills when playing with familiar peers than when they are in the presence of strange children or adults. In addition, the play environment should be familiar and should include a wide variety of play materials that are appropriate to the age range of the children.

Suggestions for Follow-Up

The Play Interaction Checklist can be used to identify when a young child's social skills are lagging behind those of age-mates. In addition, the tool can identify frequent social behaviors that result in poor or inappropriate social interaction, as well as social skills that are completely missing from the child's social interaction repertoire.

In analysis of the Play Interaction Checklist, the following questions should be asked:

- Is this skill in the formative stage? Are other children the same age or younger more skilled in this behavior?
- Is this a skill that is typically lacking in children of that age? The behavior may be missing or underdeveloped because the skill normally does not develop until a later age. This recognition can correct unrealistic expectations for the child's behavior by the parent or teacher. Unrealistic expectations may be especially problematic for children physically large for their age. In addition, gifted and talented children often exhibit dissynchronous development, and their social skills sometimes lag behind their advanced cognitive or creative abilities. Because of their advanced cognitive abilities gifted children may not relate well to age-mates. In addition, parents and teachers often fail to recognize this phenomenon and may not take appropriate steps to help gifted children develop these vital skills.
- What skills are present in age-mates but lacking for the target child? A child may use actions rather than language, for example, taking toys rather than asking for a turn. Intervention then focuses on the specific skill missing rather than on social interaction as a whole.

Children's social skills can be altered in a variety of ways. Research in social learning theory has successfully demonstrated that young children can learn new social skills from models. The teacher or therapist can role-play social interactions with the child, practicing using specific words and phrases during play. The teacher or therapist together with the child can observe children playing, directing the child's attention to successful play interaction skills. Finally, the Play Interaction Checklist can be used to identify members of the child's play group who are skilled in the interaction behaviors problematic in the target child. The child can then be paired or grouped with these children during play to allow the child to learn from the others. The most appropriate play partners for a child learning a new social skill are usually slightly younger children who are well skilled in the social behavior lagging in development in the target child.

Contraindications for Use

This tool is appropriate for use with normally developing children who are experiencing difficulties in social interaction with same-age peers. It should not be used with children with diagnosed behavior problems. Caution should be used in interpretation of results of the checklist for children with physical developmental delays, motor problems, or sensory disorders, including delayed or missing language abilities.

Readings and Resources for Professionals

Fromberg, D. and Bergen, D. (Eds.) (1998). *Play from birth to twelve and beyond.* New York: Garland.

Katz, L.G. and McClellan, D.M. (1997). *Fostering children's social competence: The teacher's role.* Washington, DC: National Association for the Education of Young Children.

Kostelnik, M.J., Stein, L.C., Whiren, A.P., and Soderman, A.K. (1993). *Guiding children's social development.* Albany, NY: Delmar Publishing.

Roopnarine, J.L. and Honig, A.S. (1985). The unpopular child. *Young Children, 40*(6), 59-64.

Trawick-Smith, J. (1994). *Interaction in the classroom: Facilitating play in the early years.* New York: Merrill.

Readings and Resources for Parents

Crary, E. and Megale, M. (1996). *I can't wait.* Seattle: Parenting Press.

Crary, E. and Megale, M. (1996). *I want it.* Seattle: Parenting Press.

Crary, E. and Megale, M. (1996). *I want to play.* Seattle: Parenting Press.

Crary, E. and Whitney, J. (1992). *I'm mad.* Seattle: Parenting Press.

Crary, E. and Whitney, J. (1996). *I'm furious.* Seattle: Parenting Press.

Crary, E. and Whitney, J. (1996). *I'm scared.* Seattle: Parenting Press.

West, D.C. and Weston, M.S. (1996). *Playwise: 365 fun-filled activities for building character, conscience and emotional intelligence in children.* New York: Jeremy P. Tarcher/Putnam.

References

Frost, J.L., Wortham, S., and Reifel, S. (2001). *Play and child development.* Upper Saddle River, NJ: Merrill Prentice-Hall.

Katz, L.G. and McClellan, D.M. (1997). *Fostering children's social competence: The teacher's role.* Washington, DC: National Association for the Education of Young Children.

Play Interaction Checklist

Observer's Name: _____ Date of Observation: _____

Child's Name: _____ Age: _____

Location: _____

Play Materials Present: _____

Peers Present (indicate age and gender): _____

    Select a time to watch the child at play with others. Do not play with the child or make any comments as you complete the checklist. This checklist can be completed by a therapist, parent, or caretaker.

    Check the child's skills for each item. Some skills may be emerging; others may be well developed. If the child is not observed interacting in some areas, such as conflict, mark the item as "NA," not available. For each item rated, describe the play activity observed.

Scale: 3 = Most of the time

      2 = Some of the time

      1 = None of the time

Play Behavior   **Examples of Play**

1. Play social interaction:

_____ plays alone

_____ plays with one child

_____ plays with a small group of children

Remarks:

2. Usual time/persistence in specific play behavior

_____ less than 5 minutes

_____ 5-10 minutes

_____ over 10 minutes

Remarks:

3. Social attraction behavior

_____ continues play as another child enters the play space

_____ physically or verbally acknowledges another child's presence

_____ plays with other child by altering play theme or incorporating child into ongoing theme

Remarks:

4. Pretending

_____ pretends with objects

_____ pretends without objects

_____ pretends with realistic objects

_____ uses common objects in fantasy way

_____ uses only simple play themes

_____ uses elaborate play themes

_____ can change roles or elaborate role-play

_____ can play off others' role ideas

_____ suggests more elaborate role-play

Remarks:

5. Group play skills

_____ generates and expresses ideas for play accepted by others

_____ joins others' play themes

_____ negotiates change in play themes

_____ attempts to enter ongoing play

_____ uses force or other inappropriate way to enter play

_____ responds to nonverbal social cues

_____ responds to verbal social cues

_____ changes own behavior to coordinate with others

Remarks:

6. Use of language in play

_____ uses words in play

_____ responds and builds on others' words inside the play theme

_____ uses language instead of physical behavior to access toys or play situations

_____ uses words to alter the course of play

_____ uses words to maintain play theme despite bid for change by others

_____ uses words to reject social interaction overtures or requests by others

Remarks:

7. Conflict management

_____ will compromise

_____ uses negotiation skills

_____ yields objects for turn taking by others

_____ waits for turn to use objects in play by others

_____ uses actions only to obtain objects

_____ uses actions only to retain objects

Remarks:

8. Self-regulation

_____ expresses temper with inappropriate actions

_____ expresses temper with inappropriate language

_____ controls temper

_____ cries easily

_____ is easily distracted

_____ stays with actions or ideas

_____ uses words to label emotions

_____ demands immediate satisfaction of wants

Remarks:

_____

Source: Adapted and developed by Karther, D. and Karns, J. T. (2001). Portions of this checklist have been adapted from "The Play Checklist." In Heidemann, S. and Hewitt, D. (1992). *Pathways to play: Developing play skills in young children* (pp. 19-29). St. Paul, MN: Redleaf Press.

SAMPLE
Play Interaction Checklist

Observer's Name: _____ Jane Doe _____ Date of Observation: _____ 8/15/01 _____

Child's Name: _____ Robert _____ Age: _____ 4 yrs. _____

Location: _____ Center for Child Development _____

Play Materials Present: _Blocks, toy trains, marbles, computer_____

Peers Present (indicate age and gender): _10 children aged 3- 5 yrs., 4 boys and 6 girls_____

Select a time to watch the child at play with others. Do not play with the child or make any comments as you complete the checklist. This checklist can be completed by a therapist, parent, or caretaker.

Check the child's skills for each item. Some skills may be emerging; others may be well developed. If the child is not observed interacting in some areas, such as conflict, mark the item as "NA," not available. For each item rated, describe the play activity observed.

Scale: 3 = Most of the time

2 = Some of the time

1 = None of the time

Play Behavior	**Examples of Play**
1. Play social interaction:	Robert plays alone with the computer even when others come near to play with him. He will play with one other friend.
__2__ plays alone	
__2__ plays with one child	
__1__ plays with a small group of children	

Remarks:

Robert has one close friend in this group. He will play with this friend but does not seem interested in playing with any other children.

2. Usual time/persistence in specific play behavior	Robert stayed the longest at the computer. However, he was not playing the entire time. He did a lot of glancing around the room.
__1__ less than 5 minutes	
__3__ 5-10 minutes	
__1__ over 10 minutes	

Remarks:

Robert seems to lose focus after a while and is easily distracted during play.

3. Social attraction behavior

__3__ continues play as another child enters the play space	While playing with the computer, Robert con- tinued playing when Eric approached. With the trains, he looked up and smiled as Steve approached.
__2__ physically or verbally acknowledges another child's presence	
__1__ plays with other child by altering play theme or incorporating child into ongoing theme	

Remarks:

Robert does not readily change his play behaviors when others enter his play activity. He often notices and responds or addresses them when they approach, but he usually continues his original play activity.

4. Pretending

__3__	pretends with objects	Used toy trains for pretend train play. He moved them around and made train noises. I didn't see any elaborate play themes. Once he said, "There is a break in the rails" and crashed his train.
__2__	pretends without objects	
__3__	pretends with realistic objects	
__2__	uses common objects in fantasy way	
__3__	uses only simple play themes	
__1__	uses elaborate play themes	
__2__	can change roles or elaborate role-play	
__1__	can play off others' role ideas	
__1__	suggests more elaborate role-play	

Remarks:

I have observed Robert's play on eight occasions and have never seen him use objects for pretend that are not lifelike. Sometimes he will use no play objects but pretend he is flying or driving something.

5. Group play skills

__2__	generates and expresses ideas for play accepted by others	Robert barged into the middle of the block area and began to run his train in the middle of the blocks. The boys there complained and he stopped and watched play for a while and then left the area. He rejoined his friend and they began to play space monsters.
__2__	joins others' play themes	
__1__	negotiates change in play themes	
__1__	attempts to enter ongoing play	
__2__	uses force or other inappropriate way to enter play	
__2__	responds to nonverbal social cues	
__2__	responds to verbal social cues	
__2__	changes own behavior to coordinate with others	

Remarks:

Robert reads social cues and responds to his friend's behavior during play but does not use the same social skills with the other children. He does seem able to generate ideas when they play. He seems reluctant to do this with the other children.

6. Use of language in play

__3__	uses words in play	Robert talked with Steve the entire time they played. He responded appropriately to Steve's suggestions and contributed some ideas of his own.
__2__	responds and builds on others' words inside the play theme	
__2__	uses language instead of physical behavior to access toys or play situations	
__2__	uses words to alter the course of play	
__1__	uses words to maintain play theme despite bid for change by others	
__2__	uses words to reject social interaction overtures or requests by others	

Remarks:

Robert and Steve converse easily as they play. With other children, Robert tends to sit back and watch rather than try to contribute play suggestions. He does ask children to leave when they approach him and Steve at a play activity. He seems to want Steve all to himself as a playmate.

7. Conflict management

__1__	will compromise	When Steve had a different idea,
__1__	uses negotiation skills	Robert tried to talk him out of it. How-
__2__	yields objects for turn taking by others	ever, when a boy approached and
__2__	waits for turn to use objects in play by others	grabbed a train and wanted to play,
__2__	uses actions only to obtain objects	Robert just grabbed it back and told
__2__	uses actions only to retain objects	him to go away.

Remarks:

Robert does not seem to have the typical four-year-old ability to negotiate or compromise during play. His strategy usually is to grab toys and turn his back physically on the other children, with the exception of his friend, Steve. He exhibits better skills with Steve but still does not use the arguments and reasoning as other four-year-olds do.

8. Self-regulation

__2__	expresses temper with inappropriate actions	Robert and Steve had a disagree-
__1__	expresses temper with inappropriate language	ment over a different way to play.
__2__	controls temper	At first Robert wouldn't listen to
__1__	cries easily	Steve's arguments but finally gave
__3__	is easily distracted	in reluctantly. He almost lost his
__2__	stays with actions or ideas	temper but took a deep breath
__1__	uses words to label emotions	and agreed to go along with Steve's
__2__	demands immediate satisfaction of wants	idea.

Remarks:

Robert gets frustrated and angry more easily with the other children than with Steve. He tolerates more with Steve than with the others. When he wants something from the other children, he will tend to grab the toy rather than ask for it. He tends to be impulsive and want his way most of the time.

Source: Adapted and developed by Karther, D. and Karns, J. T. (2001). Portions of this checklist have been adapted from "The Play Checklist." In Heidemann, S. and Hewitt, D. (1992). *Pathways to play: Developing play skills in young children* (pp. 19-29). St. Paul, MN: Redleaf Press.

SECTION IV:
DEALING WITH ILLNESS, TRAUMA,
AND BEREAVEMENT

19

Children's Understanding of Death

Jeanne Thibo Karns

Type of Contribution: Handout

Objective

The death of a family member or friend is difficult for adults. For a child, the experience can be overwhelming, with effects lasting for the rest of the child's life. A child's comprehension of and reaction to death change with development: cognitive, social, spiritual, and moral. This handout will assist caring adults in supporting children and teens through the anticipated death of someone they love.

Rationale for Use

Death has become an isolating experience in much of modern society. Parents often are confused by a child's reaction to the death of a loved one. Because they are dealing with their own grief, parents often cannot see the effects on their children.

Parents may mistakenly assume that the child does not know about the approaching death of a sibling, parent, or grandparent. Yet even children as young as infants are affected by the emotions and altered schedules surrounding serious illness or trauma. In addition, parents often have many questions concerning the activities of children during these times. Should the child visit the dying person in the hospital? Should the child attend the funeral? This handout can guide parents and other caring adults in understanding children's behavior and making appropriate decisions for children during the grieving process.

Instructions

The handout can be supplied to parents and other caregivers of children experiencing anticipatory grief. Family counselors, support group leaders, school counselors, hospital- or hospice-based social workers may all have the task of guiding families through the experience of a family member's or friend's death.

Suggestions for Follow-Up

As anticipatory grieving progresses and the terminally ill or injured person comes closer to death, the parents or other caretakers of grieving children should be reminded to revisit these guidelines. Information that was not relevant early in the process, and therefore not remembered

An earlier version of this chapter appeared in the *Journal of Clinical Activities, Assignments & Handouts in Psychotherapy Practice* (2002), 2(1), 43-50.

or applied, may offer important guidance at a later time. Those caring for children should be reminded that grief is not a linear process, nor does it have a steady increase or decrease of intensity. In the midst of their own grief, the adults important to children need to remain open and supportive of their children. In addition, anticipatory grief does not replace or lessen grief of the bereaved. The family will still need to mourn the death of the family member or friend after the death has occurred.

Professional Readings and Resources

Broome, M.E. and Rollins, J.A. (1999). *Separation, Loss and Bereavement in Core Curriculum for the Nursing Care of Children and Their Families* (pp. 82-83). Pitman, NJ: Janetti Publications.

Child Life Council (1998). *Activity Recipe Book.* Rockville, MD: Child Life Council, Inc.

Doka, K.J. (1995). *Children Mourning, Mourning Children.* Washington, DC: Hospice Foundation of America.

Doka, K.J. (Ed.) (2000). *Living with Grief: Children, Adolescents and Loss.* Washington, DC: Foundation of America.

Goldman, A. (Ed.) (1994). *Care of the Dying Child.* Oxford: Oxford Medical Publications.

Sourkes, B.A. (1995). *Armsfuls of Time: The Psychological Experience of the Child with a Life-Threatening Illness.* Pittsburgh, PA: University of Pittsburgh Press.

Virshup, E. (1993). *California Art Therapy Trends.* Chicago, IL: Magnolia Street Publishers.

Bibliotherapy Sources for the Client

Emswiller, M.A. and Emswiller, J.P. (2000). *Guiding Your Child Through Grief.* New York: Bantam Books.

McCue, K. (1994). *How to Help Children Through a Parent's Serious Illness: Supportive, Practical Advice from a Leading Child Life Specialist.* New York: St. Martin's Press.

Anticipatory Grief: Helping Children Through the Process

The Three Components of Death

End of Physical Activity

The dead person no longer has any of the physical needs of the living person. A dead person does not eat, drink, or go to the bathroom. The dead person will not feel cold or lonely or be afraid of the dark inside of the casket when buried in the ground. Young children do not understand how a person cannot have these needs. A child may ask if the casket has a light on the inside, such as in a refrigerator. School-age children are usually old enough to understand these differences. A visit to a cemetery where an adult "talks" to a deceased person may confuse a child. The child should be assured that the body in the grave no longer hears, but according to the family's spiritual beliefs, the spirit of the person in heaven can hear.

Irreversibility

When a death occurs, the person does not return to the living. Death is permanent. Children often experience loved ones going to work at the beginning of the day and returning in the evening, going on vacations, or going to visit relatives. Children learn to expect people to return from these absences. Children may become confused if death is called "going away," "passed on," or "gone to be with the maker." A young child may repeatedly ask when a deceased parent will be home or ask to go to a favorite park and play when a deceased sibling returns. In addition, children see stories on TV about someone who was close to death due to trauma or illness being revived. These miracles of faith or technology may cause additional confusion when a loved person dies and is not revived by these methods. Only when children are older and approach adolescence can they really understand the irreversibility of death.

Universality

All living things eventually die. Older children and teens may be able to understand this concept in the abstract. They may understand the life cycle from science class. Yet, well into the teen years, children have difficulty applying the idea of death to themselves and people they love. When death does occur, children and teens struggling with this idea may worry that they will die of the illness that caused the death of a sibling, or that if one parent has died, the other parent may also soon die.

Helping the Child to Understand the Approaching Death

- Be honest with children and teens. If illness or trauma is expected to cause death, explain to the child that death is expected. Children usually understand more than adults may realize. Telling the child that everything will be all right when adults are clearly upset may cause children to become confused or distrustful. Giving honest information increases children's trust.
- Use the "D" words: die, dying, dead, and death. Children become confused with terms such as "gone away" or "gone to sleep." People often go away on trips but they come back. Calling death "sleep" may cause children to fear that they will die when they go to bed at night.
- Explain death and prepare children in a manner that is appropriate to their developmental level of understanding. Help them *gradually* to understand and accept that their family member is not getting better, despite all the medicine, and that the person will eventually die.
  Example 1: "Mom is very sick, but she has great doctors who are doing everything they can to make her better. We hope the medicine works."
  Example 2: (Mom isn't responding well.) "The medicine doesn't seem to be working, and Mom is getting sicker. The doctors are trying a new medicine, and we hope this will help Mom."
  Example 3: "None of the medicines are helping Mom, and she is getting sicker. We don't know how much more the doctors can do to help Mom. She may not get better. She may even die."
  Example 4: "There is nothing more the doctors can do to try to help Mom get well. There are no more medicines to try to help her get better; her body is just too sick to live much longer. But the doctors do have medicine to stop Mom's pain."
  These messages need to be given often as the child gradually understands the extent and seriousness of the illness. Clear messages prepare the child for the dying experience, facilitate anticipatory grieving, and offer the child a chance to say goodbye.

- Children of all ages will have many questions. They should be encouraged to ask questions about any issue. The questions may be repeated several times. As children begin to understand the situation, they may repeat questions to confirm their new knowledge. Because the approaching death of a loved one is a new experience, children may repeat questions to the same person or different people to see if the answers also change throughout this new experience. Explore children's questions with them. Asking the child "What do you think?" enables an adult to identify misconceptions.
- Children commonly do not ask questions even though they are uncertain of what is happening. Caring adults may need to begin the conversation and volunteer discussion on relevant issues. For example, "When someone is very sick, people often wonder if that person is in pain. Can we talk about the medicine your mother is getting?" or "When teens know a parent is going to die, the teens often wonder what will happen to them—Who will take care of them? Where will they live? Will they need to change schools? Can we talk about these issues now?"
- Children may have difficulty talking about feelings. They may not have the vocabulary to label what they are experiencing. Adults need to label feelings such as confusion, frustration, sadness, and anger. Adults should acknowledge their own feelings as well as those of children. This gives children permission to experience these emotions by reassuring them that all people sometimes feel this way. Reinforce the idea that when some people are sad, they may cry. Crying is a normal way of expressing and dealing with sadness and grief.
- Role model stress reduction activities for children, both active and passive, should be included. Walking along a lake, sitting quietly before a fireplace, jogging, or playing basketball can be effective. Children as young as three can be taught to use guided relaxation and imagery for stress reduction (see "Soaring Above Stress," Chapter 4). Some children are very good at creating their own pleasant dreams. Try talking quietly with a child at bedtime about favorite experiences from the past.
- Be alert for children's feelings of guilt. Because children can understand events from only their own point of view, through events they have already experienced, children may feel guilty. Children commonly believe that something they did has caused the illness or trauma. A fight with a sibling just prior to the diagnosis of cancer can be viewed by the child as related. They may see the approaching death as a punishment for actual or perceived misbehavior. In addition, children may believe that if they promise to be good, the death will not occur. This magical wishing is most frequent during early childhood but can also be seen throughout the childhood and teen years. Children need to be reassured *repeatedly* that nothing they did or will do is the cause of the illness or trauma.
- Most religions and spiritual beliefs contain descriptions of what happens to the soul or spirit after death. Many of these beliefs include physical descriptions of the afterlife. These details may already be familiar to the child. Words such as "heaven" give the child a picture of the loved one after death. Children may speak of heaven as being far away, perhaps in outer space or on the other side of Mars. Spiritual beliefs may also foster guilt, confusion, or anger at God in children if they are asked to pray for someone to get well and the person later dies. Children may become angry with adults who are praying for a recovery if the child views the death as a result of the adult not praying hard enough.
- Children learn through play. During pretend play, the children may act out medical scenes, including cardiopulmonary resuscitation (CPR) on a doll, or surgery on a stuffed animal. A child may play "dead baby" over and over when a newborn sibling dies. A medical play kit can help children work on the ideas of terminal illness and death. Play may become violent with trauma or gunshots. A trusted adult can pretend play with the child. By following the child's lead in the play, the adult can discover the questions or misinformation of the child. A caring adult play partner can offer support if the emotions impacting the child and expressed through play become overwhelming to the child.
- As part of play, children may want to have funerals for "small deaths," such as those of a pet or even a dead bird found in the park. These funerals give the child an opportunity to "try on" the emotions surrounding death.
- Read stories to children about separation and death. Share information with teens about books with appropriate themes. Get the books and place them in an accessible place for the teens to read when they feel ready. Videos or movies and familiar children's shows can also be used to help children explore the issues of death. Trusted adults need to watch the videos *with* children and teens so that conversation can naturally follow the issues on the videos. Stories and videos can also act as a catharsis, breaking through the image of detachment and maturity created by teens to hide their feelings of grief.

- School-age children and teens are grounded in physical actions and objects. They may ask for gruesome details concerning the illness or death. They may become more focused on violence on TV and in video games. Explain the cause of the approaching death directly and simply. The imagination of the child is often more scary than reality. If a pet or other animal such as a bird dies, the child may want to dig up the buried animal to learn what happens to the body after death.
- Anger is a normal emotion for grieving children, just as it is for adults. The child may become angry with the dying parent or sibling. If the person would not die, then the child would not need to experience the grief. The child may also feel angry with God for causing or not stopping the death. Telling the child that "God wanted Grandma to come to heaven" can be very confusing, making heaven seem like a punishment, or making the child wonder why God is so selfish as to take away someone that he or she loves and needs. Anger is often followed by guilt. Provide safe outlets for the child's anger, such as pounding on pillows, throwing clay at a target, tearing apart phone books, stomping on bubble wrap, or hammering nails into boards or golf tees into thick styrofoam. *Be aware that teens may engage in reckless behavior,* such as driving too fast, as a vent for their anger. Help children to understand that it is perfectly acceptable to feel anger; adults feel anger too. The strength of anger can seem overpowering to an older child or teen. Adults need to stress that teens acting violently, hurting themselves or others, will not change the fact that a loved person is dying.
- Try to keep the child's regular schedule as consistent as possible. Children find assurance in the structure of their normal day-to-day activities. They need the outlet of being with their friends both as an assurance that their lives will continue as well as offering them a break from the emotions of the grieving adults.
- Be sure adults are available to listen to the child and share the grief. Children also need physical comforting. *Holding the child close and crying and talking together can be comforting, as long as the child isn't overwhelmed by the parent's grief.* But a parent dealing with the approaching death of a spouse, parent, or child may not have the physical or emotional energy needed to help the child. An aunt, grandparent, neighbor, or other loved and trusted adult should be asked to fill the role of confidant and supporter. Without this, children will feel abandoned and will not grieve well.
- Children and teens may regress in their behaviors, acting less mature than during nonstressful times. They may cling, have temper tantrums, or be disobedient or aggressive. This is a normal reaction to their own grief and the stress caused by seeing the grief of their parents or other loved ones. Grieving parents may not be able to perceive this and may react adversely to the children's behaviors. Other caring adults can help the children deal with the high intensity of these emotions by providing extra hugs and attention.
- Many children and teens become less mature in their activities, and the overwhelming emotions hinder their abilities to understand the situation. A child may easily forget to feed the dog or change the cat's litter box. A teen who could normally care for younger siblings, cook, or do laundry may not be able to carry on these responsibilities during grief. Guard against adults placing older children or teens in adult roles. *Do not allow children to place themselves in these roles.* A teenage boy with a dying father needs to be allowed to remain the father's child and not placed into the role of "the man of the family." A teenage girl should remain a daughter and not the substitute mother for younger siblings. Teens do not know how to "be strong and take care of" parents. The implication that they should take on this role may be overwhelming to them.
- Older children and teens may try to hide their grief by acting detached and grown-up. Teens may engage in reckless behaviors as a way of displacing anger, sadness, or grief. Teens may turn to sexual activities for physical and emotional comfort, or to alcohol or drugs to numb their pain, especially when they feel lonely and cut off from a parent due to the parent's own grief. Adults need to anticipate these possible behaviors and guide the teens into more positive outlets for their grief. Peer support groups should be made available to children and teens both during anticipatory grief and after the death of a loved one has occurred.
- Notify the important people in the child's regular environment. They can then be prepared to answer questions, understand changes in behaviors, and offer an ear for listening or a shoulder to cry upon. A variety of people should be contacted. Teachers in child care centers and elementary schools, guidance counselors at high schools, coaches of sport teams, and scout leaders are obvious possible choices. A child may also be close to gymnastic or music teachers, the youth leader at church, or the parents of friends of the child. *Discuss this with children first, being sensitive to what information they do or don't want shared with whom, and why.*

Some children are sensitive about how their peers will react, and their concerns need to be respected and fully explored before contacting the school.

Helping the Child to Say Goodbye

- Maintain the familiar activities of the child with the dying person. This can be reading stories, playing cards, or watching a favorite video.
- If the dying person has changed in appearance as a result of trauma or illness, prepare the child for these changes. Identity and appearance are the same to the young child, who may become confused if physical changes are great. A child may deny that the person in the hospital bed is her brother if trauma resulted in damage to the brother's face. Describe to the child any medical equipment, such as monitors, intravenous (IV) or other tubes *before* the child visits. An instant picture can help the child know what to expect so that the experience is not overwhelming. The nurse or child life specialist at a hospital is experienced in explaining these issues to children and can help prepare the child.
- Keep the child in contact with the dying person for as long as possible. The visits need to be frequent rather than long, especially if the dying person is easily fatigued.
- Give the child a job to do during the visits. Greeting cards can be arranged on a bulletin board. A teenager can brush Grandma's hair or help Grandpa shave. The job will help the child to feel needed rather than in the way.
- Between visits or if the child is unable or unwilling to visit, help the child to find other ways to maintain contact. Phone calls can be timed for when the dying person is most alert. The child can tape the person's favorite television shows. Photos can be taken of the child's activities, such as sports and club activities, to be sent to the dying person. If possible have the child write about the events in the photos or audiotape the description.
- As death approaches, help the child find outlets for the increasing grief. Drawing pictures or writing poems or goodbye letters for the dying person gives the child a concrete role. These activities also help the child express feelings that may be difficult to put into words.
- Do not force the child to visit the dying person. The child may fear the unknown. Teens may be startled by the strength of their own emotions and may fear crying in front of other adults. Keep the option of a visit available. The child may change his or her mind. Reassure the child that the visit can end as soon as the child is ready. Having an assigned task, such as picking a flower from the backyard or buying the dying person's favorite candy, may make the approaching visit less scary.
- As death approaches, explain what is happening to the dying person. If the dying person can no longer respond by voice or movement, explain that the person probably still can hear what is said and would recognize the child's familiar voice. Explain that death is usually a quiet process, unlike the fictional deaths often seen on TV. Reassure the child that medicine can keep the dying person from feeling pain.
- If the death is imminent and the family is present at the hospice or hospital, the child should be told what is happening. As the dying process takes place, children may become distressed by the emotions of their parents or other adults. Have a trusted adult relative or friend stay with the young and school-age children in another room. Teens may choose to stay at the bedside with parents or may decide to wait elsewhere. They should be given the option but will need the support of caring adults whatever their choice.
- If the death occurs at home and is anticipated, the child should be supported the same as a planned death at a hospital or hospice. If the death occurs suddenly, the child should be told immediately so that he or she does not become confused about a possible rescue or revival. All family members should know whom to call when the death occurs. Children who have had CPR or first-aid training may want to call 911. A caring adult should explain that the death was anticipated and there is nothing a rescue crew can do. The child should be given the opportunity to see and touch the dead person before the body is removed from the home. As earlier, the child should not be forced into these activities. Seeing, touching, and saying goodbye should be options made available, with the clear understanding that the child can change his or her mind and participate later.

Helping the Child During the Funeral

- Between the time of death and the funeral, try to keep the child's mealtimes, nap times, and bedtimes as close to regular as possible. Emotional stress, disruption of schedules, and too many unfamiliar visitors may keep children from eating and sleeping well. Offer nutritious snacks and rest times frequently throughout the day.

- If possible, the children should be at home in their own beds and with familiar toys. Nighttime can be especially difficult, and younger children may want and temporarily need the physical reassurance of sleeping with a parent, at least until they fall asleep. Children should not be asked to give up their beds to visiting relatives. If the family is staying at another house or motel, the children should have a bag of familiar toys and a favorite stuffed animal or doll.
- Plan for active periods during the immediate days after the death when regular school and playtimes may be disrupted. Swimming at the motel pool, playing basketball in the driveway, or other physical activities will help to release pent-up energy and vent feelings of emotional discomfort.
- Older children and teens can be given a role in planning the memorial service. They can help decide which tie the deceased grandfather should wear or what color earrings for a deceased sister. Also, older children and teens can aid in selecting the music, scripture readings, or poetry.
- Prior to visiting hours or the funeral, the child should be given the opportunity to view the body of the dead person in the open casket. A supportive adult should explain to the children how the person will look and that the skin of the person will feel dry and cool. A child may want to view the casket from a distance before approaching. A child should not be forced to view the body, touch the body, or kiss the deceased goodbye. However, they should be reassured that these actions are allowed if wanted.
- If the casket is closed or the body cremated, the child should be given an opportunity to see the casket or urn prior to the arrival of other mourners. Some children may express disbelief that the deceased body is present if it cannot be seen. They should be reassured that the body is present, but the time for looking at the body has passed.
- Older children and teens may ask questions about the embalming or cremation process. These questions should be answered simply by a caring adult or the funeral director. Reassure children that after death the body cannot feel any pain.
- Prepare children for behaviors they may see during the visiting hours or funeral service. Children may not have previously seen adults, especially men, crying. As adults share memories of the deceased, they may smile and laugh. With the heightened emotions, old grudges may result in yelling and angry behaviors. Children and teens may become confused, upset, or embarrassed by the behaviors of adults.
- Adults may wonder if children should attend visiting hours and funerals. Most children feel a need to be close to parents. They may also have curiosity about what happens during these rituals. Children not taken to visiting hours or funerals may later feel that they did not have an opportunity to say goodbye to the deceased. Funeral homes usually have a secluded family area where children can play, watch TV, or do other activities. Children should be told that they can come and go from this area, as they want. They should not be required to sit beside grieving parents as the parents talk with other adults. Again, it is important to have a caring adult be with the child during the visiting hours and the funeral. This can be a relative, family friend, or a familiar, well-liked baby-sitter. Each child should have a separate support person since not all children in the family may want to participate in the activities at the same time. A caring and known adult can also take the child home, to a park, or to a friend's home after the child's visit to the funeral home.
- A variety of "goodbye" activities should be made available to the child between the death and the funeral. Art supplies will help keep the child occupied as well as give the child the opportunity to create a last picture for the deceased. Older children and teens can write letters. An adult can write a message dictated by a young child. The pictures and letters can be placed in the casket before burial or cremation or tied to environmentally safe balloons and released. Older children and teens can plan and carry out remembrance activities, such as planting a new tree on the grounds of the school the deceased sibling attended.

20

Tips for Parents When There Is Illness in the Family

Nancee Biank
Catherine Ford Sori

Type of Contribution: Handout

Objective

This handout provides much useful information for parents on issues that might arise for children or teens when there is a serious illness in the family, such as cancer. It can be used as a psychoeducational handout and can be incorporated into family sessions and parent groups. These tips are useful in all phases of the therapy process, from goal setting to monitoring children's and parents' progress and assessing outcome. At the end of therapy this handout provides parents with a concrete summary of critical points that may arise during a chronic, serious illness.

Rationale

Therapists need to be aware of the serious impact an illness or disability can have on children and family members, and should always assess for the presence of an illness when a child or family begins therapy. It is crucial to be aware that an illness may be invisible or not openly discussed but often may be an important underlying factor in the child's or parent's presenting problem. Parents often don't recognize how an illness is affecting them or their children. For example, one mother presented with severe depression that was affecting all areas of her functioning. She and her husband attributed this to her lack of a social life. Although her husband appeared healthy, the therapist learned that he had been out of work for eight months, after he had broken both arms in a semitrailer accident. During that time his young wife had to do everything for him, including caring for all his bodily functions. Their sex life had disappeared, and the wife's mother had taken over the daily care of their child, who had become clingy and sad and had developed sleep problems. The husband had stopped attending rehab and spent most of his days watching game shows or playing video games. He rarely held their daughter due to the lingering pain in his joints. The therapist was alert to the impact these events had on all family members. She helped the parents begin to discuss all the implications of these changes in their lives, and then to be aware of how their child was being affected, and how they might help her.

The written self-report of several hundred children (Biank and Sori, in progress) indicates that children often feel abandoned by both of their parents when the family is experiencing a serious illness. Children are greatly affected by the changes that occur in these families. The well spouse directs his or her attention toward the decisions that need to be made by the person with the illness and is often preoccupied with caregiving and treatment demands while simultaneously trying to maintain the household and support family members. The person who is ill is directing all of his or her attention to decision making and treatment. In a single-parent family this problem is even more exacerbated, as the ill parent has to assume both roles and may lack

150

sufficient outside support. Parents are less available in many ways, including overseeing home-work, providing transportation to after-school activities, and hosting birthday parties, sleep-overs, or holiday celebrations. Both children and adolescents will be called upon to perform ad-ditional responsibilities within the family, which may include more chores, caring for younger siblings, and helping to care for the ill parent. For adolescents this can be an especially difficult time because they are in the developmental stage of separating and individuating, yet they are being pulled back into the family at a time when they should be gaining more autonomy and in-dependence.

The experiences of patients and family members can be very different at different stages of an illness (Rolland, 1994; Loscalzo and Brintzenhofeszoc, 1998). Rolland (1994) discusses the tasks of families during different stages of an illness. For example, when a family member is first diagnosed and treatment is initiated, families must quickly gather their resources and reor-ganize to collect crucial information and make rapid decisions about treatment. Roles and re-sponsibilities shift and are redistributed as the family organizes around the illness, and families who are close and can pull together often have an easier time than those whose members are less cohesive or more independent. However, when an ill parent or child enters a chronic phase where treatment may be long and drawn out, families must again organize for the "long haul." This requires flexibility to ensure that all family members have their own individual develop-mental needs met, while ensuring that the sick family member is cared for. A relapse or recur-rence of a serious illness such as cancer or multiple sclerosis can often be much more devastat-ing than an original diagnosis. Families can rapidly lose hope or may frantically search for alternative treatments or "miracle cures." They must quickly muster their sagging resources and once again reorganize to gather additional information and initiate new treatments, often with a terrible sense of urgency. This may be an especially difficult time for young children who are not told much about what is happening, yet sense the roller coaster of emotions their parents are experiencing. Adolescents who were preparing to leave home for college may change their plans, fearful of not being there if something happens, or feeling guilty about not being there to support other family members. Parents often are too overwhelmed, preoccupied, or just unin-formed about the serious and far-reaching implications of these events for their children.

A serious illness can occupy 50 percent or more of a young child's life. In one family with an eleven-year-old boy, the mother had been diagnosed with two different primary cancers: cervical cancer when he was two, and breast cancer when he was six. Although his mother was doing well, he could not remember a time when cancer was not a serious threat to his family, or when family emotions and activities weren't related to treatment appointments, side effects, or the latest test results.

Children want and need emotional support as well as objective information about parental ill-ness. Without accurate information, children will fill in the blanks and create a picture that often is much worse than reality. They often cannot talk to either their parents or their peers, who don't understand or can't relate to their unique experiences. This can leave children feeling fear-ful and alone, with no one to turn to for support or to answer their many questions (see Biank and Sori, in progress). Studies indicate that children's or adolescents' behavior, self-esteem, and peer experiences may be negatively affected when a parent has cancer (Lewis, 1996). Daughters of breast cancer patients have been found also to be at increased risk for experiencing emotional problems, such as dysphoria (Wellisch, Hoffman, and Gritz, 1996). All of this can impact nor-mal emotional and social development. The goal of this handout is to keep children and adoles-cents on track developmentally by helping parents share vital information, answer questions, discuss feelings and changes in the patient and family, and support their children in ways that fit the children's developmental needs. The importance of discussing these issues and tips within the family is paramount.

Instructions

The therapist should be aware of this information and be prepared to incorporate it into individual, family, and group work. It is imperative to assess families for chronic or serious illnesses or disabilities, even when these are not the presenting problem. This handout can serve as a guide for therapists to determine if children's informational and emotional needs are being met by parents in an age-appropriate manner. *Therapists should stress to parents that children usually do not ask questions or let their parents know how they are being affected.* This commonly occurs because children sense their parents don't want (or don't know how) to discuss the illness, or because children fear that sharing their worries or sadness will overtax their already stressed parents, making them even less available.

As therapy progresses and while supporting parents, therapists can introduce parents to common experiences and needs of children concerning the illness. The therapist can facilitate communication between parents and their children or adolescents to dispel myths and provide objective information about the illness. Children can be encouraged to express their fears and ask questions, while parents can be helped to support and comfort their children, and to provide age-appropriate answers to their questions. Facts can and should be shared objectively, and children should be given honest information that balances reality and hope. (If there is no longer hope for recovery, children can be given reassurance that they will always be loved and cared for, hope for quality time with parents, and hope that their lives will be happy in the future.) Parents can encourage children to play, spend time with friends, and maintain their lives as normally as possible.

If parents are too overwhelmed, the therapist can act as a holding environment and provide some of the emotional support and information to the children. At the same time, therapists can also support the parents while gradually they assume this role.

Suggestions for Follow-Up

This handout can pave the way for therapists to help facilitate more open communication among family members to share their individual experiences of how illness has impacted their lives, to highlight strengths and evidences of resiliency, and to share hopes and dreams for their future lives. This open climate can help family members decide how to work together to "put the illness in its place," and to discover how to carve out more time for enjoyable activities together (see McDaniel, Hepworth, and Doherty, 1993; Jacobs, 1993).

A reoccurrence of the illness may be an opportune time to reintroduce these guidelines or to reinforce and extend previous therapeutic work. This handout can also be used in follow-up to check for the maintenance of therapeutic gains.

Contraindications

Therapists need to be sensitive to parents' emotional states and careful to ensure that parents are stable enough to hear how the illness may be affecting their children. Parents may themselves be overwhelmed and, upon hearing how difficult this experience is for children, may feel they have failed them, may fear that they have been bad parents, or may even deny that their children are impacted at all by the illness. *Care and sensitivity must be used in sharing this information with parents, and this should be done only when the therapist believes they are ready to hear it and will be available to help and support the children.*

Therapists should always be sensitive to clients who may be illiterate or have a serious reading disability. In such cases, the therapist could read and tape-record these tips so they can be reviewed outside of sessions.

References and Professional Resources

Baider, L., Cooper, C. L., and De-Nour, A. T. (1996). *Cancer and the family*. New York: John Wiley and Sons Ltd.

Biank, N. and Sori, C. (in progress). *Tell them that we know . . . children's responses to illness and loss*.

Brown, M. (1996). Families on the tightrope: Maintaining hope while facing the possibility of death. *Cope, 6,* 17-19.

Holland, J. C. (Ed.) (1998). *Psycho-oncology*. New York: Oxford University Press.

Jacobs, J. (1993). Families under siege. *Family Therapy Networker, 17*(1), 14-15.

Jacobs, J., Ostroff, J., and Steinglass, P. (1998). Family therapy: A systems approach to cancer care. In J. Holland (Ed.), *Psycho-oncology* (pp. 994-1003). New York: Oxford University Press.

Kofron, E. E. (1993). The language of cancer. *Family Therapy Networker, 17*(1), 34-43.

Lederberg, M. S. (1998). The family of the cancer patient. In J. Holland (Ed.), *Psycho-oncology* (pp. 981-993). New York: Oxford University Press.

Lewis, F. M. (1996). The impact of breast cancer on the family: Lessons learned from the children and adolescents. In L. Baider, C. L. Cooper, and A. Kaplan De-Nour (Eds.), *Cancer and the family* (pp. 271-287). New York: John Wiley and Sons Ltd.

Loscalzo, M. and Brintzenhofeszoc, K. (1998). Brief crisis counseling. In J. Holland (Ed.), *Psycho-oncology* (pp. 662-675). New York: Oxford University Press.

McDaniel, S. H., Hepworth, J., and Doherty, W. J. (1992). *Medical family therapy: A biopsychosocial approach to families with health problems*. New York: Basic Books.

McDaniel, S. H., Hepworth, J., and Doherty, W. J. (1993). A new prescription for family health care. *Family Therapy Networker, 17*(1), 19-29, 62-63.

Roberts, J. (2000). "Sustaining families through illness." Presentation at national conference of the American Association for Marriage and Family Therapy. Denver, CO. October.

Rolland, J. (1994). *Families, illness, and disability: An integrative treatment model*. New York: Basic Books.

Walsh, F. (1998). *Strengthening family resilience*. New York: Guilford Publications.

Wellisch, D. K., Hoffman, A., and Gritz, E. (1996). Psychological concerns and care of daughters of breast cancer patients. In L. Baider, C. L. Cooper, and A. Kaplan De-Nour (Eds.), *Cancer and the family* (pp. 289-303). New York: John Wiley and Sons Ltd.

Tips for Parents
When There Is Illness in the Family

When a parent is diagnosed with a serious illness, children and adolescents face significant stress. They may find it difficult to deal with all the necessary changes in the family and sometimes become isolated from their peers because they feel different or sense that their friends can't relate to their experiences. Children often lack the skills needed to cope with the changes that occur in their families. Some experience feelings of anxiety and sadness, yet many are reluctant to share their worries with parents. Parents, too, often struggle with how to talk to their children, and how to help them cope. The following is an overview of some common reactions of children and teens when there is a serious illness in the family, and some ideas for parents to consider in helping their children cope.

When a Parent Is Ill Children Commonly:

- Wish their family could go back to how it was before the illness, or wish they could be like other families
- May feel neither parent is available, when one is ill and the other needs to assume additional responsibilities
- Worry about their parents dying
- Miss active fun times and/or special time alone with each parent
- Feel that they've lost some of the innocence and security of childhood
- May want to help out, but sometimes feel overburdened
- May not want to be with their friends as much, because they want to stay home with their parent
- May have trouble concentrating in school because they are worried about their parent

When a Parent Is Ill Teens Commonly:

- Feel drawn back into the family at a time when developmentally they should be separating and becoming more autonomous
- Distance from friends who they feel aren't interested, or who have insignificant concerns compared to what they are experiencing
- Feel angry at how the illness has changed their lives ("This isn't fair!")
- Worry about their parents dying and that their life will change forever
- Worry more about the future
- Long for their lives to be "normal"
- Often feel angry, and don't know how to handle it; think, "I can't talk to Mom or Dad, I can't tell my friends, and I feel guilty that I'm so angry!"
- Are torn because they want to help care for their parent, but part of them wants to ignore it all

Tips for Parents:

- Children want and need to know what's going on, but seldom ask their parents questions. They will often imagine things are much worse than they are.
- Talk to your children and keep them up to date on what is going on. Give them factual information in language that is appropriate for their age. Knowing they can trust you to keep them informed helps them relax and let go of worry.
- Keep your explanations simple, and encourage children to come to you with questions at any time.
- Children will respond to how you present the information, so be both matter-of-fact and as hopeful as possible. Emphasize the strengths and resiliency in your family.

- Reassure kids often, but do not make promises about your future health that you cannot keep. Emphasize that you have a great doctor and are doing many things to get better.
- Hug your children often.
- Laughter truly is the best medicine—everyone needs a daily dose!
- Children often have many misconceptions about illness that they don't express. It is vital to assure your children:
  — Your illness is not contagious.
  — They did not cause the illness.
  — They won't upset you more by telling you their concerns.
  — They can't "make it go away" by being good, getting all A's, etc.
  — It isn't their job to worry about you or make you happy—their job is to do well in school and come to you with their concerns.
  — It's okay to be a normal kid—to play, have both good and bad feelings, have friends, etc.
  — Although this is difficult for you, you are okay emotionally.
- Let your kids know when you need extra help, and tell them often (and with a hug) how much you appreciate them.
- Hold family meetings to discuss changes in the family. Allow kids to express their feelings, and validate them. Give kids choices whenever possible. This helps them have a sense of control over events at a time when their lives may feel out of control.
- If a parent is hospitalized, encourage frequent visits if the child is comfortable with this and the parent is in a good place. Be sure to prepare the child in advance for what to expect.
- Listen to your children, to their needs, their hopes, and their disappointments. Help them put their feelings into words, and tell them it is good to talk about how they feel. (What they can talk out, they won't have to act out.) Be sure to separate your own emotions from your children's.
- Protect pockets of normalcy in your family life whenever possible. This includes meals, special times together, holidays, etc. These are important to kids.
- Keep as much sameness at home as possible. Maintain as many routines as possible.
- Expect children to regress (e.g., bed wetting, thumb sucking) in times of stress.
- Be consistent with enforcing rules—this helps kids of all ages feel more secure!
- Prepare kids for potential problems or emergencies.
- Encourage and model good coping through journaling, exercise, good nutrition, and talking.

Additional Tips for Teens:

- Try not to give too many additional responsibilities and to maintain reasonable house rules.
- Schedule respite time for teens—encourage them to spend regular time with friends.
- Make it explicit when they need to be there to help, and when they can be off pursuing their own interests.
- Balance your need for them to help out with their developmental needs to pursue their education and other interests.
- Encourage them to find an appropriate adult to talk to, if needed (e.g., school counselor).

Finally:

On bad days, help kids to understand "it's the illness talking," and don't be afraid to say, "I'm sorry." Kids will feel respected and will respect you for it. Propose to "put the illness in its place" by maintaining as much normalcy as possible, and finding ways to ensure the children's individual needs are met. Balance the reality of your situation with hopefulness that there is still much beauty and joy for you and your children to experience in life. Above all, help your children to see the ways that all of you have found strength in the face of adversity (e.g., "We really appreciate one another more," and "Even though it's been hard, we're closer as a family"). Although you can't protect them from all the difficulties they'll encounter in life, you can help them grow through this experience by learning good coping skills that will benefit them for the rest of their lives.

Books for Parents

How to Help Children Through a Parent's Serious Illness: Supportive, Practical Advice from a Leading Child Life Specialist, by Kathleen McCue, MA, CCLS, with Ron Bonn (New York: St. Martin's Press, 1994).

When a Parent Has Cancer: A Guide to Caring for Your Children, by Wendy Schlessel Harpham, MD (New York: HarperCollins, 1997) (includes children's booklet *Becky and the Worry Cup*).

Books for Children

Alexander and the Terrible, Horrible, No-Good Very Bad Day, by Judith Viost (New York: Macmillan Children's Book Group, 1972).

The Jester Has Lost His Jingle, by David Saltzman (Palos Verdes Estates, CA: The Jester Co., Inc., 1995).

The Little Engine That Could, by Watty Piper (New York: Platt and Nunk, Publishers, a division of Grosset and Dunlap, 1930/1976).

Mommy's in the Hospital Again, by Carolyn Stearns Parkinson (Folsom, CA: Solace Publishing, Inc., 1994).

When a Parent Is Very Sick, by Eda LeShan (Boston: The Atlantic Monthly Press, 1986).

Why Me? Coping with Family Illness, by Anna Kosof (New York: Watts, 1986).

21

Scrapbooking During Traumatic and Transitional Events

Jeanne Thibo Karns

Type of Contribution: Activity, Handout

Objective

Scrapbooks are used in this activity to promote self-healing, self-expression, understanding, and mastery of a hospitalization, traumatic event, or other transitional process (such as family dissolution, relocation, or addition of a stepparent to a child's family). This intervention is appropriate for middle childhood through adulthood.

Rationale for Use

Scrapbooking is a popular hobby used to record a variety of positive events, such as senior year in high school, vacation trips, and the birth of a child. Scrapbooking has also long been used as a therapeutic tool in pediatric hospitals to document a child's surgery, cancer treatment, chronic illness, or recovery from trauma.

Scrapbooks can also be a useful coping method for a variety of personally challenging events. Transitions, such as a parent's remarriage and the creation of a stepfamily/blended family, or relocation due to a family member's employment, can be chronicled in scrapbooks. The family transition commonly occurs because of the actions of one family member, usually a parent. Children and teens may feel lost, ignored, or in the way during these transitions. During these family events, the scrapbook helps to document the changes experienced by the young person. The scrapbook is a place to focus on what is important to the child or teen during changes, especially those thoughts, worries, and emotions the individual may feel others are too busy to notice or understand.

Numerous psychological benefits may be gained by scrapbooking. Creating scrapbooks is an appealing activity that normalizes difficult events and benefits children in various stages of development. School-age children who have reached Erickson's stage of industry versus inferiority benefit by creating a scrapbook and adding to it each day during the transition. The activity gives the child a job that creates purposeful action when everything else seems out of control. Teens and young adults struggling with changes in identity during Erickson's stage of identity formation may feel especially unsettled by illness, trauma, or family transitions. The scrapbook is a unique product of each creator, thereby aiding the teen in exploring changes in and threats to identity. Scrapbooks shared with peers in the hospital or members of support groups enhance peer interactions. Ideas, concerns, worries, and fears expressed in the scrapbook can be used to facilitate discussion with counselors, child life specialists, and other therapists. In addition to the benefits gained through the process of creating a scrapbook, the books can be used as school reentry tools or as personal records of courage.

The process of scrapbooking includes the familiar benefits of journaling, including exploration of ideas and emotions, clarification of thoughts, and recognition of how experiences and environments impact the individual. Scrapbooks, however, can be used as a therapeutic tool with a wider variety of people. Individuals who may be intimidated by the blank page of a journal can begin a scrapbook with pictures, postcards, brochures, placemats from restaurants, and autographs. For individuals uncomfortable with writing complete sentences, the scrapbook page prompts can be completed with lists of words, pictures cut from magazines, or instant photos.

Jarboe (2001) recognizes the value of scrapbooking:

> Scrapbooks can have relevance in any practice setting and can relate to generational, cultural and unique health (or family transitional) concerns. They can be elaborate books including photos, art and poetry. Or they may be as simple as some stapled pieces of paper with penciled comments. They fit any budget yet the insight gained is priceless. (p. 85)

Instructions

A variety of materials should be made available. A partial list might include a three-ring binder, colored paper, stickers, markers, ink stamps, paints, glitter sticks, tape, glue, instant camera and film, and computer graphics software, computer, and printer.

The patient or client creates a cover for the scrapbook or a standard cover may be prepared on a computer. Preformatted pages prepared with standard computer graphics programs can be headed: People, Autographs, Places, Events. The page prompts listed in the handout at the end of the chapter can be preprinted on pages, or the scrapbooker can title the pages. Teens may want to create their own page prompts. Blend prompts on multiple subjects to keep the scrapbooks positive. Include prompts on sensitive issues and topics the person may have difficulty discussing directly. The preprinted page prompts "give permission" for the scrapbooker to express negative thoughts, emotions, and questions.

Vignette 1

Melinda, a high school senior, was involved in a motor vehicle accident resulting in multiple fractures. During her lengthy hospitalization, she had her mother bring to her hospital room the many photos and newspaper articles she had collected featuring her role as a star member of her high school's volleyball team. These items helped Melinda to retain her identity as an athletic, independent person despite being confined to a hospital bed. Her scrapbook began with these items. Cards and letters from teammates were added. Photos were used to document her recovery progress, including first steps, physical therapy, and finally dismissal from the hospital. The scrapbook also contained the newspaper stories on the volleyball team's games during the remainder of the season, thereby keeping Melinda connected with the team. When Melinda became discouraged at the slow pace of her recovery, the scrapbook helped her focus on her self-identity and her goals for rehabilitation.

Vignette 2

Mark's parents were planning a divorce. The changes planned included Mark and his mother relocating from their house to an apartment, requiring a change in schools for Mark. Mark's current friends would live too far away for Mark to visit by riding his bike or the bus. Therefore he would not be able to see them often.

Mark was supplied with an instant camera and a scrapbook. As part of the goodbye process, he took pictures of his friends and had them write something in his scrapbook. He also took pictures for the scrapbook of his school, his favorite store where he bought comic books and candy, and his old neighborhood. Mark also took pictures of his room and the view from his window. As changes were made, Mark added material to his scrapbook that was important to him. When he went with his mother to look at apartments he took a picture of the rooms that would be his bedroom. When Mark attended the custody hearing as part of his parents' divorce, he wrote about it in his scrapbook. On days when Mark was confused and angry about all the changes in his life, he made lists of all the bad things he could think of and put the lists in his scrapbook. When Mark and his mother moved into their new apartment, Mark explored the area and took pictures for his scrapbook. These pictures included his new school, the park, and the grocery store. He also drew a map of his new neighborhood, and wrote how it felt the first night to sleep in a new place. Gradually, as Mark adjusted to his new family situation, he added less and less material to his scrapbook.

Suggestions for Follow-Up

The therapist working with a child going through a transition can use the scrapbook to open discussion on new topics.

A journal page in the scrapbook may include emotions such as anger and fear that the child is afraid or unable to express verbally. Using the scrapbook entry as a guide, the therapist can role-play with the child how to tell a parent about emotions. The "wish" pages in a scrapbook can be used to begin discussion on the changes taking place, the range of possibilities for the issues important to the child, and exploration of ways the child or teen can positively impact the transitions taking place.

Using the scrapbook pages as a guide, the therapist can help the child find his or her way through the transition. By documenting the changes important to the child, the scrapbook emphasizes the importance of the child not getting lost in the transitions initiated by adults. In family therapy, the therapist and child together can introduce the scrapbook pages to include the needs of the child in the family's adaptation to the transitions that are occurring.

A teen rehabilitating from an injury may have pictures in the scrapbook of how he or she looked immediately after the accident. By guiding the teen to make comparisons between his or her dependent state in the hospital and the progress made in rehabilitation, the therapist can help the teen recognize progress and take pride in the effort required to achieve it.

The scrapbook belongs to the person who created it. The scrapbook should be considered private property. As with a journal, it should not be read without the individual's permission. During the process of compiling the scrapbook, the individual may be open to sharing the contents. After the illness, trauma, or family transition is complete from the viewpoint of the individual, he or she may want to put the scrapbook away and no longer discuss it. This may be the individual's way of putting the experience behind him or her and moving forward with life. This decision should be respected.

Professional Readings and Resources

Ashton, J. and Ashton, D. (1996). *Loss and Grief Recovery: Help Caring for Children with Disabilities, Chronic or Terminal Illness.* Amityville, NY: Baywood Publishing Company.

Goldman, L. (2001). *Breaking the Silence: A Guide to Help Children with Complicated Grief—Suicide, Homicide, AIDS, Violence and Abuse.* Philadelphia, PA: Brunner-Routledge.

Jarboe, J. (2001). Scrapbooks: Insightful Bits and Pieces. In *Proceedings for Nineteenth Annual Conference on Professional Issues of the Child Life Council*. Salt Lake City, UT: Child Life Council.

Jarratt, C. J. and Rosenberg, D. (1993). *Helping Children Cope with Separation and Loss,* Revised Edition. Boston, MA: Harvard Common Press.

Bibliotherapy Sources for the Parent, Teacher, Teen, and Older Child

Hegard, M.E. (1992). *When Mom and Dad Separate: Children Can Learn to Cope with Grief from Divorce Workbook*. Minneapolis, MN: Woodland Press.

Lagorio, J. (1993). *Life Cycle: Classroom Activities for Helping Children to Live with Daily Change and Loss*. Tucson, AZ: Zephyr Press.

Stillwell, E.E. and Olsen, C. (1998). *Sweet Memories: For Children and Adults . . . to Create Healing and Loving Memories for Holidays and Other Special Events*. Omaha, NE: Centering Corporation.

Van-Si, L. (1994). *Helping Children Heal from Loss: A Keepsake Book of Special Memories*. Portland, OR: Portland State University, Continuing Education Press.

Bibliotherapy Sources for the Young Child

Oehlberg, B. and Roth, S. (1996). *Making It Better: Activities for Children Living in a Stressful World*. St. Paul, MN: Redleaf Press.

Szaj, K.C. and Hicks, M.A. (1996). *I Hate Goodbyes!* Mahwah, NJ: Paulist Press.

Scrapbooking Page Prompts

You are making your very own scrapbook and you can put anything you desire into it. Following are some suggestions of topics or ideas that you may wish to include in your scrapbook, and some you may not want to include. It is all up to you! Be sure to autograph your special scrapbook with your name and age. Add a photo of yourself or draw a picture of yourself to be included in your book.

General Topics

Something I want people to know
   about me is . . .
My favorite color
The music I like
My favorite food
My least favorite food
The animal I like best
My pet
My dreams
What I like to watch on TV
My favorite holiday

My favorite movie
What I am afraid of
Okay. Take a deep breath! What helps me
   relax?
Sports I like
Sports I play
My favorite games
My hobbies
Things I do best
I am special because . . .

My Family

My family is special because . . .
My brothers and sisters
Silly things I know about my
   brothers and sisters

What I think about school
What I like to do on the weekend

My Friends

The thing I like best about my friends is . . .
I wish my friends would . . .
What makes me laugh . . .
   Ha! Ha! He! He! Ho! Ho! Giggle! Giggle!

The person I like to laugh with most is . . .

About Me and My Feelings

What makes me sad?
What makes me happy?
Favorite vacation I have taken
Favorite vacation I want to take
I don't like . . .
Things I like
Things that bore me
If I were rich . . .
If I could go anywhere . . .
Favorite things to do

Least favorite thing to do
Where I live
My hero
My hopes for the future
My biggest worry
My greatest wish
If I could change anything in my life,
   I would change . . .
Words of wisdom

Topics During Illness, Recovery from Trauma, and Hospitalization

I am in the hospital because . . .
Autograph and picture page, my doctors
Autograph and picture page, my nurses
Autograph and picture page, my physical
   therapist
Autograph and picture page, my respiratory
   therapist
Autograph and picture page, my visitors
Autograph and picture page, my child life
   specialist

Hospital jokes and riddles
I'd like to tell my doctors . . .
I'd like to tell my nurses . . .
I wish my parents understood . . .
Areas I'd like to explore in the hospital
Medical tests I have had
Medical treatments I have had
Medication I take to help me get better
What I think about at night when I can't sleep
When I first got sick or hurt . . .

Autograph and picture page, the person
who does my blood tests
Autograph and picture page, the person
who takes my X rays
My favorite activity in the hospital
The best part of the hospital is . . .
The worst part of being in the hospital . . .

My surgery
Menus
Pictures I have drawn
Get well cards
New toys and games
What I want to say to God

Changes

Topics during family transitions
What is changing?
Why things are changing
The new person in my family
The new place I will be
What I like best about before the changes
What I like about the changes taking place
I wonder about the new . . .
What I want to remember from before
New people
New places
I wonder what will happen next
I wish someone would tell me about . . .
I just discovered that . . .
During the move to a new home,
I wonder about . . .

Things I want to keep with me during
the move
How I want my bedroom to look in our
new home
When I heard about Mom (Dad) getting
married, I . . .
Fun things I have done with the new person
in my family
I want to tell someone . . .
Things important to me about this change
I feel left out when . . .
I get worried when I think about . . .
Things I want to teach to . . .

Source: Adapted by J. T. Karns from Jarboe, J. (2001). Scrapbooks: Insightful Bits and Pieces. *Proceedings for Nineteenth Annual Conference on Professional Issues of the Child Life Council.* Salt Lake City, UT: Child Life Council.

22

Animal-Assisted Therapy for Sexually Abused Children

Elisabeth Reichert

Type of Contribution: Activity

Objective

Animals often lower a child's anxiety, and in animal-assisted therapy, the animal serves as a bridge between the therapist and the child. By lowering the child's anxiety, the animals aid in creating a nonthreatening atmosphere whereby the child can express feelings and disclose abuse. By promoting projection and identification of the child's feelings, storytelling with the animal can be beneficial to the therapeutic process. Animal-assisted therapy can be nicely utilized as an adjunct to play therapy.

Essentially, the animal can help the therapist establish a relationship with the child. Used appropriately, the animal sets a child at ease. If the child sees the therapist treating the animal with kindness, the child will often believe that the therapist will treat her or him with kindness, too. In the presence of the animal, the child may feel more at ease and safe and will more readily disclose circumstances of the abuse.

Rationale for Use

Animal-assisted therapy has been successfully utilized with abused children (Levinson, 1969, 1972; Bruch, 1988; Peacock, 1986). The purpose of using a pet in therapy is to build a bridge and ease tension and anxiety. The use of animals to help treat sexually abused children on an individual basis can be an effective tool in the treatment process. This aspect of treatment, called animal-assisted therapy, includes the animal as part of the therapeutic process. The child may see the animal as a model, mirror, or teacher. Because the animal is nonjudgmental, it can enhance the child's sense of self-esteem and promote the expression of feelings.

The animal serves as a bridge between the client and the therapist and can be a transitional object for the child (Levinson, 1969). In other words, the child might more easily convey her or his feeling through the animal, instead of talking directly to the therapist.

Piaget found that all children go through a stage of development when it is natural for them to ascribe human traits to animals (Piaget, 1929). In fairy tales and mythology, animals play an important role in human interactions. Children often project their feelings about themselves onto the animal, which gives love, does not talk back or argue, and provides a consistent, nonjudgmental relationship. The children receive value from a living being that offers love and reassurance without criticism (Solomon, 1981). Therapists can also utilize animals to teach children affection, empathy, nurturance, responsibility, and self-acceptance (James, 1989).

To use animal-assisted therapy, the therapist needs to understand the bond between animals and humans. When a therapist uses an animal in counseling, the need for language decreases (George, 1988). For instance, a child often finds it easier to express herself or himself through physical interaction with the animal, rather than verbal communication. Consequently, the therapist may have to depend more on the child's posture, tone of voice, and facial expression than actual statements in interpreting what the child is trying to communicate (George, 1988).

The characteristics of the animal to be used in therapy are extremely important (George, 1988). A dog was used in the case vignette, although other safe, tame animals could also be used in therapy for sexually abused children. Regardless of the type of animal to be used, the animal needs to be good-natured and work well with children, who can be physically rough. Because they are loyal, easily trained, intelligent, and protective of children, German shepherds can be ideal for working with children who experience lack of love, low self-esteem, and hopelessness (Gonski, 1985). The author found that her dog Buster, a dachshund, was very loving and worked well with sexually abused children.

Instructions

The presence of an animal in therapy for sexually abused children requires a specific approach to introduce the animal to the child. For instance, the therapist can ask the child whether she or he has a family pet and, if so, what type of relationship the pet has with members of the child's family. The therapist should allow the child time to become familiar with the animal, and the animal also needs time to adapt to the child. If the child is timid or fearful, the therapist can introduce the animal to the child and talk for the animal. If the child has no pet, the therapist can ask the child what kind of animal she or he would like to have.

To help gather information from small children, indirect interviewing through the animal can be a useful approach. Instead of the therapist directly asking questions of the child, the therapist can ask questions through the animal. For example, "Buster wants to know what your favorite game is" or "Buster would like to know how old you are."

The initial discussion of the traumatizing event needs to occur when the child and therapist engage in quiet, parallel activity, such as side-by-side drawing or stroking and holding the animal. By engaging in this type of activity, the therapist can make statements at a casual pace, thus allowing the child time to absorb information. Because the child experiences anxiety and tension concerning the topic of abuse, the primary focus at this time is on play, which allows the child to distract herself or himself if necessary (James, 1989). The child can also focus on the animal if the anxiety or tension becomes too great.

Feelings of traumatized children are often either numbed or greatly intensified, with these two extremes explained by post-traumatic stress disorder (see American Psychiatric Association, 1994). Because children frequently are not aware of their feelings, an integral part of therapy is that of teaching children about feelings. Discussion of the traumatic event at the beginning of the treatment process can help relieve tension, provide assurances to the child, and identify reasons why the child is in therapy (James, 1989). This early discussion of sexual abuse also affirms that the therapist will discuss the abuse and address the child's feelings about the abuse (James, 1989).

Using an animal as the child's alter ego helps the child to express his or her feelings. For instance, I told one child that Buster had a nightmare. I then asked the child, "What do you think Buster's nightmare was about?" The child said, " The nightmare was about being afraid of getting hurt again by someone mean." The child was able to project her feelings onto the dog and talk about the dog instead of herself. By projecting her feelings onto Buster, the child was able to indirectly express her own feelings.

In cases involving disclosure of abuse, the therapist encourages the child to tell her sexual abuse story to the animal being used in the session. The child may choose to whisper her abuse story into the animal's ear. For example, children would often hold the author's dog, Buster, while they told Buster what had happened to them. One particular child initially played with Buster, who then offered the child her paw to take. The child began telling Buster about how the child's uncle had hurt her private parts. Throughout the story, the child held Buster's paw. The child continued to hold and pet Buster even after she had finished telling her story.

The mere presence of the animal may not be sufficient to persuade the child to disclose information about the abuse. Therefore, a further intervention that might assist the therapist is that of storytelling to include the animal.

The use of stories in child therapy has helped children in the treatment process (Bettelheim, 1977; Mills and Crowley, 1986). Because a child's ability to identify with characters and themes is so powerful, the child can easily relate to a story and make unconscious connections to heroes and conflicts. A story can help the child resolve problems. When the therapist tells the child a story, an animal can assist the child in acting out a role and serve as support for the child. When using stories, the therapist needs to tailor the story to the child's issue.

Vignette

The author encountered a child who displayed symptoms of sexual abuse but had not disclosed the abuse. The child was a seven-year-old boy whose older brother, age ten, had already disclosed that a neighbor had sexually abused both of them. The child's mother believed the older brother's statements about sexual abuse and emotionally supported both of her children. However, the younger child would not talk about what had happened. The child lived with his mother, brother, and another older sibling.

To help the child express his feelings and tell what had happened to him, the author told the following story (adapted from Davis, Custer, and Solarz, 1990):

Once upon a time, there was a doggie named Buster. Buster lived with her mommy and two brothers and was very happy. She loved to play, especially when she got to run in the woods, meet other doggies, and chase squirrels. One day, Buster disappeared in the park for awhile and when she returned, she was different. She was afraid of everything, wet her bed, and had tummy aches. Her family saw that she was scared. They asked her, "What is wrong, Buster?" But Buster couldn't say anything because she had gotten an invisible, magic bandage over her mouth while she was in the woods. Buster was afraid that if she took if off, something bad would happen. A few days later, Buster got a splinter in her tail. Buster could not tell her mommy about the splinter because the invisible bandage was still over Buster's mouth. Then an old dog tried to bully Buster. The old dog said, "I bet you can't even swim." Buster thought to herself, "That dog is wrong." Buster went to a pond and swam across it. The old dog had tried to trick Buster, who was a very smart dog. And now Buster started to think about the invisible, magic bandage. "I think it's a trick, too," she said to herself as she pulled it off. Nothing bad happened. Buster ran home and told her mommy all about the woods and what had happened there. The more Buster told her mommy about the woods, the safer and more powerful she felt. Buster also told her mommy about the splinter. Buster's mommy helped Buster get the splinter out of Buster's tail. From then on, Buster was not afraid to sleep and Buster's tummy felt better. Buster had figured out that the invisible magic bandage wasn't magic at all. The bandage was there simply to keep her quiet. Buster had learned a lesson she would always remember. Telling the truth about trips to the woods to grown-ups who help doggies made her feel strong and safe.

After telling the story, the author asked the child the following questions: How do you think Buster felt coming out of the woods with an invisible, magic bandage on her mouth? How do you think Buster felt when the mean old dog told her she could not swim? How do you think

Buster felt after taking off the bandage? How do you think Buster feels now? In the next session, the child disclosed the sexual abuse by his neighbor. During this disclosure, the child held Buster.

Stories and animals can also be used to address the child's negative feelings. Children commonly experience shame and guilt about sexual abuse (Gil, 1991; Marvasti, 1989; James, 1989). It is not unusual for children to believe that they brought on the abuse because they feel they did something wrong and the abuse was their fault. To help children express feelings regarding shame and guilt, the author told the following story, also involving Buster:

> Once upon a time I heard a mournful cry outside my house. I thought it was the neighbor's dog at first, but the crying kept on and on. So I went outside and there was a puppy named Buster, who was scared and frightened and all covered with fleas and ticks. Someone had put Buster there and left her all by herself. Buster thought she had been left on the wrong side of the road because she had cheated in school and she knew that this was wrong.

The therapist can end this story with the phrase "Bad things can happen to good little doggies like Buster just as bad things can happened to good little kids." The therapist can then ask the child the following question: "Whose fault was it that Buster was put on the side of the road?" The child can then respond to the story. The therapist and the child can then address issues of guilt and responsibility.

Storytelling in animal-assisted therapy helps the child disclose the abuse and express feelings. By integrating the animal into the story the therapist presents the child with the opportunity to identify with the animal and project her or his feelings onto the animal, thus facilitating disclosure and expression of feelings.

Suggestions for Follow-Up

Working through issues of shame, guilt, fear, and safety are crucial in treatment of sexually abused children. To have the animal present on an ongoing basis is helpful since those issues can be worked through with the assistance of the animal. The animal can also aid in any ongoing anxieties that surface as a result of the abuse.

Contraindications for Use

Although animal-assisted therapy can be useful for many children, this type of therapy is not appropriate for all children. For instance, children with a history of aggression toward animals should not be involved in this therapy. Also, children can be fearful of animals, or some children might have behaviors that provoke an animal. The therapist also needs to be aware of potential legal ramifications when using this intervention. Substitution of a stuffed animal may be effective for those with allergies or negative emotional reactions to animals.

Professional Readings and Resources

Davis, N., Custer, K., and Solarz, V. (1990). *Once upon a time: Therapeutic stories to heal abused children* (Revised edition). Oxon Hill, MD: Psychological Associates of Oxon Hill.

Gil, E. (1991). *The healing power of play: Working with abused children.* New York: Guilford Publications.

James, B. (1989). *Treating traumatized children: New insights and creative interventions.* Lexington, MA: Lexington Books/Washington, DC: Heath and Company.

Levinson, B. (1969) *Pet-oriented child psychotherapy.* Springfield, IL: Charles C Thomas.

Levinson, B. (1972). *Pets and human development.* Springfield, IL: Charles C Thomas.

McCulloch, M. (1983). Animal-facilitated therapy: Overview and future direction. In A. Katcher and A. Beck (Eds.), *New perspectives on our lives with companion animals* (pp. 410-426). Philadelphia, PA: University of Pennsylvania Press.

McDonald, A. (1979). Children and companion animals. *Child Care, Health and Development, 5,* 347-358.

Reichert, E. (1994). Play and animal-assisted therapy: A group–treatment model for sexually abused girls ages 9-13. *Family Therapy: The Journal of the California Graduate School of Family Psychology, 21*(1), 55-62.

Reichert, E. (1998). Individual counseling for sexually abused children: A role for animals and storytelling. *Child and Adolescent Social Work Journal, 15*(3), 177-185.

Schowalter, J. (1983). Clinical experience: The use and abuse of pets, *Journal of the American Academy of Child Psychiatry, 22*(1), 68-72.

Bibliotherapy Sources for the Client

Girard, L. W., Pate, R., and Girard, W. (1992). *My body is private.* Morton Grove, IL: Albert Whitman.

Hagans, K., Case, J., and Brohl, K. (1998). *When your child has been molested: A parent's guide to healing and recovery.* San Fransisco: Jossey-Bass.

Kleven, S. and Bergsma, J. (1998). *The right touch: A read-aloud story to help prevent child sexual abuse.* Bellevue, WA: Illumination Arts Publishing Company.

Spelman, C. and Weidner, T. (1997). *Your body belongs to you.* Morton Grove, IL: Albert Whitman.

References

American Psychiatric Association (1994). *Diagnostic and statistical manual of mental disorders* (DSM-IV) (Fourth edition). Washington, DC: Author.

Bettelheim, B. (1977). *The uses of enchantment.* New York: Vantage.

Bruch, A. (1988). Ein Hund und ein Kater in der Kinderpsychotherapie: Ein Bericht aus der Praxis. *Arbeitschrift für Individual Psychologie, 13*(4), 264-273.

Davis, N., Custer, K., Solarz, V. (1990). *Once upon a time: Therapeutic stories to heal abused children* (Revised edition). Oxon Hill, MD: Psychological Associates of Oxon Hill.

George, M. (1988). Child therapy and animals: A new way for an old relationship. In C. Schafer (Ed.), *Innovative interventions in child and adolescent therapy* (pp. 400-419). New York: John Wiley and Sons.

Gil, E. (1991). *The healing power of play: Working with abused children.* New York: Guilford Publications.

Gonski, Y. (1985). The utilization of canines in a child welfare setting. *Child and Adolescent Social Work, 2*(2), 93-105.

James, B. (1989). *Treating traumatized children: New insights and creative interventions.* Lexington, MA: Lexington Books/Washington, DC: Heath and Company.

Levinson, B. (1969). *Pet-oriented child psychotherapy.* Springfield, IL: Charles C Thomas.

Marvasti, J.A. (1989). Play therapy with sexually abused children with mental retardation. In S. Sgroi (Ed.), *Vulnerable populations* Volume 2: *Sexual abuse treatment for children, adult survivors, offenders, and persons with mental retardation* (pp. 1-41). Lexington, MA: Lexington Books/Washington, DC: Heath and Company.

Mills, J.C. and Crowley, R.J. (1986). *Therapeutic metaphors for children and the child within*. New York: Brunner/Mazel.

Peacock, C. (1986). "The role of the therapist's pet in initial psychotherapy sessions with adolescents: An exploratory study." (Unpublished doctoral dissertation, Boston College).

Piaget, J. (1929). *The child's conception of the world*. New York: Harcourt Brace.

Solomon, A. (1981). Animals and children: The role of the pet. *Canada Mental Health, 29*(2), 9-13.

SECTION V:
YOUTHS/ADOLESCENTS

23

Using Adolescents As Consultants in Therapy

C. Everett Bailey

Type of Contribution: Activity, Handout

Objective

This chapter describes a role-play intervention that therapists can use when working with older children and adolescents. The objective of this intervention is to reduce the amount of blame that adolescents feel when they are presented by parents as the identified patients in treatment. It can also change the dynamics in the parent-child relationship, from one of blaming the adolescent to helping the adolescent feel more empowered. It can help adolescents feel more like they are valued members of the family system who can contribute solutions and are not just blamed for the problems in the family. In addition, this activity provides parents with some helpful feedback, which allows them to think about the family's problem from the adolescent's perspective.

Parents often enter therapy confused about why their teenager behaves the way he or she does. They want the therapist to help them understand their teenager and, in some way, to "fix" the teenager and help change his or her behavior. Parents often are not aware of their role in the process, or what they might be doing to contribute to the problem. It may be easier for parents to hear or see their contribution to their family's problems in a role-play, in which they have "hired" their adolescent child as a consultant to help them understand the experience, thoughts, and feelings of the adolescent. In the process, this intervention gives the adolescent a "voice," empowering the teen within the therapy session and within the family.

Rationale for Use

Preadolescent and adolescent children are dealing with several developmental issues, and families often get "stuck" as they enter into this new stage of the family life cycle. Family systems have a strong tendency to maintain the status quo because change threatens the family's cohesiveness and can compromise the system's integrity. To make the transition to the new stage, parents must renegotiate their relationship with their teenager to accommodate the developmental needs of their teen. The developmental tasks that adolescents are confronted with include these:

- Establishing a sense of autonomy and personal identity
- Achieving emotional independence from parents and other adults
- Initiating the process of individuation from the family of origin

Adjusting the parent-child interactions is necessary to help the adolescent accomplish these developmental tasks. As the child enters adolescence, parent-child interactions take on two important objectives: (1) to promote autonomy and self-regulation and (2) to help adolescents develop a personal identity separate from parents. This redefining of the parent-adolescent relationship can preserve the functioning of the family system. The task that is often most difficult for parents of adolescents is to relinquish some degree of control over their child, which is necessary to help their child develop normally.

Bigner (1998) states that some behaviors of parents of adolescents provide structure and nurture:

- Showing approval for the teen's efforts to achieve developmental tasks
- Accepting the teen's feelings and sharing own past feelings to build empathy with the teen
- Not discounting the teen's behavior, feelings, and attitudes
- Understanding the teen's need for individuation and supporting efforts to establish it
- Celebrating the teen's growing independence and gains toward attaining adult status
- Encouraging, supporting, and accepting the teen's emerging personal identity, even though it may be different from what they desired or hoped for the teen

Adolescents want to be taken seriously. They want their ideas, feelings, and experiences to be considered legitimate. They want to feel heard. Often the parent-child dynamics are such that the child resents being blamed by the parent for problems in the parent-adolescent relationship. The parents' response often is to push more and insist their teenage child comply, which meets with more resistance from the adolescent. One of the reasons for this is that adolescents face the tasks of becoming more autonomous and establishing an identity of their own, separate from their parents. These developmental issues increase the need for the child to be taken more seriously, because that indicates that the adolescent is respected for being his or her own person.

The attached handout may be used to help educate parents about adolescent developmental tasks, and to provide them with a rationale for the need to modify their parenting to allow teens to develop increasing autonomy and independence. The handout can be used in conjoint sessions with parents to help couples begin discussing these issues, as well as to prepare parents for this activity.

This role-reversal activity can be an effective intervention in helping the parents and adolescents renegotiate the nature of their relationship to allow for more optimal development. This activity, in which the child becomes the "person in the know" and the parents are "clueless," allows for a dynamic whereby the parents insist and the adolescent resists being changed. This activity can also provide the parents with some understanding and insight about their child. It does this by allowing parents, for a moment during the role-play, to step out of the parental role where they often feel compelled to correct, criticize, or control their child. The role-play allows them to listen, be understanding, accepting, and empathic toward their child's experience.

Instructions

This activity is a modified role reversal. It is not a typical role reversal where the parents play a child and the child takes on the role of parent, but a role reversal where the parents are in a one-down position to their child. The parents become the consumers of wisdom and advice rather than the dispensers. At the same time the adolescent switches from a one-down position to a one-up position, in which the teen is no longer the "immature child" who does not know anything but is the "expert" on his or her own life. In addition, teens become a valuable resource to the family because their expert insight about how adolescents feel and think is something the parents do not remember or understand. The parents are then asked to take a noncritical role toward their child, accept what the child has to say, and appreciate his or her insight. This helps them to understand their child and relate better. They are encouraged not to challenge or question the expert counsel of their teenage child but instead to take it in and accept it. The parents are asked to take what they find to be useful and to leave the rest. The role-play allows parents to come out of their parental role and interact in a person-to-person manner, which is often more respectful than parent-to-child. It helps the parents shift from an "I'm in charge, you have to do what I say, and my ideas count more than yours" stance to one that is respectful and seeks to understand their child. At the same time the adolescent's status is elevated to one of importance and significance.

This activity should be used in a session where one or both of the parents and the adolescent are present. The therapist asks the family if they would be willing to participate in a role-play. The therapist states that he or she would like to "hire" the adolescent as an expert consultant to help him or her offer some good advice to some parents who happen to have a child his or her age. As a part of the role-play, the therapist explains that the parents have retained the therapist's council to help them with their teenage child, whom they are concerned about and with whom they feel out of touch. Since the therapist is not a teenager and it has been a long time since he or she was a teenager, he or she wants to hire the adolescent child as an expert consultant to offer insights to help the parents understand what their teenager might be thinking and feeling. *It is important to stay in the role-play and set it up so that it is clear that the adolescent is not the child of the parents but instead is playing the role of another teenager who just happens to be the same age as the parents' teenager.*

The therapist starts by explaining some of the concerns that the parents have and some of the recent interactions that the parents have had with their teenager. The therapist then asks the adolescent consultant what he or she thinks may be going on for this teenager that might help the parents understand him or her better. The consultant is asked what advice he or she would give these parents on what they could do to help their teenage child. It is important that the therapist help the parents to stay in a listening and receptive mode and not allow them to respond defensively to the adolescent's advice. The parents can ask questions, but only for clarification or to obtain more information, and should not ask questions that challenge the adolescent consultant. The session should end by having the parents summarize the advice that the expert consultant has offered them and describe how it will help them as parents.

Vignette

The following vignette is of a session in which I asked a thirteen-year-old boy to be an expert consultant to his parents. Dawn and Gary had five children, and thirteen-year-old David was their oldest. The parents brought David in for treatment because he was acting out at home, and Dawn was having an increasingly difficult time handling him. He was frequently disrespectful and aggressive toward his mother, and Gary had to take time off work to come home and mediate situations between Dawn and David. In the previous sessions, Dawn had been fairly critical and blaming of David for the problems in the relationship, without showing much awareness or taking responsibility for her role in the conflicts. David was often defensive and surly, blaming Dawn in return. Gary was supportive but not sure how to intervene. He often felt that Dawn overreacted to situations, and that David treated his mother inappropriately. Dawn was unaware of how she got "hooked" into conflicts with David. She would often personalize David's anger and angrily confront him. This would make it difficult for her to understand David and empathize with him.

In this, the fifth session, I spent a few minutes with the parents asking them about how the week went. They reported that David and Dawn had a few arguments during the week, and that the day before David had gotten angry and broken a chair. As we discussed the incident during the session, Dawn started to blame David. She stated that she had been doing everything she could, but that nothing seemed to make a difference with David. At that point in the session, I initiated the role-play.

THERAPIST: David, let's see if you can help us figure this out. Say you are talking to two people here who aren't your parents, but they are the parents of a friend of yours, or a kid your age. And you are consulting with them. Sometimes people hire consultants to get some expert advice. These parents come to you and they say, "Listen, we've got a kid your age. We want to know how to deal with him; we are not really sure how to respond to him. We realize we are doing a couple of things that are not really helping. In fact, they're making things worse. Since you're his age, thirteen years old, we thought you might be able to give us some ideas as to what might be helpful, and what would not be helpful." How would you advise or consult these parents of your friend, to help them deal with situations with their own teenager?

DAVID: Don't get so mad.

MOM: If we don't get mad, then what should we do?

DAVID: Just try to figure out how to handle the problem by talking.

MOM: What if the kid doesn't want to talk?

TH.: Okay, let's not go with the "what if"—let's just listen to your consultant. Remember, you're paying him big bucks. Okay, so don't yell, or don't get mad, and talk about it. And to whom should the parents talk?

DAVID: The kid.

TH.: So when your son does something you don't like, don't get mad at him, go talk to him. And how should they talk to him?

DAVID: Nicely.

TH.: And what kind of nice things should they say?

DAVID: Like, how are you going to help me fix the chair, or what are you going to do to fix the problem? Stuff like that. Ask the kid why he did it.

TH.: So, you might say, "Why did you do that?" And then what should they do? And then what if the kid says, "Well, because I hate you."

MOM: [Laughs] Yeah, that was my question. Or what if he says, "I don't want to talk to you, you make me sick"?

DAVID: I didn't say that. I didn't say any of that. [Laughs]

TH.: Oh, no, no.

DAD: We are not talking about you; we are talking about *our* son, and you're giving *us* advice.

TH.: You are giving the parents of this other kid advice. This is their experience. So, you, David, kind of laughed, right? You kind of go, "Yeah, maybe I say that a little bit too, but not out in the open. Yeah, I know kids say that when they are thirteen years old, they say that to their parents because that's their job, right?" [All laugh.] Teens are supposed to say that stuff. So now, give these parents some idea on how they deal with that? The kid says, "I hate you," or "I don't want to talk to you because I am sick of you." [All laugh.] So, what could you—

MOM: "Our" son just said that a couple of days ago.

DAVID: It was today.

MOM and DAD: No, not you, "our" son. We're not talking about *you*. So how would you deal with that?

TH.: What advice would you give them?

DAVID: But I did do that today.

TH., MOM, and DAD: No, no.

TH.: We're talking about advice. What advice would you give to them when a kid says something like "I hate you" or "I don't want to talk to you because I am sick of you"?

DAVID: Tell him that he can't watch TV until he figures out how to fix the chair. Or figures out a way that he could earn money to fix it.

TH.: What should they do with the "I hate you" and "I don't want to talk to you because I'm so sick of you"? Do you think they should still talk to him?

DAVID: Umm, probably not.

TH.: So do you think it might be a good idea for parents to ignore it when their kids say that?

DAVID: Well, that is probably what I would do, but I don't know 'cause I'm not a parent.

TH.: No, no. We are asking you from your perspective as a thirteen-year-old. So that's what you would do? You would ignore the fact that the kids says that. Don't take it personally, parents, right?

DAVID: Yeah.

TH.: Why do you think the kid is saying that?

DAVID: 'Cause he is mad.

TH.: So try to see this as the kid just being mad; it really has nothing to do with you. He could just as easily have been saying gobbledygook, gobbledygook [Mom laughs]. Right? And it's just an expression of frustration and being angry. So that sounds like some good advice! Ignore that, and instead of responding to that, what would you suggest they do?

DAVID: Figure out how to solve the problem, and the kid doesn't get to do something until he does.

TH.: So you think some punishment should be involved, if he doesn't fix it?

DAVID: I would only say that he doesn't get to do something if he said that he hated me or something. Otherwise I would just tell him to figure out how to solve the problem, and if he just did that, then I wouldn't say anything else.

TH.: So what if the kid says I'm not going to do it?

DAVID: Then I'd just say, "You can't watch TV until you do!"

TH.: So you'd have some kind of punishment fixed as to whether he solves the problem.

DAVID: But it's not permanent.

TH.: So, if he fixes it then there's no punishment, but if he doesn't fix it, then he can't watch TV.

MOM: But what if you run out of punishments? What if you don't know what punishments. What if the kid doesn't care? You know, "I don't care if I don't watch TV. I just want to stay in my room anyway." What if you can't think of anything?

TH.: [To David] What I hear this parent saying is, "Sometimes I wonder if my kid really cares what I think or what I want him to do." So how would you respond to that?

DAVID: Umm, be nice to him, and maybe he will just be nice back.

TH.: Let's say in this moment, there's a problem you're trying to work on and you're trying to get the thirteen-year-old to do something or stop doing something and he says, "I don't care. I'm not going to stop." Do you think that's true that the child really doesn't care?

DAVID: No.

TH.: So you think the child does care?

DAVID: Yeah, probably good advice is to punish him, but that's not what I would tell somebody.

TH.: So what would you tell someone?

DAVID: I would just do the opposite of punish him, just be nice to him.

MOM: Like take him out to eat?

DAVID: If he is in trouble, just say, "Come on, we're going," and just tell him that you are going out to eat, and they can just sit there and talk with him and ask him why he thinks that stuff and be nice to him and stuff. And maybe the next time he won't do it.

TH.: So maybe you can change the setting. What if you can't change the setting?

DAVID: Just do something with him, or just play Nintendo or basketball or something—anything like that would be fine.

MOM: But what if the behavior needs to be talked about?

DAVID: You can do it while you're spending time with him, while you're playing Nintendo, just talk to him.

TH.: Okay, so change the setting, maybe change the room, not just sit there, kind of try to do something different, and talk to him. Okay, what else?

DAVID: Probably the person who wasn't involved with it should talk to the kid. But you always have to talk. Probably the person could get mad but could just think of a way that the kid could fix the problem instead of making him feel like he has to suffer his whole life.

TH.: So avoid a "This is the end of the world" type of response, but instead take an approach that "Stuff happens. We need to fix this."

DAVID: Right, and help the kid to be responsible for it, to help him to see that he has the responsibility for fixing it.

TH.: I wanted to ask one more question, and then I'd like to see what kind of good ideas these parents have gotten. David, could you help these parents understand why their kid might be doing some of these things? Would that be helpful to you as parents to understand what might be going on for your son?

MOM: Definitely.

DAVID: It could be something that the parents are doing that the kid doesn't like, or that he doesn't have any friends.

TH.: So how does the kid feel when the parents are doing something he doesn't like, or when he doesn't have any friends?

DAVID: Mad, well, not if you don't have any friends—you feel like no one likes you or anything. But if it's something the parents are doing he doesn't like, then he's probably mad about it. And if they won't listen to him, then he would probably do something like that.

TH.: Okay, I think those are some good ideas . . .

MOM: I have a question that relates to that . . .

TH.: Okay, let me just kind of summarize. Sometimes his parents do things he doesn't like and they don't listen to him. And that seems as if maybe they don't like him or that makes him mad.

DAVID: It's probably never that they don't like him, but he's just mad at them or he just thinks that they don't treat him fair.

TH.: Because they won't listen to him?

DAVID: Yeah. Well sometimes they listen but they don't do anything about it.

TH.: So it seems like they might be giving him a chance to talk and they might be hearing with their ears, but they don't really make any changes. That seems like a pretty big thing for what's going on with this kid.

MOM: Well, what if, like the other day, my son was lying in the closet and I tried to talk to him, and he said, "I don't want to talk to you." I was trying to be nice and find out what was wrong with him and stuff, but he didn't want to have anything to do with me. You know, what does he expect?

TH.: What should you do then, right? [To David] You're kind of shaking your head . . .

MOM: It hurts my feelings.

DAVID: Well, the first thing she did when she came was said, "What's wrong?" I said, "I don't know. I don't have any friends." She goes, "Oh, you have friends." She just didn't start out very good.

TH.: So what advice would you give her there? What could she have done instead to start off better when her son said, "I don't have any friends"? What could she have said?

DAVID: Well, she could have tried to figure out a way that I could not be so bored and sad about stuff by saying, "Maybe we can think about a hobby or something we can do, or maybe we can call up some kid from school, a friend that you had a long time ago." Not just right off the bat say, "Oh, you have friends." 'Cause they don't really know.

TH.: It sounds to me like that kind of fits with what you were saying before, that parents don't listen sometimes. You say, "I don't have friends" and they say, "Yes you do." This makes it feel as if they don't listen?

DAVID: Uh-huh.

TH.: [To parents] Well, you've had a chance here to get some advice from an expert. What are some things that were helpful?

DAD: I think our advice there is not to take it personally because our son is just saying things because he's mad.

MOM: It was good advice [laughing]. It made me think more like a thirteen-year-old.

TH.: Mom, what was helpful to you?

MOM: Not to take things so personal. It just made me look at it differently. It made me think of using reflective listening instead of giving opinions.

TH.: So, don't take it personally, listening. Gary, anything?

DAD: Well, the part about not taking things personally.

TH.: So you agree that not taking it personally is good. That's good advice, David! Thanks for sharing that insight. Anything else that you want to thank David for?

DAD: He's just an all-around great guy. Well, *everything* he said made sense. I can't specifically think of anything else, but it all made sense.

TH.: [To mom] Anything else?

MOM: [Shakes her head no]

TH.: Okay, thanks, David.

DAD: Sounds like he would be a good parent.

TH: Yeah, or he'd be at least a good thirteen-year-old consultant, right? Maybe you could start your own business, David. How could parents understand their thirteen-year-old, huh?

DAVID: Maybe.

TH.: If you didn't really understand or you forgot something that David said, you know, maybe he might be willing to talk with you off the clock. I don't know, he might charge you [laughs]. But I think that David has given some really good advice here, and what I would really like both of you to do is to consider that advice and incorporate it into how you deal with your thirteen-year-old son. And I don't know about the buts. I guess I'm asking you not to worry about those right now and just take what was given—it was a nice gift. [Mom nods.]

MOM: Yeah.

TH.: Okay, thanks, David, good job! [The two shake hands.] So we're not going to meet for two weeks.

MOM: Or we can just go to his office [looking at David]. [All laugh.]

Suggestions for Follow-Up

Generally there is not enough time in the session both to do the role-play and to thoroughly process it. Therefore, follow-up in subsequent sessions is critical. If the therapist has videotaping capability, he or she could replay the videotape with the parents and go over some of the key issues brought up during the session. The therapist could also give the videotape to the parents to watch at home to identify some points they might have missed. Of course, the key issue to address in follow-up sessions is how the parents can renegotiate their relationship with the adolescent. It is particularly important for the parents to identify ways that they need to change to create new dynamics that are less blaming, and that will foster an environment that facilitates their child in individuating and developing his or her own identity, which is valued and respected.

Contraindications for Use

The main contraindication would be if the parents are extremely defensive and closed to any input from the child. If the parents have been abusive, the relationship may need to be repaired to some degree and some trust established for the activity to be effective. Although the activity can be effective with preadolescents, it may not be helpful with younger elementary school or preschool children.

Professional Readings and Resources

Selekman, M. D. (1993). *Pathways to change: Brief therapy with difficult adolescents*. New York: Guilford Publications.

Werner-Wilson, R. J. (2001). *Developmental-systemic family therapy with adolescents*. Binghamton, NY: The Haworth Press, Inc.

Bibliotherapy Sources for the Client

Larson, R. and Richards, M. H. (1994). *Divergent realities: The emotional lives of mothers, fathers, and adolescents*. New York: Basic Books.

References

Bigner, J. J. (1998). *Parent-child relations: An introduction to parenting* (Fifth edition). Upper Saddle River, NJ: Prentice-Hall, Inc.

Adolescent Development and Parent-Adolescent Relationships

Adolescents must deal with several developmental issues. The developmental tasks that adolescents are confronted with include

- establishing a sense of autonomy and personal identity,
- achieving emotional independence from parents and other adults, and
- initiating the process of individuation from the family of origin.

The process that adolescents go through to establish their own personal identity and to gain a sense of autonomy from their parents is called individuation. The process of individuation consists of four phases:

1. *Differentiation:* This occurs in early adolescence (twelve to fourteen years old) when teens recognize that they are psychologically distinct from their parents. Teens also realize that their parents are not all-knowing and all-powerful, as they had previously believed. This naturally leads teenagers to question their parents' values, even though these values are reasonable.
2. *Practice and experimentation:* This involves the adolescent's belief that he or she can do no wrong and does not need the advice of parents. Friends may be given more credibility than parents.
3. *Rapprochement:* This occurs in middle adolescence (fourteen to sixteen years old). Having achieved a certain amount of autonomy, the teen at times accepts parental authority. At other times teens will still challenge and question their parents.
4. *Consolidation of self:* This occurs gradually as teens approach early adulthood and they gain a sense of personal identity that is based on self-understanding and emotional independence.

Adolescents who successfully separate from their family to become mature, responsible, moral adults have democratic parents. Democratic parents are willing to share power between themselves and their teen, while the parents have veto power over their teen's decisions. As children enter the adolescent years it is important that parents be willing to redefine and renegotiate their relationship with their teens to accommodate their developmental needs. Parent-adolescent interactions take on two important objectives:

1. To promote autonomy and self-regulation by equalizing power
2. To help adolescents develop a personal identity separate from their parents

The task that is often most difficult for parents of adolescents is to relinquish some degree of control over their child, which is necessary to help their child develop normally. Some behaviors of parents that promote normal adolescent development include these:

- Supporting the teen's attempts to achieve developmental tasks
- Accepting the teen's beliefs, feelings, and attitudes; being nonjudgmental (Remember, the teen years are a time when adolescents are "trying on" new things, so give them room to explore new ideas.)
- Setting appropriate limits on behavior, not on beliefs, attitudes, feelings, ideas, etc.
- Fostering empathy with the teen by remembering some of your own feelings and behavior as a teenager
- Acknowledging and supporting the teen's need for independence and autonomy
- Appreciating the teen's formation of a unique identity even if it is different from yours or how you want the teen to be

---

Source: Adapted from Bigner, J. (2002). *Parent-child relations* (Sixth edition) (pp. 256-259). Upper Saddle River, NJ: Prentice-Hall.

24

Creating a Participating Role for Adolescents in Group and Family Therapy

Daniel J. Wiener

Type of Contribution: Activity

Objective

To induce constructive participation of adolescents in group and family therapy sessions

Rationale for Use

All therapists who work with adolescents know that many of them are unwilling or reluctant to participate cooperatively in psychotherapy sessions. Common behaviors include outright refusal to engage in conversation or answering questions, giving only minimal answers, sarcasm, challenging counterquestions, refusal to make eye contact, hostility, displays of boredom, physically leaving the office, and so on. While different factors contribute to these behaviors, a common thread is that adolescents typically are brought or sent to therapy by their parents rather than coming on their own. For many of them, answering therapists' questions without understanding their purpose or volunteering information without knowing the consequences feels unsafe. In family therapy, therapists often find themselves stymied by such lack of cooperation and focus attention on talking with other family members. The result is that the adolescent is talked about in his or her presence, making it yet more difficult to include him or her in treatment. In group therapy for adolescents, a cooperative member may be labeled by others as weak or foolish for cooperating with an adult group leader and may lose status within the group.

The technique described here aims to create and offer the adolescent client a safer role from which to participate during therapy. The role is that of a commentator on the actions of others. Initially, the commentator is a social role, meaning that the client undertakes the role as himself or herself. At a later stage, the commentator can be offered a dramatic role, meaning that the client is playing a character who functions as a commentator on the actions of others.

Instructions

The presented technique develops in four flexible phases, explained with the example of family therapy. In phase I (preparation), which occurs during the joining process at the beginning of contact between therapist and family, the therapist shifts attention away from negative emotions such as anger, fear, embarrassment, or guilt toward positive ones such as curiosity, optimism, and humor. Although the therapist shows respect for the feelings of all clients, he or she looks for opportunities to let them know that he or she is a playful person who copes with life by not taking things too seriously. During phase I the therapist labels blame statements as problems experienced by the blamer, offers everyone the opportunity to present his or her viewpoint without interruption, and honors anyone's refusal to cooperate by stating that all are welcome to contribute in their own way.

In phase II (invoking the commentator) the therapist comments on his or her own possible reactions to statements made by family members. For example, if Mother states, "John [the adolescent] won't tell us who his friends are," the therapist might comment, "If I were John I might feel resentful that you would be prying into my private life." The therapist would then turn to John and ask, "Any comment?" After John's response, if any, the therapist would turn back to Mother and say, "If I were you I might wonder whether this therapist really understands what it's like to be responsible for my son without knowing what's going on." The point is not to achieve or display accurate empathy, but to model the role of commentator.

After a number of such comments have been made by family members, the therapist points out that everybody has judgments about others going on in his or her head. What is different between individuals are their decisions surrounding if, when, around whom, and in what ways to voice their judgments. The therapist labels the voicing of frank opinions as a positive contribution to the therapy and encourages family members to listen to such comments with detachment from the feelings they bring up in oneself (even though the therapist does not expect everyone to keep his or her cool at all times).

Note that the therapist does not voice his or her own judgments but draws out the comments of family members regarding one another. Should family members point out that the therapist is not speaking his or her own opinions, the therapist agrees and adds that he or she is there to help keep the focus on the family, not to bring himself or herself into the situation.

In phase III (activating the social role of commentator), the therapist offers an open-ended task for family members to participate in together during the session. Constructing a family drawing of life at home or handing them a ball with instructions to make up a family game are examples. Even if the adolescent is willing to participate in the family task, the therapist asks him or her to stand aside, observe, and make a running commentary to the therapist on what the rest of the family is doing. The therapist and the adolescent dialogue about the performance of other family members, who are to carry on with the task and not respond at that time to any commentary overheard. The role of the therapist is to provide the adolescent with a partner who listens and responds but does not agree with or add to any judgmental comments by the adolescent. For instance, if the adolescent says, "Sis is bossing around everyone else," the therapist might say, "And Dad is sitting quietly, looking at Sis." Should the adolescent comment upon the ongoing process itself, for example, "This situation is so lame," the therapist acknowledges it with his or her own comment, "And you are looking really bored," keeping the process going.

Following completion of the task, the participating family members get to exchange observations and comments, including any that refer to the adolescent being an observer and making his or her particular comments. The adolescent is invited first to listen and then to respond with further comments on what was just said by other members. In this way the adolescent is drawn into a participatory role in the session.

In the culminating phase, phase IV (activating the dramatic role of commentator), the therapist introduces the idea of playing a character who is a professional commentator performing for an audience. One way this dramatic role may be enacted is to introduce the family to a scenario involving the broadcast of a fictional Olympic competitive event. This is accomplished by having one family member (the athlete) perform some routine physical activity in extremely slow motion, while the commentator talks to an unseen broadcast audience as a sports announcer. Adolescents who lack interest in sports may be offered a comparable role with different content (MTV announcer at a rock concert; reporter at a fashion show; host(ess) of a promotional video for some commercial activity). In setting such scenes the therapist should be sure they involve some physical action onstage, both to influence commentary and to be commented upon. Also, there should be an absurd (playful, unrealistic) element to the scenes so that these enactments do not become events involving any real skill.

The only rule for all players (clients enacting roles onstage) is that they accept whatever is done or said by other players as true, even if that changes an idea they already had for the scene. The therapist can stand outside this scene or play the part of a commentator who acts as an assistant to the main commentator character.

Vignette

John, fifteen, had been caught by his mother smoking pot with his friends in his room. The example following occurred in the third family session attended by Mother, Stepfather (of two years), John, sister April (twelve), and brother Ben (ten). Earlier, Ben and Mother had first tried this game, which was partly successful.

THERAPIST: So let's have April be the athlete this time. [April nods.] How about Olympic door-knob touching? So, April, let me place your chair. [April gets out of chair; Therapist turns it to face the office door, six feet away. April sits down again.] You get out of your chair, walk to the door, touch the doorknob, and return to sitting down. Remember, you have to move extremely slowly because the whole action should take at least two minutes. OK, John, you said you'd be willing to be the announcer, but do you want an assistant?

JOHN: Uh, okay.

TH.: So who do you want to announce with?

John: You?

TH.: OK, let's set up over here. [Therapist puts two chairs alongside each other diagonally facing both the family and the office door. John and Therapist sit down.] Now, what name do you want to give your character?

[Pause]

JOHN: Zap-man.

TH.: And I'm Joe Steele. [Therapist assumes a stage voice.] So here we are, Zap-man, broadcasting live from the Olympics. I see our next competitor in the doorknob-touching event is Stacy Lindgren, from . . . [looking at John questioningly]

JOHN: North Germany.

TH.: Yes, Zap-man, North Germany, and she's been a medalist before, right?

JOHN: Yeah, she won a bronze in the trials in Yin . . .

TH.: Korea! Yes! And what scores does she have to beat here?

JOHN: [Blankly] Scores?

TH.: Well, I see Sonia Fritz is ahead with a 9.37 for doorknob-touching. How'd Stacy do on her first attempt?

JOHN: Not so good, only a 7.

TH.: Hm, that'll be tough. But I see she's ready to begin. [Therapist motions for April to begin. She stands up normally. Therapist directs in a stage whisper, very, very slowly. April nods, sits down, and starts to rise from her chair in slow motion.] What do you make of her form, Zap-man?

JOHN: Looks wobbly to me.

TH.: Yes, I'm surprised her trainer didn't bandage her right knee after that skiing accident last month.

JOHN: She'll never make it if she can't extend her leg fully.

TH.: How true! [Excitedly] Look, what great balance! Her shoulders are perfectly level! [April straightens up as she strides in slow motion toward the door.] She's coming in for the touch! [April starts to extend her hand toward the doorknob.]

JOHN: [Importantly] Folks, this is the moment of truth! She's coming in low . . .

TH.: Will the judges penalize her for an underside touch?

JOHN: Definitely. Her arm's gotta be straight and touching the center of the knob. [April touches the center of knob.]

TH.: [Very excited] She's pulled it off! A midcourse correction, Zap-man. It hasn't been done in competition since 1992! Now, if she can only keep her form on the return. [April turns slowly to return to her chair.]

JOHN: On no! She's pulling off to the left. [April turns her head looking questioningly at John and Therapist. The therapist motions her to go to her left, whispering, "Go with it!" April leans to the left.]

TH.: A tough break . . . [April stage falls on her left knee in slow motion, right hand reaching for her chair.] Let's hope she's not hurt too bad.

JOHN: [Nodding] A tough break. Here come the medics!

TH.: [Stands up and waves his arm to end the scene] That was terrific! [He leads the family in applause. John and April are smiling broadly.]

The next ten minutes were spent in family conversation replaying what had happened on-stage. Audience family members were excited and congratulatory toward both John and April.

Commentary

The scene went very well. Both John and April entered the spirit of the pretense and cooperatively cocreated events in the scene. I had to coach April at a few points and fed John a few questions, but they both contributed strongly on their own to make the scene work. It might be observed that Zap-man's comments were of a somewhat doubting or negative character while Joe's were more upbeat. This contrast actually contributes to the interest the scene generated.

To me, John clearly enjoyed the power Zap-man's commentary had to cause Stacy to fail, but my objective was not to draw attention to this dynamic. Indeed, to do so would have increased John's self-consciousness and returned him to the initial unwelcome role of therapy client. This obviously would have been counterproductive.

Note that it is usually better for the therapist to first offer the commentator role to a cooperative family member instead of to the adolescent, since it may seem too demanding when described. Once demonstrated, though, it is typically seen by the adolescent as a fun activity that carries a low risk of personal disclosure and affords an opportunity to influence the behavior of others without seeming to risk being influenced oneself.

However the scene turns out, the therapist should praise the players for their courage to try it at all and to head off attempts by family members to critique the performances or offer even constructive criticism. If the scene falls apart, the therapist should directly and cheerfully take responsibility for its failure, saying that he or she should have better prepared the players. Such artistic failure need not be a setback for the therapy since the therapist can selectively offer the family feedback as to what aspects of the enactment *did* work, such as whatever degree of cooperation between players was manifest, their taking on of character, following instructions, using their imaginations, or, if nothing else, players' willingness to risk failure in attempting the scene.

Suggestions for Follow-Up

Once there has been even a partial success at a commentator scene involving the adolescent there are a number of constructive options: (1) returning to exclusively verbal therapy, making best use of the adolescent's increased involvement; (2) enacting another commentator scene if the adolescent is now willing to take the athlete role; (3) introducing other enactments that draw on shared control and mutual cooperation. In particular, I use three games (listed in increasing order of difficulty and described in further detail in Wiener, 1994): Poet's Corner (pp. 84-85), Little Voice (pp. 86-87), and Dubbing Scenes (p. 86). In my experience, adolescents who have had positive involvement in such scenes are more willing to do other enactments than to engage in talk-only therapy.

Contraindications

For Clients

As a playful atmosphere promotes cooperation and discovery, it is not advisable to move on to phase IV while any overt antagonism among family members is manifest in the session. Where thought disorder is displayed by the adolescent, or where there appears to be paranoid ideation, neither phases III nor IV are indicated.

Should the adolescent react negatively during or following a commentator scene, the therapist needs to assess whether this reaction is part of the initial recalcitrance or is due to a perception of failure or embarrassment. In the latter case, the therapist can attempt to offer encouragement and reframe the experience as brave and constructive.

For Therapists

To move through phase IV successfully, the therapist needs to be in touch with his or her playfulness and be unconcerned with the possibilities of the scene not working and of dealing with unexpected outcomes. Should the therapist be apprehensive, it would be better not to introduce such improvised enactments as the commentator scenes described.

Suggested Readings and Resources for the Professional

Edgette, J.S. (1999). Getting real. *Family Therapy Networker, 56,* 36-41.
Wiener, D.J. (1994). *Rehearsals for growth: Theater improvisation for psychotherapists.* New York: Norton (particularly pp. 107-108, 143-167).

25

Silent Scream: Opening Adolescent Communication

Catherine Ford Sori

Type of Contribution: Activity

Materials: Teen magazines (provided by client or therapist)

Objectives

This activity is designed to promote more open communication between adolescents and their parents. As it is described, Silent Scream is more appropriate for female teens. However, it could be adapted for males when appropriate. This intervention goes beyond a mere "communication" exercise, as teens share their inner thoughts and feelings, and parents are encouraged to listen and empathize with their children. As adolescents feel better understood they are more receptive to listening to their parents' points of view. This more intimate level of sharing strengthens family relationships and forges a bridge that allows the therapist to help the family work together to address problems. All of this is designed to keep teens on track developmentally by fostering intimacy, autonomy, and identity development.

Rationale

Often by the time an adolescent is seen in therapy there is a wide emotional gulf between the parents and teen. Teens report that their parents don't understand them, and parents are often frustrated with their troubled adolescents. The sad result often is a sense of alienation between the generations, where no one really seems to be able to listen or attempt to understand the other's point of view. Parents often turn the child over to the therapist to be "fixed"—having tried every solution they could think of, and feeling defeated and powerless to help their child (Bailey and Sori, 2000). Therapists who bite this tempting bait—that they can "save the child" where the parents have failed—run the risk of further disempowering the parents, and increasing the gap between teen and parents. The goal is to increase intimacy in family relationships, so that parents and teens find ways to bridge the generation gap. When this doesn't occur, the cost can be considerable for both teens and parents.

Adolescence is a time when several important developmental tasks need to be accomplished for teens to prepare for the next stage of the life cycle: leaving home. Conflicts at home need to be resolved for the adolescent to be able to form intimate attachments in dating and marriage. Healthy autonomy develops gradually as the child moves from pre- to late adolescence and is closely linked to identity development. During these years teens want more space as they seek to discover who they are. They also want less parental control and more freedom to make their own choices. Friends become increasingly important, and teens use peer referencing as a way to discover how they are viewed by others. Friends' opinions—whether good or bad, valid or invalid—are often incorporated into the teen's developing self-identity.

Some parents believe it is "normal" for adolescents not to confide in their parents, as they increasingly turn to peers for support. They believe it is normal for teens not to share much with parents because they are striving for autonomy and independence. Instead of promoting healthy autonomy, however, this may leave teens feeling isolated and without a wise and caring adult in whom to confide.

It is a misconception that the family is no longer important, or that teens don't want or need more parental involvement in their lives (see Taffel, 2001). Parental referencing is also vital for teens to develop a healthy identity and is often crucial to counterbalance negative or invalid peer referencing. Teens who feel unpopular, unattractive, or "less than" their peers can be helped by parents who teach their children about the lure of temporal values (such as materialism or physical attractiveness), instead emphasizing character development (such as kindness and respect). Parents esteem their children by celebrating their good qualities and strengths, and reminding them of their special value to the family. When a teen is struggling parents may share the difficulties they experienced during adolescence. Since teens have trouble looking too far into the future, parents can point out that it might be rough road right now, but there is light at the end of the tunnel. Above all, teens can be reassured that their parents are there to support them.

This type of intimate communication between teens and parents may not occur for various reasons. Some adolescents may keep their feelings to themselves in an attempt to strengthen their personal boundaries. When parents are too intrusive, adolescents may have little privacy or opportunity to experience themselves as separate individuals. Teens may struggle to differentiate and establish a personal identity in these families. Disengaged families often lack the warmth and degree of concern necessary to foster the sharing of intimate feelings among family members. In addition, some children may never have had a close relationship or secure attachment with either parent. This might occur, for example, in a stepfamily or after a custody change, perhaps when a teen is sent to live with a parent who is a relative stranger. Other teens may have attempted to share their feelings but found their parents unwilling or unable to listen and empathize. Some children (e.g., those in foster care) may never have had a parental figure who was emotionally available. These children, deprived of empathic mirroring, may really struggle to understand who they are and what they feel.

In all these cases, a careful assessment is crucial to understand the family's structure and past and present emotional closeness (Minuchin, 1974). It is important to work with parents to ascertain their readiness and willingness to listen to what is really going on with their teen. Parents may need individual and/or couple work to gain insight into their own family history, and to understand their child's needs. Some benefit from psychoeducation or improving parenting skills.

This intervention is useful for teens to begin to sort out and identify their inner thoughts and feelings, perhaps first in the safety of the therapeutic relationship, but ultimately to their parents. The overall goal is to prepare both the child and parents to come to a deeper knowledge and understanding of one another. Some teens are willing to open up to their parents with only minimal support from the therapist. Others may be too depressed, hopeless, or overwhelmed to be able to voice their deeper feelings. It is in these situations that this intervention is most useful.

Instructions

Once the therapist has a solid background and a strong working alliance with an adolescent, this activity may be used to help a teen access deeper feelings and problems. Parents are included when the teen wants to share her feelings more openly with them. However, the therapist should help prepare the parents to ensure they will respond in a way that fosters acceptance and helps the teen feel understood.

The teen should be asked to bring in a few of her favorite magazines or the therapist may provide some he or she has preselected. Initially, the therapist can spend some time just flipping through the magazines and discussing things of interest to the teen (e.g., hairstyles, clothes, cosmetics, rock music, dating, or romance articles). The therapist might comment on how many people believe the models in magazines are so beautiful that they must live perfect lives. But in reality, models struggle with many of the same issues most teens encounter. For example, models are often very critical of their looks, thinking their noses are too long or their lips too thin. They also break up with boyfriends, argue with parents, and worry about their future.

The therapist might then wonder about what worries or concerns the teen might have. If the teen is reluctant or seems unable to share, the therapist may ask to borrow the magazine to see if the therapist can "guess" how the teen feels. However, the teen is free to disagree with, correct, or confirm the therapist's guess. The teen is told that if she says nothing, the therapist will assume that the guess was correct.

The teen's body language, facial expressions, and affect are important clues in correctly identifying underlying feelings and concerns. But therapists must also employ their intuition and memories of their own adolescent experiences to begin to discover the teen's inner world. All of these factors, combined with information that has been directly shared and the therapist's observations of the teen and family relationships, are what guide this process. It is vital that therapists conduct this activity "as if" they were experiencing these feelings themselves. At the same time, extreme care must be taken that therapists not "impose" their own thoughts or feelings on clients. The goal is for the child to feel understood and accepted, never judged or criticized.

Careful attention should be paid to language, and statements should be questioning, exploratory, and tentative. For example, the therapist might show a picture of a sad-looking teen staring longingly at a couple holding hands and kissing. The therapist might comment in a soft, questioning tone, "I wonder if you think how wonderful it would be to be happy like the girl kissing this guy. She looks so confident and happy . . . and very sure of who she is. . . . But maybe sometimes you feel more like this girl, who looks sad . . . like she wishes she had a boyfriend . . . someone to love her, and be with her . . . but she might be thinking that this won't happen for her . . . maybe because she doesn't believe she's pretty enough." Throughout this slow and tentative process, the therapist should observe the teen's expression and reaction and ask if perhaps she ever felt this way, since many girls do. The teen may agree with a nod, and the therapist may then deepen the discussion. The therapist should continue in this manner as long as the teen is receptive, and until the therapist believes he or she has tapped into some core feelings (e.g., sadness, fear).

If a teen disagrees with a guess, the therapist should request her help because he or she is confused and really wants to understand her experience. Taffel (2001) emphasizes the importance of therapists (as well as parents) demonstrating genuine interest in really getting to know teens. When a teen appears extremely guarded or resistant it may be helpful first to relate the pictures to the experiences of other teens. For example, in working with a teen who moved and is struggling to break into a new peer group, the therapist might find an appropriate picture and state that the picture reminds him or her of how another teenager said she felt after moving to a new school. (Later this story might be expanded to include how that teen found good ways to cope.)

After the teen can acknowledge and discuss her feelings, the therapist can ask parents for their reactions to what their child has shared. Since parents have been prepared, the therapist need only coach them to respond with love and empathy. The therapist continues discussions until the teen feels accepted and understood and then ends the activity with each person discussing his or her reactions to the session. The therapist should acknowledge the teen's courage to talk about some deep subjects, and the parent's wonderful demonstrations of love and understanding.

Younger adolescent boys may also benefit from this intervention, since it often is more difficult for boys openly to share feelings. Once the therapist has joined well and has a good knowledge of the teen's issues, the same procedures can be followed, but using magazines that appeal to male youths. Teen boys often identify with sports figures or rock stars, so these magazines might be used to bring up issues such as power, popularity, and "being cool." With males it may be helpful to be more playful, exaggerating a position to reduce defensiveness, before probing on a deeper emotional level.

Vignette

Allison, age seventeen, was the oldest of three siblings. She, along with her fifteen-year-old sister and twelve-year-old brother, lived with their father, stepmother, and two half siblings (two girls, ages six months and three years). Allison's parents had divorced when she was five, following a long separation. The girls had lived most of their lives with Mom, who often neglected them. Allison's mom would sometimes disappear for several days, leaving Allison to care for her younger siblings. Once when Allison was eight she was caught shoplifting a jar of peanut butter and a loaf of bread. Mom hadn't been home for three days, her siblings were crying, and there was no food in the apartment. The children were placed in foster care, then were sent to live with relatives, and were eventually returned to their mother.

From early childhood Allison had assumed a maternal role in caring for her younger siblings. When they were hurt or scared, it was usually Allison who comforted them. Allison had long ago lost her childhood, as well as her innocence. Mom often brought her many "boyfriends" home late at night. When drunken fights erupted the younger children would huddle in bed, looking to Allison for safety.

Throughout their childhood the children had only minimal phone contact with their father. Mom often told Allison that her father had never wanted them. She said he was now remarried to a "skinny bitch" and had a new family. The children were repeatedly told their father did not want to hear from them.

When Allison was fifteen the family had moved north to a trailer park. They were living with Mom's boyfriend, Billy Bob, who had a prison record. When drunk, Billy Bob was often violent and abusive. It was not unusual for the children to witness their mother and Billy Bob having sex in the living room. One night after Mom had passed out, Billy Bob grabbed Allison, trying to force her to the floor. The other children began screaming and hitting Billy Bob, who quickly backed down. However, this aroused Mom, a fight ensued, and Billy Bob left Mom. Ultimately Allison was blamed.

This time, however, Allison had had enough. She had recently discovered that her father, Dave, lived only fifteen miles away and had gotten his telephone number. The next day she called Dad's house and poured out her story to her stepmother, Julie. Julie mobilized her husband; they hired a lawyer and arranged for the children to be removed from their unsafe environment. Dave eventually was awarded custody. Soon after, Billy Bob was arrested for armed robbery and was sent back to prison. Their mother just quietly disappeared.

Two years later Julie brought Allison for therapy because she had "caught her in the barn doing funny things with a boy." Allison had her top off when her stepmother walked in. Julie genuinely cared about Allison, as well as her other two stepchildren. However, she had her hands full, with two young children of her own and helping to run their small farm. Her husband abdicated all parenting duties to her. Julie was proud that she had rescued the children from "their whore of a mother." She was also thankful for how much Allison helped her with the younger kids, the cooking, and the chores.

During individual sessions Allison said she loved Julie, but she also loved her real mom. She felt guilty and responsible for Mom and worried that she wasn't okay. She had learned that her mother had recently moved back to the area and was waiting for Billy Bob's release from prison. Sometimes she would sneak out to call her mother after school, just to make sure she was okay. Allison was sad and troubled beyond her years. She longed to be "normal and happy like other teens."

Dad, a quiet and hardworking man, was not very involved with the family, except to take them to horse auctions on weekends. Allison was very distant from her dad, but Julie persuaded him to attend some therapy sessions. Julie had never parented teens, and she had very rigid rules about social and school activities. For example, Allison could talk on the phone only ten minutes a day, had to come straight home from school to help with chores, and was not allowed to date or attend school activities. The therapist worked with both parents to help them understand how Allison's past might be affecting her in the present, and to allow the older children more appropriate independence. Allison's parents were very concerned about her recent sexual behavior, fearing she would "turn out to be just like her mother." Julie was strongly encouraged not to call Allison's mother names, and to allow Allison to find redeemable "parts" of her mother that she could love and identify with, to help foster healthy identity development. Although she was well cared for, Allison still had too many responsibilities to allow her to enjoy a more carefree adolescence. The couple discussed ways to redistribute chores more equitably among the older children, and to accept Grandmother's offer to help with the younger children.

Julie and Dave both wanted to understand Allison and all that she was feeling. Allison seemed willing but unable to talk on a deeper level with her parents. As a child probably no one had recognized, labeled, or validated Allison's feelings. They had been repressed for so long that it was now difficult for Allison to access and talk about her emotions. Although she could recite the facts of her life, the emotional content was not readily available. She was not close to her father but found it easier to talk to Julie. Allison did well in school, but she had no close friends.

This activity was planned with both Julie and Dave present, since Allison wanted to be able to feel closer to both of them. The therapist believed both parents were receptive and would respond appropriately to Allison. The goal was to help Allison begin to share more deeply about herself and her peers, and to increase her parents' ability to respond appropriately to her emotional and developmental needs.

Allison brought in two popular teen magazines, and she and the therapist spent some time discussing the advertisements, and chuckling over a love advice column. When Allison felt comfortable and ready, her parents were invited in. The therapist explained that teenage girls often find it difficult to talk about how they feel, even when they wish they could. After giving Allison permission *not* to talk, the therapist explained that she would use pictures in the magazine to "guess" how Allison feels. Mom and Dad's initial role was to listen, while Allison was free to disagree, correct the therapist, or confirm the guess.

The therapist slowly flipped through the pages of the magazines, making general comments, until she stopped on an ad that showed an attractive teen. The therapist commented that most girls want to feel attractive, be popular, and have "cool clothes." When the therapist wondered if Allison sometimes wished for those things, she nodded slowly, keeping her eyes on the magazine. Next the therapist found an ad for makeup, and then one showing a teen chatting on the telephone. The therapist commented on how most teens love to spend hours on the phone with friends, and how important that is for girls to develop close friendships. Allison agreed. Then the therapist said that sometimes we feel sad if we don't have a special friend to talk with and wondered if Allison had ever felt this way. When Allison said nothing the therapist said gently, "You don't have to answer, but since you aren't disagreeing or correcting me, I assume that sometimes you might feel that way." Other pictures showed friends at parties or on dates, and the therapist normalized how teens long for these fun activities.

Then the therapist came across a picture of a girl who was lying on her bed crying. She wondered if perhaps this girl was crying because she was sad about someone she cared about. Or maybe she wished she were prettier or more popular. Allison, eyes never leaving the pictures, nodded almost imperceptibly. Next the therapist pointed out a picture of a girl who appeared to be screaming out in silent agony. She wondered if perhaps this girl felt so overwhelmed that she could only scream silently. . . . Because so much had happened in her life that maybe she would never really love herself, because maybe she wasn't lovable . . . and she wondered if she would ever be loved the way she longed to be, or if she could ever really be happy. In fact, when she looked in the mirror, she wasn't even sure who she was, what kind of person she saw looking back at her. With tears in her eyes, Allison whispered, "How did you know *that's exactly how I feel?*"

The therapist, moving closer, gently assured Allison that she had every reason to feel that way because so much *had* happened to her that had gotten in the way and blocked her ability to see all the beauty and strength and courage she had deep inside her. Motioning for Dave and Julie to move closer and touch Allison, she wondered what they might like to say to help Allison feel better, and to give her hope. Julie reached out for Allison, and they sat for several moments, holding each other and crying. Dave softly stroked Allison's back. Then, with tears welling up in his eyes, he pulled Allison's head against his chest, holding her in their first close embrace. Together, Julie and Dave soothed and comforted Allison, telling her what a good and loving and beautiful young woman she was. They assured her of their love, and that they were committed to helping her learn to love herself, and to see the beauty and good that was inside her. Julie shared how much she enjoyed their special relationship, and how happy she was to have Allison for a stepdaughter. With some coaching she gave Allison permission to love her real mother, who couldn't be "all bad." In a broken voice, Allison's father told that he had loved her from the moment she was born, and how deeply he regretted all the lost years of her childhood. He shared how proud of her he was, of the lovely young woman she was becoming. Allison responded by saying how deeply sorry she was that she had worried them and let them down. She wanted so much to make them happy and proud of her, but sometimes she felt life was so overwhelming and confusing. She wanted them to be able to trust her again.

For the first time Allison risked real intimacy and was rewarded with warm acceptance, deep understanding, nurturing love, and validation. Her parents were given a glimpse of the depth of her emotional pain and longing and drew closer in their efforts to reach out to help her. This type of intimacy fosters healthy self-esteem and was a vital first step for Allison to begin to heal from the trauma of her childhood. This intervention also provided the foundation for much of the rest of therapy for Allison and her family.

Suggestions for Follow-Up

Therapists can refer back to the pictures at different points in therapy to normalize and validate teens' emotional experiences, hopes, and dreams. They can also be encouraged to bring in new magazines periodically, especially if an article or picture particularly strikes them and they'd like to discuss it. This activity can also be done with siblings, to foster discussions about a variety of teen issues. With parents it is a great lead-in to heart-to-heart talks about opposite-sex relationships, dating, sex, and intimate relationships.

One additional helpful activity that further boosts self-esteem is to have teens cut out pictures for a collage. Pictures may depict different "parts" of themselves (e.g., "crazy," "punk," "preppy," "glamorous," and so on), various feelings, as well as things that have special meaning to them (e.g., clothes, rock stars, movies, TV shows, and so on). The collage can be shared with siblings, parents, or done as a group activity.

Contraindications

This activity would be contraindicated if the therapist suspects a teen has a thought disorder or is dissociative. In these cases a teen might have a difficult time separating her real experiences from the pictures or from the suggestions of the therapist. Much care should be taken to ensure the teen is comfortable disagreeing with a therapist's "wrong guess."

As stated earlier, the therapist should feel confident that parents are able to respond appropriately to their teen before including them in this activity. Likewise, therapists should be confident that the adolescent is strong enough and won't be overwhelmed by the emotions that might be revealed.

Therapists may want to provide teen magazines to have a chance to preselect appropriate pictures. Finally, this activity may be a better fit for therapists who are comfortable working experientially, since it requires the therapist to use both drama and deep emotional connecting.

Professional Readings

Bailey, C. E. and Sori, C. E. (2000). Involving parents in children's therapy. In C. E. Bailey (Ed.), *Children in therapy* (pp. 475-501). New York: W.W. Norton and Co.

Blatner, A. (1994). Psychodramatic methods in family therapy. In C. Schaefer and L. Carey (Eds.), *Family play therapy*. Northvale, NJ: Jason Aronson, Inc.

Keith, D. V. (1987). Intuition in family therapy: A short manual on post-modern witchcraft. *Contemporary Family Therapy, 9*(1-2), 11-22.

Minuchin, S. (1974). *Families and family therapy*. Cambridge, MA: Harvard University Press.

Taffel, R. (2001). The wall of silence. *Psychotherapy Networker, 25*(3), 52-64.

Resources for Clients

Teen magazines for girls, such as *Seventeen, Madmoiselle, YM* (Young and Modern), *Teen Beat*.

Teen magazines for boys, such as *Sports Illustrated, Rolling Stone, Wolf Marshall's Guitar One,* or magazines for specific sports.

26

The Places You'll Go: Developing Hope and Self-Efficacy

James Patrick Ward

Congratulations! Today is your day. You're off to great places! You're off and away!

Dr. Seuss, *Oh, the Places You'll Go!*

Type of Contribution: Activities/Homework, Handouts

Objective

Much of therapist training is focused on gaining knowledge and honing our skills with models and techniques of therapy, aspects that allegedly account for a small portion of change in therapy (Hubble, Duncan, and Miller, 1999). The objective of this homework is to help therapists build hope and expectancy that therapy will help the client. Investing some time building hope should increase the odds that clients will find therapy useful. Snyder, Michael, and Cheavens (1999) essentially state that people have hope when they feel their dreams can be attained. This homework can help the client identify goals, generate a plan to reach his or her goals, and achieve a new sense of agency.

Generating a plan to reach a goal, according to Stephen Covey (1989), is "to begin with the end in mind" (p. 97). This activity is very productive at any stage in life. However, it can be particularly empowering for the adolescent who is preparing to leave home. Identifying what one wants reduces anxiety and feelings of ambivalence. Organizing the steps to goal attainment produces clarity of thought, sense of purpose, and hope for the future. Working through this activity with an adolescent client will help prepare him or her for the "solo flight" of developing personal autonomy.

Snyder, Michael, and Cheavens (1999) explain that hope can be conceptualized by how people think about goals. One component of hope is the thoughts people have about their ability to achieve a workable route to a goal. This is referred to as pathways thinking. A second component, agency thinking, refers to the beliefs people have regarding their ability to start and work toward a goal. Creating a goal can be thought of as knowing exactly what you want. Pathways thinking can be conceptualized as, "I know what my goal is and this is how I plan on getting there." Agency thinking can best be summarized as, "I think I can."

Rationale for Use

Hubble, Duncan, and Miller (1999) specify four factors of therapeutic change common to all theories of therapy. The first is client/extratherapeutic factors, which are seen as the most powerful element in therapy. These are the client's circumstances outside of therapy, such as strengths, environmental support, and various events in the client's life. This factor is said to account for 40 percent of outcome variance. Second is the relationship factor, which represents variables in the client-therapist relationship, such as empathy, mutual affirmation, and warmth. The relationship factor is said to account for 30 percent of positive outcomes. The third factor is hope, expectancy, and placebo, which accounts for 15 percent of positive outcomes. This factor refers to the client's knowledge that he or she is expected to improve. The client is offered hope that therapy will help. The fourth and last factor is that of therapist model/technique, which accounts for the final 15 percent of positive outcome. By developing a sense of hope and expectancy in therapy, the client has a better chance of achieving positive outcomes. The therapist will do well to develop skills in the common factor of hope.

Instructions

Identifying Goals

Walter and Peller (1992) state that the client is the expert in identifying his or her own goals. They provide an excellent list of criteria for well-defined goals:

- State the goal in positive language, in terms of what the client *will* be doing or thinking.
- Goals should be stated in a process form. Use "-ing" endings in goals to elicit the how.
- Word the goals in the here and now so the goal is attainable in the present.
- Make the goal as specific as possible.
- Make the goal within the client's control. Action can be initiated or terminated by the client.
- Word the goal in the client's own language.

Activity #1: Using these criteria, work with the client on formulating attainable goals. Write this process down on a sheet of paper. When a goal is finalized, write it in the goal starburst on Handout 1, Goals and Pathways. Use one copy of the handout for each goal.

Constructing the Pathways

Walter and Peller (1992) assert that several paths can be constructed to arrive at the solution or goal. Focusing on positive, future-oriented change directed toward the goal is key in developing pathways. A famous (infamous for some) comedy movie about therapy, *What About Bob,* involved a psychiatrist who wrote a book titled *Baby Steps.* Although this book may be bogus, the concept of baby steps is very applicable here and is directly tied to how specific the goal is made. In creating the pathway, the steps should be very attainable and realistic for the client.

Activity #2: With Handout 1, Goals and Pathways, write down the specific steps the client plans on taking to attain the goal. Do this for each goal in a stepwise fashion. The initial steps will start at the bottom, working up the stairs toward the goal.

Developing a Sense of Agency

A key aspect to agency thinking is that people believe they are in control and have all they need to solve their problems (Walter and Peller, 1992). Walter and Peller state that one way to help a client develop personal agency is to have a conversation with him or her about how the client will achieve his or her goals, presupposing that the client has all he or she needs to achieve them. This strategy of assuming the client has the power to attain his or her goals is one the therapist can take throughout the process. In addition to this, the therapist can help the client think about things he or she can do well. Snyder, Michael, and Cheavens (1999) state that people often forget their preexisting accomplishments and successes when in a crisis. An effective strategy for encouraging pathways thinking is to review past successes with the client. A third strategy is to help the client think of environmental supports for the sense of agency. Who, or what, is in his or her "cheering section?" Encourage clients to inform key people about their goals and their plans to achieve them, and also to ask for their encouragement. The client should surround himself or herself with people who will provide encouragement rather than discouragement. The creation of such a positive climate in the client's environment will give a positive boost to the outcome element of extratherapeutic factors (Hubble, Duncan, and Miller, 1999).

Activity #3: In session, work with the client to fill out Handout 2, I Think I Can! I Know I Can! Keep in mind that the client may struggle to come up with anything that he or she is proud of or views as a personal success. Work with the client on small things first. Write down that he or she learned how to tie his or her shoelaces if this gets the list started. The therapist can also suggest that he or she be put in the client's cheering section. The therapist should advise the client to contact all people in the cheering section, asking them if they are willing to act as part of the client's support network. The client should inform them about the goal, discuss the plan to achieve the goal, and ask for their encouragement. At the bottom of the handout page is a place for a client-constructed positive self-statement memory verse. This should be constructed in the client's own language to make it meaningful.

Homework

Copy the handouts to keep in the file and give the originals to the client. Encourage the client to keep the handouts in a place where they can be referred to often. Especially important will be the client contacting and maintaining his or her "cheering section" support network.

As the client achieves steps toward a goal, the client can write beside that step the date that step was taken. This will provide visual reinforcement of both pathways and agency thinking.

Vignette

Tom, a seventeen-year-old, presented for therapy at the insistence of his parents. The parents complain that Tom, a senior in high school, has let his academic performance slide and has quit all extracurricular activities. Now, they perceive that Tom just lies around at home watching TV. The parents are worried that Tom has become depressed. In the first individual session with Tom, he reported that he does feel a little depressed, but mostly he feels that the rest of his life is hopeless. He recently received a rejection letter from the only college to which he applied, but he hasn't told his parents because this college is their alma mater and they have always planned for him to follow in his father's footsteps. Tom reports that he is secretly happy about the rejection because he felt trapped into doing what his parents wanted for him rather than what he wanted for himself. In addition, Tom is experiencing depression and anxiety because he doesn't know what he is going to do after graduation. Tom states, "I've always just gone along with my parents' plans for me. Now that I have an opportunity to do what I want, I don't know what I want to do! I've never done anything on my own and I'm afraid I'll fail."

Tom had several family therapy sessions to resolve conflicts with his parents about making his own life choices. Eventually, his parents accepted that Tom could develop his own life plan and voiced their support for this. Next, Tom worked with the therapist on identifying attainable life goals. Once a goal was identified, specific doable steps were developed to attain that goal. One Goals and Pathways handout was used for each specific goal. For instance, one of Tom's goals was to figure out if he even wanted to go to college. Steps to attain this decisional goal included taking a career interest test, interviewing people he knows who didn't go to college and those who have gone to college, and visiting some college campuses that are of interest to him.

The therapist also worked with Tom in session to develop his sense of agency. Initially Tom had difficulty identifying anything as a personal accomplishment. To illustrate this point: Tom is a very adept pianist, yet he states that his parents wanted him to learn the piano and forced him to practice. The therapist helped reframe this as something that Tom personally can do well. Even though his parents made him practice, Tom was successful in mastering the skill of playing piano. Through this exercise, Tom was able to develop a positive self-statement memory verse: "I have succeeded in the past, and can succeed in the future. I can make my own good choices." Through this activity, Tom was able to develop a clear vision of what he wanted out of life, and possible steps to attaining his current goals. Tom left therapy with a new sense of hope, agency, and self-reliance.

Suggestions for Follow-Up

This intervention requires frequent and regular follow-up. Time should be allocated each session for reviewing the client's goals and successful steps taken toward the goals. Also, the client's sense of agency should be assessed regularly. The therapist should keep in mind that he or she is in the client's cheering section throughout therapy.

Contraindications for the Activity

It will be necessary to make sure the client feels heard and understood before engaging in this activity. Snyder, Michael, and Cheavens (1999) maintain that therapists who do not listen carefully to what the client is saying run the risk of lessening hope in therapy. In addition, clients may need to spend considerable time processing their emotions and talking about their problems before they are ready to generate goals (Egan, 1994). The therapist should be warned against taking on the client's responsibility for change. Snyder, Michael, and Cheavens (1999) assert that the client should feel a sense of ownership of his or her own goals and hope. Also, if the client displays extremely rigid thinking or an "all or nothing" attitude, in other words appears set up for failure, this activity should not be done. In this case, the intervention could be detrimental rather than helpful. This type of client would first need to work toward becoming flexible and to allow himself or herself to be OK with failed attempts at change.

Suggested Readings and Resources for the Professional

Egan, G. (1994). *The skilled helper: A problem-management approach to helping.* Pacific Grove, CA: Brooks/Cole.

Hubble, M. A., Duncan, B. L., and Miller, S. D. (Eds.) (1999). *The heart and soul of change: What works in therapy.* Washington, DC: American Psychological Association.

Snyder, C. R., Michael, S. T., and Cheavens, J. S. (1999). Hope as a psychotherapeutic foundation of common factors, placebos, and expectancies. In M. Hubble, B. L. Duncan, and S. D. Miller (Eds.), *The heart and soul of change: What works in therapy* (pp. 179-200). Washington, DC: American Psychological Association.

Walter, J. L. and Peller, J. E. (1992). *Becoming solution-focused in brief therapy.* New York: Brunner/Mazel.

Bibliotherapy Sources for the Client

Covey, S. R. (1989). *The seven habits of highly effective people.* New York: Simon and Schuster.
Piper, W. (1976). *The little engine that could.* New York: Platt and Munk.
Seuss, Dr. (1990). *Oh, the places you'll go!* New York: Random House.
Weiner-Davis, M. (1996). *Change your life and everyone in it.* New York: Simon and Schuster.

References

Covey, S. R. (1989). *The seven habits of highly effective people.* New York: Simon and Schuster.
Egan, G. (1994). *The skilled helper: A problem-management approach to helping.* Pacific Grove, CA: Brooks/Cole.
Hubble, M. A., Duncan, B. L., and Miller, S. D. (1999). Introduction. In M. Hubble, B. L. Duncan, and S. D. Miller (Eds.), *The heart and soul of change: What works in therapy* (pp. 1-19). Washington, DC: American Psychological Association.
Snyder, C. R., Michael, S. T., and Cheavens, J. S. (1999). Hope as a psychotherapeutic foundation of common factors, placebos, and expectancies. In M. Hubble, B. L. Duncan, and S. D. Miller (Eds.), *The heart and soul of change: What works in therapy* (pp. 179-200). Washington, DC: American Psychological Association.
Walter, J. L. and Peller, J. E. (1992). *Becoming solution-focused in brief therapy.* New York: Brunner/Mazel.

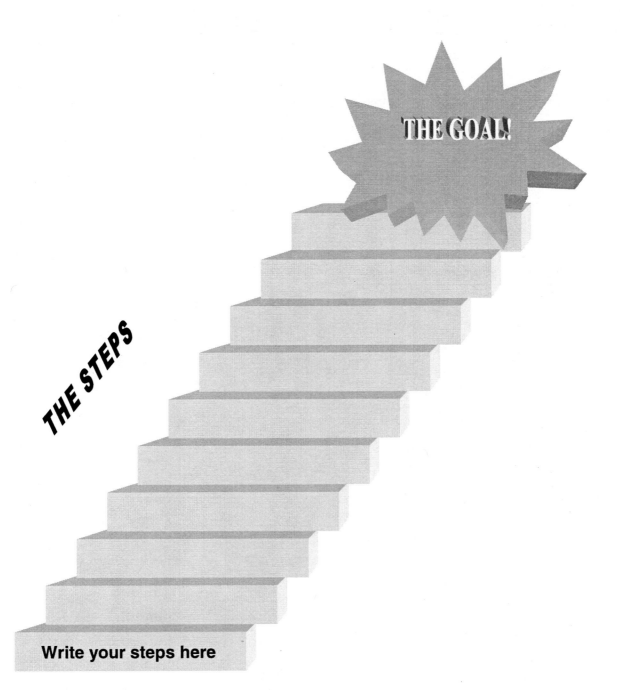

THE GOAL!

THE STEPS

Write your steps here

I Think I Can! I Know I Can!

Things I Am Proud Of ... Things I Can Do Well ...

Successes I Have Experienced ...

Who/What Is in My Cheering Section?

Positive Self-Statement Memory Verse:

_____

_____

_____

27

Therapeutic Letters to Young Persons

David Paré
Mary Ann Majchrzak Rombach

Type of Contribution: Homework/Handout

A therapeutic letter to a child or adolescent, written by his or her therapist(s), is a specialized narrative tool that simultaneously functions as a handout and homework. Letters are homework: they encourage young persons to try out more of what is working and invite them to reflect on where they might be headed if these favorable developments continue. Letters are also handouts in the sense that the child or adolescent brings home a highly individualized document that affirms her or his knowledges, resources, and breakthroughs ("unique outcomes"). Typically, we compose therapeutic letters using a tentative tone to avoid making expert pronouncements that may devalue the ideas and experiences of those who consult us.

Objective

Therapeutic letters are intended to extend the work of therapy beyond the consulting room door by continuing the meaning making that occurred in a therapeutic conversation. Suppose, for instance, during a session we have focused on drawing out the resources of a young client, and codiscovered actions he or she has already performed to take charge of his or her life. A therapeutic letter written as a follow-up to the session might echo and amplify these victories, however small, by recounting them on paper. The letter might encourage further actions, or it might simply highlight the changes and invite the client to make meaning of them in his or her own life. In addition, the letter might provide the chance for family members or other significant persons in the client's life (a teacher or principal, for example) to bear witness to the positive developments. One way to depict the objective behind therapeutic letters, then, is to see them as tools for "thickening" preferred stories in the lives of clients.

Rationale for Use

Therapeutic letter writing is associated with narrative and social constructionist therapy practices. Some of the key ideas emphasized within this practice include the following:

- We all inhabit a world of meanings constructed through language in a social context.
- These meanings tend to be organized into narratives that give coherence to our lives and identities.
- Persons who consult us can be understood to be under the influence of dominant, "problem-saturated" (White and Epston, 1990) narratives that obscure more helpful meanings in their lives.
- Therapy can be understood as inviting forward and developing experiences and meanings currently obscured by problems.

Following on these ideas, therapeutic letters provide a powerful means of committing preferred stories to paper and rendering them more concrete or real by drawing on the special legitimacy we often grant to the printed word. They also provide a vehicle for circulating what might be called counternarratives. As more favorable accounts are witnessed and reflected back by a range of people important to the clients, those preferred meanings take on more substance and occupy greater space in their lives. A therapeutic letter is a tangible, written contribution to the reclamation of a young person's identity.

Instructions

David Epston and Michael White (Epston, 1989a,b, 1991; Epston and White, 1992; White and Epston, 1990) may be credited with first experimenting with therapeutic letters. In the last decade they have taken a number of informal polls with clients to whom they have sent letters and are typically told the letters are as helpful as anywhere between three and ten therapy sessions. Therapeutic letters are now used in a variety of ways that incorporate the various styles and knowledges of therapists around the world.

I've (MAMR) developed one way of doing therapeutic letters from which my young clients seem consistently to benefit. More than anything else, the letters tend to describe thickly their knowledges and resources, because I often find problems have a way of blinding persons to their own knowledges and strengths, and because children in particular may underestimate themselves in the company of adults. There are a wide variety of helpful ways to employ therapeutic letters, and one should not feel locked in by a set template. Each therapeutic situation is different, and therapists should feel free to be creative in responding to the uniqueness of their clients.

I frequently begin a therapeutic letter by thanking the young person for being courageous enough to share his or her story with me, a virtual stranger. I underline the wisdom of reaching out and/or trusting a parent's wisdom when a client feels stuck. I then quickly remind the readers that these are merely some wonderings; if my ideas don't fit for them, then I apologize in advance and invite them to make all the changes necessary to get the story straight. Of course, all this is done in the language appropriate to the developmental ages of the clients. Also, I take great care to use the words, metaphors, and ideas of the children/adolescents to maximize a sense of congruence with their ways of making meaning.

Having granted the client editorial power over the letter, I reflect on all the resources, strengths, and knowledges that I witnessed in the previous session(s). I draw up a giant list of assets that the young person may never have considered himself or herself to possess. This can be very empowering. I find it especially empowering to notice those things the child or adolescent appears *already* to know—easily overlooked in a world where young people are frequently marginalized or discounted. Knowing what one knows, and *that* one knows, is a powerful starting point for making better life decisions.

From here, the letter usually turns to speculation about where the young person might take the knowledges and assets identified. I wonder aloud what would happen if he or she chose a certain direction over another, pulling from information gathered in the session(s). What would be the effects of certain directions over others? On oneself? On one's parents? On one's siblings? On one's teachers, and so on? I also ask identity questions: What impact, positive or negative, would that direction have on his or her sense of identity? I invite the young person to consider his or her values in relation to certain possible actions. What kind of person does he or she want to be? What kind of a reputation does he or she want? I often close the letter by inviting the child or adolescent to keep me up to date on important progress. This can be framed in playful language that matches the young person's, such as saying I'd love to hear of "any further home runs you've hit out of the park" or "all the lessons you learned from those muscle-building mistakes."

Composing therapeutic letters is an efficient way of extending the work done in a session while also capturing details of the session for records. The difference, of course, is that the notes become a public document that highlights possibilities, rather than adhering to the field's time-honored tradition of filing away a deficit-laden inventory in anticipation of some possible future practice review.

Letters to young persons provide a vehicle for playful meaning making. If composing them on a computer, the therapist can select a large type size in a casual font such as Comic Sans. The therapist might consider using the wallpaper feature increasingly common with current software or inserting clip art. Handwritten letters provide the opportunity to doodle or add drawings to illustrate the therapist's points.

Therapeutic letter writing is the outgrowth of some determinedly nonpathologizing thinking. An air of optimism and excitement reflects the separation of person from problem. It should be clear that the therapist is on the client's side against difficulties that may have been making a mess of his or her life. It should also be clear that it is the young person who ultimately knows best what is useful and meaningful to him or her. Therapeutic letters are offered, not as pronouncements of professional truth, but as tentative reflections from a supportive observer who happens to have the advantage of not being under the blinding influence of the problem(s) at hand.

Vignette

The family I (DP) will call the "Grishams" came to see me when Mom and Dad (Leona and Gordon) were concerned about their seven-year-old son's anger. Tyler was having falling-outs with other children at school and was frequently getting into arguments or hitting matches with his five-year-old sister, Morgan. After spending some time talking about and reflecting on Tyler's behavior in various contexts, we did not arrive at some *other* problem, some issue beyond these incidents, such as academic frustration or social rejection, that appeared more deserving of attention. We therefore decided that "Fighting" was a good name for the problem, and we began to look at Fighting's effects on Tyler, and on the family. This separation of persons from problems is sometimes known as externalization, a central feature of the narrative theory work of White and Epston (1990). It rests on the assumption that *persons* are never the problem; the *problem* is the problem. When problems are externalized, they can be rendered more concretely, or personified (e.g., the "Temper Monster"), which is a helpful and playful way of speaking with young persons about the difficulties they are facing.

It seemed apparent that Fighting had persuaded Leona and Gordon they must be doing something wrong as parents. This idea in turn seemed to be reflected back to Tyler, so that his outbursts were now laden with a good deal more meaning than he might originally have attached to them. They were viewed not merely for their negative impact on Tyler's sister and classmates but as evidence of some darker, deep-rooted problem likely derived from poor parenting practices.

Like every view of a clinical situation, this depiction of the Grishams' situation is influenced by a body of ideas and practices. In this case, narrative ideas encouraged me to put some space between Tyler's family and the pathologizing story of the outbursts as the ingrained evidence of poor parenting. I became curious about not only Tyler's but also the whole family's ability to defy this story by making meaning and acting in alternative ways.

After one of our conversations, I wrote a letter to the family in lieu of taking process notes. The letter was designed to thicken an alternative story about the family that was beginning to emerge from our talks together. Because it is directed to the whole family, the letter promotes shared meaning making: Leona and Gordon get to witness their children's progress and the children are reminded of their parents' support.

Dear Tyler, Morgan, Leona, and Gordon,

I was thinking about our last meeting and I thought I'd send you a note. What struck me was the way all of you seem to really value having peaceful time together as a family. I feel I've shared some of that time with you in our meetings. When we get together, you take turns talking and listening, and everyone gets a chance to say what's on his or her mind. I notice that in your family, it's okay to say what's bothering you because someone will listen.

The other thing I remember from our last meeting was learning about how Tyler and Morgan kept Fighting out of the way for almost a whole weekend. Remember we talked about whether you guys locked Fighting in the closet, or maybe pushed it out the door? Or maybe you shrank Fighting, so it was so small it got lost behind the bookshelf or under a couch pillow.

Your dad said it was "exceptional." Do you remember that big word? "Exceptional" means "really amazing." Did you realize how proud your mom and dad were of you for the way you did that?

Gordon and Leona, what could you tell me about Tyler and Morgan that would help explain how they were able to do that? What special skills do these two have that made them able to push Fighting out the door?

Tyler and Morgan, can you pay attention to how you manage to keep fighting away or shrink it or whatever, and tell me all about it when you come in next time? You might have to take notes.

Where do you all imagine your family is headed as these positive changes continue? I'll be really curious to hear back from you all next time we meet.

See you in a while,

David

As is often the case with therapeutic letters, the family reported that they had read and reread the letter after receiving it. Therapeutic letters make an emerging story tangible and provide a shared reference point for successes—in this case, both Tyler's and his family's, as Fighting became a less frequent visitor, and Leona and Gordon rediscovered faith in their abilities as parents.

Suggestions for Follow-Up

Therapeutic letters provide a bridge between sessions and a means to anchor new stories that promote personal agency. We sometimes begin a session by checking with a young person and family about their response to a letter sent out following the previous meeting. What stood out for them in the letter? What rang less true? Did any further ideas emerge from reflecting on the letter? Have they noticed ways in which the positive developments reported in the letter have continued in the ensuing days? We sometimes invite clients to respond to a letter by writing one of their own that is, for instance, addressed to the problem, to update it on the resurrection of abilities and knowledge temporarily obscured by the problem's influence, or to other significant persons in the clients' lives, reporting on the favorable developments.

Contraindications for Use

Confidentiality is always a potential issue when we mail envelopes with return addresses on them. As with any direct correspondence with clients, we check first to confirm that it's okay to send letters to a home address.

No therapeutic practices are inherently risk free; however, because narrative and social constructionist practices build largely on preferred developments, we find they offer relatively safe clinical possibilities. Nevertheless, therapeutic letter writers should be mindful that their enthusiasm for noticing successes over certain identified problems does not divert attention from other serious, but unnamed difficulties (for instance, learning difficulties at school in Tyler's case). Thoughtful narrative practice attends closely to the obstacles life scatters in our way; therapeutic letters should acknowledge the scope of the very real challenges faced by young persons in a world largely controlled by adults.

We also find it's important that a letter to a child or family feels like the outgrowth of our collaboration with someone who consults us—the product of a team effort. If we jump to naming a problem unilaterally, without drawing on family metaphors and the young person's language, our letters may be received more as an imposed story than a summary of some shared developments. In writing therapeutic letters, we try to lead from behind.

References

Epston, D. (1989a). *Collected papers*. Adelaide, South Australia: Dulwich Centre Publications.

Epston, D. (1989b). "One good revolution deserves another," *Family Therapy Case Studies* 3(2), 45-60.

Epston, D. (1991). "I am a bear." Discovering discoveries. *Family Therapy Case Studies* 6(1), pp. 15-23.

Epston, D. and White, M. (1992). *Experience, contradiction, narrative and imagination*. Adelaide, South Australia: Dulwich Centre Publications.

White, M. and Epston, D. (1990). *Narrative means to therapeutic ends*. New York: W.W. Norton.

Additional Resource for Professionals

White, M. (1995). *Re-authoring lives*. Adelaide, South Australia: Dulwich Centre Publications.

28

Parental Involvement in an Adolescent's Career Decision Process

Hemla D. Singaravelu
Tammy B. Bringaze

Type of Contribution: Activity

Objective

This activity provides an arena for conversation between parents, their adolescent, and the counselor regarding the process of career decision making. Upon completion of this activity the following will be achieved:

- Parents and adolescent will be educated on the process of selecting a study major/career.
- Adolescent will have identified her or his interests, values, and abilities.
- Adolescent will have created a list of potential study majors/careers to investigate further.
- Adolescent will have a sense of direction and career objectives.
- Parents and adolescent will have reduced the anxiety related to career indecision.
- Parents and adolescent will understand that career decision making is an ongoing process.
- Parents and adolescent will have begun to open the lines of communication regarding the adolescent's career development.

Rationale

Research has suggested a link between college attrition and the undecided student (Goodstein, 1965; Gordon, 1998; Fuqua, Seaworth, and Newman, 1998). Characteristics such as a lack of career objectives, uncertain degree expectations, inability to select a major, and anxiety have been used to describe both undecided students and factors contributing to college attrition. In addition to these shared characteristics, a positive correlation has been established between anxiety and career undecidedness. Career exploration and counseling are useful in curbing this anxiety. In addition, parents can also serve as active agents in their children's career development and decision-making process (Schulenberg, Vondracek, and Crouter, 1984; Young and Friesen, 1992) and thus help reduce some of this anxiety.

Furthermore, it has also been contended that children expect assistance with their career planning from parents more than anyone else (Burke and Weir, 1979; Mitchell, 1978; Roberts, 1979). Similarly, parents also believe they have an impact on their children's career development (Gulick, 1978); however, they may not have the knowledge and skills to encourage effective career decision making. In their enthusiasm to help their children, parents may put too much pressure on them to succeed in making a decision (Grotevant and Cooper, 1988).

Penick and Jepsen (1992) discussed the influence of enmeshed families and disengaged families on adolescents' career development. Adolescents from enmeshed families may not be able to distinguish parental goals and expectations from their own career objectives. Consequently, these adolescents may select careers within their family business. On the other hand, adolescents from disengaged families may not have the support necessary for career decision making.

To be a positive influence on their adolescent, parents must be educated about the process of selecting a major or career. Parents can further assist the adolescent in the formulation of career objectives by first differentiating between parental goals and expectations versus the desires of their children. Furthermore, it is imperative to explore and identify personal characteristics, such as interests, abilities, values, and one's future lifestyle, when deciding on a career path. Once these characteristics have been identified, the adolescent's career objectives or goals can then be successfully explored and established. The counselor can facilitate this process by providing appropriate resources and, more important, a platform whereby parents and their adolescent feel comfortable in expressing their thoughts, feelings, and concerns regarding career decision making.

Instructions

1. The three components of Carney and Wells's (1991) Venn diagram for career decision making are described to parents and the adolescent (see Handout 1, Factors to Consider in Career Decision Making).
2. Holland's (1998) Self-Directed Search (SDS), a self-scoring instrument, is administered to both parents and the adolescent. The instrument is then scored and a three-letter summary code is derived from this score.
3. The adolescent selects between five and ten occupations from the Occupational Finder (included in the SDS assessment packet) that relate to his or her three-letter summary code.
4. The selected occupations are then listed in Occupation Handout to be explored.
5. The *Occupational Outlook Handbook* (Bureau of Labor Statistics, 2002-2003) is utilized to gain career information such as the nature of the work, working conditions, earnings, training, other qualifications, and related occupations.

Vignette

Kevin, a seventeen-year-old student, and his parents came in for counseling. Kevin's parents were concerned about his lack of motivation in discussing college education and his anxiety regarding the impending decision on an academic major and career. Although Kevin is undecided about his future, he is still interested in a college education. His parents feel he will do well in the business field, but they do not know how to assist Kevin and hope that counseling will offer clarity and direction.

The counselor describes the three components of Carney and Wells's model (see Handout 1) to Kevin and his parents. According to the model, *self-knowledge* and *career information* along with the expectations/dreams of *significant others* are the three necessary factors to consider when deciding on a career path.

Self-knowledge consists of personal characteristics such as interests, abilities, values, beliefs, decision-making style, and future lifestyle, which are critical factors in selecting a satisfying major/career. With the help of his parents, some introspection, and the SDS instrument, Kevin will begin to explore and identify these characteristics.

The process of self-exploration begins with the examination of Kevin's SDS results. Kevin's three-letter code is IAS (Investigative, Artistic, Social). The counselor then describes the characteristics of an individual with the code of IAS to Kevin and his parents. Kevin then selects five to nine occupations that seem appealing from the Occupational Finder under the IAS category and creates a list of occupations to explore.

The parents' participation in the SDS assessment is aimed at helping them understand the instrument's utility in identifying interest, abilities, and occupational preferences. Furthermore, by also taking the SDS, the parents can better appreciate the decision-making process that Kevin is undergoing. It is also interesting for parents to see if their current profession coincides with their SDS results and to process this information. The counselor then facilitates the discussion between the parents and Kevin concerning the SDS results: the congruence between career aspirations, abilities, values, beliefs, and potential stereotypes regarding the world of work. The parents are reminded that the identified characteristics will change as Kevin is exposed to new ideas and environments, thus making career decision making an ongoing process. The following questions might then be discussed:

- Are they surprised that Kevin's SDS code did not include E (Enterprising) which is where the business field falls?
- What are their thoughts and feelings about his scores and the implications of his results?
- What was it like for the parents to take the SDS?
- What salary does Kevin anticipate making three years after graduation with a bachelor's degree?
- What type of lifestyle would Kevin like to live (e.g., comfortable, wealthy)? Does this matter to Kevin?

To make informed decisions, it is important to gather accurate *career information* and avoid unrealistic expectations of careers and majors. This information can be acquired through occupational interviews with individuals currently in the field and printed materials such as the *Occupational Outlook Handbook (OOH)*. The counselor then encourages Kevin and his parents to read up on the list of selected occupations. Important questions to be asked here are as follows:

- Based upon the description of this occupation, can you see yourself performing the tasks described in the *OOH* on a daily basis?
- What aspects of this occupation do you like?
- What do you think about the amount of education required for this occupation?
- What do you think of the salary listed for this occupation? How does this compare with your expectations?
- Where are the best opportunities for this field? How does the location of opportunities compare with where you want to live?

In addition to *self-knowledge* and *career information*, the dreams of *significant others* are also critical in helping develop adolescents' career aspirations. Families, partners, and friends play a large role in influencing adolescents' beliefs, values, interests, and future lifestyle, which may in turn impact the career decision-making process. A discussion follows focusing on the expectations and implications of the SDS results for Kevin and his parents. Here parental goals and wishes are further discussed and compared to Kevin's goals. Familial values, roles, and traditions are also explored and their impact on Kevin's career options is also discussed.

Suggestions for Follow-Up

1. Occupational interviews are ideal in gaining firsthand information regarding a specific career and the world of work. By interviewing individuals who are currently in the field, adolescents will have an opportunity to ask questions and receive valuable answers that may aid them in their decision-making process.
2. Job shadowing is another helpful avenue to gain career information. This allows the adolescent to be exposed to the work environment and observe the daily activities involved in a specific field.
3. Parents can play a vital role in helping the adolescent process his or her experiences and information gained through these activities.

Contraindications for Use

1. This activity may not be as effective with individuals below fourteen years of age, as skills and abilities may not be realized at this stage of development.
2. The counselor needs to be cautious and inclusive in the definition of family. The adolescent may have a nontraditional family such as one that includes a gay or lesbian parent(s). Culture is also an important consideration, as he or she may have extended family members acting in parental roles.
3. An initial assessment of family conflict should first be conducted before implementing this activity. If a high level of conflict is present between the adolescent and the parents, the adolescent may experience greater difficulty in the career decision-making process.

Readings and Resources for Professionals

Bureau of Labor Statistics (2002-2003). *Occupational Outlook Handbook*. Washington, DC: U.S. Department of Labor.

Carney, C. G. and Wells, C. F. (1991). *Discover the career within you*. Pacific Grove, CA: Brooks/Cole.

Kennedy, J. L. (1993). *Joyce Lain Kennedy's career book*. Lincolnwood, IL: VGM Horizons.

References

Bureau of Labor Statistics (2002-2003). *Occupational Outlook Handbook*. Washington, DC: U.S. Department of Labor.

Burke, R. and Weir, T. (1979). Helping responses of parents and peers and adolescent well-being. *Journal of Psychology, 102*, 49-62.

Carney, C. G. and Wells, C. F. (1991). *Discover the career within you*. Pacific Grove, CA: Brooks/Cole.

Fuqua, D. R., Seaworth, T. B., and Newman, J. L. (1988). Relation of state and trait anxiety to different components of career indecision. *Journal of Counseling Psychology, 2*, 154-158.

Goodstein, L. (1965). Behavior theoretical view of counseling. In B. Stefflre (Ed.), *Theories of Counseling* (pp. 140-192). New York: McGraw-Hill.

Gordon, V. (1998). *The undecided college student*. Springfield, IL: Charles C Thomas.

Grotevant, H. D. and Cooper, H. R. (1988). The role of family experience in career exploration: A life-span perspective. In P. B. Baltes, D. L. Featherman, and R. M. Lerner (Eds.), *Life span development and behavior* (pp. 231-258). London: Lawrence Erlbaum.

Gulick, E. (1978). *Study of parental influence on career development of adolescent youth.* Grove City, OH: Southwest City Schools.

Holland, J. L. (1998). *The self-directed search.* Odessa, FL: Psychological Assessment Resources.

Mitchell, A. (1978). *Career development needs of seventeen-year olds.* Washington, DC: American Personnel and Guidance Association.

Penick, N. I. and Jepsen, D. A. (1992). Family functioning and adolescent career development. *Career Development Quarterly, 40,* 208-222.

Roberts, J. (1979). Survey shows little change in students' college aspirations. *Public Education, 14,* 1-3.

Schulenberg, J., Vondracek, F., and Crouter, A. (1984). The influence of the family on vocational development. *Journal of Marriage and the Family, 46,* 129-143.

Young, R. A. and Friesen, J. D. (1992). The intentions of parents in influencing the career development of their children. *Career Development Quarterly, 40,* 198-207.

Handout: Factors to Consider in Career Decision Making

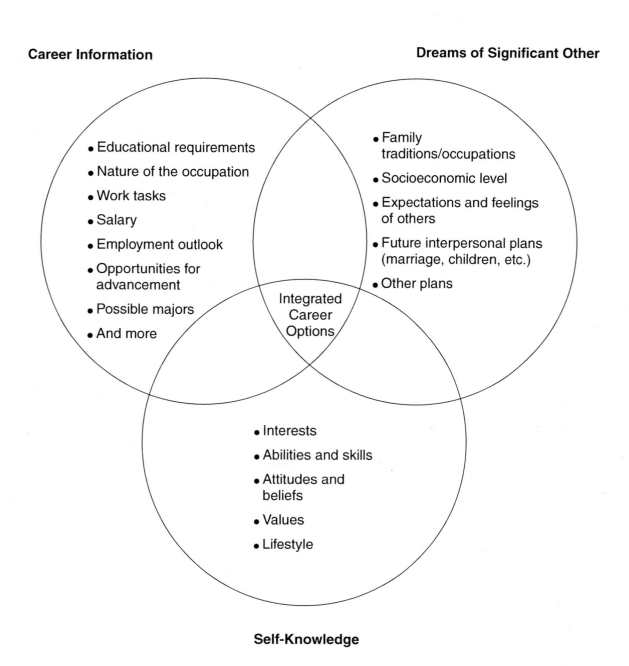

Career Information

Dreams of Significant Other

- Educational requirements
- Nature of the occupation
- Work tasks
- Salary
- Employment outlook
- Opportunities for advancement
- Possible majors
- And more

- Family traditions/occupations
- Socioeconomic level
- Expectations and feelings of others
- Future interpersonal plans (marriage, children, etc.)
- Other plans

Integrated Career Options

- Interests
- Abilities and skills
- Attitudes and beliefs
- Values
- Lifestyle

Self-Knowledge

Source: From *Discover the Career Within You,* 1991 edition, by C. Carney and C. Wells ©1991. Reprinted with permission of Wadsworth, an imprint of the Wadsworth Group, a division of Thomson Learning.

Occupation Handout

Please select and list in the space given below five to ten occupations that are of interest to you from the Occupational Finder. Your selection should be based on the three-letter code derived from the results of your Self-Directed Search. Your next task is to further explore these careers. This can be accomplished through reading about these fields in the *Occupational Outlook Handbook* and by conducting occupational interviews.

1. _____

2. _____

3. _____

4. _____

5. _____

6. _____

7. _____

8. _____

9. _____

10. _____

29

Improving Behavior and Identities of Youths: Exploring and Creating Culturally Relevant Masks

Dominicus W. So
Maia C. Coleman
Philippa S. Stuart

Type of Contribution: Activity/Intervention

Objective

This fifty-minute intervention activity is designed for therapists' use with individual African-American youths. However, we believe that it can also be used with individuals or groups of other minorities, such as ethnic minorities, gay and lesbian youths, and religious minorities. The purpose of this activity is to help the therapist and client address the specific concerns of identity development with regard to growing up black or as a member of other minority groups in America. It should facilitate discussion of racism, financial disadvantage, oppression, or discrimination. Although we focus more on the negative factors of being in a minority group, this intervention is likely to be applicable to members of privileged groups as well, if used with appropriate modifications. The activity aims at raising the youths' awareness of their identity status, improving their evaluation of their own heritage/background, and appreciating their blackness and/or other minority status. This objective is combined with the goals to increase self-awareness of internal emotional states, to help the youths modulate their otherwise explosive emotions, and to cope effectively with the environmental stressors related to their minority status.

Rationale for Use

Youths of African descent and other ethnic groups are more likely than youths from the mainstream culture to face special stressors during their identity development. In America, minority group membership often creates extra developmental tasks that teens need to fulfill. These extra developmental tasks involve the development of a positive identity related to the minority group membership. For instance, adolescents must ask, Do I like being black (Asian, Jewish, gay, or a member of any minority group)? In other words, besides developing self-esteem and a sense of who they are, minority youths also need to establish a positive cultural identity.

Clinicians then need to ask themselves if their intervention strategies are adequate for helping minority youths build a positive self-image as well as cultural identity. Another question for clinicians, then, is Are current intervention measures suitable for diverse populations of youths in order to enhance minority youths' cultural/ethnic identity? If not, what more do we need to do? This intervention activity attempts to supplement the current intervention strategies in child and adolescent psychotherapy.

Current models of racial/cultural/ethnic identity development (e.g., Cross, 1991; Sue and Sue, 1999) generally describe an individual's journey of understanding himself or herself in terms of his or her own minority culture, the dominant culture, and the oppressive relationship between them. One of those models (Sue and Sue, 1999), for example, describes five stages of cultural identity development: conformity, dissonance, resistance and immersion, introspection, and synergetic articulation and awareness. Another model (Cross, 1991) describes the black racial identity development in four stages: preencounter, encounter, immersion/emersion, and internationalization/commitment. Overall, these models hypothesize that the minority individual moves from the initial stage of preferring the dominant culture through a period of confusion and contradiction, becomes more aware of cultural differences, resists the dominant culture, feels autonomous, and then ultimately commits to one's cultural background, becoming objectively critical of the dominant culture.

Building an ethnic/cultural or minority status identity is not the youths' only developmental task during the formative years. Many youths often have self-esteem and self-identity issues intertwined with their minority identities, particularly among oppressed populations. These youths often have trouble verbalizing their emotions and actively coping with environmental stressors related to their minority status. Their development can be advanced by incorporating the development of a healthy self-image into a positive ethnic identity. In that light, this chapter focuses on the positive development of one's minority status identity and coping behaviors in difficult and culturally relevant situations.

Using the clients' cultural artifacts will help clients feel accepted. Such use also fosters the therapists' understanding of the clients' culture, while expanding the therapists' worldview and ability to work with a diverse clientele. More important, the use of cultural artifacts from the clients' heritage is intended to help the youths incorporate their cultural identity in the development of an emotionally mature and positive behavioral repertoire, while improving the cultural relevance of psychotherapy.

Instructions and Vignette

Materials Needed

- Pictures from magazines of particular cultural/minority/interest groups (These pictures or drawings may include situations that depict stress or any other emotions that are prominent in the clients' lives. Alternative resources can be found on the Internet, for example, a list of Web sites of African art, museums, and other cultural interests.)
- Ethnic (African or other culturally relevant) masks, sample artwork
- Construction paper, art supplies (e.g., color markers, safety scissors, glue, tape, and cotton strings)
- Lined paper and pencils

Introduction and Presentation of Magazine Cutouts

Therapists may begin the therapy session by communicating to the client that she or he will have a special activity during the session to help her or him express emotions and feel good about her or his own culture. For instance, the therapist may start a conversation with the client in the following manner:

THERAPIST: We have some very special artwork cut out from magazines [or Web sites on the Internet]. I would like to use them in our session today, and let's see what we can do about them? Do you have an idea what I may ask you to do with these [masks] today?

CLIENT: Uh-uh.

THERAPIST: Well, usually therapy gives people an opportunity to openly express their feelings and freely discuss things that are bothering them. Sometimes, it's really difficult to express our feelings. Sometimes, we might not even understand what's bothering us. When this happens, it might be easier to use art to express our feelings instead of words. I have some pictures here that I'd like you to look at. [Therapist then presents magazine cutouts or Web sites to client.] What do you think is happening in the picture?

CLIENT: I see a girl running around with the dog. It looks like they are playing with each other.

THERAPIST: That's right. In this picture, the little girl is running with her dog, and she has an expression that shows she is happy. What else do you think is happening? [Therapist may consider showing other picture cutouts as examples to describe the emotions expressed in different situations. Therapist may focus on a particular emotion, such as anger or joy, or continue to show the client pictures of a wider range of emotional reactions to situations.] These other pictures may show different feelings [e.g., anger, joy, or a variety of feelings] that people sometimes have.

Presentation of Culturally Relevant Masks

THERAPIST: [Displaying a collection of authentic culturally appropriate masks, Web sites, or magazine cutouts of masks. See resources for therapists.] Now, let's look at something different. You see, here is a traditional [e.g., African/Chinese/Hindu] mask. [Therapist may also briefly describe the history, purposes, and creation of these masks. See resources for therapists.]

THERAPIST: Let's now look at the patterns, colors, and facial expressions on the masks. [Therapist may briefly describe the meanings of particular colors, lines, and textures as used on the masks. See resources for therapists.] What type of feeling do you think this mask expresses as you see its patterns, lines, color, texture, or shapes?

CLIENT: I don't know. It looks like it's mad, like it's pouting.

THERAPIST: Good. Do you sometimes feel that way? [Encourage the client to relate the masks to his or her own feelings. Therapist may continue to explore each mask available and explore the emotion displayed by each mask. Therapist may also choose to focus on several masks that display a limited range of feelings, such as anger or sadness, that have been the focus of therapy.]

Creating Masks of Various Emotions

THERAPIST: Well, today during the session we can make our own masks. Here are some markers, construction paper, tape, and glue that we can use to make masks. I have some here that were done by others. [Display any masks therapist has made in the past or use the samples available from the resource list. Therapist may also demonstrate how a simple mask can be made with paper plates and markers.] It will really be fun. Do you have any questions so far?

CLIENT: I'm not very good at art. . . . I don't like art. . . . Art is boring. . . . Do I have to do this?

THERAPIST: [Encourage the client to attempt the project, but avoid a power struggle.] Well, this isn't for a grade and no one else has to look at your mask, and I'm sure that you are better at it than you think. [If older adolescents think they are too old for the task, the therapist may entice clients with more challenging techniques to keep them interested.] See, if you do this [e.g., cut two slots, and fold that part up, and glue them together in the back], you can make an angry mouth and the mask becomes three-dimensional. It looks much more real.

CLIENT: Okay. Can you show me again how you did that?

THERAPIST: Yes. . . . Now, before you begin, if I were to ask you how you were feeling today, what type of mask would you make to show how you feel?

CLIENT: Upset. [Client may mention another feeling and/or a situation in which he or she had experienced that feeling.]

THERAPIST: So, you were upset [or other feeling] when . . . [Therapist may inquire a little more about the details of the situation and, more important, how the client felt and how that feeling was expressed physiologically, behaviorally, and facially.]

CLIENT: Yeah, that's pretty much it.

THERAPIST: Now that you've got a good idea about mask making, today you get to be the artist. You can use these art supplies on the table to make a mask that expresses how you are feeling right now. Let's try to make our own masks at the same time. [While making her or his own mask, the therapist takes time to encourage the client to create a mask that best suits his or her immediate emotional state.]
Do you know how you are going to start?

CLIENT: I think so.

THERAPIST: [Allow at least five minutes for the client to work on his or her own. Thereafter, offer occasional help and discourage overly careful coloring or other techniques that may take up too much time.] That is a very nice mask. You see this [e.g., African] mask we saw earlier. It shows these marks and this pattern on the cheek. Let's make your mask more like that one, with the African pattern. [Therapist encourages the client to incorporate the cultural elements from the artifact on the client's own mask.]

Discussion About Emotions Displayed by the Mask and the Client's Coping Strategies

THERAPIST: It looks like you are almost done. Let's hold on the artwork for a little while unless you just have a little bit of work to finish. [When client is done, begin to explore the feelings portrayed by the mask. Therapist can display his or her own and model how the mask shows his or her feelings.]
Now, it's your turn to tell me about your mask.

CLIENT: He looks sad. He looks like he's about to cry.

THERAPIST: That's what the mask [e.g., pattern, lines, color] shows? I wonder why he is sad?

CLIENT: Because he had to go to school.

THERAPIST: Why would going to school make him sad?

CLIENT: Because he doesn't have any friends at school, and everybody else makes fun of him at school. . . .

THERAPIST: What usually happens when you are sad? Do your classmates make fun of you too? [Therapist may allow the client to express his or her feelings more, and to describe the situations and his or her coping strategies. But avoid being judgmental about negative coping techniques.] What will happen to you if you respond to feelings like those in the mask? [Therapist may let the client explore the pros and cons of the client's own coping strategies.]

Identify Situations in Which the Client Experiences a Particular Emotion

THERAPIST: Now let's think about situations that may cause you to feel that way [e.g., sad or angry]. Can you come up with some stories that might make someone feel sad or like crying? [Therapist may use verbal praise or rewards, such as stickers, as positive reinforcement of the client's appropriate responses.]

CLIENT: Like when somebody goes to lunch and never has anyone to sit with. Or like when somebody comes to school with cheap tennis shoes and everyone makes fun of him.

THERAPIST: Wow! Well has something like that ever happened to you? What happened the last time you felt that way? [Therapist may encourage the client to verbalize his or her own experience in those situations. If the client chooses to, the therapist may encourage other culturally relevant modalities, such as using written words, singing out, rapping, poetry, drawing out the scenarios.]

Generate Alternative Emotions and Coping Strategies

THERAPIST: How did you feel when that happened to you? What did you do? [Therapist should let client briefly describe what happened to him or her and others. Therapist may help client process emotions and develop effective coping strategies.]

CLIENT: I was so upset, so I yelled out loud in the classroom, and the teacher gave me a warning and a detention yesterday. I had to stay in school until five p.m. I hated it.

THERAPIST: It seems your response made you even more upset and it really did not help you with that situation at all. [If client lacks insight to reflect on the negative impact of his or her emotional response, the therapist may direct the client to reflect on how his or her emotions have made the situation worse for him or her and others.] Have you thought of other things you could have done that would have made the situation better for you and everyone? [Therapist may continue to spend the remaining time of the session exploring alternative responses in feelings and behaviors. If alternative masks are available, therapist may suggest the use of these alternative feelings/behaviors to respond to the same situation.] Do you remember the other masks we saw, or the one I made? Some of these show joy, sadness, and frustration. See, this one shows frustration. [Therapist may help the client use the cotton string to tie the mask on the client's head and face, to highlight the use of alternative emotional and behavioral responses.] Let's see if changing the frustration mask can change the situation. [Therapist may ask the client what frustration may do to him or her, or the therapist may offer to use a laugh mask to demonstrate that the client can just laugh at the teaser and walk away.] You see, if you had laughed about it, and walked away, you may not have gotten into trouble and detained. So, you see, in any situation, when we become upset or sad, we can deal with the anger and sadness in many ways. Some of these ways can actually make you feel better, and the situation will get better as well.

Suggestions for Follow-Up

Creative artwork, such as mask making, is likely to open up possibilities of useful therapeutic follow-up. To facilitate follow-up, the therapist may shelve/file the masks or photograph them as therapeutic artifacts (with the client's permission and protecting client confidentiality). In subsequent sessions, the therapist may bring out masks made in past sessions or by other clients to review different emotions. Also, to help the client generalize his or her behavior in real-life situations, subsequent sessions may involve psychodrama using the masks to act out the feelings, and the client may use alternative masks, emotions, and behavior to respond to the same situations. Moreover, to help the client develop a positive ethnic identity, the therapist may ask if the young client has other opportunities to view traditional masks, and if there are real-life situations in which he or she uses the emotions expressed by the masks he or she saw and made in previous sessions. In parent-child joint sessions, the parents can be trained to use the same masks to act out situations involving the youth, and to help the child use alternative masks/emotions. If the mask creation session appears to be productive, the therapist may attempt, in future sessions, other art therapy modalities (see, e.g., Oster and Gould, 1987) and encourage the client to continue exploring masks of his or her ethnic background (see bibliography for clients).

Contraindications for Use

This activity is thought to have wide application if flexibly adapted. However, in several situations, the therapist must use his or her own careful discretion to determine if masks may be countertherapeutic. First, in the ethnic identity stage models, if the client is at a preencounter stage, in which cultural and racial identity has low salience to the client, and the client is shameful of his or her cultural background or those who exclusively identify with the mainstream culture, the client may become resistant to the use of his or her culture, and thus any subsequent intervention strategies. Second, the young client or the parents with fundamentalist religious convictions or indigenous African religious backgrounds may regard the masks as idolatrous, shamanic, or divine artifacts. In such cases, the therapist needs to be sensitive to the client's religious background and be open to using alternatives of cultural relevance, but indicating clear facial expressions or emotional expression. Pictures of real people of the same ethnic background may be a good alternative. Finally, if the client's symptomatology includes any psychotic features, paranoid delusions, aggression, or dangerous use of sharp objects, the masks and certain cutting instruments may induce inappropriate reactions and behavior in the client. In those cases, the therapist needs to be particularly careful to justify the use of masks and cutting instruments and must continuously monitor the client's reactions.

Professional Readings and Resources

Atkinson, D., Morten, G., and Sue, D. (Eds.) (1998). *Counseling American minorities.* Dubuque, IA: McGraw-Hill.

Carter, R.T. (1998). *The influence of race and racial identity in psychotherapy: Toward a racially inclusive model.* New York: Wiley.

Cross, W. (1991). *Shades of black: Diversity in African-American identity.* Philadelphia, PA: Temple University Press.

Franklin, A. (1989). Therapeutic interventions with urban black adolescents. In R. Jones (Ed.), *Black adolescents* (pp. 293-308). Berkeley, CA: Cobb and Henry.

Jennings, S. and Minde, A. (1993). *Art therapy and dramatherapy: Masks of the soul.* London: J. Kingsley Publishers.

Harris, H.W., Blue, H.C., and Griffith, E.E. (Eds.) (1995). *Racial and ethnic identity: Psychological development and creative expression.* New York: Routledge.

Helms, J.E. (Ed.) (1993). *Black and white racial identity: Theory, research, and practice.* Westport, CT: Praeger.

Hutchinson, J.F. (Ed.) (1997). *Cultural portrayals of African Americans: Creating an ethnic/racial identity.* Westport, CT: Bergin and Garvey.

Lee, C. (1989). Counseling the black adolescent: Critical roles and functions for counseling professions. In R. Jones (Ed.), *Black adolescents* (pp. 309-337). Berkeley, CA: Cobb and Henry.

Oster, G. and Gould, P. (1987). *Using drawing in assessment and therapy.* New York: Brunner/Mazel.

Segy, L. (1976). *Masks of black Africa.* New York: Dover Publications.

Sue, D.W. and Sue, D. (1999). *Counseling the culturally different: Theory and practice* (Third edition). New York: John Wiley.

Tyler, F. (1991). *Ethnic validity, ecology, and psychotherapy: A psychosocial competence model.* New York: Plenum.

Bibliotherapy Sources for the Client

Baumgardner, J.M. (1993). *60 art projects for children: Painting, clay, puppets, paints, masks, and more.* Largo, MD: Crown Books.

Finley, C. (1998). *The art of African masks: Exploring cultural traditions.* North Minneapolis, MN: Lerner.

Smith, A.G. and Hazen, J. (1991). *Cut and make African masks in full color.* New York: Dover Publications.

Smith, A.G. and Hazen, J. (1999). *African punch-out masks.* New York: Dover Publications.

Vanzant, I. (1999). *Don't give it away.* New York: Simon and Schuster.

30

Judge and Jury: A Creative Approach to Discussing Sex with Teens

Liddy B. Hope

Type of Contribution: Activity

Objective

This courtroom role-play helps teens make an informed decision about whether and when to have sex. This is achieved through exploration of both sides of the abstinence argument. In addition, this activity helps foster a family environment that is open to discussing issues surrounding sex. Finally, this activity allows the therapist and parents to gain an understanding of the teen's existing sexual knowledge.

Rationale for Use

Adolescents face a variety of peer pressures, including sex. The culmination of pressure to have sex may reach its peak at any point during adolescence. For some, this may happen as early as twelve, while for others it may occur years later. Regardless, this is an issue that should be addressed by parent and child. Both peer pressure and issues surrounding sex are often difficult subjects for teens and their families to broach. Often, when parents and teens try to talk with each other about sex, it feels awkward and embarrassing. Ultimately, the conversation may end as a result of this discomfort, before anything is ever really discussed. The more parents and teens fall back into this silence, the more difficult it becomes to discuss sex. By facilitating the initial interaction, the therapist is helping the family open the door to future discussions. By approaching sexuality issues in therapy, the therapist can facilitate and lead the family in such an initial discussion. As an outsider, the therapist is less emotionally involved and can help families discuss potentially "hot" topics. This is especially important when discussing sex, particularly the sexuality of a teenage client. In addition, by using a role-play, the clients are able to "act" as a character. This can allow the person to be more open or challenging because he or she can ask the questions ascribed by his or her role. Because it is a role-play assigned by the therapist, the family is able to shrug off some of the responsibility onto the therapist, perhaps making it easier to participate in a "sex talk." As the family members begin to see that they are able to discuss the issue, even though they are "acting," they may become more comfortable continuing the discussion outside of the therapy room. Being able to turn to one's family with questions and concerns about sex is an important part of making informed and healthy decisions.

Beyond helping the family overcome discomfort surrounding the discussion of sex, this activity helps teens learn the skills important to make an informed decision. One's initial sexual experience is often life-altering and should be given a great deal of thought prior to the actual event. As with many of the pressures faced by teens, information about sex is often gathered primarily through peers. Although peers are an important resource for teens, the information given often is inaccurate. By assigning the teen the role of prosecuting attorney, the teen is required to gather accurate information from reliable sources in order to win the case. The therapist and parents can help the teen find accurate resources to use in his or her argument. These resources, as well as the process of finding and gathering information, will be something he or she carries for a lifetime.

Finally, this activity allows the therapist and parents to discover how much knowledge the teen has about sex. If the teen presents a good argument full of accurate information, the parents and therapist then know the teen is capable of gathering accurate information and is at least considering abstinence or safe sex. Then it becomes the job of the therapist and parents to discover if the arguments presented by the teen coincide with what the teen believes and practices. Either way, the teen has gathered accurate information with which to make his or her decision. Conversely, all is not lost should the teen present an ill-prepared case, full of inaccurate information. The therapist and parents are then aware of his or her ignorance and can begin to provide accurate sex education.

Whatever the outcome, this activity helps families begin an ongoing discussion about sex. Also, teens are made aware of their parents' knowledge of the pressures they face, perhaps making them more human and approachable in the eyes of the teens. Finally, through this role-play parents are able to learn just how much knowledge their teens have about sex, and therefore how much education is needed.

Instructions

This activity should first be discussed with parents or guardians to ensure their comfort level with this type of activity. As with all therapy, it is important to explore family values prior to implementing interventions that have the potential of being heavily value laden. This intervention is not for every family, nor is it for every therapist. For some, however, it presents a fun and revealing manner to explore the sexual values of adolescents and their parents.

This role-play is designed to mimic a courtroom hearing. The number of courtroom roles portrayed will depend on the number of participants in therapy. This activity can be done with as few as two participants. The most important roles are the defense and prosecuting attorneys. However, jury members, judges, and witnesses can be added to the role-play as desired. It is important that all appropriate family members participate.

The defendant is a teen who has decided to have sex for the first time. This role should be played by the therapist or by no one at all, to avoid any client feeling "prosecuted." The prosecuting attorney should be played by the teen at risk. It is the teen's responsibility to prepare his or her arguments as to why the defendant's decision lacks basis. The defending attorney will be played by the parent(s). It is also the parent's responsibility to prepare his or her arguments. An extended-family member or the therapist, as the most objective member of the group, plays the judge. The remaining clients or cotherapists can play the jury. Finally, younger children can be included when appropriate, playing such roles as bailiff, clerk, reporter, and so on.

Due to its in-depth nature, this activity may take several sessions. Clients will need time to prepare arguments and for the trial itself. The therapist should allow adequate time to "sell" the activity, ensuring that all participants get into their specific roles and take the activity seriously. Through a thorough explanation of this "pretend" activity and an invitation to participate, the therapist should be able to spark the competitive nature in the clients. This typically leads clients to take the content of their roles seriously, while enjoying the playful process of the scenario being created.

Vignette

The "Lucas" family came to therapy following a series of violent outbursts by Kristin (age twelve). Initially, only Kristin and her mother, Sharon, participated in therapy. As Kristin began to control her anger and outbursts, the focus shifted from her as an individual to the family. At this point Kristin's sister, Dee (age thirteen), joined the therapy. The focus of the therapy became Dee's lack of self-esteem, Kristin's misbehavior, and helping Sharon learn to deal with two teenagers.

Over the course of therapy, Sharon repeatedly brought the subject of the girls' possible sexual activity to the therapist's attention, but only during individual sessions. Her main concern was that Kristin would be taken advantage of by one of the older boys she hung out with, and that Dee and her boyfriend of six months were getting too serious. In general, Sharon believed sex was on the horizon for both girls. As the focus began to shift toward the girls' sexuality, the therapist began to explore how this issue was discussed at home. Sharon claimed to have "no problem" talking to the girls about sex, saying that she relied on her nursing background to educate them.

While Sharon certainly could be an excellent resource for the girls, Kristin and Dee reported that they didn't feel comfortable asking Sharon questions because she was always "lecturing" them. Usually, if they were curious about boys, they talked to their Aunt Ruth, but only about general topics such as dating. However, during individual sessions Kristin often asked the therapist questions about birth control, certain terms, and other things she'd "heard" about sex. Dee used a less direct approach and had Kristin ask her questions for her, which was a typical communication pattern for Dee, a shy girl. They were reluctant to discuss openly such issues with Sharon, even with the therapist present.

Despite their reluctance, the therapist spent several sessions suggesting this role-play activity and eventually sparked the girls' curiosity. When it was explained that Sharon would take the role of defense attorney and thus defend the decision to have sex, the girls were hooked. They found it impossible to imagine their mother in this role and were curious to see how she would handle it. Sharon had always been in favor of the activity, understanding that this would allow the girls to see a different side of her, perhaps making her more approachable.

Once all individuals had agreed to the activity, it was decided that the next session would involve planning. The entire family would meet with the therapist and roles would be assigned. In addition, the family was asked to invite Aunt Ruth to the next session.

The next week the entire family arrived in a playful mood. It seemed a healthy competition was arising over who would win "the case," Sharon or Kristin. It was agreed that Kristin, as the more vocal of the two girls, would play the prosecuting attorney. Dee was assigned the role of bailiff, per her request. Both "attorneys" agreed to Aunt Ruth playing the role of the judge (probably each believed Ruth would take her side). Finally, the therapist played the role of the defendant.

The next step was to decide on the scenario. This step can be slippery, because while the defendant should pose as being similar to the teen, it is also important that the real-life teen not feel set up. In this case, the therapist led the discussion, asking the family questions: How old should she be? Should she have a lot of friends? More girl or boy friends? The entire family made decisions, but by leading the discussion the therapist was able to shape the resulting character, ensuring the demographic similarity to the client. In the end the character of the defendant was a thirteen-year-old girl with a lot of guy friends, one with whom she had been particularly close for several years. The girl and this boy had been dating for the past few months and he was beginning to pressure her about sex, about which the girl was curious. This girl was close to her older sister but had very few other female friends. Her family consisted of her mother, sister, and father. Although this girl was not particularly close to either her mother or father, she spent more time with her mother. (It was interesting that the family chose a "traditional" family for the girl, even though they are a "nontraditional," single-parent family.) With the scenario set, the family was sent home with the assignment of preparing their cases.

The next session was devoted to helping each client with her case; the therapist especially helped the prosecuting attorneys (Kristin and Dee). Kristin and Dee had spent the week talking to friends and had discovered that of those who were no longer virgins, most of them regretted it. Kristin was full of stories of ruined reputations, boys who never spoke to the girls again, and, as she put it, overall "bad news." Still, some girls said it was no big deal. Of all the girls Kristin and Dee knew who had been sexually active, only one was happy about it. The majority of their friends were still virgins who said they were waiting for the right guy. While Kristin thought these were all good arguments, she felt frustrated because she knew her mother would have all sorts of "facts and figures."

The therapist and two girls spent the remainder of the session brainstorming about other, more factual resources. The girls thought their aunt would take them to Planned Parenthood for some information, and Kristin was also planning to go talk to her school counselor. The final resource suggested was the Internet, specifically a Web site designed for adolescent girls: www.gurl.com (2001). *It is important that any Web searches be supervised as the information may be questionable, and the potential for uncovering pornography is great.* Armed with a game plan, the girls and Sharon felt their respective arguments would be ready next week. A two-hour session was scheduled to allow for any last-minute questions or preparations, as well as the actual hearing.

There was no question as to how serious the Lucas family took this assignment. Each family member arrived in business attire. Kristin carried a briefcase, which was, in her words, "full of mind-blowing facts," and Aunt Ruth actually brought a gavel. After complimenting the family on their obvious efforts and preparedness, the therapist began the activity. Each "lawyer" declined the offer of additional prep time. After reviewing the responsibilities of each role, the trial began. Both lawyers' arguments were as well prepared and thought-out as their attire. Although the trial started out traditionally, with each lawyer questioning the defendant, the trial eventually took on a debate format. Kristin presented statistics on pregnancy and sexually transmitted diseases in an attempt to persuade the judge of the dangers of sex. Sharon's argument focused on the many feelings surrounding sex. The feeling of being left out if you don't have sex, the importance of exploration, and finally how "making love" can be a wonderful way to express love for another person. Kristin used her friends' experiences as a rebuttal, highlighting the regret and disappointment so many of the girls felt instead of the expected love. Sharon also offered a frank discussion of how difficult it would be to say "no" to a boyfriend, a very special person in the defendant's life.

Both arguments were compelling, and it was difficult for the "judge" to make a decision. But, in the end, Ruth ruled in favor of the prosecuting attorney, Kristin, due largely to Kristin's use of statistics. Ruth found it difficult to ignore the gruesome statistics concerning the frequency of teen pregnancy and sexually transmitted diseases. She understood and sympathized with Sharon's arguments but found Kristin's words "stuck in her head."

The remainder of time was spent "debriefing." Everyone was thrilled with Kristin's win, especially Sharon, although she herself had tried her best to win. The girls were amazed at how accurate their mother had been in her portrayal of a teenage girl's feelings. Previously, each girl assumed her mother's thinking to be more scientific than emotional regarding this issue. Likewise, Sharon was impressed with Kristin's use of statistics—which she admitted were more up to date than her own knowledge. Discussion of the "trial" moved easily to a discussion of sex in general. The family was encouraged to continue this discussion at home.

The next session the family reported not only continuing the discussion but also making a plan. Both girls had decided to wait for sex until they were "a lot older," and in a "very serious relationship." Regardless, Sharon asked that the girls please talk to her or Aunt Ruth before taking any action, if for no other reason than contraception. The girls agreed, joking that they would help their mother stay "up to date" on the facts.

Suggestions for Follow-Up

As one of the objectives of this activity is to help families establish open communication surrounding sex or other difficult issues, it is vital that this subject be revisited frequently. "Checking in" regularly serves as a way to mirror the desired behavior to the family. It is important that the family stops thinking about sex as a separate category reserved for a "special talk" and instead begins to view it as a normal part of everyday conversation. The clinician can aid in this process by allowing or directing the conversation toward sex and related issues. For example, a later session with the Lucas family found Kristin lamenting the skimpy clothing of her classmates. The clinician led this to a discussion about the pressure to look "sexy," which led to a discussion about the pressure to have sex.

Contraindications

It is important that a good relationship exist between the family and therapist. If the clients and therapists are not well joined, the clients may feel obligated to participate in this activity despite unwillingness. In such an instance several contraindications may result. As sex is often uncomfortable to discuss, this activity may further alienate a family from the therapist as well as from one another. Although the clients agree to participate, by doing so their anxiety and discomfort concerning the issue are raised. This can potentially lead to reinforcement of the family's inability to openly discuss sex, as well as other difficult issues. Finally, clients who are reluctant participants may not take the activity seriously, a circumstance that may cause more harm than good.

Having a parent or guardian play the role of defense attorney has many benefits when taken seriously by the entire family. However, when not taken seriously, especially by the at-risk teen, this argument may achieve the opposite of its intention. The parents' argument may indeed prove to be the "straw that broke the camel's back," convincing the teen to have sex. Ensuring a high participation level, careful follow-up, and "debriefing" can eliminate this concern.

Finally, careful attention must be paid to the creation of the defendant character. The purpose is to parallel the actual teen, while not offending or alienating the teen. Including the teen in creating the character should eliminate these feelings, as he or she will feel a sense of control over the procedure.

Bibliotherapy Source for the Client

Drill, E., McDonald, H., and Odes, R. (1999). *Deal with It! A Whole New Approach to Your Body, Brain, and Life As a Gurl.* New York: Pocket Books.

Reference

Gurl.com (2001). Access: <http://www.gurl.com>.

SECTION VI:
SPECIFIC APPROACHES OR INTERVENTIONS

31

The Use of Consultants in Play Therapy: Narrative Practices with Young Children

Susan K. Sholtes

Type of Contribution: Activity

Materials: Stuffed Animals, Furbies, Dolls

Objective

The use of a "consultant" or "helper" in the therapy relationship can be an effective way to better understand the thoughts and feelings of young children. This is a narratively informed practice that privileges the voice of children to (1) name the problem as experienced by the child using his or her own words; (2) minimize stigma or shame associated with the problem; and (3) decrease both the hierarchy of the therapeutic relationship and adult-child power issues. This sends a clear message to children that their ideas, attitudes, and feelings are important, which empowers and enlists children in their own therapy. For parents, it offers new perspectives about their children that helps to open up new options for change, thus creating more support and hope in families.

Rationale

The word "narrative" implies listening to and/or the telling or retelling of stories about people and the problems in their lives. Narrative practices in therapy are informed by the idea that hearing stories can shape new realities and alternative stories (Freeman, Epston, and Lobovits, 1997). The acceptance and use of the person's language is seen as useful, not only in respecting another's thoughts and feelings, but also deemphasizing the hierarchy in the therapeutic relationship. The genuine collaboration created between therapist and client seeks to validate and honor the client's experience of the problem. It also invites an open, creative way to mutually discover remedies for the problem, guided by the person's strengths and interests. The use of assumptions or judgments by the therapist is minimal, thereby keeping the focus solely on the person and his or her problem.

A common narrative phrase is, "The person is not the problem, the problem is the problem." This practice is called "externalization" (White and Epston, 1990) and helps separate the person from the problem. Externalizing the problem often relieves the pressure from blame and defensiveness. It tells children that instead of them being defined *as* the problem, they have a relationship *with* the problem. This allows for a lighter approach. Children's resources and ideas can be engaged to help them make unique contributions as participants in their own therapy. It also helps parents open up to new ideas about their children and the problem.

The practice of using a "consultant" is recommended primarily for children ages three to ten years old. This playful approach is experienced as a more natural way to communicate with this age group. The use of imagination and problem solving are familiar to children and can be used effectively to help them face their concerns. This promotes the belief that children's ideas and abilities are valued, and that age does not prohibit them from contributing to the work.

Instructions

Most children are new to the experience of the therapy room and have never met a therapist before. This encounter can be confusing and intimidating for many children. When asked traditional questions such as, "Do you ever have any worries or problems?" most will shy away and answer, "No." Upon first meeting children, therapists should try to hear their strengths and interests and may also tell a little about themselves. At some point in the interview, usually when the children seem curious about the room and toys and appear ready to play, therapists might tell the children about the "consultants" (or "helpers," if the children are younger). Therapists should point to the many stuffed animals, Furbies, and dolls that are visible in the room or pull them out of a toy chest together with the children.

Almost immediately, one of the toys usually catches a child's attention, and he or she is allowed to explore his or her choice. The therapist should tell the child that the objects help the therapist and other children with any problems or worries they might have, such as problems with their temper, being scared at night, and so on. Often the parents have informed the therapist of behaviors to look for, and an issue can be introduced in the same way (e.g., wetting the bed). This is done in a matter-of-fact way, as though the problem is outside of the child and familiar to the therapist. The therapist should tell children that they are allowed to choose one of the consultants from the office (or playroom), one that they feel might be helpful to them. Children seemed surprised and slightly wary of this offer at first. The therapist should explain that they can return it later for other children to use but not until they've decided that they are finished working on their problem. Children can be asked if they'd like to pick a name for their toy (e.g., Hoppy, for the choice of a stuffed rabbit). Next the therapist can ask the children what they think Hoppy can help them with. By that time most children are eager to talk about a worry or concern they have, and together the therapist and children can name the problem (e.g., the "worry monster"). The therapist can describe how Hoppy will whisper in their ear about ideas to help learn about the worry monster, and that by teaming up with Hoppy (the consultant), the therapist is sure that together the monster will be overcome!

At that time, the child might be asked a series of questions about the problem:

- When does the worry monster usually show up?
- Where does it show up?
- Is it a big monster or a little one?
- Where is it when it is not out?
- Using artwork or drawing, what does the worry look/sound/feel like (Freeman, Epston, and Lobovits, 1997)?

These questions help to draw out details and describe the problem. Children often have elaborate answers and can inform the therapist about how much of the time they are consumed by their problem.

Questions that help tease out the strengths of the child and the perseverance of the problem include these:

- What have you already done to get the worry monster to shrink in size?
- How does the problem get in the way of things you like to do?
- Does it shrink or go away when other people are around?
- Who are those people?
- How is it affecting your days? Your nights? Sleeping?
- For parents or others in the room with you, ask each person how the problem affects him or her and how he or she thinks it has affected the child.
- Does the worry monster get in the way of your playing with your friends? Leaving your house?
- Is the worry monster in the room right now?

At the next appointment, children bring their toys back with them, and all of the questions can be directed to the stuffed toys, as if the "consultants" are being interviewed, not the children. The therapist will ask if the consultants have been helpful, and if so, how.

Children usually begin to offer more details about their week and their experience of the problem. Often another problem will emerge (e.g., the problem goes from the worry monster to worry about their parents fighting). When this occurs, the therapist consults with children about whether they think their choice of helper can help them with this new problem, too. Children usually seem very comfortable by this time, and sometimes the therapist can rename the original problem (Freedman and Combs, 1996). The children consistently play along and answer for the stuffed objects as though they are familiar with this kind of conversation. They will often tell you stories about where the "consultants" sleep or whether they are allowed to take them to school, and they soon start developing stories about their lives. Asking the children what the objects whisper in their ear to help them usually leads to a rich description. This helps name some of the solutions the children have already found, and therapists can then cocreate more strategies to attack the problem.

The children repeat this at each session. It is helpful to let the parents in on these practices, what the problem has been named, and the purpose of using the consultant. It is important that the children guide the parent, and often children will share their successes when improvements are made. Some parents sit in the room during the entire process, while others are informed later during a conversation with everyone present.

Eventually, the children return the objects when they feel better about the problem. Some children invite the consultants to join their other favorite stuffed animals or blankets from home, and they bring them all in to help. Some use a different stuffed animal for each problem, returning one and replacing it with a new one until they feel free of the problem.

Vignette

Alex is an adopted, ten-year-old boy who came to therapy with his mother. His mother had very strong ideas about Alex's anger and temper problem and was sure that he was heading for a life of difficulties. She was even considering the possibility of "sending him away." She felt that they had tried a number of techniques, and that things seemed hopeless. Alex was currently attending a public grade school, but his mother worried that he would soon be placed in an alternative school due to his poor conduct.

Alex was very shy, quiet, and private about his mother's concern. Upon showing him the toy animals, the therapist remembered thinking that he might find this "consultant" practice below his age level. However, he quickly seemed intrigued with one of the larger stuffed animals. Alex remarked how he liked the Husky dog because he seemed "tough but nice." He decided to name it Braveheart, from a movie that he had seen. Although there were not any dogs in the movie, he felt certain of the name. When the therapist asked some questions about Alex's interests and his life, he brought up the lack of fun things because he always got into trouble. When asked what this was like for him, Alex said he felt "frustration." The therapist and Alex talked more about things that had been taken away from him, how he spent time in his room as punishment, and so on. He agreed with the therapist that not only did this frustrate him but it also made him very sad. Alex was asked if he thought that Braveheart might be able to team up with them and be of some help. He said yes, with resignation, but he wasn't sure how. The therapist repeated the three problems that he had mentioned and said, "You first told me about 'trouble' taking some of your life away. You also said that frustration is present, and that you also have sadness in your life. Do you know which of these problems is the biggest? Or are there any other problems that you'd like to work on first?"

Alex thought about it for a moment and said, "Frustration."

Over the course of the sessions, Alex described how Frustration ruined things in his life and described the degree to which it affected him. They discovered that Frustration liked to see him friendless, that it took away his patience, and Frustration doesn't care if he is happy. For example, Alex had been losing at a Nintendo game, and Frustration had him get mad and throw the game across the room. Then Mom punished him. Using his Husky dog, Alex answered more questions about the problem. He stated that now he felt he was not alone with Frustration, and this seemed to make a difference for him.

Over time, Alex developed strategies not to let Frustration take over, to build up his patience and to let more friends into his life. One example was that the consultant would "tell" Alex to stop getting mad, and to get up and walk around until he felt Frustration leaving.

After Alex became successful at combating Frustration, the problem then changed to "Loneliness." Loneliness invited his mother more openly to tend to him, since she viewed the problem as more manageable and less frightening to her. She was able to separate the history of his adoptive mother from Alex. (Alex's natural mother had spent time in the criminal justice system as a teenager.) Alex began allowing himself to receive support from other adults, including his mother and friends, when needed. His conduct problems lessened both at home and at school. His mother was able to enjoy the brave heart that he was revealing through his actions, and to spend more time with her son as she shared his interests. She felt proud of the work that Alex had done in therapy and even asked if the therapist had a "consultant" for her! (Mom did begin individual counseling at this point.)

Author's Note

Narrative ideas influenced the work with Alex and his mother. His adoptive mother had been feeling that the genetics of Alex's birth mother inevitably left little room for new ideas about Alex and his problems. By exploring the story of Alex's connections with his birth mother and his birth culture, his adoptive mother was able to invite new feelings and perspectives about his problems and their effects. Further work with Alex and his mother might include the unmasking of discourses that separate adopted children from nurturing connections with their birth parents and birth culture (Freedman and Combs, 1998).

Contraindications

One child, age six, did not feel comfortable with choosing to take one of the objects home. She had a problem with stealing and told the therapist that she might "lose him" if she took him home. They worked without the "consultant," and once the stealing problem was better, the child asked to take a stuffed animal home to help with a new problem.
Every object from my office that has been loaned has been returned.

Professional Resources

Freedman, J. and Combs, G. (1996). *Narrative therapy: The social construction of preferred realities.* New York: W.W. Norton and Company.

Freedman, J. and Combs, G. (1997). Before and after Lily Hua. In C. White and J. Haley (Eds.), *The personal is the professional: Therapists' reflections on their families, lives and work.* Adelaide, South Australia: Dulwich Centre Publications.

Freedman, J. and Combs, G. (1998). Reflections on dark histories. In *Gecko,* #3 (pp. 18-22). Adelaide, South Australia: Dulwich Centre Publications.

Freeman, J., Epston, D., and Lobovits, D. (1997). *Playful approaches to serious problems.* New York: W.W. Norton and Company.

Madsen, W. C. (1999). *Collaborative therapy with multi-stressed families: From old problems to new futures.* New York: Guilford Publications.

Morgan, A. (1999). *Once upon a time . . . Narrative therapy with children and their families.* Adelaide, South Australia: Dulwich Centre Publications.

White, M. and Epston, D. (1990). *Narrative means to therapeutic ends.* New York: W.W. Norton and Company.

32

Integrating Externalization and Scaling Questions: Using Visual Scaling to Amplify Children's Voices

Lee Shilts
Barry L. Duncan

Type of Contribution: Activity

Objective

This chapter presents a technique that combines externalizing the problem with scaling questions called "visual" scaling. With children, the use of visual scaling helps make change in therapy more concrete, graphic, and achievable, thereby allowing the therapist the opportunity to gauge the child's impression of change between sessions. Questions are designed to fit the emotional and intellectual development of the child, which can promote change by enlisting the child's participation in the therapeutic process (Duncan, Hubble, and Miller, 1997). The visual scaling technique offers one way to amplify the child's voice and help therapists and children arrive at solutions. The use of visual scaling invites the child into the change process.

Rationale

When the presenting problem is that of a child, it is invariably the parents or some other significant adult who is desirous of the therapy. Rarely is it the child who is concerned. This appears to be particularly the case for children in the age range of five to eleven years. Indeed, when asked by the therapist if he or she knows why the family has come to therapy, the child often has little or no idea or, if he or she does understand, doesn't care. Given such a scenario, it is the task of the therapist to tailor therapy so that a "fit" develops with the child, enabling him or her to have a voice in the process.

It is therefore imperative that therapists choose a therapeutic pathway that makes sense to a child. Questions and interventions must be within the intellectual and developmental realm of children, particularly those within the age range of five to eleven years.

Scaling Questions

Berg and de Shazer (1993) developed scaling questions to transform abstract concepts into more tangible thoughts: "Scaling questions were first developed to help both therapist and client talk about nonspecific topics such as depression or communication" (p. 22). Scales measure the

A version of this chapter was first published in the *Journal of Systemic Studies* (as "Integrating Externalization and Scaling Questions with Children," 2000, 19[1], 82-89) and represents the starting point of collaborative writing between the two authors.

client's perceptions, motivate and encourage the client, and illuminate goals, solutions, and other important aspects of the therapeutic conversation (de Shazer, 1994). Scales are designed on a zero-to-ten continuum. A "ten" usually denotes the absence of the complaint while a "zero" denotes either the present complaint or the complaint at its worst (Berg, 1994; de Shazer, 1994; Miller, Hubble, and Duncan, 1996).

The answers to scaling questions are completely self-referenced, they do not relate to external criteria. Further, scaling questions are not static. As Kowalski and Kral (1989) suggest: the scale builds on the assumption of change in the desired direction. Since a scale is a progression, the number "7" assumes the numbers "10" as well as "5", "3", or "1". It also assumes the movement (or change) in one direction or another, rather than stagnation. By virtue of this, an expectation of change is built into the process of asking scaling questions (p. 61).

By structuring the scale in this fashion, the therapist and client are able to quantify change where a "zero" becomes a lack of movement toward the client's goal and "ten" becomes the attainment of the client's goal (Shilts and Gordon, 1996). By agreeing to speak the same language of numbers, the therapist and client are then able to focus on the exceptions (de Shazer et al., 1986) that are occurring between the different levels of numbers. Berg (1994) defined exceptions as those "times when the problem could have happened but did not" (p. 91). Thus, therapists and clients can investigate the differences between a "five" and a "six" to find out what occurs when there is a difference in ratings (Walter and Peller, 1992). Quantifying abstract concepts and client change allows the therapist and client to converse jointly about what is happening and needs to continue to happen so that the change in the desired direction continues (de Shazer, 1994).

With children, the scale can be made more concrete in various ways. For example, Cade and O'Hanlon (1993) have different versions of the scale: "If this single brick stands for when you are being very noisy in class and behaving like a five-year-old, and this tall pile of bricks stands for when you have been able to behave like a ten-year-old, what pile size would stand for how grown-up you have been these past few days?" or "If this small circle on the blackboard shows me how shy you used to be, and this big circle shows me how brave you are going to be, draw me a circle to show me the bravest you have been this week" (Cade and O'Hanlon, 1993, p. 108).

This type of scaling allows children to measure their progress in concrete ways. It provides children the opportunity to picture their progress in therapy and become actively involved in change. Since children in the age range of five to eleven years often have difficulty with abstract ideas, graphically scaling progress in therapy helps children plot their successes as well as where they need to proceed to enhance the change process.

Externalization

White and Epston (1990) define "externalizing" as "an approach to therapy that encourages persons to objectify and, at times, to personify the problems that they experience as oppressive" (p. 38). Two main outcomes emerge (White and Epston, 1990): First, the person and the problem become linguistically separated; the problem is the problem, not the person. Second, those problems that were perceived as being inherent and reified take on a less-restrictive quality. Externalization encourages clients to document the ways in which they have resisted and surmounted the dominant stories of their lives—stories organized around their problems, symptoms, and socially ascribed pathologies. In describing our therapeutic practices, we have found it helpful to view the concept of "knowledge" as a plural noun and to formulate questioning strategies that elicit from the clients we work with the "solution knowledges" and the "alternative knowledges" about their lives and relationships that have been resurrected or generated in therapy. These knowledges then become more available for clients to deploy when necessary, and for others to consult as aids to their own self-development (Epston and White, 1995, p. 340). Thus, the therapist explores how family members have resisted the influence of the problem and, in so doing, discovers their competencies and successes in managing the problem (White, 1986).

Instructions

Weaving the Techniques Together: Visual Scaling

Combining externalization with scaling questions helps children initiate and maintain change within the therapeutic context. Hopefully, this language for creating change reaches beyond therapy and into the child's everyday life.

The following outlines a step-by-step description of visual scaling:

1. Upon completion of the concern definition, the therapist asks the child to describe his or her problem utilizing the externalization technique as described by White and Epston (1990). For example, if the child's (and family's) concern is fear, the therapist will ask the child to describe and measure the size of the "fear monster."
2. Next, the therapist allows the child to stand on a chair and stretch his or her hand as high in the air as possible. This encourages the child to envision the maximum size of the monster, thus allowing the "monster" to reduce or shrink as the therapy progresses. This visual picture will be utilized as the child (and family) begins to visually scale his or her concern.
3. The therapist will next pose the following question to the child: "What will you be doing to shrink the monster so he is only as tall as you?" The question is designed to turn the scale "upside down" (Molnar and de Shazer, 1987), especially in the areas where children experience anger, fears, and inappropriate behaviors. The idea behind this is to help the child purposely "shrink" the problem so that he or she can gain control over the problem. This allows a fear to be portrayed as a "downhill slide" rather than an "uphill battle" (Molnar and de Shazer, 1987).
4. At the end of the first session, the therapist assigns as a task to the child (and family) to note those times in the next week when he or she beats the monster down and, when that is done, to measure the size of the monster. Thus, each day the child will give a visual picture of the size of the monster.
5. In follow-up and subsequent sessions, clients are asked to visually scale their progress by how much they have reduced the size of their problem monster. The therapist follows this theme in subsequent sessions and monitors the size of the monster. The child is told that when he or she gets the monster to his or her size, he or she then has a fighting chance to beat the monster. Similarly, the child is told that once he or she reduces the size of the monster below his or her own height, he or she will be able to stamp out the monster and reduce it to a pile of ashes. Once this occurs, the monster no longer has control of the child and the monster will be out of the child's life forever. After a review with the family members as to how they reduced the problem, the child is asked if he or she is ready to "step on the monster and forever be rid of it." At this point, therapy is usually terminated.

In essence, externalization initiates the change and scaling provides the opportunity to gauge progress in therapy, thus maintaining change. The visual scaling process provides a developmentally appropriate way to encourage children and therapists to continue looking for information about change.

Vignette

Mrs. Brown and her eight-year-old daughter Megan entered therapy because Megan had a fear of darkness that had persisted for two years. She refused to sleep alone in her bedroom and often sought refuge in the parents' bedroom.

Session 1

During the initial session, the therapist externalized the problem by exploring the meaning of the "fear monster" with Megan. The therapist and Megan discussed the monster, his habits, how he tended to push her around, and times when the monster appeared to be at the very worst. Once Megan described the monster, the therapist next moved to get a description of just how big this monster appeared to Megan. The use of visual scaling enabled a vivid picture to emerge, rather than just an abstract idea. To enable Megan to imagine the monster as large as she possibly could, the therapist asked her to stand on a chair and stretch her arms up as far as possible. This signaled to everyone just how menacing the fear monster was and the control he exerted over Megan. When the therapist asked if this was the size of the monster, Megan (and her mother) readily agreed.

The next step was to ask Megan and her mother what Megan would be doing differently when she began to shrink the monster. The therapist arbitrarily shrunk the monster about five inches using the wall as a benchmark. Megan and her mother suggested that she would be sleeping through the night in her own room with the use of a night-light. The therapist followed this line of questioning and asked what would be going on when the monster was five more inches shorter. Megan stated that she would be sleeping in her room without needing a night-light. The session ended with the following task: Megan and her mother were asked to measure the size of the fear monster each day based on how Megan did at night with the dark and her sleeping arrangements. A second session was scheduled for one week later.

Session 2

Megan and her mother returned the next week with a list of their observations regarding the task of measuring her fear monster. After a brief discussion, the therapist asked Megan to report the size of her fear monster as she had recorded on a daily basis. Megan said that the monster had shrunk to her height on three different nights during the past week. Mother agreed with Megan's report. When asked what occurred on those nights, Megan proudly explained to the therapist that she was able to sleep alone all three nights in her bedroom without the aid of a night-light. Megan was able to do this due to her new perceptions of the sleep monster. Mother echoed the same results and stated that the whole family had never experienced such a calm week of sleep.

The therapist complimented Megan and her mother on their work and suggested that their measurement scores indicated the beginning of progress toward change. He further suggested to Megan that when she shrinks the fear monster to her size, it is probably a good sign that the monster feels that he no longer has control over her. The therapist next suggested that when she shrinks the monster to below her height, the monster would feel the need to leave her since he can no longer control and scare her. Megan nodded approval to the therapist's comments, and the same task was given to Megan and her mother. A third session was scheduled for three weeks later.

Session 3

Megan and her mother returned three weeks later for their third and final session. Megan reported that the monster was now a shrimp, only measuring to below her knees. Mother reported that she had spent the past twelve days sleeping alone in her bed. Megan proudly told the therapist that she even awakened one night for a drink of water, went to the kitchen, and returned back to her bedroom with no signs of the fear monster. To finalize the therapy, the therapist suggested that since the monster was now so small, Megan should stamp on it and leave it behind in the therapist's room. Megan did this with zeal and therapy was terminated. Before departing, Megan turned to the therapist and stated that there must be many dead monsters in his office carpet. The therapist agreed with her and stated that this is a good place for monsters to go to die.

Case Summary

This case demonstrates the integration of the techniques of externalization and scaling. Externalizing the problem offers the client the opportunity to highlight competencies over the problem and initiate change, and scaling allows the client to "measure" success concretely and identify how to maintain and increase the desired changes. The child in this case initiated change after describing the monster and then reporting ways she could shrink the monster and thereby feel more in control of her fears. Her fears became controllable and she no longer felt overwhelmed with the idea of sleeping alone. Once she built on this idea, the monster no longer controlled her and it became a nonentity in her life. Scaling questions helped her concretely describe and maintain her victories over the fear monster. The two techniques together seemed to fit naturally her developmental level and encourage her participation in the therapeutic process. A follow-up six months later revealed that the presenting problem never returned, and Megan continued to sleep independently in her own room. This proved that change was maintained and no further therapy was needed. Mother reported to the therapist that the family had not been revisited by the fear monster and reiterated that the whole family was sleeping better through the nights.

Suggestions for Follow-Up

Once the client system reports progress in the area of concern (e.g., soiling the pants) and the therapy is close to termination, parents can be encouraged to check periodically with their young children on the status and the relative size of the poop monster. This gives parents a tool to keep things in check. A chart can be kept and used to monitor the status of the monster over time, until it is deemed not necessary, usually by the parents. This process allows the family to keep up with the procedure even though the therapy has formally ended.

Contraindications

This intervention is usually inadvisable or ineffective for children beyond the age of ten, unless they are mentally challenged. From a developmental standpoint, children begin to process in the abstract and therefore the visual part of the intervention is neither appropriate nor effective.

Conclusion

This chapter suggested that therapy accommodate younger children with approaches that are tailored to fit their developmental level. Externalizing the problem coupled with scaling is one way to accomplish this task. The proposed "visual" scaling seems to naturally fit children's worldview, encourages their active participation in therapy, and provides a concrete process of measuring progress and enhancing the change process. Overall, visual scaling advocates the central philosophies of brief systemic therapy: that clients have the inherent resources to resolve problems, are seeking therapy to look for information about change, and that the therapist should focus on client-generated content and goals. Visual scaling allows children to be reliable informants of the problem and its resolution, permitting therapy to be "client informed" (Shilts, Fillippino, and Nau, 1994) with children as well.

The authors continue to explore the utility of visual scaling with children presenting a wide variety of concerns. We invite interested readers to consider the clinical and research possibilities with specific child populations and applications within a training/supervision context. We welcome your ideas and feedback.

References

Berg, I.K. (1994). *Family-based services*. Milwaukee, WI: Brief Family Therapy Press.

Berg, I.K. and de Shazer, S. (1993). Making numbers talk: Language in therapy. In S. Friedman (Ed.), *The new language of change* (pp. 5-24). New York: Guilford Publications.

Cade, B. and O'Hanlon, W.H. (1993). *A brief guide to brief therapy*. New York: W.W. Norton and Company.

de Shazer, S. (1994). *Words were originally magic*. New York: W.W. Norton and Company.

de Shazer, S., Berg, I.K., Lipchik, E., Nunnally, E., Molnar, A., Gingerich, W., and Weiner-Davis, M. (1986). Brief therapy: Focused solution development. *Family Process, 25,* 207-222.

Duncan, B., Hubble, M., and Miller, S. (1997). *Psychotherapy with "impossible" cases: The efficient treatment of therapy veterans*. New York: W.W. Norton.

Epston, D. and White, M. (1995). Termination as a rite of passage: Questioning strategies for a therapy of inclusion. In R.A. Neimeyer and M.J. Mahoney (Eds.), *Constructivism in psychotherapy* (pp. 339-354). Washington, DC: American Psychological Association.

Kowalski, K. and Kral, R. (1989). The geometry of solution. Using the scaling technique. *Family Therapy Case Studies, 4,* 59-66.

Miller, S., Hubble, M., and Duncan, B. (Eds.) (1996). *Handbook of solution-focused brief therapy*. San Francisco: Jossey-Bass.

Molnar, A. and de Shazer, S. (1987). Solution-focused therapy: Toward the identification of therapeutic tasks. *Journal of Marital and Family Therapy, 13,* 349-358.

Shilts, L., Fillippino, C., and Nau, D. (1994). Client-informed therapy. *Journal of Systemic Therapies, 13,* 39-52.

Shilts, L. and Gordon, A.B. (1996). What to do after the miracle occurs. *The Journal of Family Psychotherapy, 7,* 15-22.

Walter, J.L. and Peller, J.E. (1992). *Becoming solution-focused in brief therapy*. New York: Brunner/Mazel.

White, M. (1986). Negative explanation, restraint, and double description: A template for family therapy. *Family Process, 25,* 169-184.

White, M. and Epston, D. (1990). *Narrative means to therapeutic ends*. New York: W.W. Norton and Company.

Additional Professional Resource

White, M. (1993). Deconstruction and therapy. In S. Gilligan and R. Price (Eds.), *Therapeutic conversations* (pp. 22-61). New York: W.W. Norton and Company.

Resources for Clients

Any prop that helps young clients visualize the externalized foe will be helpful and serve to maintain an open and concrete representation and record of progress. This prop can be viewed in the home environment and simultaneously brought in to therapy on a routine basis.

33

Becoming the Author of Your Life: Writing Stories of Change

Megan L. Dolbin

Type of Contribution: Activity

Objectives

As a means of acknowledging and celebrating a child's progress in therapy, this activity is designed to be used as the child nears the termination of therapy. Arising from the framework of narrative therapy, the purpose of the activity is to help children create a rich and permanent record of their development of an alternative story about themselves. More specifically, by helping the child through the process of creating his or her own children's book about the externalized problem, this activity allows the child to document his or her new relationship with an externalized presenting problem.

Rationale for Use

Within the framework of narrative therapy, therapists often work on presenting problems through externalization. Externalization is a framework for approaching presenting problems in which the child no longer is seen as the problem. Rather, presenting problems are seen as disrupting the child's life but are not seen as intrinsic to the child. Therefore, with the use of externalization, the problem becomes the problem. For example, instead of saying that a child is angry, externalization would say that anger creeps in and takes over the child. Making the problem as something that is external to the person is especially useful when working with children. Many children feel very embarrassed and guilty about their problems and the disruption that the presenting problem is "causing" in their families. By using externalization with children and their families, feelings of blame and defensiveness often decrease. In addition, externalization allows the family and the child to tap into their creativity for the purposes of working together against the externalized problem and not against each other. Finally, externalization often empowers the child to be active in working on the presenting problem, enhances the child's sense of self-worth, and enhances the child's confidence in his or her ability to change the presenting situation.

Once the presenting problem is externalized, therapy proceeds with a deconstruction of the presenting problem. By asking questions about the problem's history, context, effects, and strategies, the child can begin to learn more about the problem and to experience the problem from a different perspective. Armed with a different perspective on the problem, the child and the therapist can then begin the process of reconstructing an alternative story. The development of this alternative story begins by identifying and exploring occasions (i.e., unique outcomes) when the child is in charge of the problem. Then, by exploring and focusing on the child's preferred outcomes and the meanings of those preferred outcomes, the therapist and the child complete the development of the rich and detailed alternative story.

When children reach a point where they have developed a positive and empowering alternative story and are nearing the end of therapy, it often is powerful to create a permanent record for celebrating and underscoring the child's progress in therapy and the changes that the child has made regarding the presenting problem. In addition to highlighting the progress made in therapy, having something to take home as a reminder of the alternative story is often very fun and enjoyable for children and their families.

This activity guides children through the process of creating a permanent record of their process of developing an alternative story about themselves and the externalized presenting problem. Using the format of a children's book, the therapist and the child work together to write and illustrate the child's alternative story of himself or herself and his or her relationship with the externalized problem. From there, the therapist and the family can work collaboratively to incorporate the child's book into a ritual celebrating the completion of therapy.

Instructions

Begin by talking with the child about how his or her relationship with the externalized presenting problem has changed over the course of therapy. That is, ask the child what has changed and how his or her life is becoming different as a result of developing a new story about himself or herself and a new relationship with the externalized presenting problem. If necessary, give the child feedback about progress that you have observed during therapy. (If working with the child's family, and assuming that family members would provide positive feedback to the child, it may also be useful to elicit each family member's opinion about the changes that the child has made while in therapy.)

> *Helpful Hint #1:* Keep a list of these changes. It will be helpful when working on the storyline of the child's book.

Next, ask the child to think about some of his or her favorite books and to describe the stories in those books. Talk with the child about how people write books for the purpose of telling a story that other people might find interesting and might like to read over and over. Explain to the child that since therapy will be nearing termination, it might be fun for the child to become the author and illustrator of a book about the changes that he or she made in therapy. Also, explain that the book will be a special gift that the child will always have and can read over and over again— even after therapy has ended.

> *Helpful Hint #2:* Have several children's books available for the child to examine. These can be helpful in giving the child some ideas about the stories in children's books and how the stories look when illustrated.

Since the child is the author, set up a "planning meeting" in which the child and therapist write the text (i.e., the storyline) of the book. This meeting may take several sessions. If the child can write, he or she can write down the story. If the child cannot write, the therapist can write the text of the story for the child. Another option for recording the text would be to use a computer to type the story. For the purposes of writing the actual text of the book, two strategies can be used:

Strategy #1: Have the story focus on the adventures of the externalized presenting problem. That is, the story can be about the struggles of the externalization, how it got itself and the child into trouble, and how it learned to become different.

Strategy #2: Have the story focus on how the child learned to take control of the externalized presenting problem. More specifically, the plot of the story could follow the stages of therapy: (1) how the externalization was disrupting the child's life, (2) how the child learned to see the externalization differently, (3) how the child discovered that there were times when he or she was in charge of the externalization, and (4) how the child was able to build a new relationship with the externalization so that the child was in charge and not the problem.

> *Helpful Hint #3:* Stories are often easier for children to write if the presenting problem has been externalized into some type of "live character." For example, instead of externalizing angry outbursts as "the temper," it may be more effective (in terms of writing a story) to externalize angry outbursts as "the temper monster."

> *Helpful Hint #4:* Depending on the child, the story can be realistic or a fantasy. The child should be encouraged to be creative and to be the sole author. The therapist's role should be to help fill the gaps in the story.

> *Helpful Hint #5:* At this stage, it is also feasible to outline the story. Then, as the child creates the illustrations, the child and the therapist can write the text of the book. Although creating the book in stages is easier (i.e., write the text and then do the illustrations), the therapist should feel free to adapt the activity as necessary to meet the needs and personality of the child.

Once the story is written, supply the child with a tablet of unlined white paper and a variety of markers, crayons, paints, pencils, and other supplies necessary for drawing the illustrations of the book. Using a published book as a model, have the child begin to draw the illustrations to go along with the story. After all the illustrations are complete, insert the text of the story. This can be done by having the child or the therapist write the text on the same pages as the illustrations. Other options include inserting pages of text between the illustrations or printing out the text (if it was stored on a computer) and gluing it onto the illustrations.

After the book is completed, have the child create a cover page. Then, between therapy sessions, take the book to a copy center and have it bound. Many inexpensive methods of binding will preserve the book and make it look more like a real children's book. At the next session, present the book to the child. This can be done in the context of a celebratory ritual that includes the child and other important family members and friends (see Suggestions for Follow-Up for a discussion of using the child's book in the context of a ritual).

Vignette

When he came to therapy, eight-year-old Jim was plagued with a variety of behavior problems. On several occasions, he had been caught lying to teachers and to his mother and new stepfather. Jim was also prone to angry outbursts in which he would punch and bite his two younger siblings. In terms of contextual information, the therapist learned that prior to his parents' divorce, Jim had witnessed a great deal of violence between his mother and biological father.

The focus of therapy was creating a context in which Jim did not feel that everything was his fault. He often talked about how bad he was and how it was his fault that he was no longer living with his mother and father. In addition, since his mother, stepfather, and teachers were very critical of his disruptive behavior, Jim informed the therapist that he had a rotten core. The therapist began the process of externalizing Jim's angry outbursts. With some discussion about the angry outbursts, Jim decided that a small blue man named Butt was the angry person who was tricking him into getting into trouble and hurting his siblings.

During therapy sessions, Jim talked at length about how Butt would get so upset that he would take over and make Jim do mean things to other people. At this point, the therapist asked Jim if there were times when Butt tried to get him to do something mean but he did not listen to him. Jim proudly recalled a story in which Butt was telling Jim to steal crayons from another child at school. Jim said that he told Butt to knock it off and convinced Butt that, instead of stealing the crayons, they would play kickball at recess. Using this unique outcome, the therapist and Jim worked on creating a new story about Butt. In this story, Butt was not bad and mean. Rather, he was a very young boy who needed someone to teach him how to express his anger more appropriately. Jim enthusiastically agreed to become Butt's big brother.

With time, Jim's behavior problems began to improve. Jim reported that when Butt wanted to do something that would get Jim into trouble, they would take a time-out and Jim would teach Butt a better way to handle the situation. Jim smiled and said that he really enjoyed being a big brother to Butt. He said that he felt important and like he was making a difference to someone. With time, Jim began to wonder how he could be a better big brother to his siblings.

As Jim neared the end of therapy, the therapist suggested that Jim write a book about Butt. Jim immediately accepted the idea and enthusiastically began talking about the story he was planning. Jim's story focused on Butt and his adventures. Because Jim was too young to write the text of the story himself, the therapist wrote the text of the story into a notebook. The story began with all of the things that Butt was doing wrong, such as beating up kids, stealing toys, breaking things, and screaming at everyone he saw. According to the story, Butt was very mad and liked to make other people feel just as bad as he did. Butt's favorite person to bother was Jim. He would tell Jim stories about how getting into trouble was fun and made you cool. In the story, when Butt got Jim into trouble, he had put a blindfold on Jim. As the story continued, Butt kept tricking Jim into doing worse and worse things. However, one day, Butt tied the blindfold wrong and Jim could see out. When Jim looked out of the blindfold, he realized that Butt was acting like a jerk and hurting other people. Jim decided that Butt should learn to treat people better. So, to teach Butt how to behave, Jim took him to "Good Person School." In school, Butt learned how to share, how to be nicer, and how to make friends with other people. After school, Jim went everywhere with Butt and made sure that he followed the rules from "Good Person School." At the end of the story, Butt and Jim became best friends. Jim promised to help Butt behave better if Butt would help Jim learn to know when he was upset and needed to talk with an adult.

After completing the text of the story, several sessions were spent illustrating the story. Jim enjoyed drawing the illustrations and, after completing each drawing, the therapist added the corresponding text. Once the book was bound and completed, Jim and the therapist planned a celebration party for Jim's mother, stepfather, and two siblings. At the celebration party, the therapist helped Jim read the book to his family. Then, the therapist interviewed Jim about the changes that Butt had made and about how Jim and Butt were going to continue to work together. The family members were also given an opportunity to ask questions about the story. In response to some questions about the future, Jim said that he would always be a big brother to Butt. However, he did ask his family for some help. Jim said that he wanted his family to help him by becoming a "Butt meter." That is, when Butt was "acting like a jerk," the family would remind Jim that the "Butt meter" was too high and that he needed to step in and help Butt. As a final portion of the celebration party, each of the family members congratulated Jim on his progress and presented him with a certificate of merit. Within a few weeks of this session, the family stopped coming for therapy. A follow-up telephone call indicated that Jim's behavior was slowly improving. Jim's mother indicated that, when Jim had bad days, the family would pull out the book and read it together as a way of reminding Jim how to be a big brother to Butt.

Suggestions for Follow-Up

The completion of therapy and the development of a rich and positive alternative story is a definite reason for celebration. One means for celebrating the child's therapeutic work is to conduct a ritual using the child's book about his or her alternative story. By highlighting the child's work in therapy (as symbolized by the child's book) within a ritualistic setting, the child can feel a sense of pride in his or her accomplishments and can be empowered to take responsibility for maintaining his or her new alternative stories and for not allowing the externalized presenting problem to creep back into his or her life.

When planning the ritual, it may be most enjoyable and meaningful for the child and his or her family if everyone works together to develop the ritual. Some suggestions for possible rituals include having the child read the book to family members, having family members interview the child about the book (e.g., a press conference), and having a book-signing party for family and friends. Family members and friends can also be asked to share how they have seen the child change and their hopes for the child's future. Other suggestions include presenting the child with a certificate of success or change, taking pictures, and making a videotape of the ritual.

Explain to the child that she or he is now an expert on the externalized presenting problem. After explaining that many other children struggle with similar problems, ask the child if she or he would like to share the book with other children. With the permission of the child, explain that a copy of her or his book will be placed in the clinic library so that when children who have similar problems come in for therapy, they can read the child's book. Most children are very proud to know that they can help children who are having similar difficulties.

Contraindications for Use

Although there are no specific contraindications for making a book with the child, developing and writing a story may be difficult for very young children. Therefore, this activity is most appropriate for older children. However, the activity can be adapted for children who are too young to write by having the therapist write the text of the story for the child. Another method of adapting the activity for younger children is to have the child draw a picture book about the externalized presenting problem.

Therapists should be cautious when using the child's book as the basis of a therapeutic and/or celebratory ritual. If family members continue to blame the child and harbor negative attitudes about the child's progress, having the child read the book to family members may not be appropriate. Thus, therapists should exercise sensitivity and judgment when considering the extent to which family members will be able to celebrate changes in the child. This activity is designed to provide the child with a positive and empowering experience. Therefore, if the family is not able to support the child's progress and success, then the therapist may want to consider having the celebratory ritual with just the child.

Professional Readings and Resources

Freedman, J. and Combs, G. (1996). *Narrative therapy*. New York: W. W. Norton and Company.

Freeman, J., Epston, D., and Lobovits, D. (1997). *Playful approaches to serious problems: Narrative therapy with children and their families*. New York: W. W. Norton and Company.

Imber-Black, E., Roberts, J., and Whiting, R. (1988). *Rituals in families and family therapy*. New York: W. W. Norton and Company.

34

Jumanji

Katherine A. Milewski-Hertlein

Type of Contribution: Activity

Objective

The purpose of this activity is to externalize the problem for children who are brought to therapy with behavior problems. When working with families who seek therapy for their "problem" children, it is likely that external factors are causing or maintaining the problem. "Externalization" is the process that allows the family to form a cohesive unit, similar to a team, to defeat the problem (White and Epston, 1990). The purpose is to get the family to "fight the problem" instead of fighting each other.

Rationale for Use

Jumanji is appropriate for use in the following situations: (1) when a parent needs assistance separating the bad behavior from the worth of the child; (2) when a family presents with a child who has aggression problems, such as hitting peers and throwing tantrums; (3) when chaotic families seek therapy; and (4) when outside sources are identified as possible factors in the cause or maintenance of a problem.

Externalization of the problem is a concept that stems from narrative therapy. Narrative therapy was popularized by Michael White, David Epston, and Michael Durant in the 1980s and is based on the assumption that there are two "stories" that a person uses to interpret events and experiences: a dominant story and a subjugated story (White and Epston, 1990). An individual's dominant story is a set of assumptions he or she believes about the world around him or her. In other words, it is a lens through which one views the world. The dominant lens allows one to assign meaning to situations, events, and experiences. The subjugated story is the secondary lens through which the client does not typically view his or her world and experiences. According to White and Epston (1990), interpreting events through the "dominant story" can be problematic when using that lens is no longer effective, and it is this which brings people to therapy. Therefore, therapy consists of moving from the old, ineffective dominant story to an effective, new subjugated story until the subjugated story becomes the new dominant story. "Externalization" of the problem is one way in which this is accomplished.

Externalization is the process whereby one attributes problems one experiences to external factors (White and Epston, 1990). By attributing the problems to something external (or objectifying them), one attempts to defeat the problem. White and Epston (1990) assert that externalizing problems in child cases is important, as most members of the family attribute the problem to the child or identified client. For example, White and Epston (1990) recount a case in which a family sought therapy for a child with a history of encopresis. The clinician and the family termed the problem "Sneaky Poo," and the child and parents as a team became determined to outwit Sneaky Poo. By externalizing the problem, or making the encopresis an external problem rather than something tied to the child, the family created a "team" and fought against Sneaky Poo, resulting in significantly fewer incidents of the appearance of encopresis. In Jumanji, a similar process is happening in that the problem is related to an external factor (which, instead of Sneaky Poo, is known as Jumanji) and outwitted by the family.

Many times, it is difficult for parents to separate the child's negative behavior from the child. Parents, by the time they seek help, attribute the cause of the problem to the child, labeling the child "bad." When parents do come to therapy, they are often exhausted from having to deal with the "problem" child, resulting in an even greater difficulty separating the negative behavior from the child. Externalizing the problem will help to separate the behavior from the child. This is helpful because it will contribute to solidifying the unit between family members, creating a team against the problem. In other words, parents versus the child becomes entire family (parents plus child) versus the problem.

Once parents and child are on the same team, the child is reframed in the family's mind as one who is *also* plagued with the problem and desires resolution. The child is viewed as just another member of the team. The reframe is helpful because, once established, the parents can spend a portion of their energy responding to the *positive* behaviors in which their child engages. Suddenly, the child is viewed as another family member suffering the same consequences of the behavior—frustration, sadness, helplessness, and so on—inevitably encouraging opportunities for cooperation among family members.

In addition, reframing increases the probability that all family members, including the identified client, will work more cooperatively. Working together, especially as a team, is likely to increase dialogue among members, as opposed to monologues about the problem that previously resulted in holding the identified child responsible for the problem. Finally, it allows the family to take a lighter approach to the problem (White and Epston, 1990). In summary, externalizing the problem and attributing it to external factors creates a team of family members pitted against the ailment rather than the child. Parents are no longer frustrated with the child and work with the child to help him or her through the problem.

Instructions

In Jumanji, the therapist and family participate in making up a game, and then the entire family plays the game against the problem, eventually defeating the problem. To prepare parents for this intervention, the therapist should explain the procedure and rationale for the intervention to the parents privately. This gives the clinician an opportunity to emphasize the concept that the child is not what is negative, only the behavior. The more people in the family who are able to externalize the behavior, the more successful this intervention is. If the parents react negatively to the therapist and the children engaging in this behavior or are not willing to participate in the activity, there may be two reasons for this: the therapist and family are not properly joined, or the parents are not willing to externalize the behavior. In either case, the therapist should explore with the parents their concerns and reactions.

This activity takes place during a family therapy session. The children, parents, and therapist are all to be present. It is helpful if the children sit together. The clinician begins to tell a story and asks the children to help as he or she continues. The clinician reads the following format:

> Once upon a time, there was a man walking through the jungle. He saw many things in the jungle. He saw trees, bugs, and animals. What kind of animals do you think he saw? . . . [Following discussion of animals] The man in the jungle then saw a hole in the ground. It was hard to see because it was covered with leaves, but he could see it. So the man peeked

in the hole. He saw an animal. What kind of animal do you think he saw? . . . [Following discussion of animal] The animal was very surprised to see the man and called all of his jungle friends. His jungle friends began to run to the hole, jumping, romping, yelling, and creating chaos. Can you act like the animals?

The children jump and yell and are encouraged by the therapist to throw a tantrum. The therapist concludes with the following:

> The jumping and yelling that you just did, just like a tantrum maybe at home, is Jumanji [or ask the children to come up with the name].

It is not necessary that the clinician follow this exact format, however. Although the story can revolve around anything, it should lead to a situation where chaos breaks out.

It is noted that the specific label of Jumanji fit this family. For other families, a name tailored to fit the family's interests, likes, and cultural heritage is recommended. For example, some names are Delicious Devil, Ornery Octopus, Hairy Havoc, and Jesse Messy.

After this activity, the therapist leads a discussion surrounding the causes and effects of Jumanji (or whatever name the family chooses for the activity). The therapist explores how the chaos, tantrums, and so on, are maintained within the story of Jumanji by asking questions (White, 1995). Appropriate questions following the introduction of Jumanji include these:

- When are the times that Jumanji is not around?
- What feeds Jumanji?
- What are things that make Jumanji go away?
- How does Jumanji affect you?
- What does Jumanji tell you?

In other words, the therapist asks questions about the behaviors, the antecedents (or events that precede the problematic behaviors), and consequences (events that follow the behaviors), without labeling the child as bad and perpetuating the idea that the identified client *is* the problem. It is imperative that the clinician continue with the Jumanji theme after presenting the idea to promote the reframe of the child to parents or other family members, to maintain the family as a team, and to increase dialogue among family members.

Vignette

Gina was a six-year-old girl referred to therapy. Her mother reported that Gina threw tantrums on a daily basis and was highly aggressive, both at home and at school. The clinician asked Gina and her older sister, Maria, if they had ever heard of Jumanji. The children said no. The therapist told the story in which a man was walking through a jungle and saw many animals. The therapist asked the children to tell about the kinds of animals that the man saw in the jungle. The children discussed the kinds of animals. The clinician stated that the man in the jungle saw a hole in the ground. The man peeked in the hole. The clinician then asked the children what was in the hole. The children responded, naming a type of animal. The clinician stated the animal was surprised to see the man and called all of the animals. The jungle friends began to romp, scream, and jump in the jungle, creating *chaos*. The clinician jumped around and threw a tantrum and then asked the children to throw similar tantrums, pretending to be the animals in the jungle. The therapist explained that the chaos, yelling, screaming, and jumping around is Jumanji.

Once the children were calmed down again, the therapist asked the following questions: "Why does Jumanji stay away when you come to see me?" and "What kinds of things make Jumanji go away?" The response from both girls was their mother saying "stop" would make Jumanji leave. The next part of the session was spent with Gina and Maria rehearsing making Jumanji leave. They practiced throwing tantrums and stopping when directed by Mom.

In the following session, the therapist inquired about the ways the family learned to tame Jumanji. Mother indicated that visits from Jumanji were significantly less frequent, and the school reported that Gina's behavior had improved considerably. Over the remainder of the course of therapy, there was only one reported incident in which Gina became extremely aggressive at school. The therapist maintained the idea of Jumanji and continued questioning, reinforcing ways in which Jumanji could be controlled. This incident was the only revisit of Jumanji noted during the course of therapy.

Suggestions for Follow-Up

It is pertinent that the clinician follows up the Jumanji intervention with appropriate questions. Part of the narrative model includes questions and should continue session after session as a normal course of the therapy. This will aid in maintaining the theme around externalizing the tantrums to Jumanji.

A follow-up technique involves the closure of therapy sessions and takes approximately two sessions to complete, one of them being the last session. At a session sometime before the last session, the clinician asks the identified client to draw a picture of his or her Jumanji. Other family members are also instructed to draw pictures of their Jumanjis. This activity can also be assigned as homework. If the clinician allows the family to do the activity as homework, he or she asks the family to bring the pictures in at the last session. After all pictures are complete, each client places his or her picture in a separate envelope and seals it. The clinician keeps the sealed envelope until the last session.

To prepare for the last session, the clinician attempts to procure two to three environmentally safe helium balloons, tied together. When the family arrives for the final session, the children tie the envelopes onto the balloons and, with the clinician and the entire family, go outside to release the balloons. The family should release the balloons as a whole, with each family member having their hands on the strings and counting down together until the release of the balloons. In this sense, the clinician and family are still maintaining the theme of Jumanji and externalizing the problem, no longer labeling the child negatively. As the family members place their hands on the balloons and release, they achieve the goal of working and communicating together. This also addresses the goal of examining the lighter side of a serious problem. The externalized problem flies away, representing Jumanji's flight from the family.

Optional: The clinician, if possible, can provide enough balloons for the children to take home with them as a tangible reminder of the event.

Contraindications

The therapist should be very cautious of how he or she frames the problem. In the event the problem is framed as a monster, it may frighten the children to whom the intervention is targeted. Another consideration is the way in which the clinician presents Jumanji. If the clinician presents Jumanji in such a way that it appears the clinician does not in fact believe it, the likelihood that the client will not believe it is higher. In addition, children who are too young may be frightened of this intervention and children who are too old may not believe it. Therefore, the age of the child is critical to the success of this intervention. This intervention seems to be most effective with elementary school-age children.

This intervention may not be as effective with children with severe impulse control problems. These children may have a difficult time calming after the story. However, it is up to the clinician to determine the child's ability to control his or her behavior while in session.

Readings and Resources for the Professional

Freeman, J., Epston, D., and Lobovits, D. (1997). *Playful approaches to serious problems.* New York: W.W. Norton and Company.

White, M. (1995). *Re-authoring lives: Interviews and essays.* Adelaide, South Australia: Dulwich Centre Publications.

White, M. and Epston, D. (1990). *Narrative means to therapeutic ends.* New York: W.W. Norton and Company.

Bibliotherapy Sources for the Client

Dinkmeyer, D.C., McKay, G.D., and Dinkmeyer, D. Jr. (1997). *The parent's handbook: Systematic training for effective parenting.* Circle Pines, MN: American Guidance Services.

References

White, M. (1995). *Re-authoring lives: Interviews and essays.* Adelaide, South Australia: Dulwich Centre Publications.

White, M. and Epston, D. (1990). *Narrative means to therapeutic ends.* New York: W.W. Norton and Company.

35

A Picture Is Worth a Thousand Words:
Getting to Know a Child's World Through Photographs

Anna L. Bower
Lorna L. Hecker

Type of Contribution: Activity

Objective

Children often are reticent when they come to therapy for any number of reasons. In addition, at least initially many are reluctant to discuss verbally their inner lives with a strange adult. The objective of this activity is to increase verbal communication between clinicians and child clients. The A Picture Is Worth a Thousand Words activity is designed to aid therapists in getting to know the child's world in a manner such that the child doesn't feel interrogated. Instead, the clinician invites children to share their world in an exciting and rather unique way.

Rationale

Because younger children may not be able or initially willing to express ideas and feelings in words, it is especially important for clinicians to be able to observe their behavior and directly interact with the children. It is essential to begin by establishing a friendly atmosphere and winning the children's confidence. It is usually better to begin with a discussion of neutral topics, such as pets, play activities, favorite toys, friends, and so on before proceeding to the presenting problem. This activity allows the children to share their world without numerous inquiries, and emphasizes the children's views of what and who are important. As children share their photographs the therapist is allowed to view aspects of the children's world that the clinician may never have "seen" in a conventional interview or session. When children are invited to tell stories about the pictures, their subsequent descriptions and stories shape the realities of the children's world. These pictures and stories can serve as bridges of meaning between children and therapists, and may help facilitate healing interactions. The language and emotions children use to tell their stories about the pictures can shape the therapeutic dialogue.

When a therapist assesses a child, he or she often asks lots of questions. Some children, when faced with a stranger, will become shy, defeating therapists who rely on talk to make therapy work. Typically, the therapist will need to show investment in the child before he or she will trust the therapist. This activity allows the therapist to meet the child on his or her terms and explore with the child what has meaning in his or her world.

The therapist can glean a wealth of information and assessments from this activity. Allowing the child to be in more control of the information-giving, rather than information-taking, process can create more neutrality in beginning sessions and help to build trust. Creating a scrapbook and sharing stories allows the child to demonstrate his or her creativity, decision-making ability, and manual dexterity, all of which provide information regarding the child's emotional, cognitive, and physical development. The therapist's respect and interest communicates an investment in the child and in what he or she values.

Instructions

The therapist should query the child's parents about utilizing this intervention prior to implementing it and explain to the parents that one useful way to get to know a child is on his or her own terms, by allowing the child to take pictures of people or things that are important to him or her. The therapist should indicate the need for a disposable camera for this activity and be sure that the family can afford the expense of both the camera and developing the pictures. Parents should be reasonably comfortable with the child taking pictures and willing to aid the child in getting the photographs developed. A nondisposable camera can also be used, but a disposable camera is recommended so that the child does not have to worry about damaging a camera; a disposable camera may also be easier to transport than a more bulky regular camera.

The therapist then tells the child to buy (or have parents buy) a disposable camera. The child is told that the therapist would like it very much if he or she would take pictures that tell about the child's life. Children should pretend that they are telling the therapist all about themselves and their lives, and that they are telling a story about themselves as they snap the pictures. The therapist may make limited suggestions about the subjects of the pictures, such as pets, favorite toys, family members, their room, and so on. However, suggestions should be limited so as not to influence the content.

A special project begins when children bring their pictures to the therapy session. The child is given paper, fasteners, or a binder to use to make a scrapbook. The child puts the pictures in whatever order he or she wishes, and the therapist asks the child to tell a story about himself or herself with the pictures in his or her scrapbook. The therapist gives very little direction at this point. The child is instructed to put the scrapbook together in any way he or she would like, and the child is reminded that it is his or her personal scrapbook, not the therapist's. The therapist uses the child's reaction to the scrapbook in his or her assessment. Noting if the child is chaotic, if the child is overly careful, or if the child is worried he or she is not doing it "right" provide useful information in making initial hypotheses about the child and his or her family dynamics. The child can be reassured that there is no wrong way to complete the scrapbook, and that however he or she chooses to construct it will be fine. When the scrapbook is completed, children can give it any title they like and/or draw a picture on it to let everyone know it is their personal scrapbook.

Vignette

Ryan, a seven-year-old boy with symptoms of oppositional defiance behavior who had been diagnosed with attention deficit disorder (ADD), was brought to counseling by his mother. The mother stated that Ryan's teachers were having difficulty managing him in the classroom, and that she also was experiencing problems with his behavior (e.g., bedtime schedules, getting ready for school on time, and verbally communicating with his mother). Ryan's parents were recently divorced and the mother and son lived together, although Ryan had weekly contact with his father. Mother openly disparaged Ryan's father in front of him and was discouraging the boy from spending time with his father. The mother expressed to the therapist that she and the child were exceptionally well "bonded," and that they did most things together. Ryan remained silent during the first session, and when asked about his problems when his mother was in the room, he refused to comment. When the therapist saw Ryan alone, he was more talkative and shared limited information about his school activities but would not comment on his situation with his mother and father.

The therapist asked Ryan if he had ever taken pictures before. He said he had not, indicating that his mother didn't like him touching her camera. The therapist explained that she had arranged for Ryan to get his own disposable camera. She explained that it was one that he would not have to worry about breaking, as it was made of plastic. She asked Ryan if he might like to take some pictures of his own. Ryan said that he would be willing to try it. The therapist explained that she would like Ryan to take pictures of things that were important to him. She asked him to get the disposable camera (which his mother had already approved) and, when taking pictures, to pretend he was telling her all about himself and his life. Ryan became more animated as the therapist talked about some of the possibilities of the assignment. He found the idea of having his very own camera to complete the project quite appealing! He asked if he could take a picture of his dog, and the therapist said she would love to "meet" his dog through the picture. The therapist cautioned Ryan's mother that this was an assignment that Ryan was to complete on his own, with no help except in getting the pictures developed.

Ryan returned to therapy with a packet of pictures in hand, eager to share them with the therapist. The therapist and Ryan sat on the floor, and she gave him the materials (construction paper, glue, and scissors) to assemble the scrapbook. She told him to put the pictures in the order he would like for the scrapbook. He became very animated and intent on deciding the order of pictures for his presentation. When he was ready, he excitedly told the therapist his story. The therapist watched and listened as Ryan openly shared, through pictures, his life. His story included his dog, pictures of his bedroom, neighbor children, and, once he was comfortable, he starting showing pictures of his father. While doing this activity, Ryan became less timid about talking about his relationship with his father.

The therapist asked very few questions as the pictures were presented, except to compliment him or ask for a clarification when appropriate. Pictures and conversation about his mother were absent from the mix. Ryan completed the scrapbook in one session, and through the photographs and storytelling, the therapist was then acquainted with Ryan's perceptions of his world. Ryan chose to show the scrapbook to his mother but to give the photographs/scrapbook to his father.

For three sessions the therapist allowed Ryan to talk about his relationship with his mother and father. Then his mother was brought into the sessions for periods of time to talk about Ryan's behavior before and after visitations with his father. It was apparent that Ryan's anxious, defiant behavior increased both prior to and after visits with his father. Ryan and his mother worked to forge agreements regarding bedtime and preparing for school on time in the mornings. In an individual session Ryan's mother was offered an opportunity to talk about her feelings regarding Ryan's relationship with his father. A psychoeducational approach was used to empower Ryan's mother to support their father-son relationship, without interjecting any negative comments about his father. Using much of the information shared in the making of his scrapbook, the therapist explored activities that might offer Mother and Ryan more opportunities to interact and would encourage verbal communication on an emotionally nonthreatening level.

Ryan's classroom teacher identified target behaviors (staying in his seat and completing his classroom assignments) that were followed throughout the therapy. The teacher reported that Ryan was less anxious and able to remain seated during structured classroom time. She also reported that Ryan had improved concentration and follow-through with classroom assignments by the seventh therapy session.

The photographs allowed several things to happen in therapy. First, they allowed the therapist to enter Ryan's private and distinct world. The format of the activity allowed the therapist to join with Ryan and understand him and show interest in his life. Second, the absence of Mother in the photographs led the therapist to hypothesize that the mother and son had become enmeshed, following the divorce of Ryan's parents.

It became apparent to the therapist after working with Ryan that following his parent's divorce, he had become very close to his mother and had been elevated in the family hierarchy almost to the level of an adult. His acting-out behaviors were attempts to be his own person, separate from his mother, and had the systemic effect of pulling the estranged father back into the family system.

In part because of the intervention, the therapist was able to support Ryan's development and help Ryan's mother deal with her anxieties and insecurities in a different way—one that freed Ryan from being responsible for his mother's well-being. In later sessions Ryan's father was consulted, and a plan was developed regarding rules and consequences that was largely consistent in both households. The therapist supported Ryan's mother in following through on rules and consequences. Special techniques to deal with some of the more arduous parenting of ADD-type behaviors were chosen and implemented.

Suggestions for Follow-Up

As therapy progresses, new pages can be added to the scrapbook, and the therapist can continue to query about aspects of the pictures that may relate to the therapeutic agenda. One way in which this activity can be used to facilitate closure of therapy is to include a blank page at the end of the scrapbook. On the last day of therapy, a Polaroid picture may be taken of the therapist and the child to adhere to the last page. The child can be encouraged to write down on this page three things he or she learned in therapy or three things he or she liked best about therapy. The scrapbook is then sent home with the child as a closure to therapy.

Contraindications

If the cost is prohibitive this intervention should be altered. When parents are reticent for the child to take part in the activity, reasons for the reticence should be explored. Parents or children should not be forced to participate in the activity.

Readings and Resources for the Professional

Cerio, J. (2000). *Play therapy: Do-it-yourself guide for practitioners*. Alfred, NY: Alfred University Press.

Kissel, S. (1990). *Play therapy: A strategic approach*. Springfield, IL: C.C. Thomas.

Kottman, T. (2001). *Play therapy: Basics and beyond*. Alexandria, VA: American Counseling Association.

McMahon, L. (1992). *The handbook of play therapy*. New York: Routledge.

Minuchin, S. (1974). *Families and family therapy*. Cambridge, MA: Harvard University Press.

Wallerstein, J., Lewis, J., and Blakeslee, S. (2001). *The unexpected legacy of divorce: A 25-year landmark study*. New York: Hyperion.

Bibliotherapy Sources for the Client

Phelan, T. (2000). *All about attention deficit disorder* (Second edition). Glen Ellyn, IL: Child Management.

Phelan, T. (2000). *More 1-2-3 magic: Encouraging good behavior, independence and self-esteem*. Glen Ellyn, IL: Child Management.

Phelan, T. (2001). *"I never get anything!" (How to keep your kids from running your life)*. Glen Ellyn, IL: Child Management.

Wallerstein, J., Lewis, J., and Blakeslee, S. (2001). *The unexpected legacy of divorce: A 25-year landmark study*. New York: Hyperion.

36

Champion Pack

Katherine A. Milewski-Hertlein

Type of Contribution: Activity/Homework, Handout

Objective

The purpose of this activity is the tracking of both positive and problematic behaviors for children. Tracking problematic behaviors and events that precede them allows the clinician to discover the antecedents (events that precede) and consequences of the child's negative behavior. Tracking positive behaviors will allow the child and parents to notice the child's successes and give the child a feeling of empowerment in overcoming the problematic behavior.

Rationale for Use

The Champion Pack is a fanny pack a child carries with him or her to keep track of his or her successes. The pack includes a pad of paper, a pencil, and stickers. One main reason to implement the Champion Pack is when a child's success in behaving better goes unnoticed by the child. Tracking successes allows the child to experience success. Many parents discipline by telling a child what not to do and rarely give alternatives about what to do in a situation. For example, a parent often tells a child not to scratch at chicken pox bumps but rarely will tell him or her what to do instead of scratching. This impairs the child's ability to experience success because he or she is not accustomed to hearing about his or her successes. Second, the Champion Pack is a fun and creative way for the child to complete the homework associated with the activity.

Two behavior modification principles are at work when children are punished or rewarded for behavior—positive reinforcement and punishment (Martin and Pear, 1992). Positive reinforcement refers to consequences following a behavior that result in an increase of that behavior. For example, if Johnny is playing quietly with his toys in the bedroom and Mother tells Johnny that she likes it when he plays quietly and gives him a piece of his favorite candy, Johnny is more likely to play quietly in his room the next time he plays. He is positively reinforced for the behavior. Punishment, or something aversive following a behavior, results in the decrease of that behavior. Considering our first example, if Johnny's mother sees him playing quietly and begins screaming at him for not letting her know where he was and confines him to the time-out chair for ten minutes, Johnny is less likely to play quietly in his room in the future.

Parents impose consequences on children for their inappropriate actions but rarely reward children for appropriate behavior or interaction. For example, a child is sent to his or her room for hitting his or her sibling, but when he or she is playing quietly with the sibling, the parent says nothing. Even though the child is not receiving a negative consequence, he or she is not receiving a reward or reinforcement for *not* fighting. Rewarding positive behavior is critical to allow children to experience success.

Keeping track of successes positively reframes a child for parents. Rather than viewing the child as the one causing problems in the house, the parents begin to view him or her as a victim of the problem afflicting the whole family. Placing stickers in a book as used in the Champion Pack, for example, is a visual reminder to both parents and child that the child is experiencing success, which in turn allows *parents* to reward the child's successes. Once rewarding or reinforcing appropriate behavior begins, parents begin to see other times the child is successful (or a champion) in solving the problem. And once parents observe success, they no longer view him or her as the "problem" and start reacting to him or her differently. This is helpful because it promotes even more successes for the child.

Finally, the child is separated from the behavior in a technique known as externalization (White and Epston, 1990). The entire family, including the identified client, unite as a team to defeat the negative behavior, which is also likely to engender success for the child. This is helpful because the problem is no longer the child, but an "it" afflicting both child *and* family. For example, White and Epston (1990) provide an example of externalization with a child who was suffering from encopresis. The clinicians termed the behavior "Sneaky Poo" and, along with the family, identified areas in which Sneaky Poo affected individual members of the family, including the child. The child decided he was not going to be outsmarted by Sneaky Poo any longer, and the family came together to defeat the foe as a cohesive unit (White and Epston, 1990). Therefore, if the clients externalize a problem, it separates the behavior from the child's worth and allows the family to come together to defeat the problem.

Clinically, the Champion Pack is a concrete way to record when the child succeeds and ultimately when the problematic behavior occurs, assisting the clinician to track antecedents and consequences of the behavior. Antecedents are those events that precede a behavior. Consequences are those events which follow a behavior. Both antecedents and consequences are viewed as powerful controls of behavior (Martin and Pear, 1992). Therefore, when an inappropriate behavior occurs, clinicians utilizing behavior therapy examine the roles of antecedents and consequences in relation to the behavior. Documented successes facilitate the clinician's ability to access information regarding antecedents and consequences through conversation surrounding the Champion Pack.

Finally, when the entire family is present, a memo book included in the Champion Pack is used to generate conversation concerning inappropriate behaviors, examining powerful controlling effects of the antecedents and consequences. The discussion focuses on ways in which antecedents can be decreased or eliminated, as well as aversive consequences to the behavior that will decrease its frequency or discontinue it altogether.

Instructions

The Champion Pack is a pack of materials to aid the child in recording the times when he or she does not engage in the problematic behavior. It includes a three-by-five-inch memo book, one or two pencils (preferably colorful), and a small package of stickers put together in a fanny pack. The memo book is dated in pencil by the child and stickers are used to record incidents when the child does not engage in the inappropriate behavior. The child can write anywhere else in the notebook, as it is his or her personal notebook. The memo book is brought to every session and discussed.

To begin implementing the Champion Pack, ask the parents of the child if they are able to provide the child with a fanny pack. The clinician or the parents provide the following materials: the memo book, pencils, and stickers. Each item (with the exception of the fanny pack) is more than likely available at a local store for $1 or less.

The clinician prefaces this activity by asking if the child likes to play games. Most children respond "yes." It may be helpful if the clinician pretends the child does not truly want to play and make note that this game is only for children who really like to play games. The child who begs to play typically has a vested interest in the game and the Champion Pack. This increases the probability of experiencing success. Once the child agrees to play the game, the clinician explains the rules. The clinician can choose to explain the rules in the following format:

> This is a game for you to play against the [fill in the behavior]. When you think about doing the behavior and do not do it, you win the game. Then you put a sticker in the memo book and write the date so we know which day you won the game. The times that the behavior wins, you do not put anything in the memo book. And remember, you can write whatever you want in the book. It's your book.

The game pits the child's positive behavior against the problematic behavior. At the next session, the clinician examines the number of times in which the child's positive behavior succeeded in defeating the problematic behavior. The fanny pack allows the child to take the memo book, stickers, and pencils throughout the day. The clinician and child decide on a name or use the Champion Pack name.

Vignette

Jack was a ten-year-old foster child who had been in placement for five years as a result of his mother's drug habit. He was brought to family therapy by his foster parents of three years as a result of his stealing. Jack typically would steal food from other areas of the house in the middle of the night, eat the food, and hide the wrappers behind his bed. In addition, when confronted about whether or not he stole food, Jack consistently lied about it, even when his foster parents encouraged him to tell the truth. His foster mother was extremely frustrated with his behavior and felt she could no longer trust Jack to walk around the house freely. This was also of special concern to the parents as Jack's younger sisters, who were placed with Jack's foster parents at the same time Jack was placed, were beginning to follow his example of lying about Jack's behavior as well as their own.

The therapist asked Mom why she believed Jack was stealing. Mom stated she believed one reason was to get attention. However, she stated she and Jack's foster father had tried numerous other ways to give Jack attention for positive behavior, but these ways seemed to be ineffective. Mom also believed the adoption process she and her husband were going through to adopt the children was having an effect on Jack.

After other discussions between the therapist and Mom, homework was assigned for family members to reward Jack for appropriate behavior. Although this was minimally effective, the family still emphasized the incidents in which Jack stole or lied. The family was continually encouraged to provide Jack with positive feedback about his actions, both in and out of session.

The clinician asked Jack's mother if the family owned a fanny pack; the mother stated that each of the children owned one. The clinician provided the memo pad, the pencils, and the stickers. The clinician requested that Mom bring the fanny pack to the next session.

At the next session, the clinician explained the activity using the aforementioned format. The clinician asked Jack, "Are you good at playing games?" Jack replied that he was very good at playing games. The clinician stated she knew of a game Jack could play but was uncertain if Jack was interested in playing. Jack stated he was indeed interested and begged to play the game. The clinician agreed.

The clinician presented Jack with the memo book, pencils, and stickers and described to him that the game was between him and "Stealing." When Jack feels the need to steal and does not, he is to place a sticker in the memo book, recording the date of the event near the sticker. The clinician explained that when Jack returned the next week, he was to show the clinician his memo book and inform the clinician of the number of games he won over the week. Jack agreed. The clinician asked Jack to guess the number of times he would beat Stealing during the week. Jack and the clinician decided on one. At the end of this part of the session, Mom was brought into the room so Jack could have an opportunity to explain the game to her. Mom thought the game was a good idea. All of the children were brought into the room and, at the therapist's direction, began discussing the positive behaviors Jack had experienced that week which would be acceptable to write in the notebook.

At week two of the activity, Jack indicated he had won two games against Stealing. The clinician praised Jack for his accomplishment and discussed with Jack the reward, should Jack win a total of ten games. Jack and the clinician agreed that after ten wins, Jack would be rewarded with a fun activity during that particular session. At week three, Jack stated that he had won two games that week, for a total of four wins. A report from Jack's mother stated she had noticed him stealing significantly less often. In addition, she was involved between sessions with Jack's Champion Pack, reminding him to put stickers in the book if he had a successful day or reminding Jack about the notebook if he was beginning to have a bad day. By the third session, the other children in the family were also carrying around their fanny packs.

At this point, the therapist and Jack began to focus on the days in which he was a champion in defeating Stealing. The notebook was helpful in recording the days of the week when Jack was successful, usually Mondays, Wednesdays, Thursdays, and Saturdays. The family was able to use the notebook to generate conversation about why those days Jack was able to experience more success than others. Discussions revealed that Jack had difficulty on days just before school began for the week and days after he visited his biological mother. As a result, therapy began to focus on using the notebook to track the days in order to set goals. For example, if Jack was going to see his biological mother on a Thursday, the goal would be for Jack to be successful on Friday, *in addition* to being a champion on the same days he was able to in the previous week, Monday, Wednesday, and Thursday. Focusing on the dates of visits with his biological mother also opened up conversation between Jack and the therapist *and* between Jack and his parents about Jack's feelings on adoption, his biological family, and his previous experiences in foster homes.

The only problem that arose during the therapy was when Jack and his family went on a one-month vacation in the middle of therapy. During this time the parents felt Jack's behavior was not changing. However, the therapist, Jack, and his parents reviewed his notebook after vacation. This gave Jack's parents the opportunity to review Jack's successes in a way they had not been able to over vacation. Although Jack's successes over vacation were less frequent, there still were some. Jack's parents stated he was stealing less over vacation than he had before beginning therapy. Jack and his family resumed weekly sessions, with notably more incidents of Jack defeating Stealing, and consequently becoming more trustworthy.

Over the last one and a half months of therapy, the clinician phased out the Champion Pack to allow Jack to continue successes after the completion of therapy. Jack was able consistently to refrain from stealing and significantly decreased lying. Overall, Jack had stolen only once in the final three months of therapy and had been more consistent about asking for items. This change was reported by Jack, his family, and his school.

Suggestions for Follow-Up

This activity allows the clinician to form questions about positive behaviors, or behaviors the client utilizes to win games against the negative behaviors. Appropriate follow-up questions could include, "What did you do to win this game?" "What ways helped you to win this game?" and "What's important about you that you were able to win this game?"

Another suggestion for follow-up is to teach parents how to positively reinforce children for successes. As aforementioned, parents typically punish inappropriate behavior but do not always positively reinforce appropriate behavior. This activity allows parents to observe and reinforce when the behavior does not occur and reframe the child for parents.

Finally, after the child demonstrates some significant success with this game, the clinician creates a certificate (included at the end of this chapter) to document the child's successes. This solidifies for the child and family the success he or she has already achieved and inspires him or her to succeed more. In the previous example, Jack received a certificate stating that he was "becoming more trustworthy." The certificate should be filled out in positive terms, emphasizing the positive things the child is doing or demonstrating, as opposed to listing negative behaviors the child is learning to overcome, and signed by the clinician.

Contraindications

This activity, framed as a game, may not be as effective with children who do not enjoy playing games or feel they are not talented at playing games. In these instances, it may be helpful if the clinician frames the activity as something else that would be appealing to that particular child. This activity also may not be appropriate for children who are too young to record successes in winning the game. The clinician should assess the child's ability to complete this activity prior to assigning it to avoid setting the child up for failure.

Note: There is also the possibility that the child lies about the date on which he or she had a good day. A therapist can handle this through encouraging parental/familial participation. Parent or other family members can affirm the child's good days as well as reminding the child to record the champion days between sessions.

Readings and Resources for the Professional

Freeman, J., Epston, D., and Lobovits, D. (1997). *Playful approaches to serious problems.* New York: W.W. Norton and Company.

Martin, G. and Pear, J. (1992). *Behavior modification: What it is and how to do it* (Fourth edition). Englewood Cliffs, NJ: Prentice-Hall.

White, M. and Epston, D. (1990). *Narrative means to therapeutic ends.* New York: W.W. Norton and Company.

Whiting, R. A. (1988). Guidelines to designing therapeutic rituals. In E. Imber-Black, J. Roberts, and R. A. Whiting (Eds.), *Rituals in families and family therapy* (pp. 84-109). New York: W. W. Norton and Company.

Bibliotherapy Sources for the Clients

Dinkmeyer, D.C., McKay, G.D., and Dinkmeyer, D. Jr. (1997). *The parent's handbook: Systematic training for effective parenting.* Circle Pines, MN: American Guidance Services.

This

Champion certificate

is hereby presented to

for

on this date,

Keep up the good work!

Signed by _____

SECTION VII:
FAMILY ISSUES

37

The Family Play Planner:
Playing Together, Staying Together

Toni Schindler Zimmerman

Type of Contribution: Activity, Handout

Objective

The objective of the Family Play Planner is to encourage family members to think creatively and proactively about fun ways to spend time together for brief or extended periods. They can think of activities to increase family connection and togetherness, to expand family creativity and imagination, and to increase the quantity and quality of family play.

Rationale for Use

According to Greenspan (1999), playing together as a family is more than just fun and games. Playing forges a powerful bond between parents and children. Such intimate interactions give parents a unique chance to understand and enhance their child's development, help their child overcome challenges, and boost vital skills. When parents are good playmates, their child reaps the benefits at every stage of life. Playing challenges children to think smarter and harder and enhances skills such as attention span, language, independence, and creativity. Playing gives parents the opportunity to have fun with their children, relax together, be spontaneous, and enjoy time with the people they love.

A study done by Mader and Recker (1995) showed that much of a family's time together is spent watching television. However, the families in their study expressed an interest in learning ways to spend more quality time together while having fun. This suggests that many families need help in the area of learning to play together. Teaching families to play is an important aspect of family interaction.

Some families struggle with a sense of disconnection from one another. They lack family togetherness and have a limited sense of creativity and imagination in their fun and family play. Families frequently say things such as, "We're too busy," "We don't take time to plan things to do for fun," "We forget when fun events are going on that we could have attended," "We don't have enough money to do something that would be fun," "We all want to do different things," "When free time is available we tend not to have an idea in mind," "We're not planful about our fun," "No one takes the lead in terms of motivating us to go do something together," "When there is thirty minutes here or an hour there, the tendency is to move to activities such as opening up the mail, checking the phone messages, turning on the television, or getting chores done," or "Another weekend passed and we didn't play much." The tendency for some families is not to take off for small or extended periods of time on a regular basis for fun, play, creativity, and imagination, which are critically important for sustained connectedness, togetherness, and expression of love for one another. The Family Play Planner encourages families to maintain an ongoing list to turn to for fun ideas. Instead of having to think of something on the spot when a free moment arises, families can look to the list for ideas (reminders) of ways to spend time together.

When families put ideas out in the open where others can hear and see them, they are more likely to build play into their lives as a priority. For instance, if a family needs to cut the grass, wash the laundry, and go grocery shopping on a given Saturday, family members are far more likely to work efficiently and expediently as a team if they know that when they are done they are going to do a half-day hike at the local reservoir. However, when chores are being done on a Saturday and there is no vision or plan about how fun time will be spent afterward, family members are less motivated to get things done quickly. Families are less efficient with their time, slower at their tasks, and less excited about their togetherness if there is no vision about the play that will follow. Many families do not have a vision of how they want to spend their Saturday morning and so are drawn into an endless spiral of "getting things done." Often the time for play and family togetherness is not a priority. Families need to hear the message that they will benefit from planning as seriously and proactively for play as they do for work, school, or household tasks. Play needs to be a priority in their relationships and in their everyday lives. Regardless of the amount of time and money a family has available, it is critical to have playful activities on a regular basis.

Some families will find themselves so busy that they do not have time for play. Sometimes this busyness can be from extensive hours at work, but sometimes it is from getting into a habit of saying "yes" to too many opportunities. When families say "yes" to soccer, baseball, dance classes, Parent-Teacher Association (PTA) meetings, city governance meetings, bowling leagues, softball leagues, and bridge clubs they create an over-booked schedule. When families capitalize on too many opportunities, they frequently find that they have no Saturdays to take walks, no movie nights, no hiking time, and no time to play the piano, toss the ball, walk the dog, or paint a picture.

When families use the Family Play Planner, they begin to articulate and prioritize their use of time. They can decide if they would prefer to play soccer every Saturday morning for eight weeks or if they would prefer to do some of the half-day activities they have listed on the planner instead. If they prefer to spend eight weeks on the soccer field, then they should be encouraged to do that. After the eight weeks are over, they can decide if they want to spend the next eight weeks at basketball games and practices or if they would rather spend the next eight weeks doing activities from their list. Sometimes families get so caught up in team practices and games that the original intent is defeated—the team sports become a stressful obligation rather than an opportunity for family fun. Balance of work, team sports, and other activities listed on their planner is the goal.

Frequently, busy families want to cut back on the things they have said "yes" to and spend more time doing other things, such as simple outdoor activities. Without a structured way such as the Family Play Planner to brainstorm possibilities for fun, it is sometimes hard for families to compare all of the activities they are already doing to other options. They frequently do not consciously realize that if they say "yes" to the bowling league, they will not have time for other evening events. When they go through the process of listing ideas, both simple and complex, they can compare the opportunities for new activities with the ones they have already said "yes" to. As families consciously and proactively spend their time, they frequently choose more times for connection, togetherness, and a more balanced sense of saying "yes" and "no" to the many opportunities that come their way.

Particularly at young ages, it is very helpful for children not to have too many obligations, to be hurried off to this practice and that practice or this club or that club. It is important to have time to hang out in the backyard, sleep in, go hiking, rake leaves into a pile and jump in them, walk with their parent(s) to the ice cream store, or read five or six stories in front of the fireplace, and not always to have family time that involves getting in the car and hurrying to the next event. Team sports, club memberships, and other such activities have significant benefits for children and teens. However, if these opportunities are not balanced into family play time or relaxation time the benefits may not be realized for the child.

When families are stressed, they are even more likely to leave play and fun out of their routines. For example, a single mom working full-time and going to school full-time may come home in the evenings extremely tired and worn-out. It is difficult for her when she looks at the clock and realizes she has two hours before bedtime to think of an activity that would be fun for her and her son after dinner. Instead of having to conjure up creativity or imagination at that point, she can instead look at their list for ideas under thirty minutes or one hour. She could say, "Let's pick from this. We've talked about going for a walk around the block or riding our bikes to the ice cream store down the street. Let's do that tonight. Or we talked about getting out the playdough that we made last weekend, so let's do that." Many times just having ideas available to look at and turn to keeps families from turning on the TV together or turning away from one another and spending that valuable one hour before bedtime getting things done that could be left for another time.

It can also be fun and empowering to integrate social justice or community service activities into family playtime. Families can practice "random acts of kindness" for their fun time together, such as doing something special for another family, a neighbor, or the environment. They can plan to go on a picnic at a local park and spend the first twenty minutes picking up trash. They can bake brownies and take them to a homeless shelter or take flowers to a nursing home. These acts of community service can help create special meanings and close bonds for members of the family.

Another important benefit for using this planner is that when families plan to have more fun together, they tend to have more spontaneous fun together. If families are thinking more proactively about how to spend their time together, they are far more likely to spend quality spontaneous time together as well. For instance, the family that has "play catch outside" on their list is far more likely to end up in a spontaneous game of leaf tag because they are already outside and they have created a sense of playfulness together. A family that has started taking walks together, reading together, and spending playful time together is more likely to integrate fun into their errands and chores. While they are making dinner, they may find themselves being playful with one another, listening to music, laughing as they are cutting up vegetables and adding ingredients in bowls. As they increase their playfulness in planned ways, they are more likely to enjoy the spontaneity of splashing in a bubble bath, giggling through the grocery aisles, and singing in the car commuting to and from school.

The ultimate goal of this intervention is to get families to integrate playfulness, creativity, and imagination into the very weave or fabric of their relationships with one another. Many families need to start by planning these activities, but the ultimate goal is to incorporate more playful spontaneity when doing their everyday routine such as saying hello and goodbye, nighttime rituals, and homework. Frances La Barre (1999) defines quality time in families as any time parents achieve an intimate connection with their children. Doing one fun activity motivates us to do another because we feel close and connected and loved. Some ideas are worth doing a hundred times while others may only be done once a year, but having them in our vision is helpful for motivating people toward play. Fun times together, whether planned or spontaneous, produce more quality time together as a family. As Mather and Goodwin (1998) emphasize in their article by the same title, "Parenting can be fun!"

Instructions

The Family Play Planner provides families with a structured way to be planful and proactive about their playtime together. As shown in the handout, the far left-hand column is "time increments." This allows families to come up with ideas they can do for thirty minutes, one hour, three hours, half a day, or a full day. Activities family members can think of that might be fun and rewarding will be different depending on how much time is available.

One family moved to an area of the city that had open space so they could take walks, but years have gone by and they have not taken family walks in the open space. Another family bought a family dog so that they would go out in the backyard and play Frisbee with the dog, but they rarely do this. These kinds of activities can be done in thirty minutes if families are more proactive about putting their ideas on the planner and saying, "Let's get up early and go for a walk in the park" or "Let's go outside and play ball with Pepper for half an hour before dinner."

Across the top of the planner there is room for each family member's name. This is to ensure that all members are contributing ideas, and that anyone who thinks of an idea he or she would like to do can write it down. If someone is not contributing, another member might encourage or help him or her by asking what kinds of things that person would like to do. Having a space specifically for each person encourages each member to contribute.

It is a good idea to hang the planner on a refrigerator, pantry, or other central location where anyone at any time can add something to it. When it gets full, another sheet can be added. When a family member drives by the local park on the way home and thinks, "It would be fun to take dinner one night to the park and have a cookout," he or she can think how long that might take and add it to the proper time category. For the youngest members of the family who cannot yet write, older family members can listen when they mention an idea and ask if they would like to add it to the family list.

It is helpful for parents to evaluate which ideas are expensive and which ideas are free or low-cost by putting an "F" or a "$," "$$," or "$$$" near them so that they can have a balance of high/low-cost versus no-cost ideas. It is also helpful to encourage families to try to have a balance between activities in the home and outside of the home. Getting out in the community is important for families, but it is also important to enjoy their home or apartment. A client once reported, "It's amazing when I stand on my deck and look at the beautiful, manicured lawns around me and see how few people are actually sitting on their decks or playing in their backyards in the evenings." The more families are encouraged to think how they would enjoy the spaces they have created, as well as their neighborhoods and communities, the more likely they are to use them.

Families can also get a one-year calendar that can be seen in its entirety. As family members notice something they might like to do that has specific dates for that event, they can put it on the calendar. For instance, if a family member drives by an advertisement for trick-or-treating at a nursing home, he or she can write on the calendar the date and time it is happening. If someone notices in the newspaper that a children's festival is taking place on a certain weekend, he or she can write the details on the calendar.

This planner can also facilitate spending one-on-one time together. This includes couple one-on-one time as well as parent-child one-on-one time. Ideas under the one-hour category can be used for one-on-one time, such as playing a board game or crazy eights with one child. Parents can each take one child and do an activity with him or her before dinner to achieve some one-on-one time. Couples can pick an item from the list after the children are in bed, such as sitting on the porch watching the stars and drinking lemonade. Couples can even create their own list separate from the family's list to enhance couple playtime.

Vignette

A family with a mother and father and two young children ages six and eight entered therapy feeling very frustrated for a variety of reasons. One of the primary issues was feeling disconnected, disjointed, hurried, and rushed. At one point the father said, "I'm not having any fun." Many issues such as communication, conflict resolution, gender equity within the marriage, and parenting were addressed. The issue that is highlighted here is creating a sense of fun and family togetherness.

The father reported that he felt disconnected from both of his children and did not have an intimate relationship with them or with his wife. After looking closely at how they spent their time the family seemed overobligated to work, social events, and all kinds of activities. When asked to fill out the Family Play Planner, they had a difficult time even beginning to think what they would do if they did have time. They were coached with examples and asked to do some visioning about play. By the end of the session they were able to put down several ideas for each category of time. Their homework was to think of as many ideas as they could. Over the next few weeks they were able to fill their planner with ideas they had not thought about for a long time. The husband and wife each carried an extra copy of the list so that when each thought of something at work or while driving somewhere, he or she could jot it down.

They began to assess their work schedules and cut back to more reasonable hours. They also cut back on some of the obligations they had signed up for, such as riding lessons and club leadership. They had originally thought that activities such as clubs and sports would promote togetherness, yet they realized these were taking them away from each other and making their lives more hurried. They made conscientious choices about what to be involved in and what not to be. They made decisions as parents to allow their children to pick two activities per semester. For instance, they could be in 4-H and soccer, or they could be in basketball and karate, or they could be in student council and band. They had to make choices so that they were not overobligated to practices and games and meetings, yet able to benefit from these important activities.

They realized that many of the activities they were doing had a low cost-benefit ratio. They would hurry to the event, rush through it, get home, and be exhausted. Instead they decided to create free blocks of time in their schedule on a regular basis before dinner, after dinner, on the weekends, and in the mornings to introduce more ways to spend their time together that are less rushed and more rewarding.

One evening the entire family drove just two miles away and made a bonfire and watched the sun go down while they made S'mores. They reported that this was one of the closest times they have had in a long time. They could not imagine what would have motivated them to spend the evening laughing around the fire if they had not envisioned it, written it down, and motivated one another to get in the car, get some wood, and follow through on a good idea.

Another change this family made was to start keeping a family schedule that had time blocked out that they agreed would not be filled up. They made a commitment to certain amounts of time every week in the evenings or on the weekends to do something from their list. The father also started spending time with his children by using ideas from the list. He reported that he had frequently thought about spending one-on-one time with his children, but he often was not sure what to invite them to do. He had gotten comfortable sitting in the stands at an event or driving his children places and had not really given thought to how to spend more time with them really interacting. Small changes such as asking one of the children to go for a walk down the street or to pick a book from which they could read chapters together made an enormous difference for him. He stated that he felt comfortable selecting an idea from the planner rather than needing to think of one on the spot. Being able to turn to a list for ideas was relieving and empowering for him.

The couple also turned to the list frequently for their own activities. They had not played cards together in years, but one of the children had written down card playing, so they started using some of the time together after the children were in bed to play cards with each other in the backyard. The planner provided many ideas for this family to spend quality and quantity time together. Once they created the habit of play, the benefits were rewarding enough to continue to play on a regular basis.

Suggestions for Follow-Up

Suggestions for follow-up with families utilizing the Family Play Planner is to encourage families to revisit their list on a monthly basis and assess which activities they are doing or not doing. They can ask themselves the following four questions: (1) When we reflect on our play, what do we like the most and what do we feel the most proud of? (2) What do we want to stay the same based on our observations of our play? (3) What would we like to change about our play? (4) What are some goals we can set for change? For instance, families might notice that they mostly do activities that take half a day and do not take opportunities for shorter play time. They might notice that they only do the shorter activities and do not spend a full day or a weekend together, or they may want to improve at using everyone's ideas, not just using one or two people's ideas. If they are only doing things that cost money and are not taking advantage of things that are free they may want to adjust this. If they notice that they are mostly doing things away from home, and they might want to have more of a balance of staying home and going out into the community, they can create ideas for this goal. Families can assess their activities and set goals for themselves either to keep things the same or to make some changes in how they are spending their playtime together.

Contraindications for Use

Sometimes family conflict is very high, as in instances of domestic violence or extreme power inequities, and couples and families have difficulty spending any positive time together. These families should first address issues of gender inequity, power, conflict, violence, and communication as expediently, proactively, and overtly as possible. The integration of play and togetherness may need to be introduced more slowly. It is important to build a sense of togetherness and intimacy to sustain couples doing the hard work of therapy. However, they may not succeed at positive activities together when they cannot make shared decisions, problem solve, communicate openly, express their needs or wants, and listen to and acknowledge one another. Having playful ideas and activities are good for practicing communication and conflict resolution, but it is important to send people on hikes or into games of leaf tag armed with some skills that will decrease their frustrations with one another so that the playful activities contribute to their increased closeness.

Professional Readings and Resources

Greenspan, S. I. (1999). Power play! *Parents, 74,* 78-80, 82.
Levine, J. B. (1988). Play in the context of the family. *Journal of Family Psychology, 2,* 164-187.

Mactavish, J. B. and Schleien, S. J. (1998). Playing together growing together: Parents' perspectives on the benefits of family recreation in families that include children with a developmental disability. *Therapeutic Recreation Journal, 32,* 207-230.

Mather, L. and Goodwin, C. (1998). Parenting can be fun! In *Parenting in the 90's and beyond: Dealing with the difficult issues: 3rd national conference on parenting, Melbourne, Feb. 1998* (pp. 77-80). Melbourne: Parenting Australia.

Primeau, L. A. (1998). Orchestration of work and play within families. *American Journal of Occupational Therapy, 52,* 188-195.

Rickerson, W. (1979). *Family fun and togetherness.* Wheaton, IL: Victor Books.

Bibliotherapy Sources for the Client

Bennett, S. J., Bennett, R., and Bennett, S. (1993). *365 outdoor activities you can do with your child.* Holbrook, MA: Adams Publishing.

Bennett, S. J., Bennett, S., and Bennett, R. (1996). *365 TV-free activities you can do with your child.* Holbrook, MA: Adams Publishing.

Elkind, D. (1988). *The hurried child: Growing up too fast too soon.* Reading, MA: Addison-Wesley.

Ellis, G. (1999). *The big book of family fun.* Grand Rapids, MI: Baker Book House Company.

Ellison, S. and Gray, J. (1995). *365 days of creative play: For children 2 yrs. and up.* Naperville, IL: Sourcebook, Inc.

Erickson, D. (1989). *Prime time together with kids: Creative ideas, activities, games, and projects.* Appleton, WI: Augsburg Fortress Publishers.

Erickson, D. (1992). *More prime-time activities with kids.* Appleton, WI: Augsburg Fortress Publishers.

Erickson, D. (1997). *Donna Erickson's great outdoors fun book.* Appleton, WI: Augsburg Fortress Publishers.

Good, P. P. and Good, M. (1997). *303 great ideas for families.* Intercourse, PA: Good Books.

Haynes, C. and Edwards, D. (1999). *2002 things to do on a date.* Avon, MA: Adams Media Corporation.

Hilton, J. (1998). *Family funbook: More than 400 amazing, amusing, and all-around awesome activities for the entire family!* Philadelphia, PA: Running Press Book Publishers.

Krane, G. (1998). *Simple fun for busy people: 333 free ways to enjoy the ones you love without spending money.* Berkeley, CA: Conari Press.

Krueger, C. W. (1997). *1001 more things to do with your kids.* Nashville, TN: Abingdon Press.

Krueger, C. W. (1999). *1001 things to do with your kids.* Edison, NJ: BBS Publishing.

MacGregor, C. (1995). *Creative family projects, games, and activities: Exciting and practical activities you can do together.* New York: Carol Publishing Group.

Partow, C. and Partow, D. (1996). *Families that play together stay together!* Minneapolis, MN: Bethany House Publishers.

Perry, S. K. (1996). *Fun time, family time: More than 700 activities, adventures, recipes and rituals to help bring parents and their children closer.* New York: Avon Books.

References

Greenspan, S. I. (1999). Power play! *Parents, 74,* 78-80, 82.

La Barre, F. (1999). Redefining quality time. *Child, 14,* 78-80.

Mader, S. L. and Recker, N. (1995). Quality family togetherness with "family fun times." *Journal of Extension, 33*, 2p.

Mather, L. and Goodwin, C. (1998). Parenting can be fun! In *Parenting in the 90's and beyond: Dealing with the difficult issues: 3rd national conference on parenting, Melbourne, Feb. 1998* (pp. 77-80). Melbourne: Parenting Australia.

Family Play Planner

Time	Name:	Name:	Name:	Name:
30 minutes				
1 hour				
3 hours				
1/2 day				
1 day				
Overnight				
Weekend				

F = free
$ = low cost
$$ = medium cost
$$$ = high cost

38

Kidsculpt:
Children's Role in Marital and Family Therapy

Catherine Ford Sori

Type of Contribution: Activity, Handout

Objectives

The main objective of this activity is to disrupt marital or family patterns of interaction that are negatively affecting the children, and to promote more intimate family relationships. As children sculpt their family they are able to express their anxieties and fears, and parents are able to see things from their children's perspectives. This is often a powerful catalyst for change by reducing defensiveness and blame and promoting more honest and intimate communication. Old patterns are less likely to occur in the future, since the rules and affect attached to them have changed. This can move the family toward common goals, where each person takes responsibility for his or her own behavior to bring about change.

Rationale

For Involving Children in Therapy for Marital Issues

A panel of renowned experts in children in family therapy in a recent Delphi study overwhelmingly recommended that children be included in family therapy for almost all presenting problems, including marital issues (Sori, 2000). In fact, this panel of experts recommended that children be excluded from sessions only for two types of discussions: adult sexual issues and initially while parents are deciding on how and what to tell their children about painful subjects (such as parental terminal illness or divorce). In addition, the panel highlighted the importance of children being seen at some point even if they are initially excluded, since children are affected by individual adult and marital issues (Sori, 2000).

However, research indicates that children are largely being excluded from family therapy sessions because therapists are uncomfortable working with children (Johnson, 1995; Korner and Brown, 1990). Hines (1996) found that most therapists were more comfortable doing marital therapy than working with families that included children. Although many have long believed that marital therapy would have a "trickle down" effect on children, little evidence suggests that this is true. Children may remain anxious, worried, or depressed even after their parents receive marital therapy. Wachtel (1991) points out that even when "relieved of his or her role as symptom-bearer for the family, a child may remain troubled" (p. 46). Things may be better at home, but if the child's concerns haven't been directly addressed he or she may be waiting for the sword of Damocles to fall.

Other times parents resist bringing in their children even when a therapist does ask them to attend. Parents often believe that children are doing fine, and that they are oblivious to couple or family problems. Nothing could be further from the truth. Most often children are aware that something is wrong, but having only partial information they fill in the blanks with misinformation. Most children imagine things are worse than they are. And when misinformation stems from magical thinking (e.g., "It is my fault") and becomes embedded, it can be extremely difficult to overcome the resulting feelings, such as guilt or fear (Fogarty, 2000). Other parents who fight more openly may acknowledge that their children know there are problems but insist they are "doing fine" and don't need to attend therapy.

Yet research suggests that children want to be involved in family sessions (Cederborg, 1997). In fact, *they want to be included whether the presenting problem is a child or an adult issue.* They also make it clear that being included does not mean sitting in the waiting room. Children are aware of problems in the family and want to be part of the solutions.

Couples often become entrenched in patterns of criticism and blame, where neither partner feels listened to or understood, and neither is getting his or her needs met. As cycles escalate it is not unusual for one or both parents to try to elicit the support of a child by openly criticizing the other parent. Cross-generational coalitions can result when children are caught in a loyalty conflict, where it is not okay to like the other parent.

Couple therapy that does not include these children is ignoring the context in which the relationship and conflicts are embedded. It is almost impossible to bring about change when only working with part of the system that is maintaining the problem. It is also not ethical to discount the impact on the child. Children are the least powerful family members and often are not allowed to comment on the unhealthy position in which they have been placed. Therapists need to consider the needs of all family members when designing treatment for marital or family problems.

Yet just having the children physically present is not enough. Cederborg (1997) found that when the therapists in her study actually did include children, they were not actively engaging them in the process of therapy. In fact, children spoke only 3.5 percent of the total words in family session! When asked to comment the therapists reported that theoretically they believed children should be there, but they were unsure of what children's role in family therapy actually was.

Historically children were believed to be vital to the process of family therapy, and many of the founders of the field included children to treat most problems (e.g., Ackerman, Whitaker, Minuchin, Satir). Montalvo and Haley (1973) clearly envisioned the "child's contribution as regulator of the speed of therapy, as moderator of the pace of change" (p. 234). Minuchin (2000, personal interview) emphasized that including children changes the atmosphere of the session. In a personal interview (Sori, 2000), Minuchin stated:

> Now, one of the things that is important is to understand that when children are in a session, the adults behave differently. So let's say you have a couple that comes for therapy and the couple is a couple involved in conflict. You bring in an infant, and at the point at which you include the infant in the session you introduce nurturance. *You change from the symmetry of conflict to the complementarity of parents, and all the ways in which the parents involve the child in the conflict. So I include children even when the issue is not the child's issue, but it is the parents' issue. Because then you move the parents to deal with the conflict and see in what way they involve the child.* The issues of triangulating the child. The issues of "be loyal to me and not loyal to the spouse"—that's one of the issues, but also the issue of the fact that at the point at which you have children in the room, then the spouses' transactions change in nature by having the children as witnesses. (p. 238, italics mine)

Minuchin further points out that the technique of putting the children as witnesses is also used by such postmodern narrative therapists as Michael White, Jill Freedman, and Gene Combs.

While some children can be quite open and honest about what goes on at home (I remember one eight-year-old who commented that "Mommy doesn't like to sleep with Daddy anymore. I wonder why that is? Why does she sleep with me instead?"), many can't or won't openly share. Children may be obeying a family "rule" about what can and cannot be talked about, they may be maintaining a loyalty to one parent, or perhaps they believe that they are the cause of the problem (as the boy did in the previous example). Young children may also lack the cognitive and language skills to communicate about family dynamics. This allows parents to go on believing that their children are "fine" and not affected by marital or family problems. It also leaves the children with no one to help relieve them of their own distress.

But *how* to involve children—in ways that engage them and their parents, and that prevents further damage from parents who are caught in patterns of bitter criticism and blame. One way to stop "more of the same" behavior is, of course, to do something different, such as a family sculpt.

For Family Sculpting

Some unhappy couples have had previous therapy (most often individual and/or marital) that has not been helpful. Often these couples say that talking hasn't worked, and they feel increasingly hopeless. One of the major goals of therapy is to interrupt the "blame game" and move couples toward a more collaborative set (Jacobson and Margolin, 1979). Marital contracts won't work, however, when one partner continues to viciously attack the other, insisting the therapist take sides and be judge and jury against the other spouse. (How often have you had clients tell you previous therapy was not helpful, and even maybe harmful, because they always left feeling blamed and shamed?) Sculpts are often useful to change the emotional tone of a session, opening the possibility of changing vicious cycles into more virtuous cycles.

Both Minuchin and Satir often functioned as directors in therapy, bringing the drama of the family to life in the therapy session (Blatner, 1994). Virginia Satir was known for her use of sculpting to enhance family communication and promote intimacy. Sculpting is a type of psychodrama that shifts to a level of metacommunication, allowing family members to take a self-reflective position and gain some distance from their entrenched role. This step back allows them to consider what their action is really about, and how others perceive them. This deepening sense of awareness can shift couples from blame to negotiation. The action contains two incongruous elements, the playful sculpting and the real-life serious drama of the problems. Rigid interactions, old perceptions, and set patterns of thinking are broken, freeing individuals to consider new perspectives. Empathy is encouraged as parents listen to each other, and especially their children. This increases family members' sensitivity and understanding of one another's positions. The masks come off their hidden feelings and attitudes are revealed, which allows for more authentic interpersonal experiences (Blatner, 1994).

This exercise is designed to provide children with a way to express their true feelings. This helps parents recognize how marital or family problems are affecting their children and may begin to break the blame cycle. It also "spreads the problem" throughout the system and gives the family a common vision. Further, it allows everyone to see his or her role in maintaining the problem, and what each needs to change to help the family become closer and happier. A cognitive shift occurs when the family begins to work together toward a family goal, and when each one accepts responsibility for individual changes.

Instructions

Setting It Up

Blatner (1994) warns that care must be taken to "set the stage," or to create a context of playfulness. Sculpts are spontaneous, and "spontaneity is the root of creativity." This spontaneity cannot be forced but must include elements of both the conscious and the unconscious. The therapist, as director, needs to model spontaneity and encourage participants to explore new avenues. Performance anxiety can be reduced by assuring family members that they can't really make a mistake, since even "mistakes" offer the possibility of new alternatives (Blatner, 1988).

The Explanation

Explain that instead of talking about the problem (again) today the family is going to have the opportunity to try a nonverbal technique to explore their situation. One of them (called the *protagonist*) will enact a recent or typical family conflict by positioning the others as if they were silent mannequins, using spatial arrangement and nonverbal expressions (Blatner, 1994). While describing the scene, the protagonist will place family members in appropriate proximity, position their bodies, gestures, and facial expressions to depict the scene as if it were frozen in time. Family members are not allowed to comment but must hold the poses they are given. While initially there may be smiles or giggles at the playfulness of this activity, the therapist should encourage family members to "get into character" and allow ample silence for them to really connect with how they feel when this scene actually occurs.

After everyone, including the protagonist, is in place, one by one family members are invited to discuss how each feels, frozen in that position. Since everyone is "frozen" and not allowed to comment, they are forced to listen. The therapist directs each to explore his or her feelings on a deeper level, moving beyond anger and resentment, to pain, sorrow, fear, or hopelessness. At the end, others may be asked what they heard that was new or surprising.

The Ending

Next, invite the protagonist to change the sculpture by placing everyone in position for the "end of the scene," which depicts how the argument ends. Encourage each person to get "into the role" and really experience this event as if it were actually occurring. Then gently probe for each person's experience, with special focus on the impact on the children. Again, invite each to share what he or she learned about the others. Being careful to maintain a nonblaming attitude, parents may be gently probed to see if they had been aware of their children's feelings.

The Ideal Ending

Finally, the protagonist is asked to sculpt a new ending—to place each family member into an ideal position, and to talk about why this is ideal. Family members are again asked to hold those poses, and to internalize the feelings. Then they are asked individually to discuss their feelings, and how these feelings differ from the previous "real" ending.

Role Reversal

Spouses and siblings are asked to reverse roles (e.g., husband plays wife, wife portrays husband) (Blatner, 1994). The family resculpts the original scenes, but this time the therapist spends time exploring each member's perception of the other in that role. For example, a wife portraying her husband must talk about how she feels as her husband. Empathy is increased as she steps into his shoes and shares his perspective. Siblings who may be polarized are also helped to understand each other better.

New Beginnings

Finally, the therapist can direct the family to act out new and alternative solutions. Family members are also encouraged to create new behaviors. They are encouraged to recognize that just as each had a role in the problem, each has a role in the solution. Together they begin to articulate goals for how they want their family to be. Then individually each one is helped to develop a personal goal of what he or she can do to alter his or her "role" within the larger context of the family goal. The family goal is written in the center of the sun on the Goals to Brighten Our Days handout. Next, each person writes his or her name on a ray from the sun, and then lists his or her personal goal that will help the family get along better and meet the overall family goal. The handout can be taken home and put on the refrigerator to remind everyone to work on his or her own goals, while maintaining the new vision for the family.

Vignette

Dolores B., an elementary school teacher, first initiated therapy for herself because she felt anxious and depressed. At her first session Dolores said she had been in individual therapy off and on for several years to deal with her anger at her husband, Herb. The couple had two children, Beverly, age eight, and Darla, age eleven. They had been in marital counseling with two previous therapists, which had not been helpful. (Herb, a high-power corporate attorney, later reported that previous therapy had, in fact, left him feeling blamed, misunderstood, and increasingly hopeless to the point that he was considering divorce.) Dolores's chief complaint was that Herb tried to "dictate" to her and the kids, often yelling and screaming at them to clean up the house. Dolores admitted she usually did the exact opposite of whatever Herb wanted. For example, after he told the kids they couldn't get a pet until they showed some responsibility by keeping their rooms picked up, Dolores "surprised" the kids by bringing home, not one, but two large dogs (who still were not housebroken!). She also confessed that she tried to protect the kids from Herb when he got angry, yelling at him to "be more understanding" and "let them alone."

Dolores used a few individual sessions to review years' worth of complaints against her husband, blaming him for all her unhappiness and their problems with the children. However, she had almost no willingness to look at her own behavior or contributions to the problems. She openly criticized Herb to the children and encouraged them to ignore his directives. The therapist hypothesized that Dolores and Darla were in a cross-generational coalition against Herb. Neither child had much of a relationship with her father. Darla was anxious, not doing well in school, and had few friends. She was often openly angry and defiant with her mother and her father, and sometimes aggressive toward Beverly. Beverly had frequent stomachaches and didn't want to go to school. She was less openly defiant, usually just ignoring whatever she was asked to do. It was apparent that no one in this well-to-do family was doing well!

The therapist pointed out that since Dolores's problems were relational and involved the whole family, everyone needed to come in. Initially Dolores resisted, wanting yet more time to vent against her husband. The therapist pointed out that years of individual therapy hadn't helped to change her marriage, and that more might even make the situation worse. Dolores finally agreed, since she was very concerned about the effect the highly charged atmosphere at home was having on their children.

The first few family sessions were spent getting to know and hear from each of the family members. The therapist established ground rules that included no blaming and encouraging everyone to speak for himself or herself. This seemed to have little impact on Dolores or Herb, however, who continued to blame and criticize each other, even after the children cautiously shared how much the constant bickering upset them. The therapist took a strong stance of blocking and interrupting these behaviors, but little progress was made. Clearly this family was entrenched in old patterns of relating and needed a new and broader perspective of the problem.

Very early in the next session the therapist said that they were going to try something new today—a nonverbal way to help the therapist understand what the arguments looked like, and how they were affecting everyone. She invited someone to volunteer to sculpt the family in a recent or typical argument. Beverly's hand shot up immediately. She explained the scene: Dad was leaving to play golf on Saturday morning, and she positioned him with a hand on the door, poised to leave. He was looking over his shoulder at Dolores, his expression hostile and his mouth open in a silent rebuke. Dolores stood at the top of the stairs, hands on hips, leaning forward and silently screaming, "How dare you go off and play and leave me here with this mess! What do you think I am—a slave?" Dad was silently shouting that if she ever supported him the kids wouldn't leave messes everywhere. Bev placed Darla lying on her bed with the dogs, listening to music. She placed herself in the family room playing Nintendo.

Herb described his feelings of anger, overwork, and not feeling appreciated. Dolores was frustrated and extremely angry at Herb for putting her down and never wanting to be home. Darla stated simply that she just wished they would stop. When the therapist probed gently, Darla revealed that she just couldn't stand it when they fought all the time. It made her head hurt, and even when she turned up her music, she couldn't block out her awareness of the hostile exchanges. Bev said that her stomach always started hurting when her parents fought, and she was secretly afraid that someone would get hurt (although this had never happened).

Next Bev moved the family into a position to represent how the fight usually ends. Dad stormed off to the golf course, tires screeching down the driveway. Dad said he felt "really pissed off" and just wanted to get as far away as possible. Mom was placed yelling at the kids to get dressed—they were going to the mall (where Mom would buy expensive items to soothe herself and annoy Herb). She felt angry and defiant and was thinking "I'll show him I'm not the slave, and he can't treat me this way!" Darla positioned herself with her head buried in her dog's fur, trying to block it all out. The therapist asked her gently what she was feeling, and she said she felt nothing—nothing at all. The therapist mentioned that sometimes we have feelings that are painful, so we may put a mask on and pretend they aren't there. But if they are there they will find a way to come out—maybe in anger, or perhaps headaches. Darla's look softened, and very quietly she said, "I just feel so bad." When asked what "bad" means, she said she felt so mad at Mom for always being mean to Dad, and she worried that she would grow up to be as unhappy as her mother. She also thought that Dad probably blamed her and felt guilty that she was somehow responsible for their troubled relationship. Bev placed herself down in the basement, feeling very scared, and trying to get as far away as she could. She said she was so afraid that her parents would divorce, that Dad would go away, and that Mom would be so mad that she wouldn't allow her to visit. She also worried about what would happen to them, fearing they wouldn't have a home or enough money for food.

The therapist spent some time asking each person what he or she learned from this experience. Dad responded quickly with tears in his eyes, saying that he hadn't cried in years, but he could cry thinking of how guilty Darla felt. It reminded him of himself as a child when his own parents fought. Mom's expression softened as she said, "I had no real idea of how much we've been hurting our children. This has to change."

Finally Bev sculpted her family in an ideal ending to the fight. First she placed Darla next to Dad, with his arm around her. Dad instinctively held that pose, saying it had been so long since he'd held his little girl, and that she wasn't to blame for anything. Next she positioned Mom close to Dad and squeezed herself between Mom and Darla. She put both Mom's and Darla's arms around her. The therapist asked each how this felt, and how it was different from the feelings in the other ending. Each responded with very positive feelings. The therapist slowly walked around the sculpture, encouraging the family to experience this closeness with all their senses, and to remember these good feelings. Slowly, Herb's and Darla's arms encircled each other.

After several moments they came apart, and a discussion ensued in which everyone thought about his or her role, and what changes each needed to work on. Herb said he was going to try not to criticize Dolores, and not to yell at his children. We briefly discussed using natural and logical consequences to help the children become more responsible and happier. Darla said she wasn't going to "smart off" when asked to do her chores and, grudgingly, said she'd try to do them without complaining. Bev said she wouldn't provoke fights with her sister as much, and she'd also do her chores better. Then it was Dolores's turn. As everyone looked at her she said, "My goal is to think about how all this affects the kids, and to stop blaming Herb. I want us to find a way to work together to be a happier family."

The family was given the Goals to Brighten Our Day handout and together decided their family goal was "to stop yelling and be more respectful to each other." In turn, each listed his or her individual goals adjacent to a ray of sun. They were reminded to take responsibility only for their own goals. The therapist also suggested they take note of the next argument that might be sculpted in a future session.

The session ended with the children bouncing and hugging the therapist, and Dolores saying that for the first time she really saw that her family could change and work together to be happier. They all agreed that they'd never experienced anything like this before. The family left feeling much more hopeful, and with each having made a clear resolution to work for the common goal.

Suggestions for Follow-Up

In the previous session time did not allow for playing role reversals. Future sessions could return to the original sculpt and incorporate these role-plays, especially if partners need to increase their empathy and understanding of each other.

Future arguments that occur between sessions can also be sculpted. This often can serve as a deterrent to fighting, since parents or children know the argument will be sculpted in the next session.

It is often useful to videotape sculpts to give family members. The family could be given an assignment to watch a certain segment of the tape. For example, a family could be asked to watch the sculpt of the ideal ending, reconvene that pose, and hold it for a timed three minutes. The videotape could be reviewed periodically, especially at termination, to assess the degree of overall change.

The handout can be used and revised throughout the course of therapy to help family members track their progress toward their goals. Scaling questions can be used to assess each person's assessment of his or her own improvement in helping more sun to shine in the family.

Contraindications

Extremely cognitive adults may have a difficult time getting into psychodrama activities. However, if persuaded to participate, they often glean a lot from being asked what they *thought* (not felt) about each segment of the sculpts.

Sometimes a parent will participate but subtly refuse to try to learn anything about others' perspectives. This might indicate that partner has a secret agenda, such as sabotaging therapy to justify leaving the marriage.

Sculpts usually work well with both quiet and very active children. However, a hyperactive child who is caught in the middle of bitter conflict may become extremely anxious and over-stimulated. The child will be soothed by a therapist who maintains a strong director's stance, limiting and directing verbal interactions, and balancing the seriousness of the content with a playful approach to the process of the activity.

Professional Readings and References

Blatner, A. (1988). *Acting-in: Practical applications of psychodramatic methods,* Second edition. New York: Springer.

Blatner, A. (1994). Psychodramatic methods in family therapy. In C. Schaefer and L. Carey (Eds.), *Family play therapy* (pp. 235-256). Northvale, NJ: Jason Aronson Inc.

Cederborg, A. D. (1997). Young children's participation in family therapy talk. *American Journal of Family Therapy, 15,* 18-38.

Fogarty, J. A. (2000). *The magical thoughts of grieving children: Treating children with complicated mourning and advice for parents.* Amityville, NY: Baywood Publishing Company, Inc.

Hines, M. (1996). Follow-up survey of graduates from accredited degree-granting marriage and family therapy training programs. *Journal of Marital and Family Therapy, 22*(2), 181-194.

Holtzworth-Munroe, A. and Jacobson, N. S. (1991). Behavioral marital therapy. In A. S. Gurman and D. P. Kniskern (Eds.), *Handbook of family therapy* (pp. 96-133). New York: Brunner/Mazel.

Jacobson, N. S. and Margolin, G. (1979). *Marital therapy.* New York: Brunner/Mazel.

Johnson, L. and Thomas, V. (1999). Influences on the inclusion of children in family therapy. *Journal of Marital and Family Therapy, 25*(1), 117-123.

Korner, S. and Brown, G. (1990). Exclusion of children from family psychotherapy: Family therapists' beliefs and practices. *Journal of Family Psychology, 3*(4), 420-430.

Montalvo, B. and Haley, J. (1973). In defense of child therapy. *Family Process, 12*(3), 227-244.

Sori, C. E. F. (2000). "Training family therapists to work with children in family therapy: A modified Delphi study." Unpublished doctoral dissertation, Purdue University, West Lafayette, IN.

Wachtel, E. F. (1991). How to listen to kids. *Family Networker, 4,* 46-47.

Goals to Brighten Our Days

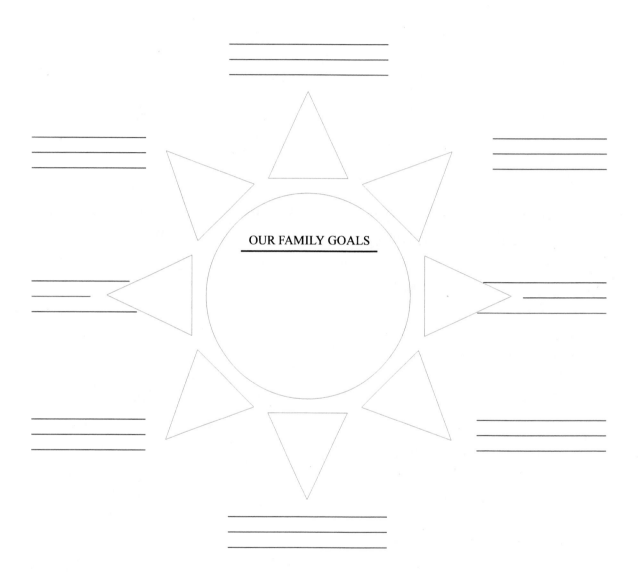

39

Special Time Activities

Jody R. Kussin
Ann-Marie Martinez

Contribution: Activities, Handouts

Objective

Although it seems intuition alone should work, many parents are not skilled in the most basic of child rearing "techniques": establishing a genuine parent-child relationship, with both parties forming positive and healthy attachments to each other. For various reasons, parents sometimes need help in shaping a relationship with their child or children. The objective of the following Special Time Activities, therefore, is to provide a structured approach to assist parents in forming a warm, meaningful relationship with their children. These Special Time Activities can be introduced to parents in a group format (such as a parenting class) or individually.

Rationale for Use

In 1999, 709 teens in the Los Angeles area participated in a survey and were asked "What would you most like to improve?" To the surprise of many, the answer with the highest percentage of responses was "My relationship with my parents/family" (LA Youth, 1999). Despite youths' desire for close and meaningful relationships with their parents, the media and parents continue to minimize the importance of the parental role in the lives of children, thinking instead that children are most interested in and influenced by other youths.

Many parents require formal training in the area of organizing their time and energy to best establish an environment through which they can connect with their children. In addition, they need lessons in what to do during interactions that will result in the formation and maintenance of a healthy, positive parent-child relationship. For instance, many parents do not realize the importance or worth of appropriate child-directed or child-driven parent-child interactions. Also, parents are often not aware of how little eye contact they have with their children, or of how little fun and humor they incorporate into their interactions. While other adults in their lives may perceive them as supportive and funny, sometimes their own children see them as punitive and dry.

The purpose of these activities, therefore, is to help parents learn how to effectively carve out time and space to establish a positive relationship with their children. All activities can be tailored to meet specific needs of parents and children. The essence, however, is that parents need to be taught how to arrange parent-child Special Time Activities and how to engage with their children during those established times.

Instructions

General Special Time

Tell parents that the first "technique" they will be learning is called Special Time. Give them the following instructions: Sit down with your children and announce that you are setting up a once a week "date" (with only one child at a time). Bring a weekly calendar. Agree on a day and time, note it on the calendar, and post it on the refrigerator or some other prominent place in the home. Together, brainstorm a list of possible activities. Promise a total of one uninterrupted hour for the week. List everything the child expresses interest in, even if it is inappropriate or repugnant to the parent (e.g., laser tag, Barbie dress-up). Finally, select the top three mutually agreed-upon activities and engage in at least one of these activities to fulfill Special Time for the week. Make sure the activities are age appropriate and realistic (see Parent Handout 1, Special Time Suggested Activities List).

Use the following rules in implementing the General Special Time activity:

1. The activity must be *prearranged.*
2. The selected activity must be *fun* and *child directed* (no homework, tutoring, or doing anything that is construed as unpleasant by the child).
3. The selected activity must be *interactive* (no television, movies, video games, computer games) and allow for eye contact (car/travel time does not count!). (See Parent Handout 2, Special Time Activities Rules to Remember.)

The parent needs to focus on having fun, interacting with his or her child, and allowing for communication. This should be a *judgment-free zone* for the child. Let parents know that they can tailor this assignment to best meet the needs of their family and children. For instance, younger children may benefit more from two half-hour activities on two different days. Families with more than one child may decide to have one child per week receive Special Time with a custodial parent and have the other children that week receive Special Time with another significant adult (grandparent, aunt, uncle, neighbor, baby-sitter).

Dinnertime Special Time

Inform parents that recent research findings suggest a relationship between families who eat dinner together and more positive child outcomes. Results from the *LA Youth 1999 Health Survey* indicated that having a good relationship with parents or family is not only a top priority, but that teens who eat dinner with their parents are more health conscious and engage in less risky, potentially self-destructive behavior (cigarette smoking, alcohol consumption, and so on). Tell parents that, therefore, in addition to continuing with their General Special Time activity each week, they will now add a Dinnertime Special Time. Parents should plan ahead and begin by choosing the night of the week carefully. It should be a night when the majority (if not all!) of the family members will be present. The type of food served is not important, although parents should try to avoid fast-food take-out. (General Special Time activities that week could include arts and crafts projects that result in personalized place mats or baking brownies that will be served for dessert.)

Be very specific and give parents the following rules:

1. No television or telephone interruptions (unplug the phone and do not leave on the answering machine if you can hear it when it picks up).

2. Think of a few neutral questions to ask. Do not ask questions that are likely to lead to conflict or confrontation (e.g., "Why did you fail the algebra test?").
3. Practice responding with praise and encouragement and open-ended statements (e.g., "Wow, that sounds very interesting. Tell me more!"). (See Parent Handout 3, Dinnertime Special Time.)

Bedtime Special Time

Inform parents that yet another opportunity for building a warm, supportive relationship with their child comes nightly, with bedtime rituals. All families should have some sort of structured nighttime routine. Children should know what time they are supposed to go to bed and what rituals precede bedtime. For younger children, Bedtime Special Time is story time. It involves five minutes of sitting with your child at bedside and reading or telling a story. It can include "the story of your life" (about either the parent or the child) or "the story of the lives of your grandparents," or it can include reading childhood favorites. For children over twelve, Bedtime Special Time can be a five- to ten-minute "checkin" about how the day went and what's on the agenda for the following day.

To summarize, rules for Bedtime Special Time include

1. establishing a routine for bedtime that includes a consistent time for beginning the ritual, a nightly hygiene program, and a plan for setting up for the following day and
2. nightly bedtime stories (for younger children) or a wind-down chat (for older children/adolescents).

When there is more than one child in a family, it is suggested that bedtimes be staggered (when possible). If this is not possible, it is preferable to have Bedtime Special Time individually with each child, alternating who gets to go first. (See Parent Handout 4, Bedtime Special Time.)

Vignette

School personnel referred an eleven-year-old male and his father for therapy services at a community mental health center because the child was exhibiting school refusal and the father was not successful at remediating the situation. At the time of intake, the father was in his early sixties. In gathering information, it was discovered that, within the past year, the child's mother left the family abruptly and moved to a different state. The father was left as the sole caretaker of the child and continued to have the responsibility of economically supporting both himself and his son. A combination of emotional upheaval from being left by his wife, the need to work long hours for economic reasons, and the fact that he was older when his child was born (and thus was lacking the energy and stamina that younger parents often have) resulted in virtually no parent-child interaction (only the "necessities" were taken care of, such as preparing meals, washing clothes, and so on), and a child who became very lonely and depressed to the point that he did not have enough motivation or energy to attend school.

Therapeutically, several issues were addressed, such as abandonment by the biological mother. Increasing and improving the parent-child interaction, however, became the focus of treatment. The importance of quality interaction was discussed with the child and his father and then the components of Special Time were explained. Initially, the father was resistant to the idea. He said he didn't have enough time, and when some time was available, he was just "too tired." The therapist empathized with the father and provided support and encouragement while continuing to stress the significance of parent-child interaction that goes beyond the necessities of everyday life.

The therapist assisted the father and son in planning for Special Time, and they gradually worked up to one hour per week. Special Time became a consistent "date" for the father and son; their fun-filled hour together generally took place before the therapy session each week. The park across the street from the agency is where they would go to play catch, shoot hoops, or simply sit on a park bench and talk. After this routine began, the child no longer refused to go to school.

In addition to General Special Time, the therapist explained and assigned Dinnertime Special Time (to occur at least three times per week) and, a short time later, Bedtime Special Time (specifically, a ten-minute "checkin" every night). Approximately four months after the referral was received, termination took place. The child was highly motivated to attend school; he had made new friends, joined extracurricular activities, and was doing well academically. The child's mood also improved significantly and he no longer exhibited signs of depression. In addition, the father's mood improved and he was greatly relieved that his son's functioning was so much better both at school and at home.

At the end of treatment, the child said, "My dad never used to do anything fun with me and I couldn't talk to him because he was always too busy or sleeping. Now, we do stuff together all the time—it's what I always wished for, especially after my mom left us."

Suggestions for Follow-Up

It is recommended that therapists inquire about Special Time activities on a weekly basis. Standard "homework" sheets can be provided in which the caregiver is reminded of the important components of a form of Special Time and asked to note a few things about the activity. Parent Handout 5 provides a sample of how this may be done for General Special Time. It also includes blank spaces for the parent to fill in.

The purpose of following up on a weekly basis is to (1) ensure that caregivers have a clear understanding of the reasons for and components of Special Time, (2) confirm that parents/guardians are routinely engaging in Special Time activities with their children, and (3) brainstorm, problem solve, and make modifications as needed when difficulties arise or Special Time does not seem to be as effective as it could be.

It is ideal for parents to have the experience of working on this "technique" one-on-one with a therapist, as well as in a group-type setting. Special Time activities are fully explained and emphasized in *Catch Them Being Good: A Guide to Positive Parenting* (Kussin, 1995). This book is based on a parenting class facilitated by two therapists. Parents are walked through various hands-on techniques and are asked to practice what they learn and provide feedback regarding their experiences. The group-type format has been found to be quite successful and desirable by parents because it provides them with an opportunity to exchange support and encouragement with other caregivers who are experiencing similar family circumstances.

Contraindications for Use

These parenting techniques are applicable to any parent. However, therapeutic experience has resulted in the discovery that teaching parents with chronic mental illness, cognitive impairment, and/or long-term chemical dependency problems requires more intensive intervention than is presented here. For instance, many parents with chronic mental illness do not grasp metaphors or abstract teaching methods. They appear to benefit from additional hands-on techniques to teaching this material, which can include an adult play therapy component and videotaping of parent attempts at Special Time. (Some parents are shocked to see on video that they lack affect, eye contact, and spontaneity!) Conversely, grandparents who are raising grandchildren as dependents tend not to be as needy in this area of parent-child relationship formation. Grandparents often have a different set of needs and issues, and, therefore, these particular interventions may be irrelevant.

Professional Readings and Resources

Barolec, S.J. (2000). *Yelling, threatening and putting down: What to do instead.* Salt Lake City, UT: Gold Bell Productions.

Gardner, R.A. (1998). *The talking, feeling, and doing game.* Cresskill, NJ: Creative Therapeutics.

Kussin, J. (1995). *Catch them being good: A guide to positive parenting.* Glendale, CA: Verdugo Mental Health Center.

LA Youth (1999). *LA youth 1999 health survey.* Los Angeles, CA: Youth News Service Los Angeles.

Metcalf, L. (1996). *Parenting toward solutions: How parents can use skills they already have to raise responsible, loving kids.* New York: Prentice-Hall.

Bibliotherapy Sources for the Client

Crary, E. (1995). *365 wacky, wonderful ways to get your children to do what you want.* Seattle, WA: Parenting Press, Inc.

Crary, E. (1996). *Help! The kids are at it again. Using kids' quarrels to teach "people" skills.* Seattle, WA: Parenting Press, Inc.

Durkin, L.L. (1986). *Parents and kids together.* New York: Warner Books, Inc.

Ilg, F.L., Ames, L.B., and Baker, S.M. (1992). *Child behavior: The classic child care manual from the Gesell Institute of Human Development.* New York: HarperCollins Publishers.

Kurcinka, M.S. (1992). *Raising your spirited child: A guide for parents whose child is more intense, sensitive, perceptive, persistent, and energetic.* New York: Harper Perennial Library, a division of HarperCollins Publishers.

Special Time
Suggested Activities List

Preschool-Aged Children (6 and younger)	Latency-Aged Children (7-12)	Adolescents (13 and older)
Arts and Crafts • put stickers on paper • decorate a frame • draw with crayons • glue items to paper • decorate a box • fingerpaint • string beads (large ones)	**Arts and Crafts** • make holiday decorations • glue sticks together • build and paint models • bulid and paint birdhouses • paper bag/paper plate masks • nature mobiles • photo collages • string beads (smaller ones)	**Arts and Crafts** • decorate a diary/journal • make friendship bracelets • make key chains • make hair accessories • tie-dye clothing • decorate own wrapping paper • shape modeling clay • make jewelry
Bake and Cook • make sandwiches • make "cut and bake" cookies • decorate cupcakes or cookies • celery with peanut butter and raisins • go to the market for 4-5 items • make own playdough	**Bake and Cook** • bake goods from a mix • make parts of dinner • make pancakes • make cookie-cutter cookies	**Bake and Cook** • prepare dinner together • make lunches for next day • bake things from scratch • go to a farmer's market to shop • make bread from scratch • learn to barbecue • plan a holiday meal together
Sports Activities • play with a ball • go for a walk • tricycle ride • toddler scooter	**Sports Activities** • play catch • go for a hike • play HORSE (basketball) • bike riding • flag football • skate boarding/roller blading • scooter ride	**Sports Activities** • batting cages • go for a hike • play basketball • bike riding • football/skateboarding/roller blading • scooter ride
Out for Food • ice cream, frozen yogurt • bakery • fast food with playland • "eatery" at the mall	**Out for Food** • breakfast at diner-type place • fast food with playland • ice cream, frozen yogurt	**Out for Food** • any meal is okay • ice cream, frozen yogurt • coffeehouse • local college campus

Story Time • tell a story • sing songs	**Story Time** • read to your child • play instruments	**Story Time** • chat about the day • listen to music
Play Games • Candy Land • Hungry Hungry Hippos • Pretty Pretty Princess • Chutes and Ladders • Memory Bingo • Peek-a-Boo	**Play Games** • SORRY! • Twister • Clue • Boggle • card games (go fish, war) • Hide and seek • Tag	**Play Games** • RISK • Monopoly • Dungeons and Dragons • Chess • Pictionary • card games (poker, hearts) • scavenger hunts
Build Things • use big empty boxes • build with blocks • stack things up and knock down	**Build Things** • Legos, K'nex, Lincoln Logs	**Build Things** • work on car/bike • put together furniture
Imaginative Play • dolls • puppets • play dress-up • build forts	**Imaginative Play** • puppets • charades	**Imaginative Play** • charades
Out and About • go to park and play • walk around local mall • library for story time • zoo • pet store, reptile/fish store	**Out and About** • garden • picnic • park • age-appropriate museum • zoo • pet store, reptile/fish store	**Out and About** • plan and plant garden • visit local college campus • museum • shopping (with limits set) • movie (with food stop)

**Special Time Activities
Rules to Remember**

1. Prearrange the day and time

Set this up one week in advance with your child. Note the day and time on a calendar and hang it on the refrigerator or another prominent place in your home. Choose a time that is "doable" for you. Try to arrange a time when your other children are otherwise occupied. For younger children (six and under), set up three twenty-minute time slots. For older children, use your best judgment. You can either set up a one-hour time slot, two thirty-minute time slots, or three twenty-minute time slots.

2. Plan an activity that is fun for the child and that is child directed

You can set limits (for example, activities must be free or inexpensive; activities must be child and adult safe; activities must fit into parameters you've established in Step #1). When you engage in Special Time, it is important that you sit back and let your child "direct" the activity. For instance, if you decide to bake brownies, let your child crack the egg, even if it's likely he or she will make a small mess (or else do not agree to bake as a Special Time activity!). When playing board games and/or sports, do not let yourself take over and play competitively. Remember that the purpose of these activities is to create a time and space where you and your child can enhance your relationship and attachment to each other. If losing SCRABBLE to a very clever eleven-year-old frustrates you, then play something else (or control your frustration!). If your child wants to play Barbie, and Barbie is annoying to you, remind yourself that your child will thoroughly enjoy the activity and that this will likely lead to a stronger parent-child bond.

3. Prepare to be interactive

Special Time activities that are NOT OKAY are types of activities that do not allow for one-on-one, eye contact included, interactive time. For example, although you can have a good conversation while driving your child to soccer practice, you cannot possibly drive safely and have one-on-one, eye contact included, interactive time. Therefore, the following activities DO NOT constitute Special Time*:

- having a conversation while driving
- watching TV or a movie or a video
- playing video or computer games
- shopping
- going to an amusement park

* Sometimes it's necessary to consider one or more of these activities when planning Special Time with a teenager.

Dinnertime Special Time

Making dinner special in your house:

1. **Choose a night of the week that is the least hectic for you and your family.**

2. **Plan ahead:** Either prepare dinner in advance (as part of Special Time with one of your kids) or make sure it's a night that you'll have time to prepare (or pick up) dinner.

3. **Involve everyone in setup and cleanup:** Younger children can decorate the table (for example, as part of Special Time, make place mats or table runners); middle school children can set the table; older children can clear the table after dinner.

4. **Minimize distractions:** Turn off the television, unplug the phone, turn off radios, remove pagers, and close the front door.

5. **Set the stage for pleasant conversation:** Choose a few topics beforehand OR have a jar with topics written on slips of paper in the middle of the table and let each person take turns "choosing" a topic for discussion. Use conversation topics that are neutral. Suggested topics include current events (from the day's newspaper headlines), funny things that happened during the day, upcoming festivities, favorite accomplishment of the past week, etc. Introduce topics with questions such as "What funny thing happened today at school?" Be nonjudgmental in your responses and DO NOT discuss "minefields" such as grades, poor behavior, and adolescent style of dress!

6. **Respond positively to contributions to the discussion:** "Wow, that sounds interesting . . . tell us some more!" OR "You have got to be kidding! That is amazing!" OR "I had no idea! I'm so glad you're letting us know!"

7. **Have everything you need on the table before you sit down to eat:** Include salt and pepper shakers, napkins, juice, margarine/butter, etc.

8. **Be prepared to match the length of the meal to your child's developmental stage:** Pre-school-aged children typically tolerate ten-minute meals, while older children and adolescents can "last" for fifteen to thirty minutes.

9. **Conclude Dinnertime Special Time by setting a date for the next family meal:** Encourage ideas from other family members to help make the next meal a success.

Bedtime Special Time

Making bedtime work AND special in your house:

1. **Establish a routine for bedtime in your home.**
   Consider the following:
   - Decide on an actual bedtime for each child
   - Work backward from that time and set up a schedule for the following tasks:
     — dinnertime
     — bath or shower time
     — checking of homework (and placing it in backpack)
     — signing of school notes (and placing in backpack)
     — teeth brushing time
     — putting out clothes for the following day
     — choosing nighttime music or stuffed animal
   - Write out an approximate time line for each child (can use pictures instead of words for younger children)

2. **Implement the routine for one to two weeks before adding Bedtime Special Time.**

3. **Add Bedtime Special Time at least three nights per week.**

4. **Engage in a Bedtime Special Time activity that is appropriate and enjoyable, according to your child's age and developmental stage.** Some examples of Bedtime Special Time activities include:
   - Preschool-aged children (six and younger)—five minutes
     — tell your child a story (about the child or about your childhood)
     — sing a few short songs with your child
     — read a story to your child (don't choose anything scary!)
     — look at a family photo album with your child
     — make up a story together (you start, the child adds, you continue . . .)
   - Latency-aged children (seven to twelve)—five to ten minutes
     — read a story to your child
     — begin a book with chapters and read a little each night
     — have your child read to you (if your child is struggling with reading, don't do this as part of Bedtime Special Time, but instead build time in with homework for practice)
     — make a photo album on a specific topic (e.g., "My Pets" album)
   - Adolescents (thirteen and older)—five to ten minutes
     — sit on the edge of your teen's bed and chat about the highlights of the day
     — ask about concerns for the following day or days
     — check in about any needs (e.g., new sneakers, gym shorts, haircut)

Parent Handout 5

Special Time Activity
Parent Homework

Reminder: Prearrange the day and time
            Plan an activity that is fun for the child and that is child directed
            Prepare to be interactive (no driving, no video games, no movies)*

Date and Amount of Time	Child's Name and Age	Special Time Activity	Child Reaction	Parent Reaction
SAMPLE September 18 30 minutes	Christy Sanchez 8 years old (latency age)	We played dress-up for half an hour. I let Christy try on "fancy dresses" that I keep in a trunk. We took a few pictures of her with the Polaroid camera. She seemed really happy and not worried about her homework so much.	She had a great time. She was laughing so much. She looked just like my mother's mother. I told her that. For bedtime she asked to see pictures of her great-grand-mother!	I couldn't believe that she could have so much fun and it didn't cost me any money. I felt like a nice mom. I also was happy to think about my grand-mother, who was nicer to me than my own mother was/is.

*Special Time with teens may involve some of these activities, if necessary.

Special Time Activity
Parent Homework

Reminder: Prearrange the day and time
Plan an activity that is fun for the child and that is child directed
Prepare to be interactive (no driving, no video games, no movies)*

Date and Amount of Time	Child's Name and Age	Special Time Activity	Child Reaction	Parent Reaction

*Special Time with teens may involve some of these activities, if necessary.

40

Anger Collage

Katherine A. Milewski-Hertlein

Type of Contribution: Activity

Objective

The objective of this activity is to help family members express feelings of anger in a safe environment and appropriate manner and to improve joining with children and family members. Families appropriate for this activity are those whose members internalize anger or express anger in inappropriate ways, such as tantrums and aggressive behavior toward others.

Rationale for Use

Children express anger in a variety of ways, such as acting out, fighting with peers, throwing tantrums, becoming defiant, and so on. At times it is extremely difficult for the child or other family members to express anger at all. Expressing anger to a parent, for example, results in negative consequences in some cases. In these instances, anger is bottled up, also resulting in negative consequences.

One who continuously internalizes difficult emotions such as anger is more likely to have difficulty managing stress appropriately. In addition, parents should not wait for children to begin throwing tantrums or being aggressive or violent toward others before helping the child to learn how to express anger or other difficult emotions.

It is important to note that the children, entire family, and therapist should already have established a joined relationship through doing other quiet activities, such as drawing pictures, before the therapist begins to expect the clients to express anger verbally.

This activity is a fun and effective method for children to express anger in a safe environment. It promotes the therapeutic relationship with the child, which ultimately will encourage the child to confide in the clinician, another safe way of expressing anger. This activity is also versatile in that it can be used in family therapy, as well as a homework assignment for families to complete between sessions.

Instructions

It may also be wise for the therapist and children to discuss which aspects of the collage they are willing to share with their parents, if the children are doing the collage without the parents in the room. Some children may want to share some of the aspects of the collage with their parents or to complete the activity with their parents. Others may not want to share any aspect of their collage with their parents and do it independently. Unless, through this exercise, the therapist discovers the children are in danger, the therapist should ask permission of the children before sharing information with parents for two reasons: First, this maintains trust between the therapist and the children. Second, a therapist talking to parents does not encourage an open relationship between parents and children, especially if part of therapy is based on family members increasing open communication.

Before beginning the collage, the therapist should assess whether this is going to be an activity for the identified child, a subsystem of the family (such as the sibling subsystem), the entire family, or whether it will be assigned as homework. Identifying which system the task is for will allow the clinician to better structure the activity. Since this activity is so versatile, the structure of the activity will vary from case to case. For example, if a clinician and family determine the family needs more quality time at home, it may be better assigned as homework rather than used as an in-session task. Again, this is more useful if a family has reached the point at which family members feel comfortable talking. It also provides the family with an opportunity to talk outside of session, creating an opportunity for change to continue after therapy is terminated.

This activity can be used as a last-session activity with families who have improved in communicating with one another to highlight the changes the family has been able to make. However, if a clinician determines that a family needs practice in sharing emotions, it may benefit the family more if the collage is completed in session with the clinician.

Materials needed are several pieces of construction or other colored paper, tape, and glue. In addition to the construction paper, the clinician sets aside two pieces of paper upon which the collage is to be constructed. This activity takes approximately one session. Two collages will be created: an Anger Collage and a Feel-Good Collage.

Although the clinical setting may be equipped with a desk or table, this activity is more effective if the clinician places the materials on the floor before beginning, sits on the floor, and asks family members to join him or her. The clinician explains the Anger Collage activity using the following format:

> We are going to make a collage. Do you know what a collage is? A collage is a picture made up of different pieces of paper. We are going to rip up these smaller pieces of paper [pointing to the smaller pieces of construction or colored paper] and glue them to this larger one [pointing to one of the larger pieces of paper].
>
> First we are going to make a "mad" collage. We'll both take turns ripping pieces from the smaller sheets of paper and gluing [or taping] them onto the bigger paper. But every time someone puts a piece on the collage, he or she has to say something that makes him or her mad. You can rip the paper as big as you want or as small as you want, and you can use any color you want.

The clinician and the family members take turns. The clinician demonstrates to the family how the game is played. In this method, the clinician models how to express anger appropriately. It also serves the purpose of joining with the family. The clinician uses situations that may provoke anger in family members, such as taking one another's property, and so on. The clinician rips a piece of the colored paper and announces that he or she is mad at a friend who borrowed a book and did not return it. The clinician secures the ripped piece of paper to the paper designated as the background for the collage. Both the family and clinician are making one Anger Collage together, so when it is the next person's turn, he or she places his or her ripped paper on the same background. The clinician instructs the family member to rip a piece off any of the colors he or she desires, state what things contribute to that family member's anger, and secure it to the collage. Each family member takes turns until the collage is full. *Note:* When it is the clinician's turn, it is more effective if the clinician discusses situations to prompt the clients into speaking about issues similar to their own. For example, if the clinician is aware that there is conflict between siblings due to one person's taking of the other person's toys, the clinician's statement is, "I feel mad when others take my things without asking."

After the Anger Collage is completed, it is important not to allow the family to leave the session while feeling angry. One suggestion is to continue with a Feel-Good Collage. The Feel-Good Collage stems from the same instructions and rationale as the Anger Collage, with one key exception: scraps of paper attached to the collage represent happiness and "feeling good." The clinician explains that in this collage, they focus on feeling good. The clinician can ask family members to go first this time. Again, after a statement is made about something that makes a person happy or feels good, a scrap of paper is secured to the second collage. Continue taking turns until the end of the activity.

Vignette

The Thompson family, Jane (mother), Pete (eight years old), and Dave (six years old) came to therapy as a result of Pete's physically aggressive behavior toward peers at school and toward Dave at home. Jane stated that Pete's problems had begun during the summer and were continuing to escalate both at school and at home. At school, Pete frequently initiated fights with other peers and reportedly was disruptive in class. At home, the family reported when Pete became angry at Dave, he would physically beat him up, not stopping at Jane's directives to do so. Jane stated she found it difficult to discipline Pete because he was defiant toward her. As family therapy progressed, the symptoms Pete was experiencing began occurring less in Pete but became more frequent in Dave. Jane's belief about the problem was that her children were "angry" about something. During sessions, she frequently asked the children why they were so angry, to which the children continually responded that they did not know.

As therapy progressed, one of the interventions the family found useful involved weekly family meetings prescribed by the therapist. Jane stated she felt the family benefited because they had more opportunity for communication. The therapist and Jane decided another opportunity to increase communication, such as the Anger Collage, would also benefit the family.

The clinician placed the materials on the floor, sat down, and asked the family, "Would you sit on the floor with me?" Jane, Pete, and Dave sat on the floor. The clinician explained the activity as described in the instruction section.

The clinician went first, ripping a moderate-sized piece of paper and stated, "I was angry when my brother hit me." The clinician secured the piece of paper to the larger sheet with tape. Next, it was Pete's turn. Pete selected a piece of paper, ripped a small piece, and said, "I was mad when my friends were making fun of me at recess." Pete secured the scrap of paper to the collage. After Pete secured his piece of paper to the collage, the family asked questions about his statement. Pete and Jane continued to discuss how Pete handled the situation, and Jane emphasized to Pete that she would be willing to listen to him tell about events such as the recess incident.

This continued, with the family members and clinician taking turns, until the collage was full. Over the course of the activity, the family members expressed anger toward several things: Jane's anger toward the boys when they do not listen to her, Dave's anger toward Pete for hitting him, and Pete's anger toward Dave for taking his things without asking.

After the Anger Collage was completed, the clinician asked the family to make a Feel-Good Collage. The clinician asked Dave to go first. Dave ripped a piece of paper and stated that he felt happy when he received a birthday present he had wanted for a long time. Dave secured the scrap of paper to the collage. The clinician ripped a piece of scrap paper, stated that she felt good when she received a good grade on a homework assignment, and secured the scrap to the collage. They continued taking turns until the Feel-Good Collage was full. Once both collages were complete, the session ended. The family decided they were going to take the collages home and hang them on the refrigerator.

In later sessions, the clinician inquired about the effectiveness of the collages. Jane stated that Pete and Dave had created another collage together after the session, and this was beneficial as they took turns and worked together. Pete reported that he moved one of the collages to his room, and Dave moved the other collage to his room. Jane stated that she was able to use the collages between sessions. For example, when Pete and Dave began to act out, the boys were more receptive to talking to her about what was bothering them.

Suggestions for Follow-Up

Another function of the collage is to introduce topics for discussion. When a family member states that he or she is angry about something, the clinician inquires about it during the time of the activity or in later sessions. After issues are initiated by the family members, the clinician gears questioning around these items identified by the family members as problematic. For example, if a child stated he or she was angry at his or her mother's new boyfriend, the clinician would follow up by asking questions about Mom's new boyfriend. The items mentioned in the Anger Collage have opened up new topics for communication between the therapist and child.

Another way to follow up is through questioning. For example, if a child states in a session following the creation of the Anger Collage that Dad did not pick him or her up again last weekend, the clinician can ask these questions:

- If you had the Anger Collage here, what color would you pick to put on that collage?
- How big would the piece of paper be?
- Where would you put that paper on the collage?
- Do you think other kids would put that on their collages?

This creates opportunity for more conversation between family members and the therapist, providing another appropriate channel for members to express their anger to one another. One modification of this exercise is to use this as a homework activity or an individual task, as it increases communication among family members.

Another suggestion applies to children who are nonverbal. These children may not feel comfortable or be able to tell a therapist their feelings. In this case, it may be easier for children to draw pictures of how they feel and then discuss them with the therapist.

Contraindications

In cases where parents have encouraged the child not to express his or her feelings, the child will feel caught between therapist and parents. In this situation, the clinician should work with the parents about the importance of appropriate expression of emotion. Once the parents are able to achieve this, they may be able to emphasize its importance to their child, thus increasing the likelihood of effectiveness for this activity.

Again, this may not work initially with nonverbal children. It is the job of the clinician to assess the child's ability to do the collage. If the child still is not comfortable with the therapist, the clinician may have to spend more time joining.

Readings and Resources for the Professional

Freeman, J., Epston, D., and Lobovits, D. (1997). *Playful approaches to serious problems*. New York: W.W. Norton and Company.

Shapiro, L. E. (1997). *Tricks of the trade.* King of Prussia, PA: The Center for Applied Psychology, Inc.

Bibliotherapy Sources for the Client

Dinkmeyer, D.C., McKay, G.D., and Dinkmeyer, D. Jr. (1997). *The parent's handbook: Systematic training for effective parenting*. Circle Pines, MN: American Guidance Services.

41

Director's Chair

Katherine A. Milewski-Hertlein

Type of Contribution: Activity, Handout

Objective

The purpose of this interactive activity is to (1) improve communication between family members, (2) rehearse appropriate behavior in difficult situations, and (3) improve joining with children. Through framing behavioral rehearsal as a game, children are more likely to engage in the activity both in the therapy room and at home. More important, by practicing appropriate behavior, the client is more likely to engage in the rehearsed behavior in real-life situations.

Rationale for Use

Director's Chair is a behavioral rehearsal technique that allows children and parents to understand the role each plays in difficult situations and provides options for better responses. Parents often bring children to therapy, stating that their child is "acting out." Acting out includes throwing tantrums, screaming, hitting others, throwing objects, and disobeying rules at both home and school. Behavioral rehearsal techniques are appropriate when a child is consistently acting out in a particular situation. Director's Chair is especially useful when the family can specify when the acting out takes place (i.e., after what event). Finally, Director's Chair is a valuable assessment tool. By asking the family to re-create situations in which the acting-out behavior occurs, the therapist gains insight into factors maintaining the problem as well as the family's definition of the child's misbehavior.

The specific behavior modification principle of positive reinforcement is at work in this intervention. Positive reinforcement states when something positive occurs after a behavior, the behavior is more likely to be repeated. Positive reinforcement in this activity is the approval of the parents and clinician when the child behaves appropriately. In Director's Chair, the therapist and family members discuss individual and familial strengths that were evident through the scenes. The more strengths discussed, the more reinforcing for the child and, ultimately, the rest of the family.

The whole family is involved in this game, increasing times family members are working together collaboratively. Working together (rather than the child versus the parents) inspires positive family dialogues about the problematic behavior. It also allows the family to take a lighter approach to the problem. Reframing decreases stress around the problem, paving the way for the family to handle the problem more effectively.

This technique also allows children to express feelings. Just as a child can practice appropriate behavior, parents can practice asking children about their feelings as well as learning appropriate ways to respond when their child describes hurt or anger. The therapist can be an integral part in training parents about how to respond to a child's expression of hurt.

Instructions

In Director's Chair, the therapist and family rehearse the problem and solutions as if the family members are actors and the therapist is the director. Family members re-create the times when the problem exists. Family members are to "act" how they typically behave when the problem occurs. For example, if a child typically acts out when Mom is on the phone, Mom would pretend that she is on the phone when the scene begins. The identified child acts his or her part by throwing a tantrum, yelling, and so on. The therapist rates the acting ability of each individual through emphasizing the strengths displayed in each scenario by each member. For example, the therapist emphasizes the parts of the scene in which the child was not engaging in the defiant behavior. At the end of each scene rehearsed, the therapist gives feedback about what strengths he or she saw. At this point, the therapist also asks family members to give their own feedback about other members' strengths. For example, after the therapist emphasizes the strengths of the child not engaging in defiant behavior, the therapist turns to Mom and asks her to describe other strengths she saw. Mom may offer that she liked the way the child came into the room, or other strengths the child exhibited through the scene.

The game lasts at least three rounds. The first round consists of the family and child acting out the problem. For example, if the child is acting out when returning from weekend visits at Dad's house, the family re-creates the situation, starting from when the child walks through the door. The child pretends to act out and parents or other family members respond in the manner in which they typically respond. The therapist addresses strengths within the scene and then asks for input about each member's strengths. The second round consists of the parents and child acting out a situation where the child is behaving perfectly. Using the previous example, the child walks through the door. Parents respond as they would if the child did act in that manner. Again, the strengths are emphasized and discussed. Finally, the third re-creation is a combination of the first two. The clinician instructs the child to begin the scene acting as if he or she is truly in a bad mood, as in the first scene, and to end the scene as if he or she is feeling better, as in the second scene. The strengths of each family member are again discussed.

It is helpful if the therapist and family discuss the most strengths in the last scenario, where each family member practices controlling his or her actions and reacting appropriately. If the strengths are discussed in the scenario where the child acts or family members act perfectly, the idea that family members should not communicate true feelings, or that it is better to "act" feelings, may be communicated. The benefit of discussing the most strengths in the last scene, where the family encounters a difficult situation and works through it, teaches family members that they have a right to emotions but emphasizes the strengths used to deal with those emotions.

In all three scenes, the clinician can focus on the strengths of the identified child. Variations on this activity include, after the three rounds, other family members playing the role of the primary director and generating strengths about other family members. The therapist should not expect the scenes to run exactly as they do in real life, but to strive for that. After all, children may be unwilling to throw the tantrum that they threw at home or in the car in the therapy room. At this point, it is the responsibility of the clinician to direct the child (or other family members) to do the best he or she can to re-create the scene.

At times in therapy, it is necessary for the clinician to coach the parents on how to respond to their child in a positive manner when a child is throwing a tantrum. For example, if a child states that he or she is angry or feels hurt about his or her divorced parents' living arrangements, a parent may respond by saying something negative about the other parent. This can be damaging to the parent-child relationship and make the child feel uncomfortable about sharing feelings with parents. In these cases, it may be necessary for a clinician to teach the parents appropriate responses to make the child feel comfortable talking about feelings.

After each scene, the clinician asks each person how he or she felt about the scene, what he or she was thinking during the scene, and how he or she wished others to respond.

Some specific questions for the identified child:

- What were you feeling?
- What were you thinking when you said that to Mom? Dad?
- Has this ever happened before?
- How would you have wanted Mom/Dad to respond?
- How did they respond?

For parents:

- How would you have wanted your child to respond to you?
- How did your child respond?
- What were you feeling?
- What were you thinking?

For all family members:

- How were the other children in the family responding to the tension between the identified patient and parents?
- How do they usually respond?
- When has this scene been prevented?
- What did the child do differently?
- What did the parents do differently?
- What are you feeling now?
- What are you thinking now?

These questions begin discussion of feelings between the child and parents, opening the door for further communication as well as allowing everyone to understand what other family members are feeling.

Vignette

Lisa brought her eight-year-old son Jacob to therapy because she believed Jacob was not adjusting well to the divorce between herself and Jacob's dad. She felt Jacob had an "attitude" when he returned home from weekend visits to his father's house. Jacob threw tantrums, became defiant toward Lisa, and did not talk to Lisa about what had gone on over the course of the weekend.

During the course of therapy, the clinician noticed Lisa consistently made negative comments about Jacob's father in front of Jacob. Therefore, before this intervention took place, the therapist and Lisa alone discussed the impact of negative statements about Jacob's father on Jacob and the potential discomfort Jacob may feel talking about his feelings. Lisa stated she understood and made a consistent effort to minimize negative comments in the presence of Jacob. After Lisa was able to demonstrate this, the therapist and Lisa discussed the Director's Chair game. Lisa responded she thought this would be helpful.

The therapist asked Jacob to describe exactly what happened when he returned home from his father's house on the weekends. Jacob said he yelled at Mom and did not do what he was told. The therapist asked for Jacob's help in understanding what happened when he returned home since the therapist did not live in the house and was unsure of how events usually occurred. To do this, the therapist suggested the family and therapist play a game called Director's Chair. Jacob and Lisa agreed to play the game. The therapist explained the following rules:

> This is a game to see who is a better actor, you or your mom. In this game, the two of you are going to pretend that it is Sunday night and you just got dropped off at home by your dad. Show me exactly what happens when you come home. I will be the director and I will tell you what you did well.

The therapist told Jacob to wait outside the door just as if he were coming home from his father's house. Jacob waited outside the door. Lisa opened the door. Jacob came into the therapy room and threw a tantrum. When Lisa asked what was wrong, he slumped down in a chair and sulked. When she tried to talk to him about what he did while he visited, he began to yell at her. She directed him to take a shower and to go to bed. Jacob became defiant. At the end of the scene, the therapist stated that the strengths in the scene were Jacob's eventual compliance with the request and Lisa being calm when she opened the door initially to start the scene.

The therapist asked Jacob (1) what he was feeling during the scene and (2) what he generally feels when he comes home from his father's house. Jacob stated he felt mad that he had to come home and that sometimes he does not get to see his dad when his dad says he will. Jacob also stated he does not understand why he has to go to bed when he comes home from his dad's house. The therapist also asked Lisa the same questions. Lisa stated she felt sad during the scene as well as when this occurs because she does not know how to help Jacob. When the therapist asked Jacob how he wanted his mother to respond, Jacob stated that he did not want Lisa to tell him to go to bed. Lisa stated that she did not want to send him straight to bed either, but he knows the rules in the house. Lisa stated that she wanted Jacob to respond by talking to her if something was bothering him.

In the next scene, the therapist directed Jacob to exit the room, and this time to enter as if he were coming home with a positive attitude. The scene progressed much like the first with the exception of Jacob behaving perfectly, as if he were not angry. Jacob came into the room experiencing no discomfort and behaved perfectly. Lisa asked what things Jacob had done over the weekend. Jacob told her. At the close of the scene, when Jacob had gone upstairs to shower, the therapist named the strengths as Jacob's completing the directions and Lisa's asking about Jacob's trip. When the therapist asked both Lisa and Jacob to comment on the strengths, Lisa stated she appreciated the respect Jacob had for her within the scene. Again, the therapist and family discussed how they felt about the scene. At this point, the therapist addressed the issue that the concern was not so much for the times when Jacob comes home feeling happy, but the times when he comes home feeling angry and is unable to talk about it with his mother.

In the final scene, Jacob was directed first to enter the house with a negative attitude and, over the course of the scene, to end up feeling better. As Jacob entered through the door, he acted in a foul mood. Lisa inquired about why Jacob was angry, and Jacob responded that he did not want to come back home and wanted to stay later at his father's house. Lisa stated that she understood how Jacob felt, and she would be upset as well. Lisa asked what she and Jacob's father did over the weekend. After Jacob told her, Lisa said it sounded like fun. As the scene progressed, Jacob responded more positively to Lisa. By the end of the scene, Jacob was engaging in appropriate behavior. The therapist concluded the scene by discussing the following strengths: that Jacob was able to tell his mother how he felt *and* was able to complete the task Lisa had directed him to do. Lisa stated the strength she observed was that Jacob treated her with respect. Jacob stated he noticed that Lisa did not yell at him and that he felt his mom understood.

The therapist and family continued to discuss how Lisa and Jacob felt during the scene. Jacob stated that although he was angry earlier in the scene, he felt better talking to his mother about it. Lisa also felt better about the scene because she and Jacob did not go to bed on angry terms.

Suggestions for Follow-Up

One specific follow-up technique is to create a "prize" for the child after he or she plays the acting game. This follow-up takes place shortly after the game or the first session after the Director's Chair that the family reports the child has engaged in the appropriate behavior at home. The clinician and child create a King/Queen of Good Attitude crown in session. A pattern for the crown is provided at the end of this chapter. The clinician can use the pattern to trace a crown outline on construction or other paper. After the clinician cuts the crown out of the paper, the clinician, child, and family decorate it.

Contraindications

As aforementioned, this intervention is contraindicated if the parents are likely to respond negatively to children expressing their feelings. In this instance, it is beneficial for the clinician first to coach the parents on how to respond to what the child may say. This can take a great deal of time in therapy, as some parents may not know how to handle their feelings when their children are hurting or angry. However, if parents respond negatively to the child when he or she does try to express feelings, the child may be less likely to talk about those feelings.

This intervention is not as effective for children who have little control over their behavior, such as those with impulse disorders. It is designed to teach the child that he or she has control over his or her own behavior. In cases where the child is truly unable to control behavior, assigning this activity may be setting the child up for failure.

Readings and Resources for the Professional

Freeman, J., Epston, D., and Lobovitis, D. (1997). *Playful approaches to serious problems.* New York: W. W. Norton and Company.

Shapiro, L. E. (1997). *Tricks of the trade.* King of Prussia, PA: Center for Applied Psychology, Inc.

Bibliotherapy Sources for the Client

Dinkmeyer, D., McKay, G. D., and Dinkmeyer, D. (1997). *The parent's handbook: Systematic training for effective parenting.* Circle Pines, MN: American Guidance Services.

King/Queen of Good Attitude Crown

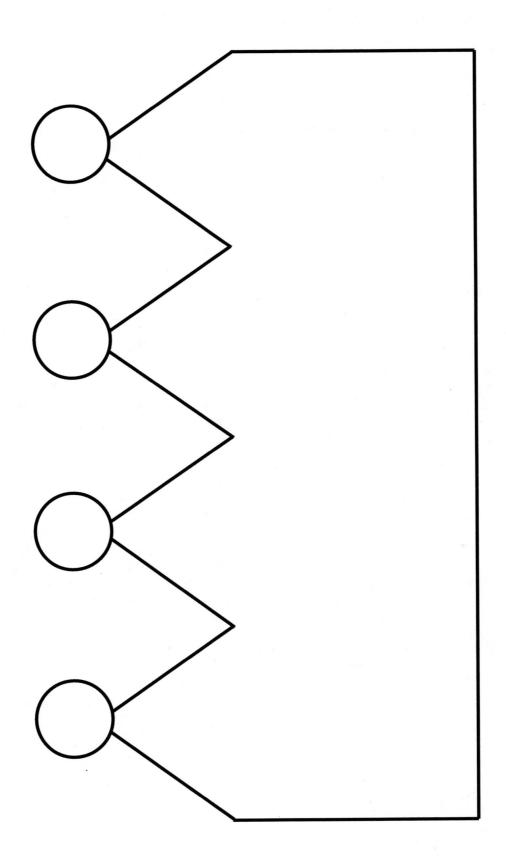

42

Using Children's Books in Family Therapy

Linda Wark
Julie Johnson
Lisa Abrahamson

Type of Contribution: Activity, Handout

Objective

The therapeutic value of using children's books in therapy and tips on reading to children are discussed in this chapter. A lengthy handout of children's books is offered that can be used by both therapists and parents or other adult caretakers with children between the ages of three and twelve. Each book is categorized according to common concerns of children and their families in therapy. The table of contents organizes the categories alphabetically. The applicable age range is noted for most of the books. Where the information was available, illustrations that portray people of color are noted. A few books are not in print but can often be borrowed from local libraries.

Rationale for Use

Stories for children have great therapeutic value in either written or verbal form (Mills and Crowley, 1986; Freeman, Epston, and Lobovits, 1997). The use of children's books to assist in therapeutic problem resolution is focused on in this chapter. Children enjoy telling and listening to stories (Gardner, 1971), which gives books excellent potential for use in therapy. Stories also have value for the cognitive development of children. Storytelling is one of the foundations of play (Engel, 1995; Pearce, 1992), and the enormous cognitive and social benefits of play cannot be overestimated (see Chapter 9). Telling or reading stories over and over again stimulates the imagination, facilitates attentiveness, and aids the conceptualization that children need to work through difficult concerns (Pearce, 1992). With these skills built, eventually the inner world of possibilities can be connected to the outer world of behavior.

Instructions

The selection of books for therapy can be made from the list according to the presenting concern. Young children are attracted to books in which animals are the characters (Pearce, 1992). Older children relate well to books in which children are the characters and have lives and problems that they can relate to, or lives that they would like to have (Pearce, 1992). However, the selection of books could be left up to children, who will vary in their tastes. Children can understand more complicated books than they could read to themselves (Cullinan, 1993) so books can be chosen above a child's reading level when the story or book will be read to him or her.

Stories are effectively read to children by parents or therapists, and some children will like to read them aloud to the family or younger siblings. It doesn't matter who reads books in therapy sessions. However, younger children particularly experience nurturing when they are read to by parents, and older children can benefit from this nurturing as well. Children of all ages can enjoy being read to, and reading to the entire family creates a shared experience and can build positive memories for them.

In therapy, books can be used in different ways. Some books have overt messages with a number of them written expressly for therapeutic intervention. Other books are metaphorical and are intended to evoke personal experiences and feelings of which people are less aware (Mills and Crowley, 1986). All books can be springboards for discussion and can be connected to broader-scale interventions (Freeman, Epston, and Lobovits, 1997). The books on the list provided can be used for numerous reasons: facilitating adjustment to life changes (going to school for the first time, stepfamilies/divorce, the death of a family member or friend); understanding difficult experiences in one's own family (alcoholism, parental conflict); enhancing relationships (racial relations, making friends); healing from damaging experiences (sexual abuse); and overcoming personal struggles (attention deficit disorder [ADD], placement in a foster home).

Children are a somewhat captive audience when an adult is reading to them. It should be noted certain topics of books are not comfortable for all children and that they may not know how to express their discomfort. When reading, the adult should look for signs of discomfort and ask children if they would like to put the book aside for a while or talk about how they feel. Some comfort with difficult topics may be promoted when books are left in the therapist's waiting room. Children can explore books on their own to develop a basic level of exposure and familiarity.

Reading to children can be enhanced with a few simple skills. Make eye contact with the children if they are sitting facing you as you read and read the story at a moderate pace with interest and enthusiasm in your voice. Vary the level and tone of your voice *moderately* to fit the plot and emotional tone of the story. Adding dramatic physical movements or abrupt voice changes may disrupt the listening process (Kimmel and Segel, 1983). Turning the book to display the illustrations can also disrupt the listening process. On the other hand, children can be distracted from the story by wondering what the reader is seeing in the book that they cannot see. Therefore, provide structure for the reading by explaining that you will read for a while, and then show illustrations periodically. If you are reading to only two or three children in a family, they may be able to sit close to the book, and special efforts to display the illustrations are not necessary.

The first time through a book, younger children will need breaks in the reading to absorb the information. Very young children love the repetition of stories read the same way over and over again. By age four, though, children benefit from a few pauses, elaboration, and questions interwoven into the reading of the story as long as they do not overwhelm the story itself. For example, such questions as "Has that ever happened to you?" "What do you think will happen next?" or "Do you feel a little like she does?" asked during the story can enhance it and make it more personally applicable. Therapists should not be concerned if a child begins a conversation relevant to the concerns in therapy before the book is completed because then the book is doing what it was intended to do. Conversely, once a book is finished, children may not feel like responding because they are absorbing the content. Thus, questions immediately asked after a book ends are often poorly timed. Parents can be guided to ask questions at home or therapists can implement activities during the next session to draw out children's thinking regarding the topic of the book.

Children of different ages in the family will not always agree on which book is to be read. To resolve conflicts of interest, turns can be taken. At times, children will not show an interest in having a book read to them or in reading a book. Interest in books for therapy can sometimes be cultivated by first reading a book simply for entertainment or to join with the children. For example, *The Stinky Cheese Man and Other Fairly Stupid Fairy Tales* (Scieszka, 1992) delights middle to older school-age children. Therapists can trade off reading their selections with joke and riddle books read by children.

Vignette

Chad, age five, and Stephen, age eight, came to therapy with their mother and stepfather. Stephen was very verbal and talked as much in the session as he engaged in more child-oriented activities. Chad focused solely on play and ignored questions from both the therapist and parents. In general, Chad's manner was defensive. Both children were not adjusting well to either the divorce or remarriage, but the mother was grateful that she at least knew what Stephen was thinking and could talk to him about it. Chad, on the other hand, was uncommunicative and touchy when she tried to approach him, and these behaviors seemed evident in the therapy session. However, when the therapist suggested that she read a book to Chad, he showed a lot of interest. The therapist asked him where they should sit to read a book, and he chose to sit next to her on the couch. The therapist chose the book *Dinosaurs Divorce* (Brown and Brown, 1988). During the reading of the book, Chad's face softened, and he talked in detail about the dinosaurs and asked numerous questions. The therapist used his questions to educate him about divorce and healing from the painful aspects of his family's divorce. This special time with Chad lasted about a half hour. The mother was quite impressed with this different type of behavior from Chad. The therapist suggested that she purchase or borrow the book and read it to him on a regular basis. She also suggested that the mother primarily discuss the dinosaur family's divorce situation in response to Chad's questions about them until a future time when Chad initiated questions regarding their own family. In addition, the therapist provided names of other books on divorce and stepfamilies for children.

Suggestions for Follow-Up

Typically, it is easy to detect whether a book has had an impact on children in therapy sessions because they will build on the story with questions or comments, respond to questions and comments from adults, or display changes in mood, such as becoming very quiet. After books are used in therapy, as in the vignette, the therapist can check in with parents regarding the continued effectiveness of the story for eliciting new ideas or questions from the child. The therapeutic value of the stories enjoyed by children can be extended by asking children to make up additional storylines for the characters within the context of the concern for therapy. This activity can be done verbally, in dramatizations, or in artwork. For example, Chad could be asked what else the dinosaur parents should do to help the dinosaur children feel better.

Contraindications

Inclusion of a book on the list does not necessarily indicate an endorsement although we have our personal favorites. However, the large list provides options for differences among families and the therapist's perception of which ones would be most useful for them. Be sure to screen the books you select for values. Be sure they fit with your client families. It is noted, where information was available, whether a book has a religious message. This message may be very useful for some clients and not for others.

The authors recommend that therapists not limit themselves to the list here and consider the therapeutic value of other books. Therapists have successfully used fiction and fantasy stories that do not have obvious therapeutic content (Mills and Crowley, 1986). Finally, therapists will want to be aware of the level of literacy of their clients before asking either adults or children to read aloud in the therapy session or at home.

Professional Readings and Resources

Cullinan, B.E. (1993). *Let's read about.* New York: Scholastic, Inc.

Engel, S. (1995). *The stories children tell: Making sense of the narratives of childhood.* New York: Freeman Press.

Freeman, J., Epston, D., and Lobovits, D. (1997). *Playful approaches to serious problems: Narrative therapy with children and their family.* New York: W.W. Norton and Co.

Kimmel, M.M. and Segel, E. (1983). *For reading out loud.* New York: Dell Publishing Co., Inc.

Mills, J.C. and Crowley, R.J. (1986). *Therapeutic metaphors for children and the child within.* New York: Brunner/Mazel.

Bibliotherapy Sources for Clients

See handout of children's books that follows.

References

Brown, L.K. and Brown, M. (1988). *Dinosaurs divorce.* Boston: Little, Brown and Company.

Cullinan, B.E. (1993). *Let's read about.* New York: Scholastic, Inc.

Engel, S. (1995). *The stories children tell: Making sense of the narratives of childhood.* San Francisco, CA: Freeman Press.

Freeman, J., Epston, D., and Lobovits, D. (1997). *Playful approaches to serious problems: Narrative therapy with children and their family.* New York: W.W. Norton and Co.

Gardner, R. (1971). *Therapeutic communication with children: The mutual storytelling technique.* New York: Science House.

Kimmel, M.M. and Segel, E. (1983). *For reading out loud.* New York: Dell Publishing Co., Inc.

Mills, J.C. and Crowley, R.J. (1986). *Therapeutic metaphors for children and the child within.* New York: Brunner/Mazel.

Pearce, J.C. (1992). *Evolution's end.* New York: HarperCollins Publishers.

Scieszka, J. (1992). *The stinky cheese man and other fairly stupid fairy tales.* New York: Viking.

Therapeutic Books for Children and Their Parents in Family Therapy

CONTENTS*

Abuse (Emotional Abuse; Physical Abuse; Sexual Abuse and Body Safety)

Adoption and Foster Families

Alcohol and Drug Abuse in the Family

Attention Deficit Disorder

Death and Dying (death of parents, siblings, grandparents, friends, and pets)

Disabilities (differently abled children with physical and developmental disabilities)

Diversity (Race Relations and Racial and Ethnic Diversity; Sexual Diversity)

Divorced Families, Remarried Families, and Single Parenting

Emotions

Ethical/Moral/Responsible Behavior

Family Relationships (adjusting to a new baby, sibling relationships)

Friendships/Peer Relationships

Illness and Health: Child's or Family Member's

Parent and Child Attachment

Self-Esteem

Separation from Parents/Being at Home Alone (going to school for the first time, temporary separation from parents)

Stress

Therapy (what it's like to attend therapy)

Toilet Training/Bed-Wetting

Abuse

Emotional Abuse

Adler, C.S. (1985). *Good-bye, pink pig.* A girl is neglected and ignored by her mother; ages ten to thirteen.

Anderson, D. and Finne, M. (1986). *Michael's story.* Emotional abuse; ages seven to ten.

Boulden, J. and Boulden, J. (1995). *Tough times.* Physical and verbal abuse; features people of color; ages seven to twelve.

Loftis, C. (1994). *The words hurt.* Dealing with the trauma of verbal abuse; ages six to twelve.

Physical Abuse

Anderson, D. and Finne, M. (1986). *Jason's story.* A boy's mother is physically abusive and he is placed in a foster home; ages seven to ten.

Bernstein, S.C. (1991). *A family that fights.* Henry's father hits his mother.

---

*The authors wish to acknowledge that descriptions of some of the books for the handout were excerpted from (1) a list compiled by Stern's Books, Chicago, Illinois, 1-773-883-5100; (2) the "Courage to Change" catalog, Newburgh, New York, 1-800-440-4003; (3) the Creative Therapy Store catalog, Los Angeles, California, 1-800-648-8857; and (4) the Childswork, Childsplay catalog, Secaucus, New Jersey, 1-800-962-1141.

Davis, D. (1984). *Something is wrong at my house*. Physical abuse.

Paris, S. (1986). *Mommy and Daddy are fighting*. Helps kids talk about and understand parental conflict.

Roberts, W.D. (1977). *Don't hurt Laurie!* A girl is abused by her mother; ages ten to thirteen.

Russell, P. and Stone, B. (1986). *Do you have a secret?* Written to encourage abused children to seek help; ages ten to fourteen.

Trottier, M. (1997). *A safe place*. A mother and her daughter go to a shelter to escape a violent husband; ages six to nine.

Velasquez, G. (1998). *Rina's family secret*. A Puerto Rican teenager describes her abusive stepfather and a counselor who helps her.

Sexual Abuse and Body Safety

American Girl Library (1998). *The care and keeping of you: The body book for girls*. A preteen's guide to basic health and hygiene, including healthy eating.

Boulden, J. and Boulden, J. (1993). *Secrets that hurt*. A new stepfather makes advances to a young girl; ages six to twelve.

Brown, M. and Krensky, S. (1982). *Dinosaurs, beware!* Sixty safety tips for home, camping, etc.

Freeman, L. (1983). *It's MY body*. Teaches young children how to say no to unwanted touching; ages four to six.

Freeman, L. (1985). *Loving touches*.

Gaines, J. (1986). *Chilly stomach*. A girl's uncle crosses the line with affection; ages four to eight.

Gil, E. (1986). *I told my secret*.

Girard, L.W. (1984). *My body is private*. A girl's growing awareness of her body and the topic of sexual abuse; ages five to eight.

Girard, L.W. (1985). *Who is a stranger and what should I do?* Ages six to twelve.

Gordon, S. (1992). *A better safe than sorry book*.

Griffin, P.R. (1992). *Hobkin*. Two sisters escape from an abusive father and are happily reunited with their mother; ages nine to twelve.

Hall, L. (1984). *The boy in the off-white hat*. A boy is sexually abused; ages eleven to fourteen.

Hoke, S. (1995). *My body is mine, my feelings are mine*.

Hyude, M.O. (1987). *Sexual abuse: Let's talk about it*. Instructional book for both males and females; ages eleven and up.

Johnson, K. (1986). *The trouble with secrets*.

Kehoe, P. (1987). *Something happened and I'm scared to tell*. Ages three to seven.

Kline, S. (1985). *Don't touch!*

McCoy, D.L. (1986). *The secret: A child's story of sexual abuse*. Ages seven to ten.

McGovern, K.B. (1985). *Alice doesn't babysit anymore*. The baby-sitter molests children.

Nathanson, L. (1986). *The trouble with Wednesdays*. A relative is a child molester; ages eleven to fourteen.

Newman, S. (1985). *Never say yes to a stranger*. Ages four to ten.

Sanford, D. (1986). *I can't talk about it*. Religious; ages five to eleven.

Sanford, D. (1993). *Something must be wrong with me: A boy's book about sexual abuse*. Latino family is featured; religious.

Sanford, E. (1990). *Don't make me go back, Mommy: A child book about satanic ritual abuse.* Religious; ages five to eleven.

Satullo, J.A.W., Russell, R., and Bradway, P.A. (1987). *It happens to boys, too. What to do if it happens to you.* Ages nine to twelve.

Sweet, P. (1985). *Something happened to me.* Ages eight to eleven.

Wachter, O. (1984). *No more secrets for me.* Sexual abuse; ages seven to ten.

Wachter, O. (1986). *Close to home.* How to stay safe; ages eight to eleven.

Adoption and Foster Families

Banish, R. (1992). *A forever family.* Eight-year-old Jennifer Jordan-Wong tells the story of her adoption; ages seven to eight.

Blomquist, M.S.W. and Blomquist, P. (1990). *Zachary's new home: A story for foster and adopted children.* Ages three to eight.

Bloom, S. (1992). *A family for Jamie.*

D'Antonio, N. (1997). *Our baby from China: An adoption story.*

Girard, L.W. (1986). *Adoption is for always.* Ages six to ten.

Girard, L.W. (1989). *We adopted you, Benjamin Koo.* Korean Benjamin, age nine, explains being brought up by parents from another culture; ages seven to ten.

Greenberg, J.E. (1987). *Adopted.* Ages six to nine.

Hickman, M.W. (1995). *Robert lives with his grandparents.*

Katz, K. (1997). *Over the moon.*

London, J. (1993). *A koala for Katie.*

Rosenberg, M. (1984). *Being adopted.* What it's like to be adopted by a family of a different race; ages eight and up.

Rosenberg, M. (1989). *Growing up adopted.* Reassuring and inspiring stories of adoptees from eight to forty-eight; ages eight and up.

Sanford, D. (1993). *For your own good: A child's book about living in a foster home.* Religious.

Schwartz, P. (1996). *Carolyn's story.* Ages six to eleven.

Stinson, K. (1998). *I feel different: A book about being adopted.* Ages five to eleven.

Wasson, V. (1977). *The chosen baby.* Ages four to six.

Alcohol and Drug Abuse in the Family

Black, C. (1982). *My dad loves me, my dad has a disease.* Father is an alcoholic.

Brack, P. (with Brack, B.) (1990). *Moms don't get sick.*

Carbone, E.L. (1997). *Corey's story: Her family's secret.* Father is an alcoholic; ages seven to twelve.

Chaplan, R. (1992). *Tell me a story; Paint me a sun.* A father-daughter relationship is interrupted by alcoholism; ages seven to eleven.

Deaton, W. (1994). *Drinking and drugs in my family.* Therapeutic book with guide for therapists; ages seven to thirteen.

Langsen, R.C. (1996). *When someone in the family drinks too much.* Therapeutic book with guide for therapist; ages five to eleven.

Sanford, D. (1998). *I can say no: A child's book about drug abuse.* Religious.

Seixas, J.S. (1989). *Living with a parent who takes drugs.*

Tabor, N.M.G. (1999). *Bottles break*. How it feels when a parent drinks.

Vigna, J. (1988). *I wish daddy didn't drink so much*. A little girl learns to deal with her father's alcoholism; ages five to twelve.

Vigna, J. (1990). *My big sister takes drugs*.

Attention Deficit Disorder

Caffrey, J.A. (1997). *First star I see*. Paige finds her "focusing knob."

Corman, C.L. and Trevino, E. (1995). *Eukee: The jumpy, jumpy elephant*.

Dwyer, K.M. (1991). *What do you mean I have attention deficit disorder?* School-age children are featured in black-and-white photographs.

Galvin, M. (1988). *Otto learns about his medicine: A story about medication for hyperactive children*.

Gehret, J. (1991). *Eagle eyes*. A child with attention deficit disorder.

Gordon, M. (1991). *Jumpin' Johnny, get back to work*. Ages five to twelve.

Janover, C. (1997). *Zipper the kid with ADHD*. Late grade school.

Nadeau, K.G. and Dixon, E.B. (1997). *Learning to slow down and pay attention*. Includes worksheets and activities; ages six to thirteen.

Pincus, D. (1989). *Shelley the hyperactive turtle*. Ages four to eight.

Quinn, P.O. and Stern, J.M. (1991). *Putting on the brakes: Young people's guide to understanding attention deficit hyperactivity disorder*. Ages eight to thirteen.

Shapiro, L. (1993). *Sometimes I drive my mom crazy, but I know she's crazy about me*. Ages five to ten.

Shore, M. (1994). *Jumpin' Jake settles down: A workbook to help impulsive children learn to think before they act*. Ages five to ten.

Death and Dying

Barker, P. (1984). *What happened when Grandma died*. Includes information for parents; ages five to eight.

Biale, R. (1997). *My pet died*.

Boyd, C.D. (1985). *Breadsticks and blessing places*. A girl's best friend is killed by a drunk driver—this book is novel length; features African-American families; ages eleven to fourteen.

Buscaglia, L. (1982). *The fall of Freddie the Leaf*. Grade school through adulthood.

Cohen, J. (1987). *I had a friend named Peter*. Betsy's questions about death are answered; ages six to ten.

Ellis, S. (1988). *A family project*. A baby sister's crib death.

Greene, C. (1994). *Beat the turtle drum*. The friendship between two sisters.

Heegaard, M. (1991). *When something terrible happens*. Dealing with death; ages nine to eleven.

Holden, D.L. (1989). *Gran Gran's best trick: A story for children who have lost someone they love*. Ages four to eight.

Jordan, M. (1989). *Losing Uncle Tim*.

Kaldhol, M. and Wenche, O. (1998). *Goodbye Rune*. The accidental death of a best friend; ages five to eleven.

LeShan, E. (1976). *Learning to say good-bye: When a parent dies*. Ages seven and up.

Mellonie, B. and Ingpen, R. (1983). *Lifetimes*. Life and death are explained.

Moser, A. (1995). *Don't despair on Thursdays!* Responding to loss and emotional pain; ages four to twelve.

Old, W.C. (1995). *Stacy had a little sister.*

O'Toole, D. (1989). *Aarvy Aardvark finds hope.*

Palmer, P. (1994). *I wish I could hold your hand.* A child's guide to grief and loss.

Paterson, K. (1977). *Bridge to Terabithia.* How a boy handles the sudden death of his best friend; a regular-length book for ages ten to thirteen.

Prestine, J.S. (1993). *Someone special died.* A little girl loses a special friend.

Rogers, F. (1988). *When a pet dies.* Ages five to seven.

Romain, T. (1999). *What on earth do you do when someone dies*? Ages five to ten.

Sanford, D. (1985). *It must hurt a lot.* Joshua is overwhelmed when his puppy is hit by a car; ages four to eight.

Simon, N. (1992). *The saddest time.* Stories of the deaths of an uncle, a classmate, and a grandfather; ages six to twelve.

Smilansky, S. (1987). *On death: Helping children understand and cope.*

Stein, S. (1974). *About dying.*

Temes, R. (1992). *The empty place: A child's guide through grief.* A young boy's older sister dies; ages six to ten.

Thomas, J.R. (1988). *Saying good-bye to Grandma.* Seven-year-old Suzie is curious and fearful about Grandma's funeral.

Thurman, C. (1989). *A time for remembering.* A grandfather dies; ages five to eight.

Vigna, J. (1990). *Saying goodbye to Daddy.*

Viorst, L. (1987). *The tenth good thing about Barney.* A family holds a funeral for a pet who has died.

Walker, A. (1988). *To hell with dying.* Older children.

Winsch, J.L. (1995). *After the funeral.*

Disabilities

Amenta, C.A. (1992). *Russell is extra special: A book about autism for children.* Explains autism to children; ages four to eight.

Aseltine, L., Mueller, E., and Tait, N. (1986). *I'm deaf and it's okay.*

Bergman, T. (1989). *Finding a common language: Children living with deafness.* A six-year-old Swedish girl attends a school for the deaf; ages five to nine.

Bergman, T. (1989). *On our own terms.* Physically disabled children; ages eight and up.

Bergman, T. (1989). *Seeing in special ways.* Unsighted and partially sighted children talk about their disabilities and how they use their other senses; ages six to ten.

Bergman, T. (1989). *We laugh, we love, we cry.* Developmentally disabled children; ages eight and up.

Brandenberg, F. (1985). *Otto is different.* An octopus discovers that eight arms can be an advantage; ages four to eight.

Brown, T. (1984). *Someone special just like you.* Black-and-white photographs tell the story of learning-disabled preschool children; ages five to eight.

Byers, B. (1970). *The summer of the swans.*

Cairos, S. (1985). *Our brother has Down's syndrome.*

Cummings, R. and Fisher, G. (1991). *The school survival guide for kids with LD.* Ages eight and up.

Fisher, G. and Cummings, R. (1990). *The survival guide for kids with LD.* Ages eight and up.

Gallico, P. (1992). *The snow goose.* A painter with a disability rescues a World War II soldier.

Gartenberg, Z. (1998). *Mori's story.* An autistic brother.

Gehret, J. (1992). *The don't-give-up kid.* Inspiration for learning-disabled kids to keep on trying; ages six to ten.

Greenberg, J.E. (NA). *What is the sign for friend?* Information for hearing children and support for the hearing disabled; ages seven to nine.

Helfman, E. (1993). *On being Sarah.* Twelve-year-old Sarah has cerebral palsy.

Janover, C. (1988). *Josh: A boy with dyslexia.*

Levinson, M. (1985). *And don't bring Jeremy.* A boy is embarrassed by his brother who has a neurological impairment; ages nine to twelve.

Litchfield, A.B. (1985). *A cane in her hand.* Physical disabilities.

McNey, M. (1996). *Leslie's story.* The school and home life of a twelve-year-old girl with developmental disabilities.

Metzger, L. (1992). *Barry's sister.* A brother with cerebral palsy.

Pridmore, S. and McGrath, M. (1991). *Julia, Mungo, and the earthquake: A story for young people about epilepsy.* A young girl has epilepsy; ages seven to eleven.

Rosenberg, M.B. (1988). *Finding a way: Living with exceptional brothers and sisters.* Physical disabilities: diabetes, asthma, and spina bifida; ages seven to ten.

Seligman, M. (1991). *The family with a handicapped child.*

Shyer, M.F. (1978). *Welcome home, Jellybean.* A sister comes home after spending most of her life in an institution for mentally handicapped children; ages nine to thirteen.

Stern, J. (1996). *Many ways to learn.* A young people's guide to learning disabilities.

Wood, J.R. (1992). *The man who loved clowns.* An uncle with Down's syndrome; ages eleven to fifteen.

Wright, B.R. (1992). *My sister is different.* Carlo has a mentally handicapped sister.

Diversity

Race Relations and Racial and Ethnic Diversity

Adoff, A. (1982). *All the colors of the race.*

Adoff, A. (1992). *Black is brown is tan.*

Carr, J. (1995). *Dark day, light night.* Manda's aunt Ruby helps her to deal with some angry feelings by making lists of all the things that they would like in the world.

Davol, M. (1993). *Black, white, just right.*

Gainer, C. (1998). *I'm like you, you're like me.* Understanding and celebrating each other's differences.

Garza, C.L. (1990). *Family pictures/Cuadros de familia.* Author talks about her life in a Mexican community in Texas; ages seven to eight.

Goble, P. (1992). *Crow chief.* A legend from the Plains Indians; ages seven to eight.

Hallinan, P.K. (1994). *A rainbow of friends.* Race relations.

Hamanaka, S. (1994). *All the colors of the earth.* Ages three to eight.

Hoffman, M. and Binch, C. (1991). *Amazing Grace*. Classmates tell Grace that she cannot play Peter Pan in the school play because she is black. Grace decides that she can do anything; features African-American children.

Herron, C. (1997). *Nappy hair*. People at a backyard picnic offer comments on a girl's nappy hair.

Imai, M. (1994). *Lilly's secret*. Animal friends are concerned about their differences.

Kissinger, K. (1994). *All the colors we are*. How people get skin color; Spanish/English.

Oughton, J. (1992). *How the stars fell from the sky: A Navajo legend*. A creation legend; ages seven to eight.

Rosenberg, M.B. (1986). *Living in two worlds*. Explanations of race; children with biracial heritage; ages eight to twelve.

Surat, M.M. (1983). *Angel child, dragon child*. Ut has just come to the United States from Vietnam.

Vigna, J. (1996). *Black like Kyra, white like me*. Ages six to ten.

Yarbrough, C. (1979). *Cornrows*. Features people of color; middle to late grade school.

Sexual Diversity

Bosche, S. (1983). *Jenny lives with Eric and Martin*.

Brown, F. (1991). *Generous Jefferson Bartleby Jones*.

Elwin, R. and Paulse, M. (1990). *Asha's mums*.

Heron, A. and Maran, M. (1991). *How would you feel if your dad was gay?*

Newman, L. (1989). *Heather has two mommies*. Biological mother is gay.

Newman, L. (1991). *Gloria goes to gay pride*.

Valentine, J. (1991). *The duke who outlawed jelly beans*.

Valentine, J. (1992). *The day they put a tax on rainbows*.

Vigna, J. (1995). *My two uncles*. A young girl worries about the family relations between parents, grandparents, and two gay uncles.

Willhoite, M. (1990). *Daddy's roommate*.

Willhoite, M. (1991). *Families: A coloring book*.

Willhoite, M. (1993). *Uncle what-is-it is coming to visit*.

Divorced Families, Remarried Families, and Single Parenting

Divorce

Banks, A. (1990). *When your parents get a divorce*.

Brown, L.K. and Brown, M. (1988). *Dinosaurs divorce*. Ages three to nine.

Christiansen, C.B. (1989). *My mother's house, my father's house*. A girl spends half the week with Mom, half with Dad; ages six to nine.

Deaton, W. (1994). *A separation in my family*. Therapeutic workbook; ages seven to thirteen.

Field, M.B. and Shore, H. (1994). *My life turned upside down, but I turned it rightside up*. Coping with divorce; ages five to twelve.

Holmes, M.S. (1997). *Daddy doesn't live here anymore*.

Ives, S.B., Fassler, D., and Lash, M. (1988). *The divorce workbook*. Ages five to twelve.

Johnson, J.R., Breunig, K., Garrity, C., and Baris, M. (1997). *Through the eyes of children: Healing stories for children of divorce*. Ages five to fifteen.

Krementz, J. (1984). *How it feels when parents divorce.* Children from ages seven to sixteen talk about living through a divorce; ages nine to thirteen.

Mayle, P. (1988). *Why are we getting a divorce?* Why parents split up and how children can handle their wide variety of feelings; ages eight to twelve.

Peck, R. (1992). *Father figure.* When their mother dies, eight years after her divorce, two brothers get the chance to know and forgive their father; ages twelve and up.

Pincus, D. (NA). *The divorce workbook.*

Sanford, D. (1985). *Please come home: A child's book about divorce.*

Stern, Z. and Stern, E. (1997). *Divorce is not the end of the world.* Young adolescents have written this book to help children cope.

Weninger, B. (1997). *Good-bye, Daddy!* A young bear learns that even when his father bear has to live in another home, love and caring never go away; ages four to ten.

Stepfamilies

Berry, J. (NA). *About stepfamilies.* For older children.

Boyd, L. (1987). *The not-so-wicked stepmother.* Ages six to nine.

Boyd, L. (1990). *Sam is my half brother.* Ages three to six.

Bradley, B. (1982). *Where do I belong? A kid's guide to stepfamilies.* Tips on living in stepfamilies; ages eight to eleven.

Drescher, J. (1986). *My mother's getting married.* Ages six to ten.

Evans, M. (1988). *This is me and my two families: An awareness scrapbook/journal for children living in step-families.* Ages four to twelve.

Jukes, M. (1984). *Like Jane and me.* Alex thinks that he doesn't have much in common with his step-father.

Mayle, P. (1989). *What am I doing in a stepfamily?* Ages six to ten.

Park, B. (1989). *My mother got married (and other disasters).* Ages ten to twelve.

Sanford, D. (1993). *My real family: A child's book about living in a stepfamily.* Religious.

Schab, L. (1996). *My dad is getting married again.* Dealing with a prospective stepparent; ages five to twelve.

Single-Parent Households After Divorce

Dolmetsch, P. and Shih, A. (1985). *The kid's book about single-parent families.*

Evans, M. (1988). *This is me and my single parent: A discovery workbook for children and single parents to work on together.* Ages four to twelve.

Girard, L.W. (1987). *At Daddy's on Saturdays.* Katie accepts her new schedule after her dad moves out and comes to accept his home as her home too; ages four to ten.

Lindsay, J.W. (1991). *Do I have a daddy?*

Miller, M.J. (1992). *Upside down.* When her mom dates the fathers of two classmates, Sara must find the strength to accept change; ages eight to twelve.

Simon, N. (1983). *I wish I had my father.*

Vigna, J. (1997). *I live with Daddy.*

Emotions

Aborn, A. (1994). *Everything I do you blame on me!/Why should I? It's not my birthday.* Two books in one on controlling anger; ages five to twelve.

Anholt, C. and Anholt, L. (1994). *What makes me happy?*

Berry, J.W. (1996). *Let's talk about feeling afraid.*

Berry, J.W. (1996). *Let's talk about feeling angry.*

Berry, J.W. (1996). *Let's talk about feeling sad.*

Berry, J.W. (1996). *Let's talk about needing attention.*

Bourgeois, P. (1986). *Franklin in the dark.* Franklin is afraid of dark places, which is a problem because he is a turtle who can't go into his shell.

Cain, B.S. (1990). *Double-dip feelings: A book to help children understand emotions.* Highlights the confusing experience of having two feelings at once; ages four to eight.

Conlin, S. and Freedman, S.L. (1991). *Let's talk about feelings at preschool: Nathan's day.* Features people of color; ages three to seven.

Crary, E. (1992). *I'm frustrated.* Ages four to ten.

Crary, E. (1992). *I'm mad.* Ages four to ten.

Crary, E. (1992). *I'm proud.* Ages four to ten.

Crary, E. (1994). *I'm furious.* Ages four to ten.

Crary, E. and Steelsmith, S. (1997). *When you're happy and you know it.* Ages three to five.

Crary, E. and Steelsmith, S. (1997). *When you're mad and you know it.* Ages three to five.

Crary, E. and Steelsmith, S. (1997). *When you're shy and you know it.* Ages three to five.

Crary, E. and Steelsmith, S. (1997). *When you're silly and you know it.* Features people of color; ages three to five. Crary and Steelsmith's books are sometimes sold as a set.

Delis-Abrams, A. (1993). *ABC feelings.* Explore feelings from A—accepted to Z—zippy; ages four to ten.

Duncan, R. (1989). *When Emily woke up angry.* Overcoming frustration; ages four to eight.

Dutro, J. (1992). *Night light: A story for children afraid of the dark.* Ages three to seven.

Formby, C. (1997). *Tristan's temper tantrum.* Tristan is a volcano.

Friedman, S.L. (1989). *All my feelings at home: Ellie's day.* Ages three to seven.

Krueger, D.W. (1993). *What is a feeling?* Recognize, communicate, and value emotions; ages three to seven.

Lachner, D. (1997). *Andrew's angry words.* The importance of expressing anger appropriately; ages four to ten.

Lankton, S. (1988). *The blammo surprise! book: A story to help children overcome fears.* Ages four to eight.

Lobby, T. (1990). *Jessica and the bad wolf: A story for children who have bad dreams.* Ages three to seven.

Marcus, I. and Marcus, P. (1990). *Scary night visitors: A story for children with bedtime fears.* Ages three to seven.

Moser, A. (1994). *Don't rant and rave on Wednesdays.* Ages four to twelve.

O'Neill, C. (1993). *Relax.*

Pincus, D. (1995). *How I learned to control my temper.* A storybook and workbook.

Schaefer, C.E. (1992). *Cat's got your tongue? A story for children afraid to speak.* Deals with anxiety with strangers and new situations; ages three to seven.

Shapiro, L. (1993). *All feelings are OK—It's what you do with them that counts*. Ages four to ten.

Shapiro, L. (1994). *The very angry day that Amy didn't have*. Anger management; ages four to ten.

Shore, H. (1995). *The angry monster workbook*. Anger management; ages five to twelve.

Simon, N. (1974). *I was so mad*. Ages three to seven.

Trower, T. (1995). *The self-control patrol workbook*. Anticipating consequences of behavior; ages seven to twelve.

Whitehouse, E. and Pudney, W. (1996). *A volcano in my tummy: Helping children to handle anger*. Stories, exercises, and games; ages six to fifteen.

Ethical/Moral/Responsible Behavior

Brainard, B. (1992). *You can't sell your brother at the garage sale: The kid's book of values*. Ages six to ten.

Crary, E. (1987). *Finders, keepers*. You find a wallet. Do you keep it?

Crary, E. (1990). *Pick up your socks*. Teaching children responsible behavior; ages five and up.

Gardner, R.A. (1990). *The girls and boys book about good and bad behavior*. Understanding the effect of behavior on others; ages six to twelve.

Humphrey, S.M. (1997). *If you had to choose, what would you do?* Twenty-five situations to help children develop their sense of moral conduct; ages six to twelve.

Moser, A. (1999). *Don't tell a whopper on Fridays*. Ages five to ten.

Naylor, P.R. (1992). *All but Alice*. Alice has to make some difficult choices in the seventh grade; ages nine to ten.

Schwartz, L. (1991). *Monkey see, monkey do*.

Schwartz, L. (1991). *The responsible rascal*. Taking responsibility; ages three to five.

Schwartz, L. (1993). *What do you think?* A guide to daily dilemmas such as dealing with ethnic jokes, being ignored, talking on the phone, having a forbidden friendship; grades three to seven.

Scott, S. (1989). *Too smart for trouble*. Standing up to peer pressure; ages five to ten.

Shapiro, L.E. (1995). *How I learned to be considerate of others*. Features photos of children of color.

Shapiro, L.E. (1995). *How I learned to think things through*. Ages seven to twelve.

Family Relationships

Annunziata, J. and Nemiroff, M.A. (1998). *Why am I an only child?* Ages four to seven.

Arnold, E. and Loeb, J. (1987). *I'm telling! Kids talk about brothers and sisters*. Ages eight to eleven.

Brainard, B. (1992). *You can't sell your brother at the garage sale: The kid's book of values*. Ages six to ten.

Brown, L.K. (1989). *Baby time*. For all big brothers and sisters; ages five to six.

Cole, J. (1998). *The new baby at your house*.

Frankel, F. (1996). *Good friends are hard to find*. Ages five to twelve.

Grant, E. (1991). *Will I ever be older?* Sibling conflict; features African-American children.

Hamilton, M. (1992). *Little sister for sale*. Kate discovers that being a big sister isn't so bad after all; ages four to eight.

Hendrickson, K. (1990). *Baby and I can play* and *Fun with toddlers*. Two-book set.

Henkes, K. (1990). *Julius: The baby of the world*. Lilly is convinced that the arrival of her new baby brother is the worst thing that has happened to her.

Hoban, R. (1993). *A baby sister for Frances*. Frances decides to run away after her sister is born.

Lakin, P. (1985). *Don't touch my room*. Aaron makes room in his heart for baby brother; ages four to six.

Lansky, V. (1987). *A new baby at Koko Bear's house*. Koko Bear experiences the key stages of pregnancy, birth, and homecoming of his younger sibling.

Manushkin, F. (1984). *Baby, come out!* Each family member tries his or her hand at coaxing a reluctant baby to be born.

Moon, N. (1997). *Something special*. Charlie takes his new baby sister for show and tell; ages two to six.

Pevsner, S. (1978). *And you give me a pain, Elaine*. After her mother dies, Andrea must work extra hard to get along with her sister; ages ten to twelve.

Sachs, M. (1992). *What my sister remembered*. Two orphaned sisters meet after eight years and must deal with a terrible secret; ages nine to thirteen.

Simon, N. (1970). *How do I feel?* A boy has a hard time dealing with a twin and an older brother; ages eight to thirteen.

Weninger, B. (1997). *Will you mind the baby, Davy?* Davy Rabbit adjusts to the new baby; ages three to nine.

Friendships/Peer Relationships

Adler, C. (1988). *Always and forever friends*.

American Girl Library (1996). *The care and keeping of friends*.

Bosch, C.W. (1988). *Bully on the bus*.

Boulden, J. and Boulden, J. (1994). *Push and shove*. Workbook; grades two to five.

Bourgeois, P. and Clark, B. (1993). *Franklin is bossy*.

Canning, S. (1997). *Friendship, Annie's fair-weather friend*. Annie is upset about the loss of a friendship until a buffalo tells the story of a young Indian who is a true friend.

Carey, D. (1992). *Will there be a lap for me?* Making room for a new baby in the house; ages three to five.

Carlson, N. (1990). *Arnie and the new kid*.

Carlson, N. (1994). *How to lose all your friends*. Humorous way to discuss keeping friends.

Cohen-Posey, K. (1995). *How to handle bullies, teasers and other meanies*.

Crary, E. (1982). *I want to play*. Ages three to five.

Crary, E. (1983). *My name is not dummy*. Ages three to five.

Danziger, P. (1974). *The cat ate my gymsuit*. Marcy overcomes having no friends and being overweight; ages nine to ten.

DeGroat, D. (1997). *Roses are pink, your feet really stink*. How can Gilbert be nice to children who were not nice to him?

Doyle, T.W. (1995). *Why is everybody always picking on me? A guide to handling bullies*. Nonviolent approach; conflict resolution; ages eight to twelve.

Falon, J.R. (1998). *Kissed the girls and made them cry: Helping children understand sexism in our society*. Become aware of gender issues, sexism, and appropriate behavior in schools.

Fox, M. (1985). *Wilfrid Gordon McDonald Partridge*. Ages five and up.

Killilea, M. (1992). *Newf*. Ages five to ten.

Krischanitz, R. (1999). *Nobody likes me!* Buddy is a shy dog who gets advice on making friends; ages four to ten.

Millman, D. (1991). *Secret of the peaceful warrior.* How to resolve conflict peacefully; ages five to eleven.

Petty, K. and Firmin, C. (1991). *Making friends.* Friendship is a two-way street.

Pfister, M. (1996). *The rainbow fish.* Learning to share; ages three to five.

Pincus, D. (1983). *Sharing.* Stresses self and other awareness; ages four to eight.

Reider, K. (1997). *Snail started it!* How cruel words hurt; how to set things right; ages three to ten.

Romain, T. (1997). *Bullies are a pain in the brain.* Dos and don'ts for dealing with bullies; ages eight to twelve.

Rowland, A. (1995). *How I learned to make friends.*

Sachar, L. (1993). *Marvin Redpost: Why pick on me?* Nine-year-old Marvin almost becomes an outcast in his third-grade class, then figures out what to do.

Schwartz, L. (1991). *What would you do?* A guide to tricky situations; grades three to seven.

Shapiro, L. (1995). *Sometimes I like to fight—But I don't do it much anymore.* Ages four to ten.

Shreve, S. (1995). *Joshua T. Bates takes charge.* What it's like to be an outcast and a hero.

Wrightson, P. (1992). *The sugar-gum tree.* Ages seven to eleven.

Zimmerman, T. and Shapiro, L. (1996). *Sometimes I feel like I don't have any friends—But not so much anymore.* Developing skills to make friends; ages five to twelve.

Zolotow, C. (1969). *The hating book.* A little girl is hurt by a friend and then learns there was a misunderstanding.

Illness and Health: Child's or Family Member's

Bahr, M. (1992). *The memory box.* Grandpa has Alzheimer's and starts a memory box with his grandson.

Banks, A. (1989). *Hospital journal: A kid's guide to a strange place.*

Berg, F.M. (1997). *Afraid to eat: Children and teens in weight crisis.* Eating disorders are defined and means for healthy change are explained; 319 pages; ages six and up.

Berry, J. (1990). *Good answers to tough questions about weight problems and eating disorders.*

Ciliotta, C. and Livingston, C. (1992). *Why am I going to the hospital?*

Day, S. (1995). *Luna and the big blur.* A story for children who wear glasses.

Gaes, J. (1987). *My book for kids with cancer.* Ages four to nine.

Girard, L.W. (1991). *Alex, the kid with AIDS.*

Guthrie, D. (1986). *Grandpa doesn't know it's me.* A young girl tries to understand her grandfather's Alzheimer's disease; ages five to eight.

Hamilton, D. (1995). *Sad days, glad days.* How to cope with a parent's depression; ages six to nine.

Laskin, P. and Moskowitz, A. (1991). *Wish upon a star: A story for children with a parent who is mentally ill.* A young girl deals with her feelings revolving around one parent who is mentally ill and incapable of parenting; ages three to seven.

London, J. (1997). *The lion who had asthma.* Ages three to seven.

Mills, J.C. (1992). *Little tree: A story for children with serious medical problems.* Ages four to eight.

Moritz, E.K. (1998). *Blink, blink, clop, clop: Why do we do things we can't stop?* Explains obsessive-compulsive disorder to children; ages three to six.

Mulder, L. (1992). *Sarah and Puffle: A story for children about diabetes*. Ages four to eight.

Ostrow, W. and Ostrow, V. (1989). *All about asthma*. An eight-year-old boy has his first asthma attack.

Pace, B. (1987). *Chris gets ear tubes*.

Peterkin, A. (1992). *What about me? When brothers and sisters get sick*. Ages four to eight.

Pirner, C.W. (1991). *Even little kids get diabetes*. Ages five to ten.

Rogers, A. (1987). *Luke has asthma, too*. An illness that affects one of every twenty children; ages three to seven.

Rogers, F. (1988). *Going to the hospital*. What happens during hospital stay.

Schilling, S. and Swain, J. (1989). *My name is Jonathan (and I have AIDS)*.

Sessions, D. (1984). *My mom is different*. A child discusses her parent with multiple personality disorder.

Smith, L. (1991). *Glasses: Who needs 'em?*

Tasker, M. (1988). *Jimmy and the eggs virus*. A boy contracts AIDS.

Vigna, J. (1993). *When Eric's mom fought cancer*. Ages six to nine.

Parent and Child Attachment

Brown, M.W. (1942). *The runaway bunny*.

Cooke, T. (1994). *So much*.

Eisenberg, P.R. (1992). *You're my Nikki*.

Hazen, B.S. (1981). *Even if I did something awful*.

Joose, B.M. (1991). *Mama, do you love me?*

Lewin, H. (1981). *Jafta's mother*.

Lindbergh, R. (1993). *Grandfather's lovesong*.

Mastrangelo, J. (1988). *What do bunnies do all day?*

McBratney, S. (1994). *Guess how much I love you?*

Melmed, L.K. (1993). *The first song ever sung*.

Melmed, L.K. (1993). *I love you as much . . .*

Modesitt, J. (1993). *Mama, if you had a wish*.

Munsch, R. (1986). *Love you forever*.

Schlein, M. (1963). *The way mothers are*.

Scott, A.H. (1972). *On Mother's lap*.

Smalls, I. (1992). *Jonathan and his mommy*.

Turner, A. (1990). *Through moon and stars and night sky*.

Self-Esteem

Brooks, J. (1994). *Princess Jessica rescues a prince*. Girls can do anything; ages four to ten.

Carlson, N. (1990). *I like me!* Ages three to seven.

Carroll, J. (1987). *Let's learn about magnificent me!*

Crary, E. (1983). *My name is not dummy*. Ages three to five.

Gardner, R.A. (1990). *The girls and boys book about good and bad behavior*. Behaviors related to self-esteem; ages six to twelve.

Gehret, J. (1996). *The don't-give-up kid.*

Kaufman, G. and Raphael, L. (1990). *Stick up for yourself!*

Lansky, B. (1998). *Girls to the rescue.* Folk tales and fairy tales where the "heroes" are all girls; ages eight to thirteen.

Loomans, D. (1991). *The lovables: In the kingdom of self-esteem.* Twenty-four animals in the kingdom have special gifts to contribute.

MacGuire, A. (1995). *We're all special.* All children are unique; ages three to eight.

Mather, A.D. and Weldon, L.B. (1991). *The cat at the door.* 181 stories about childhood to enhance self-respect and healthy values; ages four to twelve.

Moser, A. (1991). *Don't feed the monster on Tuesdays!* Enhancing self-esteem; ages four to twelve.

Patterson, C. and Quilter, L. (1994). *It's OK to be you.* Facts about preteen physical, social, and emotional growth; ages eight to twelve.

Payne, L.M. (1994). *Just because I am.* All children are special.

Robertson, J. (1993). *Oscar's spots.* A young leopard is unhappy with his appearance.

Sanford, D. (1986). *Don't look at me: A child's book about feeling different.* Religious.

Shapiro, L. (1995). *My best friend is me!* Ages three to eight.

Separation from Parents/Being Alone at Home

Ahlberg, J. and Ahlberg, A. (1990). *Starting school.* First day of preschool; ages two to six.

Banks, A. (1989). *Alone at home: A kid's guide to being in charge.*

Crary, E. (1985). *I'm lost.* Ages three to five.

Crary, E. (1986). *Mommy don't go.* Ages three to five.

Minarik, E.H. (1957). *Little Bear.* Little Bear is comfortable having adventures because his mother is always waiting for him at home; preschoolers.

Penn, A. (1998). *The kissing hand.* Reassurance for temporary separation from family; ages four to eight.

Stanek, M. (1985). *All alone after school.* Latchkey.

Tompert, A. (1988). *Will you come back for me?* Four-year-old is worried about being left in day care for the first time.

Viorst, J. (1988). *The good-bye book.* Parents go out for the evening; ages six to eight.

Zerafa, J. (NA). *Nathan's day at pre-school.*

Stress

Bunting, E. (1991). *Fly away home.* A young boy tells of his homelessness; ages five to six.

DiSalvo-Ryan, D. (1991). *Uncle Willie and the soup kitchen.* A boy works with his uncle one day to feed the homeless.

Hazen, B.S. (1979). *Tight times.* A young boy's father loses his job.

Hertensten, J. (Ed.) (1995). *Home is where we live.* Life at a shelter through a young girl's eyes.

Howe, J. (1994). *When you go to kindergarten.*

Leiner, K. (1986). *Both my parents work.* Nine children tell their stories; ages seven to ten.

Moser, A. (1988). *Don't pop your cork on Mondays!* Dealing with stress; ages four to twelve.

O'Neill, C. (1993). *Relax.* Explanations and relaxation exercises.

Romain, T. (1997). *How to do homework without throwing up*. Jokes and cartoons give homework pointers; ages eight to thirteen.

Sanders, C. and Turner, C. (1983). *Coping*.

Williams, M. and Burke, D.O. (1990). *Cool cats, calm kids*. Ages seven to twelve.

Therapy

Galvin, M. (1988). *Ignatius finds help: A story about psychotherapy for children*. Ages four to eight.

Galvin, M. (1988). *Robby really transforms: A story about grown-ups helping children*. Ages four to eight.

Koplow, L. (1991). *Tanya and the Tobo Man: A story in English and Spanish for children entering therapy*. Ages four to eight.

Nemiroll, M.A. and Annunziata, J. (1996). *A child's first book about play therapy*. Ages four to six.

Schwartz, J.L. (1986). *Shrink*. Mike goes to a psychiatrist because of poor grades; talking to a doctor is not the disgrace he thought it would be; ages eleven to fourteen.

Toilet Training/Bed-Wetting

Toilet Training

Cole, J. (1989). *Your new potty*. African-American and European-American children are the subjects of black-and-white photo illustrations.

Frankel, A. (1980). *Once upon a potty*. Ages one to three.

Gomi, T. (1993). *Everyone poops*. Ages three to five.

Lansky, V. (1986). *Koko Bear's new potty*.

McGrath, B. (1996). *Uh oh! Gotta go!* Children of several racial and ethnic groups are portrayed in the illustrations.

Reiner, A. (1991). *The potty chronicles: A story to help children adjust to toilet training*. Ages two to six.

Russ, A. (1990). *I have to go*. Sesame Street muppet babies.

Worth, B. (1997). *I can go potty*. Sesame Street muppet babies.

Bed-Wetting/Soiling

Boelts, M. (1994). *Dry days, wet nights*.

Galvin, M. (1989). *Clouds and clocks: A story for children who soil*. Ages four to eight.

Mack, A. (1990). *Dry all night*. Written for both parents and children.

Mills, J.C. (1988). *Sammy the Elephant and Mr. Camel: A story to help children overcome bedwetting while discovering self-appreciation*.

SECTION VIII:
PARENT EDUCATION AND INTERVENTION

43

The Parent's Guide to Good Divorce Behavior

Lorna L. Hecker
Catherine Ford Sori

Type of Contribution: Handout

Objective

When parents are in the throes of divorce, intensely emotional issues can cloud their view of their children's well-being. Even the most loving parents can find themselves inadvertently doing things that may harm their children simply because they are so occupied with their own feelings, they have less ability to regard the needs of their children. Other, less optimal parents may be carrying out a long marital pattern of putting children in the middle of parental conflict. Some parents will present children in therapy unsure why their children are reacting the way they are to the divorce, worried about the children, or simply wanting to make sure the children are adjusting adequately to the family transition. Other parents will find their way to a therapist's office by way of a court order where the judge recognizes harm is befalling the children as a result of the divorce, but the parents may be unaware. The handout developed herein is to give the therapist an aid for parents to use to evaluate their own behavior and correct problems that may be negatively influencing their children. Parents are often grateful for this information, or grateful for information they can pass on to an ex-spouse who may be involving the children inappropriately in the parental divorce.

Rationale for Use

The Parent's Guide to Good Divorce Behavior can be utilized simply as a psychoeducational tool for parents navigating the transition of divorce. Even the therapists who can make their points in the most eloquent manner can be buttressed by written material on the subject at hand. Printed material can help stress the importance of the topic. In addition, some parents welcome guidelines during this time to ease the stress of the divorce on their children.

Instructions for Use

The Parent's Guide to Good Divorce Behavior can be utilized at the therapist's discretion in the therapy context. It can also be placed in therapy waiting rooms to serve as client educational material. The therapist may elect to go through the guide with the parent and discuss difficult points. It may be that parents are unaware of times they are putting a child in an unfair position, and they may more readily recognize the problem with help from the guide.

Vignette

Maryann brought her nine-year-old daughter Melanie for individual therapy at the suggestion of Melanie's pediatrician. Over the past eight months Melanie had begun to scratch and pick at the skin on her hands and lower arms, and her condition had worsened to the point she had to wear long-sleeved shirts during the day and gloves at night. (Maryann called for an appointment after the doctor suggested restraining Melanie's hands by tying them to the bedposts at night!) Despite consultations with dermatologists and allergists, no medical explanation could be found to explain Melanie's condition. When asked, Melanie simply stated that her skin "bothered" her. The doctors concurred that her condition was psychosomatic.

The therapist learned that shortly before Melanie's symptoms broke out her parents had finally decided to divorce, following years of acrimony. Both of Melanie's parents were high-powered litigation attorneys, and the divorce proceedings had become increasingly bitter and vengeful. Attempts at mediation had failed, and Melanie, an only child, was caught in a custody battle, with each parent vying for her loyalty. Currently Melanie alternated weeks with each parent, who continually argued and threatened each other over any slight deviation or infringement of the temporary agreement. The therapist also learned that Melanie had become more withdrawn from her friends at school, that she rarely had friends over anymore, and that her grades had slipped in recent months. It seemed to the therapist that Melanie was caught in a terrible place between two warring parents, and that her hands were (almost literally!) tied (see Griffith and Griffith, 1994).

Maryann requested individual therapy for Melanie, and although Maryann agreed to some family sessions, she would not even consider including her husband, Benjamin, in family therapy sessions. For several weeks the therapist worked individually and in family sessions with Melanie and Maryann. Melanie was helped to externalize her problem, labeling it "Scratch" (see White and Epston, 1990). She discovered that Scratch got the best of her when she was relaxing (e.g., watching television), lying in bed, or just doing nothing. She learned ways to defeat Scratch, by doing things such as telling Scratch to "get scratched yourself!" by reading a book, getting on her computer, or talking to Mom. She discovered her best weapon against Scratch after she drew a picture of Scratch, and wrote "Dr. [therapist's name] says 'Begone'!" After this, Melanie said she could often banish Scratch by standing tall and loudly proclaiming, "Dr. _____ says, 'Begone'!"

Sessions with Maryann were aimed at helping her realize the deleterious effect the continued battles had on their daughter. With support and encouragement, Melanie began to share with her mother how awful it was for her to be placed in the middle of a custody dispute. She said that when her parents are screaming at each other she just wants to be dead because she can't stand how they hate each other, and that she feels so helpless to make it better. After a moment of silence Maryann responded, and in a softened voice she promised Melanie that the fighting would stop—no matter what it took.

At this point the therapist introduced the Parent's Guide to Good Divorce Behavior handout. She discussed each point with Maryann, who sorrowfully recognized several harmful things she herself had done, which she now saw had probably contributed to her daughter's distress. Before they finished the handout, Maryann sat forward and exclaimed, "Benjamin has got to see this! But I don't think he'll hear it from me. Can we come in alone next week, to discuss all this?" The therapist, of course, was delighted—as was Melanie!

This was a turning point in therapy, as it allowed the focus to shift from Melanie's Scratch issue to the underlying parental conflict. The therapist met with both parents for a couple of sessions to discuss the handout and how they might begin to communicate about their problems in ways that weren't so destructive for Melanie. After this they were referred back to a mediator, and a custody agreement was quickly reached.

The therapist continued to see Melanie for a few more months, with sessions gradually being spaced further apart. Her hands and arms were visibly much improved, and she no longer had to wear long sleeves to conceal her self-inflicted wounds. Her physician was pleased with her progress but would continue to check her at regular intervals. The therapist asked Melanie what was different since coming to therapy. Melanie reported happily that she felt so much better because her parents didn't fight nearly as much, and when they did start to argue, now they usually stopped quickly. Melanie said that now, if she got upset or worried, she told her mom, who was good at listening. She also seemed happy with the custody arrangement, saying she loved having her own room in both homes. When asked how much Scratch still bothered her, she replied, "Hardly ever! Remember I have power over him—I just tell him, "Dr. _____ says, 'Begone'— and he goes!"

Suggestions for Follow-Up

The handout may always be followed up as part of therapy. Therapists may ask how clients found the list helpful, or they may use the list as a way to suggest that parents alter behaviors based on the criteria of the list. Therapists also want to be sure that clients are not misconstruing any items on the list to fit their own purposes at cost to the children involved.

Contraindications

No contraindications are noted.

Readings and Resources for the Professional

Freeman, J., Epston, D., and Lobovits, D. (1997). *Playful approaches to serious problems*. New York: W. W. Norton.

Griffith, J. L. and Griffith, M. E. (1994). *The body speaks: Therapeutic dialogues for mind-body problems*. New York: Basic Books.

Ricci, I. (1997). *Mom's house, Dad's house: A complete guide for parents who are separated, divorced, or remarried*. New York: Fireside.

Simons, V.A. and Freedman, J. (2000). Witnessing bravery: Narrative ideas for working with children and families. In C. E. Bailey (Ed.), *Children in therapy: Using the family as a resource* (pp. 20-45). New York: W. W. Norton and Company.

Smith, C. and Nylund, D. (1997). *Narrative therapies with children and adolescents*. New York: Guilford Publications.

Wallerstein, J.S., Lewis, J.M., and Blakeslee, S. (2000). *The unexpected legacy of divorce*. New York: Hyperion.

White, M. and Epston, D. (1990). *Narrative means to therapeutic ends*. New York: W.W. Norton.

Bibliotherapy Sources for the Client

Blackstone-Ford, J., Ford, A., Ford, S., Ford, S., and Ford, M. (1998). *My parents are divorced, too: A book for kids by kids*. Washington, DC: Magination Press.

Brown, M.T. and Brown, L.K. (1988). *Dinosaurs divorce: A guide for changing families*. Boston, MA: Little, Brown and Company.

Coleman, W.L. (1998). *What children need to know when parents get divorced.* Minneapolis, MN: Bethany House.

Kalter, N. (1990). *Growing up with divorce: Helping children avoid immediate and later emotional problems.* New York: Free Press; Collier MacMillan, Ltd.

Krementz, J. (1988). *How it feels when parents divorce.* New York: Knopf.

Lansky, V. (1996). *Divorce book for parents: Helping your children cope with divorce and its aftermath.* Deephaven, MN: The Book Peddlers.

Lansky, V. and Prince, J. (1998). *It's not your fault Koko bear: A read-together book for parents and young children during divorce.* Deephaven, MN: The Book Peddlers.

Monroe, R.P. and Ackelmire, C. (1998). *Why don't we live together anymore? Understanding divorce* (Comforting Little Hearts Series). St. Louis, MO: Concordia Publishing House.

Moser, A. and Melton, D. (2000). *Don't fall apart on Saturdays! The children's divorce-survival book.* Kansas City, MO: Landmark Editions.

Nightingale, L.V. and Apodaca, B. (1997). *My parents still love me even though they're getting divorced: An interactive tale for children.* Yorba Linda, CA: Nightengale Rose Publications.

Schneider, M. and Zuckerman, J. (1996). *Difficult questions kids ask about divorce.* New York: Fireside.

Smith, M.F. (1999). *Families are forever! Kids workbook for sharing feelings about divorce.* New York: Changing Lives Publications.

Spelman, C.M. and Parkinson, K. (2001). *Mama and Daddy Bear's divorce.* Chicago, IL: Albert Whitman and Co.

Parent's Guide to Good Divorce Behavior

Parents naturally worry about the well-being of their child or children during the transition of divorce. In addition, in a heightened emotional state, parents may not always act in a way they normally would in relation to their children. The following information is presented as a guide to protect your child as best a parent can from emotional harm that can befall him or her in the midst of parental conflict.

1. *Do not put your child in the middle.* Communicate to your ex-spouse directly; do not ask children to carry messages. Do not have them avenge you or manipulate your ex. Never pump your child for information regarding your ex. Children of divorce have enough burdens to bear without parents weighing them down in this way. Communicate to the child that it is okay and normal for him or her to have two families, and that he or she can love all members of both families.

2. *Do not ask your child to choose a parent.* This may occur literally, as in a parent who says, "You like your Daddy better than your Mommy, don't you?" This may also occur more indirectly, such as discouraging your children to be interested in your ex-spouse's religion. Children need to feel free to love both parents.

3. *Do not assign fault to the divorce.* Like it or not, marriages are made up of two people contributing to the problem. If you need to vent, choose a friend, clergy, or professional counselor. Children need not be privy to your need to see your ex as the villain. Above all, do not tell children things they do not need to know that will hurt their relationship with either parent. For example, divulging an affair to your child by you or your ex will not aid your child in any way.

4. *Do not talk negatively about your ex.* For the children's sake, not yours or your ex-spouse's, do not talk negatively about your ex-spouse within earshot of the children. Children know they are part of both you and your ex-spouse, so to portray one parent as bad gets internalized, and children often assume they must then be bad too. Even relatively minor comments such as "We divorced because your father changed . . . he was different" places blame on the ex-spouse. This means that you may have to walk a fine line between telling the truth and not being disrespectful. Except in very severe cases, the child will need to continue to love your ex, flaws and all. Talking negatively may be very tempting during the initial stages of the divorce; some people make it a lifelong hobby. If you cannot refrain from this behavior, seek professional help.

5. *Keep appropriate boundaries with your children.* Do not allow children to assume a parental role, or that of your personal counselor about your feelings about the divorce and any ensuing hardships caused by the divorce. Your children are also in a vulnerable state, and they need to be allowed to be children, and not to take on adult roles before they are adults. Your child may like this added power, but not everything a child likes is good for him or her. Do not allow children to sleep with you on an ongoing basis. Children need to know they are cared for and secure, but they also need to develop independence in order to gain that security as they grow older. Parents often may take a child into their bed when the child is sick, only to delay returning the child to his or her bed upon recovery. It is tempting to think this is good for a child because you may feel lonely as well.

6. *Keep transitions to a minimum.* Moving, starting a new school, and quick remarriages will not aid in the child's transition. The child needs familiar things in both homes. For small children, you may want children to have a "transitional object" they take between your home and your ex's home. A teddy bear that is carried back and forth between homes can serve as a comforting object that is consistent between both homes.

7. *Stay involved in your child's life.* For some people, divorce is so painful that they may try to sever ties not only to the ex-spouse but also with the children. While this may result in short-term relief, it will bring long-range problems in the child's development, and ultimately in your relationship with your child. The child did not choose the divorce, and it is your responsibility to manage the pain of transition while guiding and nurturing him or her as well as possible. The child may already feel abandoned; don't make it worse.

8. *Do NOT engage in conflict with your ex-spouse in front of the children.* If you cannot speak civilly to your ex, don't say anything at all. Meeting in a public place to make the child exchange is sometimes helpful. When you need to converse with your ex and are prone to lose your temper, write letters or e-mails. Try to treat the former marriage like a business partnership. You now have a partnership to raise your children, even though you are no longer married to each other. If you cannot control your temper, seek professional help. Continued conflict can be very damaging for children.

9. *DO tell the children that the divorce is not their fault.* Children often assume that the parent left the family because they were bad. This needs to be repeated at each developmental level of the child's life because they incorporate information differently at each stage.

10. *DO take care of yourself and get on with your life as best you can.* Children adjust to divorce in direct proportion to how well their parents adjust. Do whatever you need to do to handle stress, conflict, depression, anger, grief, etc., in order to leave negative feelings behind and begin a new life. Divorce can be a great time for development and living your life in a way that resonates with yourself. Although no one plans to get a divorce, for many it can be a "flight into health."

11. *DO allow your children to express their feelings.* While it may be hard for you to hear their feelings, find ways for your children to be expressive of their inner selves. You may find a "feeling chart" helpful; talking about feelings without assigning guilt or blame can be a very large help for children. Art can be another way to encourage your child to express his or her feelings. When looking at his or her art don't say things such as "What's this?" (the child will feel hurt if you don't understand what he or she drew); instead say, "Tell me about your drawing." Try to not ask "yes" or "no" questions. For example, instead of asking, "Did you have a good weekend at Mom's house?" try, "What did you do at Mom's this weekend?"

12. *Transitional times between homes.* Transitional times going to or coming home from the other parent's home can be difficult for a child. Parents often mistake this for bad parenting on the part of their ex. Most children have difficulty adjusting to the transition, as you probably would too, if you thought about it. Try to have reentry rituals such as having dinner ready to eat, or having a movie and popcorn time, or having a particular special snack that serves as a regular ritual that tells the child he or she is now with you. If your child is angry and destructive once he or she comes home, do not fail to discipline. However, it can usually be quite helpful to provide an avenue for the child to express his or her feelings. If a child is destructive, you tell him or her

it is OK to be angry, and it is even understandable, but he or she cannot express it by wrecking furniture or hitting siblings. Find a way together for the child to physically express the anger. Keeping a rolled-up newspaper under the sofa that the child can pull out and hit the sofa with when he or she is angry can prove useful.

13. *Arrange for your child to have as much access to both parents as possible* (IF it is healthy for him or her. Just because you may not like or respect your ex, does not mean that his or her interaction with the children will not be healthy. Consult professionals if needed if you have concerns in this area). Parents should arrange parenting plans that adapt to the children's needs. For example, if changing your work schedule is possible and allows you to see your child more often, do it. If you cannot agree, try to use noncourt means of negotiation whenever possible. Unfortunately, the legal system in this country is set up to be adversarial, which is the opposite of what children need from their parents. There are divorce counselors, family mediators, family therapists, etc., who can help you with this task. Do NOT deny visitation if support payments are late. That is a separate business arrangement and the children's time and affections should not be mixed in with parental business.

14. *Listen to your child.* Do not try to take the pain or anger away from your child but simply listen. In addition, divorce can also bring positives, and your child may also be able to discuss those. Children can see advantages in divorce (such as two birthday parties) that we may not think about.

15. *When children ask why you and your ex divorced, try to respond in a developmentally appropriate way.* For example, you can talk with smaller children about how they like to drink chocolate milk and orange juice. Both taste good individually. Then ask the children if it would taste good if you mixed the chocolate milk with the orange juice. When they make a face, you can explain that that is how Mommy and Daddy are: they each taste good alone, but when you mix the two of you, it is like mixing orange juice with chocolate milk. For older children, a more direct *non-blaming* explanation may be in order: "Mommy and Daddy grew apart." Try to explain the process of two people growing apart, rather than focusing on exactly how Mommy and Daddy grew apart. Be sure to emphasize that the parents divorced each other, but that they will never divorce the children. Explain that you will always be their parent, no matter what. It is also normal for children to want their parents back together. You can explain that once divorced, it is very unlikely people will ever get back together.

16. *Provide reading materials on adjustment to divorce for your child.* For younger children, there are many fine storybooks that normalize divorce and aid in transitions. For older children, there are also books that explain what they might be feeling and why they are feeling this way in the crux of a divorce. Do not force them to read these books; simply make them available to your children.

17. *Allow your children to enjoy their visits with the alternate parent.* Try to be positive about them leaving, and be sure to ask them (without interrogating about your ex) what specific events they did over the weekend. Be interested in their lives, even if you may not like your ex-spouse. Children should be allowed to develop relationships with BOTH parents without fear of recrimination or hurting the other parent's feelings. View the time away from the children as your chance to recharge.

44

Ten Commandments for Stepfamilies

Catherine Ford Sori
Lorna L. Hecker

Type of Contribution: Handout

Objective

This handout is a psychoeducational tool that offers vital and succinct information for stepfamilies. Although the content is critical for healthy stepfamily formation and functioning, the Ten Commandments format conveys this serious information with some levity. It can be used simply as a handout, or the content and issues may be integrated in couple and family psychotherapy sessions.

Rationale for Use

Clients often find educational information useful to augment therapy. At times, seeing information in print makes it more digestible for clients and can be a less toxic way to introduce topics that may be sensitive for some families. Although many clinicians encourage clients to use bibliotherapy, such as *How to Win As a Stepfamily* (Visher and Visher, 1991), clients often do not follow through with these suggestions. Even when they do, clients may miss crucial points or may become upset when spouses refuse to read passages they have marked to highlight the new spouses' mistakes. This handout provides a summary of major "shalts" and "shalt nots" that therapists can discuss with both spouses in session, highlighting specific issues that pertain to particular families. This handout provides couples with a concrete summary of topics that can be discussed in future sessions or at home (for additional reading, see Visher and Visher, 1988, 1991). It can serve as a general guide for families in transition. The handout may also spur couples to read other suggested materials. It is especially useful in brief therapy, or when a family is rapidly headed toward a crisis.

Instructions

The handout can be used as an augment to psychotherapy. Topics can be gone over in therapy, adding client input, or the handout simply can be used as waiting-room reading to benefit families.

When used in therapy, the Ten Commandments for Stepfamilies handout can serve as an assessment and goal-setting device for couples in initial conjoint sessions. Therapists can encourage couples to assess themselves on each of the "commandments." They should be encouraged

---

This chapter is dedicated to the memory of Emily Visher, PhD, champion of stepfamilies, a source of great inspiration and encouragement, and cofounder with her husband, John Visher, MD, of the Stepfamily Association of America.

to recognize both their strengths (e.g., their deep love and commitment to each other) as well as their growth areas (e.g., not allowing children to "divide and conquer"). Information gleaned can be a springboard for more intimate communication (e.g., their hopes and dreams for their new relationship), to strengthen couple attachment bonds (e.g., why they fell in love and decided to marry), or to problem solve specific issues. This assessment information may also alert therapists to particular struggles children may be experiencing. While it is often recommended that couples be seen conjointly for initial sessions to strengthen the spousal bond and the boundary around this new relationship, children may need to be seen for individual (or subsystem) assessment and treatment prior to family therapy sessions (Visher, 2000, personal communication). The handout can then be used to help couples target specific problem areas and formulate goals.

Keeping the Ten Commandments posted on the refrigerator serves as a concrete visual reminder of healthy stepfamily functioning. When problems arise posttherapy, couples can refer to the commandment list to determine where they may have stumbled. Finally, couples can be told that because they are human, they will probably break at least one or two of the commandments at times. Forgiveness and love are two very important ingredients in stepfamilies.

Suggestions for Follow-Up

The therapist can ask couples if they have questions or concerns emanating from the handout. As stated earlier, families can use it to continue to monitor their "health" after termination.

After the couple has established a solid relationship, children can be included in discussions and educated about their role in the commandments. It is often very freeing and helpful for children to see and explicitly be told this information in the presence of the therapist (e.g., that they have permission to enjoy visits with the other parent, or that their new stepparent encourages their natural parent to spend one-on-one time with them regularly). Children may ask for an extra copy of the Ten Commandments handout to share with their other parent, especially if they are experiencing loyalty conflicts on that front. The handout also highlights for children the boundaries and rules around the new couple relationship.

Using the handout in later sessions with all parents and children present allows the therapist to address directly covert parent-child alliances, stepsibling problems, or other issues that may not be evident. The children and parents may be asked if they would like to add any additional commandments to the list, based on their own special needs. For example, children may come up with their own list of Commandments for Stepsiblings, or Commandments for Stepchildren and Stepparents. Younger children may draw pictures of what each commandment would look like (e.g., two stepsisters cleaning their room together, or a child getting a happy smile and a wave from Mom and Stepdad as she drives away with her biological dad). Children are more amenable to this project since they are explicitly being freed from loyalty binds and are allowed to love their natural parents without being pushed too quickly to love a new step-parent. This provides a springboard for new families to begin working together to create the specific rules for their own new family. This activity alone can serve as an early ritual that helps children and families develop their own separate and unique identity.

Contraindications for Use

Some clients may object to the religious overtones or the implied reference to the Ten Commandments from the Old Testament Bible. In this case, the items can simply be numbered.

References

Visher, E. B. and Visher, J. S. (1988). *Old loyalties, new ties: Therapeutic strategies with stepfamilies*. New York: Brunner/Mazel.
Visher, E. B. and Visher, J. S. (1991). *How to win as a step-family,* Second edition. New York: Brunner/Mazel.

Professional Readings

Hodges, W. (1986). *Interventions for children of divorce*. New York: Wiley.
Martin, D. and Martin, M. (1992). *Stepfamilies in therapy*. San Francisco: Jossey-Bass.
Wallerstein, J. S., Lewis, J. M., and Blakeslee, S. (2001). *The unexpected legacy of divorce: A 25-year landmark study*. New York: Hyperion.

Bibliotherapy Sources for Children

Berman, C. (1992). *What am I doing in a step-family?* New York: Carol Publishing.
Boyd, L. (1987). *The not-so-wicked stepmother*. New York: Puffin Books.
Boyd, L. (1990). *Sam is my half brother*. New York: Puffin Books.
Coleman, W. (1992). *What you should know about getting along with a new parent*. Minneapolis, MN: Augsburg Fortress.
Drescher, J. (1989). *My mother's getting married*. New York: Pied Piper.
Heegaard, M. (1993). *When a parent marries again: Children learn to cope with family change*. Lincoln, NE: Stepfamily Association of America.
Phillips, C. (1981). *Our family got a stepparent*. Ventura, CA: Regal Books.
Supe, G. (1991). *What kind of family do you have*? New York: Twenty-First Century Books.

Resources for Adult Clients

Burns, C. (1986). *Stepmotherhood,* First perennial library edition. New York: Perennial Library.
Kaplan, L. (1986). *Coping with stepfamilies*. New York: Rosen Publishing.
Mala, B. (1989). *Stepfamilies stepping ahead*. Lincoln, NE: Stepfamily Association of America.
Prilik, P. (1990). *Stepmothering—Another kind of love*. New York: Berkley.
Savage, K. and Adams, P. (1988). *The good stepmother.* New York: Crowne Publishing.
Visher, E. B. and Visher, J. S. (1991). *How to win as a step-family,* Second edition. New York: Brunner/Mazel.
Wallerstein, J. and Kelly, J. (1980). *Surviving the break up*. New York: Basic Books.
Wallerstein, J. S., Lewis, J. M., and Blakeslee, S. (2001). *The unexpected legacy of divorce: A 25 year landmark study*. New York: Hyperion.

Additional Suggestions

Stepfamily Association of America Inc., 215 Centennial Mall South, Lincoln, NE 68508-1834; (402) 477-STEP.
Learning to Step Together. Palo Alto, CA: Stepfamily Association of America.

Ten Commandments for Stepfamilies

I. **Thou shalt keep thy priorites in order.** For the new family to prosper it needs a firm foundation. This foundation is built on a solid relationship between new spouses. Each spouse must care for his or her own spiritual and inner self to care for, support, respect, and cherish each other, thus building a strong relationship. Then, together, they can focus on the needs of the children.

II. **Thou shalt set aside time each week to nourish your couple relationship.** Remember this special time together is sacred, and let nothing or no one interfere. Discuss your individual and conjoint hopes and dreams, worries and fears, triumphs and disappointments. Highlight your strengths and address your concerns. Above all, find time to play together, laugh together, love together, and enjoy being in each other's company. This fosters mutual love and respect and deepens a couple's confidence that, together, they can handle whatever difficulties lie ahead.

III. **Thou shalt support each other and parent carefully, as a team.** You and your spouse must share your joys, concerns, and problem-solving needs. Do NOT allow children to play the "Divide and Conquer" game, which is when a child complains to his or her biological parent about the stepparent. If a parent listens to the child's complaint, there are several results. The biological parent feels caught between the child and his or her new spouse; the stepparent will feel that his or her spouse is siding with the child, therefore causing the new spouse to feel alienated or outside of the new family. This blocks marital intimacy. These strong emotional reactions may also interfere with establishing a relationship between the stepparent and child.

 In new stepfamilies it is wise for the biological parent to do the majority of the parenting of his or her own children. The new partner should be encouraged to nurture a relationship with the child before beginning to assume a more active role in disciplining. Authority as a parent should be assumed only gradually by the new stepparent. In the meantime, assume a supporting role. This is one of the most common mistakes made by many benevolent and loving stepparents. Kids will resent and resist an "outsider" who moves in and attempts to tell them what to do. They may even feel they are losing a part of their parent and become fearful or angry. First bond with your spouse, then with stepchildren, and only later assume more parenting responsibilities.

IV. **Thou shalt avoid blaming the ex-spouse, present spouse, children, or relatives for problems.** *No one wins the "blame game"! Parents should not attempt to block a relationship with a biological parent, either through blame or cutting off the parent-child relationship.* Children will not respond positively to a stepparent when they are being asked to give up a biological parent. Cutoffs work against the stepfamily because the child creates an idealized image of the absent parent with which no stepparent can compete. It is common for children to become angry or aggressive, to be sad or even depressed, to have a decline in school performance, or later to experience problems with intimate relationships. Remarriage dashes children's hopes that their parents will reunite, thus facilitating a resurgence of feelings of loss. It is important to talk about the feelings of loss and anger, and what they mean to the child. Blaming keeps the child from adequately processing these important feelings.

V. **Thou shalt honor *all parents:*** Biological (or adoptive), stepparents, and all grandparents. *Give children permission to love all parents, and DO NOT put down or criticize your ex-spouse.* Children will internalize that there is something wrong with them, since they know that they came in part from both parents' families. Children know that their parents (and other relatives) are part of them. For children to develop their identity and self-esteem, they need to be able to love and appreciate at least aspects or parts of these people. Allow them to love or like all family members. *Encourage children to maintain contact with both biological (or adoptive) parents and grandparents.* Parents should model treating all people in the child's life with respect, even those with whom they have difficulty getting along. (*Note:* Thornier issues, such as abusive or neglectful family members, should be discussed with your therapist or attorney for more specific guidance.)

VI. **Thou shalt encourage children to enjoy time with the other parent.** Reassure children that you will be fine while they are gone and encourage them to enjoy their special visiting time. Children feel loyalty conflicts and if they sense you are uncomfortable with them leaving, they may worry about you or feel guilty if they have a good time. Facilitate easy transitions when they return (rituals such as dinner or a quiet family game or book reading might prove helpful). Do not interrogate children about what occurred in your ex's home; do not make them message bearers because of your discomfort in dealing with your ex-spouse. This burden does not belong to your children. Talk directly to your ex-spouse about child-related issues. If you can't talk directly, write a note or an e-mail.

VII. **Thou shalt allow relationships to develop in their own time.** Stepfamilies are not "instant families." Relationships take time to develop, and stepfamily relationships can tap many conflicting feelings for all involved. New spouses romanticize the new relationship and may be oblivious that their children do not share their enthusiasm. Spouses often fantasize about creating the "perfect" family (ala the Brady Bunch). Reality seldom matches the ideal. *It takes shared memories and time for feelings to develop in new stepfamilies.* In addition, *allow each spouse to have one-on-one time with each child. Until solid relationships have developed, stepparents should not be put in charge of parenting.* It is hard to build a friendship and be a parent at the same time.

Children can feel loyalty conflicts concerning a noncustodial parent. For example, it is common for children to feel that a stepparent is trying to replace their parent, which frightens children. Parents might suspect that noncustodial parents are sending messages to the child that any affection shown the stepparent hurts the "real" parent. This can prevent children from allowing themselves to develop a caring relationship with a stepparent and can cause tremendous inner conflict. When this occurs the children are the biggest losers, and all parents must work carefully to protect children from this trap.

VIII. **Thou shalt not covet the affection children feel for natural parents**. As a new stepparent, *do NOT try to replace the natural parent.* Talk with the children about all of their losses (e.g., pets, schools, friends, home) *and* feelings (e.g., how we can have two feelings at the same time). Do not expect or demand love but initially aim for friendship and respect. Love needs freedom to grow, but it is not a finite resource. The more affection and love children can give and receive, the richer their lives will be. Give permission to your children to love *both* parents; it is the best gift you can give a child of divorce.

IX. **Thou shalt cast out unproductive anger.** "Unproductive" anger serves no useful function. Work through your past anger, resentment, or disappointment from your previous relationship. If you are stuck, consider getting help. In the new stepfamily, when tensions grow and conflicts arise, the family often splits into former groups: parent and biological children against parent and biological children. This leads to increased distance between the two camps and emotional isolation between the spouses. "A house divided cannot stand." Couples may despair when reality doesn't match their fantasies. Forming a stepfamily takes lots of love, patience, and understanding. There are enough current feelings to manage without bringing old ones that you can do nothing about.

X. **Thou shalt make family a safe and secure place.** Set good boundaries around and within your family. Try to establish routines and rituals in your family that are healthy and foster family unity. Having dinner together, for example, is an important ritual, and should be encouraged. Let children help plan holiday celebrations for your new family. Be flexible and consider the children's developmental and emotional needs concerning regular and holiday visitations.

Children need special care during the transition time into a remarried family. A new relationship for a parent may leave a child feeling insecure, craving attention, or feeling loss. Remember that "stepfamilies are born of loss." Children feel this loss and should be encouraged to express those feelings. Home should be a place where all feelings can be appropriately expressed, and successes shared and celebrated. Family rules should be made clear so that everyone knows what is acceptable and unacceptable, without having to guess or test to learn the limits. Hold family meetings where children and parents are encouraged to share their gripes and successes, and to negotiate and brainstorm possible resolutions. Plan a weekly family fun night—with no TV, but with board games, reading together, outdoor activities, or art projects. Above all, remember how hard all these changes are for children and teens who have had little to say about decisions their parents have made—decisions that have profoundly changed their lives. Listen to their voices—with your ears and your hearts. They will love you for listening and understanding their world and will be more accepting of your world.

45

Helping Parents Understand and Use Natural and Logical Consequences

Dana Edwards

Type of Contribution: Activity

Objective

To assist in teaching parents how to use successfully natural and logical consequences.

Rationale for Use

Clinicians are often asked by parents which discipline methods reap the best results. Many counselors have found the use of natural and logical consequences (Dinkmeyer, 1963; Dinkmeyer, McKay, and Dinkmeyer, 1997; Dinkmeyer, McKay, Dinkmeyer, and McKay, 1998) to be most helpful and suggest their use to parents only to discover less than successful results. Perhaps the reason for this is that most parents, and even some therapists, do not really know how to use consequences appropriately. If clinicians are going to suggest that parents use consequences, they must educate parents how best to use them.

First, it is important to understand the distinct differences between random punishment and reward and discipline. If parents choose punishment as their means of training a child, then their motive is to punish severely enough so the child will "pay" for his or her misbehavior or to "hurt" or inconvenience the child so he or she won't misbehave again. In this approach to managing children, there is a sense of anger and/or revenge in the parents and the children often respond in kind. After being punished, a child openly fights back or quietly "plots" to get even. Although this method may at times be successful, it often hurts the parent-child relationship and may leave parents feeling guilty, causing them to be more permissive the next time the child misbehaves. Punishment also tends to be random, and changes from misbehavior to misbehavior, depending upon the mood and means of the punisher.

To promote good behavior, often parents will reward the child with candy, toys, money, privileges, and so on. When we choose to reward good behavior, often the child expects more and more, or when we ask the child to do something kind, his or her response often is, "What will I get for it?"

The goal of discipline using natural and logical consequences is, first, to promote good decision making and, second, to promote behavior change. Discipline is not concerned with the severity of punishment or amount of reward but is concerned with showing children that if they choose to continue the misbehavior there will be a consequence with which to contend. In this approach the consequence makes good sense. And although they do not admit it, children feel that this makes better sense too. Most important, natural and logical consequences do not jeopardize the parent-child relationship.

So what are consequences and how can a parent implement them? First, one must distinguish between natural and logical consequences. Natural consequences are what result naturally from behavior—both good and bad. For example, getting burned is a natural consequence of touching a hot stove and getting good grades is a natural consequence of studying. With natural consequences, there is no parental intervention. Parents simply let nature takes its course. It is important that parents not "rub a child's nose in it" when a natural consequence occurs. For example, if a child's toy is broken by someone stepping on it or is carted off by the family dog because the child chose to leave the toy out, the parent may be tempted to say, "See, I told you if you did not put away your toys this would happen!" Instead the parent is encouraged to say nothing or to say something to the effect of, "I'm sorry your toy is now broken. What do you think you could do to avoid this happening again?"

One problem with natural consequences is that sometimes they do not occur, such as in the case of children's teeth rotting out because they do not brush them. For some reason, even children who do not take good care of their teeth still have good dental checkups. Another problem is that the natural consequence may take too long to occur, such as in the example of a child failing a subject because he or she never studies. A third problem is that the natural consequence may be too dangerous to allow to happen, such as when a child is hit by a car because he or she chose to run out into the street. When natural consequences can occur promptly and safely, however, parents should allow them to. They are excellent teaching tools.

Logical consequences, on the other hand, are engineered by the parent and, ideally, created with the child's input. The most successful logical consequences are those that the child has conferred on—even children as young as two years of age. For example, when a misbehavior occurs, the parent should ask the child what he or she believes the consequence should be. At times, the child may think of a more severe consequence than the parent or may think of a consequence that will not serve the purpose of teaching the child about good and bad choices. The parent may wish to say something such as, "I would like you to help me come up with a consequence for your misbehavior. After I hear your suggestions and we discuss the pros and cons of each, I will decide on the correct consequence." In this case, the parent gets the final say on the appropriate consequence, but the child knows that his or her opinion is heard and valued even if not used. By getting the child's input, often complaints of "This is unfair" or "You're always picking on me" can be avoided. This idea of consulting with the child on the appropriate logical consequence may seem foreign or even ridiculous to some parents. If parents choose to create a logical consequence without the help of the child, the consequence can still be successful. However, it is important to note that when children have some say, even if minimal, in the things that concern them, they are more likely to comply. It is imperative to reiterate that the purpose of using logical consequences is to train children about good and bad choices, not simply to find another way for parents to assert their power.

Sometimes the child may not choose to cooperate in coming up with logical consequences. In this case, the parent will have to do this alone but should consult the other parent, if available, to provide a united approach to discipline. When giving a logical consequence, the parent may wish to follow this guideline: "I would like you to [state behavior you want, e.g., clean your room, put your toys away, do your homework], but I know that I cannot make you. But if you continue to [state misbehavior, e.g., not clean your room, leave your toys out, and so on], I need to let you know there will be a consequence. And the consequence for [state misbehavior again] will be [state logical consequence]."

Although using this guideline makes the use of logical consequences seem easy, often they are not. Creating consequences that are actually logical can be difficult. The reason is because we have been so entrenched in the use of rewards and punishment as parents and as children growing up in our own families of origin that doing something different is complicated. However, Albert (1996) suggests three things to consider to make developing logical consequences easier:

1. Is the consequence related?
2. Is the consequence reasonable?
3. Is the consequence respectful?

If "yes" is the answer to these three questions, then the consequence is logical and one that will be successful.

Is the consequence related? In other words, does it make sense? Having a child sit in time-out is not logical if the misbehavior it is trying to correct is leaving out toys. It is simply not related. However, time-out would be related to the misbehavior of hitting another child. This makes sense.

Is the consequence reasonable? Is it reasonable in terms of the child's developmental maturity? In most cases, it would not be reasonable to take away the privilege of playing Nintendo for one month for a child who failed a math test. Instead, what might be more reasonable would be not to allow the child to play Nintendo until after math homework or practice is completed each day. It is important to note that if we use logical consequences for poor school performance, we do so only in cases of lack of trying, not lack of ability. In the case where the child lacks ability, the logical consequence will serve no purpose other than to frustrate the child and the parent. For the consequence to be reasonable, the parent must also consider the developmental age of the child. For example, it would be more reasonable for a child of three to be placed in time-out for five minutes than for an hour. And although parents might want to restrict a teen from using the phone for a month, a weekend or one week would be more reasonable.

Is the consequence respectful? In other words, is the consequence given or stated in a calm, matter-of-fact (logical) way, rather than with a degrading voice that makes the child feel "stupid" or devalued? It is easy to be quick to anger. The key to successful parenting is to do the opposite. One of the best ways to practice handling anger is to give yourself a time-out. For example, your seven-year-old has just ruined his new shoes by jumping in all the mud puddles from Johnny's house to your house when you had previously told him to take off those shoes before going to Johnny's. It is understandable that you might be furious. Instead of reacting as you might be tempted to, say, "I am angry right now that you disobeyed me by wearing your new shoes when I asked you not to. I need some time to cool off and think about what I am going to do. Please remove your shoes and put them outside while I take some time to calm down."

Not only does putting yourself in time-out allow you to deal with your anger, but it also models to your child what to do when he or she is angry. Time-out need not always have a negative connotation attached to it, but it should be thought of as a place to go "chill out" until you can think and behave logically again. Once you have dealt with your anger, you can think rationally about the appropriate consequence to use. Having the child clean the shoes, purchase a new pair with allowance money, or repay you for a new pair by doing odd jobs around the house are all examples of logical consequences that meet the "three Rs" criteria.

Vignettes

Two common areas where discipline is needed in almost every family are dinnertime and getting ready for school on time. If the child refuses to eat when and what the family does, a loss of dinner would be an appropriate logical consequence as illustrated in the following vignette.

Vignette One

Ten-year-old Janie often does not like what her mother serves for dinner. She picks at her food, without eating much of it. In the past, her mother has served as a "short order cook" by fixing any number of dishes so Janie would eat. She has also "made" her sit at the table until she cleaned her plate. This usually resulted in Janie crying and her mother yelling—leaving both feeling manipulated and exhausted after the ordeal.

After learning about consequences, Janie's mother decided to try another approach. Mother discussed the problem with Janie at dinner, asking, "How do you feel when we fight at dinner about what you eat? I do not like fighting with you. I want to enjoy our time together at the dinner table. How do you suggest we handle it?" Janie responded that she does not like to fight with Mother either, that she doesn't want to be made to eat, and that she thinks she is old enough to decide if she is hungry. Mother agreed that she was old enough to decide, then said, "When you don't like what I fix for dinner, you often ask me to fix something else for you to eat. In the past I have done this, but I have decided that from now on I am only preparing one meal for the family. I hope you will eat it, but you can decide whether or not to eat what I have prepared, or not eat dinner at all. You will still sit at the table so we can visit together but eating is up to you." Janie's mother knew that she would not starve as a result of missing one meal. The next evening when Janie refused to eat what was prepared, Mother said nothing. At the end of dinnertime, dishes were cleared. A couple of hours later, Janie began to complain that she was hungry. Mother simply responded by saying, "I bet you are hungry. Maybe you will decide to eat dinner tomorrow night."

There are several possible logical consequences for the misbehavior of not getting ready for school on time. Going to bed earlier so the child can get up on time, missing breakfast, losing the privilege of watching a morning television program, and setting an alarm clock, thus giving the sole responsibility for waking up to the child, are all appropriate. In the following vignette, another approach is used.

Vignette Two

Five-year-old Steven had difficulty getting ready for school on time. Instead of dressing and eating in a timely fashion, he chose to dawdle. The father decided to use a modified version of the suggested sentence stems to set up the logical consequence, saying, "When you don't get out of bed and dress in the morning, it makes both of us late. I would like you to get out of bed and begin dressing the very first time I ask you to each morning. I can't make you get up and get dressed, but if you decide to stay in bed we will still leave the house by 7:30 and you will have to eat your breakfast and dress in the car." The next morning, Steven chose to dawdle and refused to dress in the car. Dad simply waved goodbye to Steven as he left the car, still dressed in his pajamas but carrying a bag with his school clothes in it. As quickly as he could, Dad got a message to Steven's teacher to explain what he was trying to accomplish. The teacher helped support the consequence by informing Steven that he could not play outside for recess until he changed into the proper attire.

In most cases, a child will choose to dress in the car, but Steven wanted to test the limits. In this situation, it was imperative to enlist the support of the teacher.

Suggestions for Follow-Up

There is no doubt that creating and implementing logical consequences takes time. Handing out random punishment and giving stars or money for good behavior are often much easier but usually work for only a short while. Parents can find lasting results with natural and logical consequences but, most important, they will find a happier relationship with their child.

It is important for the therapist to encourage the parents to choose their battles wisely. In other words, know when to leave and let go and when to stand their ground. For example, if the child has chosen not to perform his weekly chore of taking out the trash for the third time this month, the parent may decide that a discussion and consequence is needed. However, if the child has a habit of picking out and wearing clothes to school that do not particularly match, the parent may decide that this is a battle he or she does not wish to fight simply because it is not that important that the child wear matching clothes. Instead, the parent may let the child's peer group teach him or her about "proper attire" or simply wait for the child to learn in his or her own time. The parents who are most effective at discipline know when to be quiet.

Contraindications for Use

As with any change in parenting, parents may meet some resistance when using natural and logical consequences. Things can even get worse before they get better. When using logical consequences for the first time, it is suggested that parents discuss with their children the whole idea of consequences. Parents can verbalize that they have not enjoyed fighting, yelling, struggling, and so on with them, or the toll it has taken on their relationship. Parents may want to say that they want their children to take more responsibility managing their behavior and that they believe logical consequences will help their children do this. Discussions of this kind are especially important when parenting teens.

To be consistent, the most important ingredient when disciplining children, the parent must choose a consequence with which they can live. For example, if a fifteen-year-old continues to throw dirty clothes all over his or her room as opposed to the clothes hamper, the parent might be tempted to use the very logical consequence of refusing to wash anything that is not in the hamper on washing day. This may sound great and meet all three Rs, but in reality when push comes to shove, the parent cannot go through with it because it is important for the child to have clean clothes. If this is the case, it would be better to come up with another consequence, rather than using one he or she cannot abide. Perhaps in addition to the three Rs, the parent should consider another R—Really. Is the consequence one that a parent can really follow through?

If you have used logical consequences in the past but have found them to be unsuccessful, consider a few things:

1. What did I try?
2. Why didn't it work?
   - Did I ask for the child's input?
   - Was the consequence related?
   - Was it reasonable? Too much? Too little? Age appropriate?
   - Was it respectful? What kind of tone did I deliver it in?
   - Was it realistic? Did I follow through?
3. Did I give it enough time to work (at least two to three weeks) or did I give up too soon?
4. Did I feel as though I was giving up too much of my power as a parent? Was I afraid that the child might take advantage of me?

Parents might be surprised to find out what really happens when children feel a sense of control over their own lives. The result is not anarchy, but cooperation. Individuals are more willing to cooperate with someone who believes they can make good decisions and take responsibility for their own behavior. When parents use logical consequences that teach good decision making, they are treating the child with respect rather than making the child feel inferior by attempting to "control" his or her behavior by using rewards and punishment. Again, the biggest payoff with using natural and logical consequences is a happier, more respectful relationship between parents and children.

Professional Readings and Resources

Albert, L. (1996). *Cooperative discipline*. Circle Pines, MN: American Guidance Service.

Dinkmeyer, D. Sr., McKay G., Dinkmeyer, D. Jr. (1997). *Systematic training for effective parenting*. Circle Pines, MN: American Guidance Services.

Dinkmeyer, D. Sr., McKay, G., Dinkmeyer, D. Jr., and McKay, J. (1998). *Parenting teenagers*. Circle Pines, MN: American Guidance Services.

Dreikurs, R. and Grey, L. (1968). *Logical consequences: A new approach to discipline*. New York: Hawthorne Press.

Gilbert, L. (1986). Logical consequences: A new classification. *Journal of Individual Psychology, 42*, 243-254.

Sweeny, T. (1998). *Adlerian counseling: A practitioner's approach*. Bristol, PA: Accelerated Development.

Wright, L. (1986). The use of logical consequences in counseling children. *The School Counselor, 30*, 37-49.

Bibliotherapy Resources for Clients

Dinkmeyer, D. Sr., McKay G., Dinkmeyer, D. Jr. (1997). *Systematic training for effective parenting*. Circle Pines, MN: American Guidance Services.

Dinkmeyer, D. Sr., Mckay, G., Dinkmeyer, D. Jr., and McKay, J. (1998). *Parenting teenagers*. Circle Pines, MN: American Guidance Services.

Dreikurs, R. and Stoltz, V. (1987). *Children the challenge*. New York: Plume.

Nelsen, J. (1987). *Positive discipline*. New York: Ballantine Books.

Popkin, M. (Ed.) (1998). *Active parenting: Parents' handbook*. Marietta, GA: Active Parenting Publishers.

Walton, F.X. (1993). Winning children over: A manual for teachers, counselors, principals, and parents. Columbia, SC: Practical Psychology Association.

References

Albert, L. (1996). *Cooperative discipline*. Circle Pines, MN: American Guidance Service.

Dinkmeyer, D. (1963). *Encouraging children to learn: The encouragement process*. Englewood Cliffs, NJ: Prentice-Hall.

Dinkmeyer, D. Sr., McKay G., Dinkmeyer, D. Jr. (1997). *Systematic training for effective parenting*. Circle Pines, MN: American Guidance Services.

Dinkmeyer, D. Sr., McKay, G., Dinkmeyer, D. Jr., and McKay, J. (1998). *Parenting teenagers*. Circle Pines, MN: American Guidance Services.

46

Helping Parents Use the Time-Out Procedure

Lorna L. Hecker
Catherine Ford Sori

Type of Contribution: Intervention, Handout

Materials: A hand-held kitchen timer with a buzzer, beeper, or bell to signal when time is up

Objective

The objective of this intervention is to provide parents with concrete guidelines on successful implementation of a time-out procedure when disciplining their children.

Rationale for Use

Time-outs have long been taught by parent educators as a form of logical consequences to stop undesirable child behaviors, such as screaming, fighting, or throwing temper tantrums. When a child is calmly given a time-out the parent breaks a cycle that may be escalating and takes or sends the child to a quiet location to calm down. Physiological soothing is necessary for children and parents to calm down enough for parents to be able to discuss upsetting behavior with their children.

Therapists have long recommended time-outs, yet parents often struggle with both understanding how to utilize time-out procedures, as well as consistency in the use of the time-outs. Often when the subject of time-outs is broached in therapy parents become exasperated, saying, "We've tried that, and it didn't work!" Yet this usually is because there was some problem in how parents tried to implement time-outs. This handout provides clients with a rationale and detailed instructions on how to use time-outs successfully as a discipline procedure.

Often there are other serious problems in the family or with the parent-child relationship. Yet helping parents to reduce a child's acting-out behavior is often a crucial first step to lessen parental frustration, to empower parents and strengthen generational boundaries, and to reduce friction. These successes allow therapists to then address other, softer emotional issues with parents and their children.

Instructions

The handout with this chapter can be given to parents who are struggling with how to discipline their children. For parents who are familiar with the concept of time-outs, the therapist should go through the procedure step by step, asking how the parent has utilized time-outs in the

---

Catherine Ford Sori would like to thank her father, Marvin Ford, for demonstrating to her when she was a child how to successfully use "One-two-three—go to your room!"

past, and uncovering reasons why prior attempts to use time-outs have not been successful. The therapist should assess specific problem areas with this procedure and coach parents on how to overcome these problems, while encouraging them to adhere carefully to the suggestions in the handout.

For parents who are unfamiliar with the concept of time-out, the procedure should be discussed in detail, and any questions parents have should be thoroughly addressed. Therapists can role-play with parents how to implement time-outs to boost the parents' confidence in the procedure, as well as to troubleshoot any potential problem areas that may arise when they introduce time-out into their discipline regime. They can also playfully practice using "pretend" time-outs with the child in the therapy room, role-playing, or using dollhouse figures or puppets. This playfulness can help change the rules around previous unsuccessful attempts to use time-outs.

Vignette

LaShonda brought her four-year-old son Matthew to session complaining that she was very frustrated with him, and that his preschool told her that Matthew will be expelled if his behavior did not improve. Matthew had been biting the other children, not following the rules, and destroying school property. During the session, the therapist joined with LaShonda and talked with Matthew about his preschool, his pet cat, and the backpack filled with toys that he wore to session. The therapist noticed that while she talked to LaShonda, Matthew interrupted, pulled on LaShonda's arm, and demanded to leave. Soon he began to pick up objects in the therapist's office to examine them. LaShonda ignored Matthew's behavior and continued to relate her concerns about losing her day care for Matthew, stating that she needed to have him "fixed." The therapist noted the situation and quickly took action. She addressed Matthew with enthusiasm and captured his attention by stating the following:

THERAPIST: Matthew, have you ever been to an office like this before?

MATTHEW: The preacher at church kind of has an office like this.

THERAPIST: Oh, does your preacher have a window in her office too?

MATTHEW: Yes, and some stuffed animals like you do, too.

THERAPIST: Do you like stuffed animals?

MATTHEW: Yes, I like your tiger the best.

THERAPIST: Yeah the tiger is great. It's kind of like a zoo in here. Matthew, do you think there are any rules at the zoo?

MATTHEW: Yeah, I think the animals are supposed to stay in their homes. I think they also are only supposed to eat their own food.

THERAPIST: I'll bet you are right. I'll bet the animals are not supposed to fight with one another, too, right?

MATTHEW: Yep.

THERAPIST: Do you know that, like the zoo, I have rules here, too? Let's see . . . what are the rules for my "zoo"? We have three important rules. One rule is, We talk one person at a time. Another is, We only play with things with permission. Another is, We can't be too loud.

THERAPIST: Mom, do you have rules at your "zoo," too? What are they?

Subsequently, the therapist engaged LaShonda in a discussion of the rules of the home, so that Matthew was clear on the rules at his house. Preschool rules would be discussed with Matthew later. It is recommended to start initially with house rules, since parents have more control over these behaviors. After the child's behavior improves at home the therapist can address school behavior problems (Polson, 2000). First, the therapist worked with LaShonda to clarify three house rules. Polson (2000) recommends starting with no more than three rules for younger children, but older children can understand and integrate more complicated versions of the home rules. The therapist queried LaShonda and found out that she had not utilized time-outs with Matthew, but because Matthew was a very bright child, she relied on reasoning with him. Unfortunately, reasoning does not work with all four-year-olds and may often tire the parent and frustrate the child.

Later, when Matthew grabbed markers in session without permission, the therapist reminded Matthew to ask for permission to use the markers. When Matthew grabbed the markers for the second time without permission, the therapist began to initiate the 1-2-3 warning system by saying, "Matthew, put the markers down or you will go in time-out. That's one." Matthew was a quick learner and put down the markers. In the future when Matthew acted out, the therapist asked mother to institute the time-out procedures. This helped to reinforce the procedure with Matthew, and it offered Mother a place to rehearse time-out with some support and guidance from the therapist. In addition, asking the mother to perform the time-out in the therapy room validated her position of authority with her son.

Suggestions for Follow-Up

Therapists should follow up with parents to learn how successful they are in using time-out procedures at home. Any difficulties can be problem solved and possible solutions can be discussed. Consistent use of time-out should eventually allow the parent to start counting the warning to time-out: "one . . . two . . . (three will be time-out)."

It should be noted that good parenting involves much more than successful disciplining. Therapists must also assess the "softer side of hierarchy" (Keim, 1997), which involves the warm and nurturing aspects of parent-child relationships. Often, when children's emotional and attachment needs are met, they are more compliant and amenable to parents' efforts to set reasonable limits on their behavior.

Contraindications for Use

None noted. Parents who have deficits in other areas of parenting will need to have those addressed, along with being taught time-out procedures. Time-out is not a substitute for the loving guidance of a parent in other areas of a child's life.

Some parents may be too overwhelmed to implement time-outs consistently or correctly, either due to personal problems or because of the child's relentless misbehavior. These parents may need individual or couple therapy or, if they are very depressed or withdrawn, an evaluation for possible medication. Other parents may enthusiastically attempt to implement time-outs but fail repeatedly, despite the therapist's best efforts to locate and eliminate problem areas. Parents may be unconsciously reinforcing a child's negative behavior to avoid looking at underlying marital or other family issues. Time-outs should always be used as only one component of a complete assessment and treatment plan for children and their families.

Professional Readings and Resources

Everett, C. A. and Everett, S. F. (1999). *Family therapy for ADHD: Treating children, adolescents, and adults.* New York: Guilford Publications.

Keim, J. (1997). "Oppositional children and adolescents." Presentation at the American Association for Marriage and Family Therapy National Conference, Atlanta, GA. October 23-24.

Polson, M. (2000). Attention-deficit/hyperactivity disorder: Working with children and their families. In C. E. Bailey (Ed.), *Children in therapy: Using the family as a resource* (pp. 308-338). New York: W. W. Norton and Company.

Bibliotherapy Sources for the Client

Dinkmeyer, D. and McKay, G. D. (1982). *The parent's handbook: STEP: Systematic training for effective parenting*. Circle Pines, MN: American Guidance Service.

Phelan, T. W. (1995). *1 - 2 - 3: Magic! Training your preschoolers and preteens to do what you want* (Second revised edition). Glen Ellyn, IL: Child Management Corporation.

Using Time-Out Procedures with Children:
A Handout for Parents

"Time-out" is a discipline procedure that parents have used in various forms for generations. You may remember it as sitting in a chair, standing in a corner, or being sent to your room. "Time-out" is exactly that for a child who is misbehaving: time out or away from the problem behavior. If used *consistently,* it can be a very effective technique that can help parents avoid yelling, shouting, screaming, hitting, or other nonproductive behaviors. It also is respectful of the child while still setting limits on his or her behavior. The parent should try to avoid expressing high levels of anger or resentment when a child misbehaves but simply put that energy into instituting a time-out in a matter-of-fact way. The goal of time-out is not to shame or ridicule a child to make him or her feel bad, but to teach the child that the current behavior needs to change. Discipline is about *teaching,* not punishment per se.

In addition to using time-outs when children misbehave, it is very important that a parent also "catch the child being good." That is, the parent needs to praise positive things the child does. (The more praise a child gets for good behavior, the less time parents will have to spend punishing for bad behavior.)

Supplies needed: One hand-held kitchen timer with a buzzer, beeper, or bell to signal when time is up.

Decisions to Be Made Prior to Instituting Time-Out Procedures

1. **Clearly tell children the household rules.**
   Even if they've been discussed before, it is helpful to children if parents make the general rules of the household clear prior to instituting time-out procedures.
2. **Begin with three basic rules.**
   Although a parent cannot always predict the need for every rule, general rules such as "no hitting," "no talking back," "no destroying property," or "no fighting" should be established in every household. If the children don't know the rules of the home, the only way for them to find out is to misbehave. To ensure success, start time-out procedures with easier problems first.
3. **Decide a good spot in your home for a time-out.**
   A time-out spot should be free from distractions, safe, and nonstimulating (i.e., boring or dull). A lower stair in a stairwell may be a good spot, a chair facing a wall is another option, or a room with few distractions. (*Note:* sending a child to a room full of distractions such as a stereo, TV, books, games, and toys is NOT a good time-out spot—You may as well buy the child a trip to Disneyland for misbehaving—it will have the same effect!).
4. **Decide how long a time-out should be.**
   A general rule of thumb is to allow one minute of time-out for each year of a child's age. For example, a six-year-old would spend six minutes in time-out (per incident). Have a kitchen timer available to set for the amount of time the child will be in time-out.
5. **Explain time-outs to children.**
   Tell your children that you will be using something called time-out when they misbehave, and that they will be expected to sit in X (X = their time-out spot) when you have told them to go to time-out. Explain that they will be expected to stay in time-out; tell the children how many minutes they will be in time-out per offense. Explain to the children that if they choose to sit quietly, when the bell rings they can leave time-out. If they choose to whine, argue, or misbehave, they will receive additional minutes in time-out.

Using Time-Out

Here are the specific steps to instituting time-out.

The Three-Part Warnings

In addition to a child knowing the rules he or she is not to break, a child should be given a warning system used for most problem behaviors. *If the behavior is very disturbing (such as hitting a sibling), you do not have to give a three-part warning but may just order the child to time-out.*

In most instances, however, you want to train your child in a warning system that eventually will allow you not to rely on time-outs, but on the ability simply to warn the child with a count that time-out is approaching. When you first start giving time-out warnings, you will start by saying something such as: "Annie, I want you to stop [fill in the behavior you want to stop, e.g., throwing the ball in the house]" or "Annie, I want you to [fill in the behavior you want to start, e.g., pick up your room]." When the child does not comply, the parent states, "That's one . . . three will be time-out." If the behavior continues, the parent states, "That's two . . ." If the behavior persists, the parent simply states "time-out" and escorts the child to the designated time-out spot.

Example: When a child misbehaves or does not follow the rules or command a parent states, a time-out warning is given. The parent then puts out a firm command. "Jamie, I want you to stop putting your feet on the wall." If the child complies, praise is given. If the child does not comply, a time-out warning is given. *Example of warning:* "Jamie, I want you to get your feet off the wall immediately, or you go to time-out." If the child complies, a "thank you" may be stated.

If the child does not comply, the warning system begins. "Jamie, take your feet OFF the wall, that's one . . . two . . . ("three will be time-out") . . . three." If the child does not comply by the count of three, he or she is taken to the time-out spot (for additional ideas see the book *1-2-3: Magic!* by Dr. Thomas Phelan).

Begin Timing

If the child goes to time-out voluntarily, the timer is set for the appropriate number of minutes. A statement is made to the child: "When the bell rings, you may come out of time-out." (A timer bell is used so that the parent can stay out of the disciplining as much as possible—otherwise, the child will badger the parent for his or her "release time").

When a Child Refuses to Go to Time-Out

If the child does not go to the time-out spot voluntarily, the child is warned that additional minutes will be added to the time should the child not comply with your wishes. (Statements such as "I like time-outs" or "I don't care if I go to time-out" or the like should be ignored by the parent and simply considered normal child manipulations).

Ignore the Child While in Time-Out

Unless the child's behavior is disruptive or destructive to the environment or the child is not staying in time-out, ignore the child. Avoid eye contact and do not verbally address the child. If disruptiveness occurs, warn the child that additional time will be added to his or her time-out. If the child is being destructive, add to time-out and find another time-out spot that has fewer distractions for the child. A chair in the middle of a quiet room where the child cannot touch things usually suffices.

> *Note for parents of challenging children:* When parents are first instituting time-out, they may have to physically lead the child to the time-out spot. For more behaviorally challenging children, they may initially be held in time-out. If you have to hold your child in the time-out spot for the first few times, restrain the child gently, DO NOT get into any verbal interchange with your child, and gently but firmly hold the child from behind (such as in a bear hug) until the time is up. Explain to the child that in the future, time-outs will be shorter if the child stays in the time-out spot on his or her own. Add minutes to the time-out until the child stays voluntarily in time-out.

Be Consistent!

The time-out procedure must be utilized consistently to be effective. If you are having trouble with the time-out procedure, do not simply discard the technique. Troubleshoot or talk with your therapist about what part of the procedure is not working. Often when parents say time-outs do not work, it is because they *are inadvertently reinforcing the problematic behavior in some way.* For example, talking to a child when he or she is in time-out teaches the child that he or she can get individual attention from a parent by acting out.

Traps for Parents to Avoid

Avoid disagreeing about parenting in front of the children. Take the conversation to a private place. If children see any disagreement between parents, they will capitalize on the inconsistencies.

Summary of Time-Out

1. **State the wish or rule clearly to the child.**
   Warn the child of the offending behavior; e.g.: "Jamie, you will go in time-out if you don't stop using such a loud voice."
2. **Use a verbal counting warning.**
   If the behavior is particularly offensive and the child does not comply, send him or her to time-out immediately. If this is not the case, a three-count warning system should be used. "Jamie, that's one." . . . "That's two. Three will be time-out." . . . "That's three. Time-out."
3. **Place in time-out; set timer for minutes to be served. Extra minutes are added for additional infringements.**

Index

 **easy ways to order!**

PHONE
1.800.429.6784
Outside US/Canada: 607.722.5857

FAX
1.800.895.0582
Outside US/Canada: 607.771.0012

E-MAIL
orders@haworthpressinc.com

WEB
www.HaworthPress.com

MAIL
The Haworth Press, Inc.
10 Alice Street
Binghamton, NY 13904-1580 USA

❑ **YES!** Please rush me the following book(s)

❶ ❑ **The Therapist's Notebook**
Homework, Handouts, and Activities for Use in Psychotherapy

❑ $49.95 soft. ISBN: 0-7890-0400-3 _____ Quantity

Order this book online at: www.HaworthPressInc.com/store/product.asp?sku=1567

❷ ❑ **The Therapist's Notebook for Children and Adolescents**
Homework, Handouts, and Activities for Use in Psychotherapy

❑ $39.95 soft. ISBN: 0-7890-1096-8 _____ Quantity

Order this book online at: www.HaworthPressInc.com/store/product.asp?sku=4742

❸ ❑ **The Therapist's Notebook for Families**
Solution-Oriented Exercises for Working with Parents, Children, and Adolescents

❑ $39.95 soft. ISBN: 0-7890-1244-8 _____ Quantity

Order this book online at: www.HaworthPressInc.com/store/product.asp?sku=4645

❹ ❑ **The Therapist's Notebook for Lesbian, Gay, and Bisexual Clients**
Homework, Handouts, and Activities for Use in Psychotherapy

❑ $39.95 soft. ISBN: 0-7890-1252-9 _____ Quantity

Order this book online at: www.HaworthPressInc.com/store/product.asp?sku=4743

Order Today!

PAYMENT OPTIONS

❑ BILL ME LATER. ($5.00 service charge will be added.) (Not available on individual orders outside US/Canada/Mexico. Minimum order: $15. Service charge is waived for jobbers/wholesalers/booksellers.)

P.O.# _____

Signature _____

❑ PAYMENT ENCLOSED. $ _____
Payment by check or money order must be in U.S. or Canadian dollars drawn on a U.S. or Canadian bank.

❑ PLEASE CHARGE TO MY CREDIT CARD:

❑ Visa ❑ MasterCard ❑ AmEx ❑ Discover ❑ Diners Club ❑ Eurocard ❑ JCB

Account _____

Exp. Date _____

Signature _____

May we open a confidential credit card account for you for possible future purchases? ❑ Yes ❑ No

FINAL TALLIES

COST OF BOOK(S)	
POSTAGE & HANDLING See chart at right.	
IN CANADA Please add 7% for GST. NFLD, NS, NB: Add 8% for province tax.	
State Tax NY, OH & MN add local sales tax.	
FINAL TOTAL	

POSTAGE AND HANDLING:

If your book total is:	Add this amount:
up to $29.95	$5.00
$30.00 – $49.99	$6.00
$50.00 – $69.99	$7.00
$70.00 – $89.99	$8.00
$90.00 – $109.99	$9.00
$110.00 – $129.99	$10.00
$130.00 – $149.99	$11.00
$150.00 – and up	$12.00

US orders will be shipped via UPS; Outside US orders will be shipped via Book Printed Matter. For shipments via other delivery services, contact Haworth for details. Allow 3–4 weeks for delivery after publication. Based on US dollars. Booksellers: Call for freight charges.

• If paying in Canadian funds, please use the current exchange rate. Payment in UNESCO coupons welcome.
• Individual orders outside the US/Canada/Mexico must be prepaid by check or credit card.
• Prices in US dollars and subject to change without notice.

ADDITIONAL INFORMATION

Please fill in the information below or **TAPE YOUR BUSINESS CARD IN THIS AREA.**

NAME _____

INSTITUTION _____

ADDRESS _____

_____

CITY _____

STATE/PROVINCE _____

ZIP/POSTAL CODE _____

COUNTY (NY Residents only) _____

COUNTRY _____

PHONE _____

FAX _____

E-MAIL _____

PLEASE PRINT OR TYPE CLEARLY.

May we use your e-mail address for confirmations and other types of information? ❑ Yes ❑ No

We appreciate receiving your e-mail address and fax number. Haworth would like to e-mail or fax special discount offers to you, as a preferred customer. We will **never share, rent, or exchange** your e-mail address or fax number. We regard such actions as an invasion of your privacy.

THIS FORM MAY BE PHOTOCOPIED FOR DISTRIBUTION.

Order from your local bookstore or directly from
The Haworth Press, Inc.

10 Alice Street • Binghamton, New York 13904–1580 • USA
Telephone: 1.800.429.6784 • Fax: 1.800.895.0582
Outside US/Canada: Telephone: 607.722.5857 • Fax: 607.771.0012
E-mail: orders@haworthpressinc.com

Visit our website at: www.HaworthPress.com

CODE: BOF02